Appalachian Whitewater
Volume II The Central Mountains

Appalachian Whitewater

Volume II The Central Mountains

The Premier Canoeing and Kayaking Streams
of Pennsylvania, West Virginia, Maryland,
Delaware, and Virginia

Ed Grove, Bill Kirby, Charles Walbridge,
Ward Eister, Paul Davidson, and Dirk Davidson

Menasha Ridge Press
Birmingham, Alabama

Copyright © 1987 by Ed Grove, Bill Kirby,
Charles Walbridge, Ward Eister, Paul Davidson,
and Dirk Davidson

All rights reserved

Second printing, 1988

Printed in the United States of America

Library of Congress Cataloging in Publication Data
Main entry under title:
Appalachian whitewater.
Compiled by Bob Sehlinger and others.
Vol. 2 compiled by Ed Grove and others.
Includes indexes.
Contents: v. 1. The Southern mountains : The premier canoeing and kayaking streams of Kentucky, Tennessee, Alabama, Georgia, North Carolina, and South Carolina— v. 2. The Central mountains : the premier canoeing and kayaking streams of Pennsylvania, West Virginia, Maryland, Delaware, and Virginia.
1. White-water canoeing—Appalachian Region—Guide-books. 2. Kayak touring—Appalachian Region—Guide-books. 3. Appalachian Region—Description and travel—Guide-books. I. Sehlinger, Bob, 1945–   . II. Grove, Ed, 1940–   .

GV776.A55A67 1986   917.5   85-29762
ISBN 0-89732-030-1 (pbk. : v. 1)
ISBN 0-89732-031-X (pbk. : v. 2)

Cover photo of Diana Kendrick on Big Sandy Falls (Wonder Falls), Big Sandy Creek, by Paul Marshall

Menasha Ridge Press
P. O. Box 59257
Birmingham, Alabama 35259-9257

Contents

Acknowledgments *vii*
The Appalachian Mountain System *1*
How to Use This Guide *3*
Paddler Information *6*
Stream Dynamics *15*

Pennsylvania
  Lower Youghiogheny River *22*
  Slippery Rock Creek *26*
  Wills Creek *28*
  Dark Shade Creek, Shade Creek, and Stony Creek *31*
  Pine Creek *34*
  Loyalsock Creek *38*
  Lehigh River *44*
  Nescopeck Creek *49*
  Tohickon Creek *51*
  Delaware River *55*
  Muddy Creek *60*

West Virginia
  Upper Gauley River *64*
  Lower Gauley River *71*
  New River *75*
  New River Gorge *78*
  Back Fork of the Elk River *84*
  Little River, Forks of the Greenbrier, and the Greenbrier *86*
  Middle Fork River *96*
  Tygart River and Gorge *98*
  Laurel Fork of the Cheat River *105*
  Blackwater River *107*
  Big Sandy Creek *109*
  Cheat River *113*
  Lost River *120*
  Cacapon River *122*

Maryland and Delaware
  Top Youghiogheny River *126*
  Upper Youghiogheny River *129*
  Savage River *134*
  North Branch of the Potomac *138*
  Sideling Hill Creek *145*
  Antietam Creek *148*
  Shenandoah and Potomac Rivers *151*
  Gunpowder Falls *156*
  Prime Hook Creek, DE *158*
  Pocomoke River, MD *162*

Virginia
  South Fork of the Shenandoah River *166*
  Passage Creek *169*
  Potomac River *172*
  Thornton River *178*
  Aquia Creek *181*
  Rappahannock River *184*
  Tye River *186*
  Maury River *189*
  James River *194*
  Appomattox River *197*
  Johns Creek *199*

Glossary *201*
Appendixes *203*
  A. Commercial Raft Trips and Expeditions *203*
  B. Where to Buy Maps *203*
  C. Other Menasha Ridge Press Guidebooks *204*
Stream Index *205*

About the Authors *207*

Acknowledgments

Ed Grove first must thank his wife Carol for her saintly patience while he worked on this book. He is also deeply indebted to numerous fellow paddlers for their timely and invaluable contributions, which have made this book truly a work of the paddling community.

In particular, Ed wishes to thank Pope Barrow for his narrative on the Upper Yough; Paul Marshall for the book's cover picture, as well as for his description of the new Cheat Canyon after the November 1985 flood; Sam Chambliss for a delightful introduction to Muddy Creek; Frank Miles and Ron Mullet for information on Johns Creek; and Jonnie Elliott, Dave Bassage, Glenn Goodrich, and Paul Breuer for additional data on the New and the Gauley.

Ed also appreciates the help from Pat Appino, Gordon Bare, Debbie Welling Barna, Dave Brown, David L. Brown of Knoxville, Ron Canter, Cabell Chenault, Clark Childers, Phil Coleman, Roger Corbett, Joyce Decot, Greg Doggett, Stan Dunn, Steve Ensign, Mike Fetchero, Steve Ferendo, Geff Fisher, Doug Fogel, Walter Foster, Les Fry, Steve Garrison, Ed Gertler, Richard Goldsmith, Bob Grabus, Tom Gray, Lou Hannen, John Heidemann, Warren Heppding, Carl Homberg (and some friendly Keel-Haulers), Doug Howell, Josh Hubbard, Gary Johnson, Janet Kegg, Howard Kirkland, Chris Koll, Colleen Laffey, Chris Lea, Steven Michael Lowe, Louis Matacia, Mike May, Barb McKee, Gregg McWilliams, Dave Meyer, Bill Millard, Mary Miller, Kathy Mullet, Pat Munoz, Bob Opachko, George O'Shea, Tim Palmer, Steve Park, Ed Rader, Hoyt Reel, Keith Roberts, Glenn Rose, David Schmidt, Stephen Shaluta, Whitney Shields, Kirk Simon, Pete Skinner, Ron Smith, Ron Snow, Jim Snyder, Otto Spielbichler, Gary Staab, Walt Stillman, Attila and Janet Szilagyi, Bob Taylor, Steve Thomas, Al Thompson, Mac Thornton, Ron Vlascamp, Bob Wallace, Bill Warren, Steve White, Jesse Wittamore, and Jim Zoia.

Bill Kirby would like to thank the following people: Ed Gertler for advice on the whole question of guidebook writing; Ed Grove for all manner of support and assistance; all the members of the Canoe Cruisers Association and the West Virginia Wildwater Association with whom he has paddled over the years. He joins Ed Grove in thanking the following people for their contributions: Glenn Rose, for his assistance with the text of the Maury River chapter; and, for the Johns Creek chapter, Ron Mullet for his photo, and both Mullet and Frank Miles, for the information they provided.

Menasha Ridge Press would like to give special thanks to Paul Davidson, Ward Eister, and Dirk Davidson for use of the excellent material drawn from their books, *Wildwater West Virginia, Volume I, The Northern Streams* and *Volume II, The Southern Streams*.

The Appalachian Mountain System

The Appalachian Mountain system extends from the Gaspé Peninsula in Quebec, Canada, southwestward 1,500 miles to northern Georgia and Alabama. Only 80 miles wide in its northernmost reaches, the mountain range broadens to a considerable 350 miles in the south. Elevations vary from 300 feet above sea level at the far eastern edge of the range to lofty peaks exceeding 6,000 feet. The highest peak in the range is Mount Mitchell in North Carolina with an elevation of 6,684 feet.

The Appalachian Mountains are seldom considered in their entirety. Explored, settled, and named by a dozen nationalities over more than a hundred years, the Appalachians are more familiar to most of us when discussed in terms of component sub-ranges. Extending southwest from Quebec and Maine are the White Mountains with its Presidential Range containing Mount Washington, the highest peak in the northeastern Appalachians at 6,288 feet. Just west of the White Mountains are the Green Mountains of Vermont, with its gradually lesser foothills, the Berkshires of Massachusetts, and the Litchfield Hills of Connecticut. The Green Mountains attain their highest peaks in northern Vermont at Mount Mansfield (4,393 feet). Both the Green and White mountains are beautifully forested and embellished by spectacular highland lakes.

West of the Hudson River in New York are the Adirondacks, and to the south, the Catskills. A long plateau running along a southwesterly axis from the Catskills is known as the Allegheny Plateau in the north and as the Cumberland Plateau in the south. The Allegheny Plateau runs from the Mohawk Valley in New York to southeastern Kentucky. The Cumberland Plateau encompasses much of southeastern Kentucky, east-central Tennessee, and northeastern Alabama. For the most part the Allegheny Plateau, which contains the Catskills and the Pocono and Allegheny mountains of Pennsylvania and northern West Virginia, is more rugged and mountainlike than the limestone ridges of the Cumberland Plateau.

The Blue Ridge Mountains begin in southeastern Pennsylvania and extend south to northeastern Georgia and northwestern South Carolina. To the immediate west of the Blue Ridge are the Cumberland Mountains of western Virginia, the Pisgah, Bald, and Black mountains of North Carolina, and the Unakas, containing the Great Smoky Mountains in North Carolina and Tennessee. These ranges boast some of the highest summits in the Appalachian system, as well as some of the greatest diversity of plant and animal life. Trees that are typical of northern states such as spruce, birch, hemlock, and fir grow on many of the southern mountain tops.

The Blue Ridge and its adjacent ranges are separated from the Allegheny and Cumberland plateaus to the west by a series of river valleys known collectively as the Great Appalachian Valley. Beginning in the north with the St. Lawrence River valley and moving southwest, the Hudson River valley in New York, the Kittatinny valley in New Jersey, the Lebanon and Cumberland valleys in Pennsylvania and Maryland, the Shenandoah valley in Virginia, the Tennessee valley in Tennessee, and the Coosa valley in Georgia and Alabama all combine to form the Great Valley. While some sections of the Great Valley exhibit the broad, verdant river valley that its name suggests, much of the Great Valley consists of long, narrow, steep parallel ridges.

Born of powerful upheavals within the earth's crust and forged by the relentless force of moving water on the surface of the continent, the Appalachians are among the oldest mountains on earth. Yet, old as the mountains are, some of the rivers within the Appalachian system are older. Northeast of the New River in Virginia the major Appalachian rivers flow into the Atlantic Ocean, sometimes through dramatic passages called water gaps. Southwest of the New, however, the rivers (with only a couple of exceptions) flow to the Ohio River. During the upheavals and "folding" which thrust the mountains up, these ancient rivers were blocked from their westward course to the prehistoric sea which

New River Gorge, near Fayette Station. Photo by Bill Kirby.

once covered mid-America. During the ensuing millenia these rivers sculpted the landscape of the eastern United States, carving new routes to the sea and in the process creating the spectacular canyons and gorges which make the Appalachians a joy to the whitewater boater.

The entire Appalachian system is laced with a complex network of rivers, streams, and springs. Owing to its elevation, there is an abundance of rainfall, exceeded in the United States only along the northwest Pacific coast. Much of the annual rainfall, averaging 69 inches a year over most of the system, comes in great downpours of comparatively short duration. This, coupled with the steep gradient of many streams, accounts for water levels changing radically in very little time.

There is enough whitewater in the Appalachians to last the most avid paddler a lifetime. Many streams are seasonal, but a few of the larger as well as those which are dam-controlled are runnable year round. Level of difficulty ranges from splashy and scenic Class I through the absolutely unrunnable. Throughout, the scenery is spectacular with river travel often the only means of enjoying a true wilderness environment in the heavily populated eastern United States.

This series of guidebooks on the whitewater of the Appalachian Mountains is divided into three volumes. Volume I covers the Appalachian streams of Tennessee, North Carolina, South Carolina, Alabama, Kentucky, and Georgia. Described in Volume II are the mountain streams of Virginia, Maryland, Delaware, West Virginia, and Pennsylvania. Volume III includes the Appalachian whitewater of the northeast, from eastern New York State through the New England states. The emphasis in each volume is on the favorite streams, though a number of lesser known but no less spectacular streams are also included. No attempt is made to review a river from source to mouth. Rather, only the better whitewater sections of each stream are detailed.

How to Use This Guide

For each stream in this guide you will find a general description and at least one stream data list and map. (A stream is flowing water and may be a river, a creek, or a branch or fork of a river.)

Stream Descriptions

These are intended to give you a feel for the stream and its surroundings, and are presented in general, nontechnical terms.

Stream Data

Each stream data list provides the necessary technical and quantitative information for each of the streams listed, as well as some additional descriptive data. Occasionally certain facts will be covered in both the general description and in the data list for added emphasis. Listed below are fuller explanations of many of the categories found on the data lists.

Each list begins with the specific stream **Section** to which the data apply and the **Counties** in which the stream is located.

USGS Quads The names of the seven-and-a-half minute and fifteen minute topographical maps are included here to give the paddler a reference for the contours of the land and river involved. To order these maps, see the address list in "Where to Buy Maps" in Appendix B.

Suitable for While most streams described in this book are best suited to *day cruising*, some provide the opportunity for *canoe camping*. A few, because of their convenient access and configuration, are designated as being good for *training* runs.

Skill Level This item was included strictly for convenience. For a better idea of whether or not a listed stream is for you, evaluate yourself according to the paddler self-evaluation format on pages 8–9. For definitional purposes, *families* connotes adults of various skill levels who want to take nonswimming adults or children in the canoe with them. We always assume that personal flotation devices (PFD's), e.g., life jackets, will be worn by all parties on moving water. We also assume that no passengers will be carried in whitewater.

Beginners are paddlers with a knowledge of strokes and self-rescue who can maneuver their boat more or less intuitively on still water (lakes and ponds). True *intermediates* meet all beginner qualifications, have a working knowledge of river dynamics, have some ability in rescuing others, and (for our purposes) are competent and at home on Class II whitewater. *Advanced paddlers* (not experts) are paddlers who possess all the foregoing qualifications in addition to specialized rescue skills, and who are competent and at home on Class III and IV whitewater. *Experts* are paddlers who easily exceed all the foregoing qualifications. Needless to say, these definitions could be refined or elaborated ad infinitum. They are not intended to be all-inclusive but rather to give you a reasonable idea of how to classify yourself and how experienced practitioners of the sport may tend to class you.

Months Runnable The months given are based on the average rainfall for a year. Different sections of rivers may be runnable at different times. Some rivers are not necessarily runnable at a given time of year but are only runnable after a heavy rainfall or when a dam or powerhouse is releasing enough water.

Interest Highlights This category includes special *scenery, wildlife, whitewater, local culture and industry, historical* locations, and unusual *geology*.

Scenery Taste is relative, and in the absolute sense ours is no better or worse than anyone else's. Our preference is that you form your own conclusions about the comparative beauty of the streams listed in this guide. Knowing, however, that it takes a long time to run all of the states' major drainages, we were presumptuous enough to include a comparative scenery rating based strictly on our own perceptions. The ratings run from *unattractive*, to *uninspiring*, through gradations of *pretty* and *beautiful*, to *spectacular*. To indicate how capricious taste is, some popular canoeing streams are rated as follows:

Little Miami River (Ohio): Pretty in spots to pretty
Whitewater River (Indiana): Pretty in spots to pretty
Nantahala River (North Carolina): Pretty to beautiful in spots
Current River (Missouri): Beautiful in spots to beautiful
Elkhorn River (Kentucky): Beautiful in spots to beautiful
New River (West Virginia): Beautiful in spots to beautiful
Red River (Kentucky): Exceptionally beautiful to spectacular
Chattooga III–IV (Georgia): Exceptionally beautiful to spectacular

Difficulty The level of difficulty of a stream is given according to the International Scale of River Difficulty (see page 11, item V). Such ratings are relative and pertain to the stream described under more or less ideal water levels and weather conditions. For streams with two International Scale ratings, the first represents the average level of difficulty of the entire run and the second (expressed parenthetically) represents the level of difficulty of the most difficult section or rapids on the run. Paddlers are cautioned that changes in water levels or weather conditions can alter the stated average difficulty rating appreciably. We strongly recommend that paddlers also assess the difficulty of a stream on a given day by using the river evaluation chart (table 1).

Average Width Rivers tend to start small and enlarge as they go toward their confluence with another river. Pools form in some places, and in other places the channel may constrict, accelerating the current. All of these factors affect the width and make the average width an approximate measure.

Velocity This represents the speed of the current, on the average, in nonflood conditions. Velocity can vary incredibly from section to section on a given stream depending on the stream's width, volume, and gradient at any point along its length. Velocity is a partial indicator of how much reaction time you might have on a certain river. Paddlers are known to describe a high velocity stream as "coming at them pretty fast," meaning that the speed of the current does not allow them much time for decision and action.

Rivers are described here as *slack, slow, moderate,* and *fast*. Slack rivers have current velocities of less than a half mile per hour; slow rivers have velocities over a half mile per hour but less than two miles per hour. Moderate velocities range between two and four miles per hour, and fast rivers are those that exceed four miles per hour.

Gradient Gradient is expressed in feet per mile and refers to the steepness of the streambed over a certain distance. It is important to remember that gradient (or "drop" as paddlers refer to it) is an average figure and does not tell the paddler when or how the drop occurs. A stream that has a listed gradient of 25 feet per mile may drop gradually in one- or two-inch increments (like a long, rocky slide) for the course of a mile, or it may drop only slightly over the first nine-tenths of a mile and then suddenly drop 24 feet at one waterfall. As a general rule, gradient can be used as a rough indicator of level of difficulty for a given stream (i.e., the greater the gradient, the more difficult the stream). In practice, gradient is almost always considered in conjunction with other information.

Runnable Water Level (Minimum) This represents the lowest water level at which a given stream is navigable. Where possible, water levels are expressed in terms of volume as cubic feet per second (*cfs*). The use of cfs is doubly informative in that knowledge of volume at a gauge on one stream is often a prime indicator of the water levels of ungauged runnable streams in the same watershed, or for other sections of the gauged stream, either up- or downstream.

Runnable Water Level (Maximum) In this book, "runnable" does not mean the same thing as "possible." The maximum runnable water level refers to the highest water level at which the stream can be safely run (this may vary for open and decked boats). With few exceptions (which can only be run when flooded), this categorically excludes rivers in flood.

Hazards Hazards are dangers to navigation. Because of the continuous action of the water, many of these hazards may change and new ones might appear. *Low-hanging trees*, which can be a nuisance, may become *deadfalls, blowdowns, and strainers*. Human intervention creates hazards such as *dams, low bridges, powerboat traffic,* and *fences* (an especially dangerous "strainer"). Some watersheds have soils that cannot retain much water and the streams in that watershed may have a *flash flood* potential. Additionally, geologically young rivers, usually whitewater rivers, may have *undercut rocks, keeper hydraulics, difficult rapids,* and a *scarcity of eddies*.

Scouting This guidebook attempts to list spots on specific rivers where scouting is required, i.e., recommended for the continuation of life and good health. Because many hazards may change in a short period of time, this guidebook also subscribes to the rule of thumb that you should scout any time you cannot see what is ahead (whitewater or flatwater and even on familiar rivers). That small, turning drop that

Glenn Rose running Devil's Kitchen, Maury River, Virginia. Photo by Paul Marshall.

you have run a thousand times may have a big log wedged across it today.

Portages This book adheres to the rule that dams should be portaged. Additionally, portages are recommended for certain rapids and other dangers. The fact, however, that a portage is not specified at a certain spot or rapid does not necessarily mean that you should not portage. It is the mark of good paddlers to be able to make safe and independent decisions about their own ability for a given river or rapid.

Rescue Index Many of the streams in this book run through wild areas. A sudden serious illness or injury could become an urgent problem if you can't get medical attention quickly. To give you an idea of how far you may be from help, a brief description is given of what might be expected. *Accessible* means that you might need up to an hour to secure assistance, but evacuation is not difficult. *Accessible but difficult* means that it might take up to three hours to get help *and* evacuation may be difficult. *Remote* indicates it might take three to six hours to get help; and *extremely remote* means that you could expect to be six hours from help and would need expert assistance to get the party out.

Source of Additional Information Various sources of additional information on water conditions are listed. Professional outfitters can provide both technical and descriptive information and relate the two to paddling. TVA and the various hydraulics branches of the respective district Corps of Engineers offices can provide flow data in cfs but will not be able to interpret the data for you in terms of paddling. Other sources listed (forest rangers, police departments, etc.) will normally provide only descriptive information, e.g., "The creek's up pretty good today," or, "The river doesn't have enough water in it for boating."

Maps

The maps in this guide are not intended to replace topographic quadrangles for terrain features. Rather, they are intended to illustrate the general configuration of the stream, its access points, and surrounding shuttle networks.

Some of the maps are congested to the point that access letters may not be exactly where they should, but are only in the general vicinity. You may have to scout the area before launching. Approximate river miles and car shuttle miles from one access point to the next are provided with the maps. Additionally, the names of the seven-and-a-half-minute topographic quadrangles on which the streams appear are provided with the maps. To order these maps, see the address list in "Where to Buy Maps" in the appendix, item B.

Paddler Information

Rating the River—Rating the Paddler

For several years concerned paddlers have sought to objectively rate rivers. Central among their tools has been the International Scale of River Difficulty. While certainly a useful tool, and by no means outdated, the International Scale lacks precision and invites subjective, judgmental error. A more objective yardstick is the recently developed Difficulty Rating Chart that is based on a point system. While more cumbersome, it does succeed in describing a river more or less as it really is. Gone is the common confusion of a single rapid being described as Class II by the veteran while the novice perceives a roaring Class IV. Also eliminated is the double standard by which a river is rated Class III for open canoes but only Class II for decked boats. Instead, points are awarded as prescribed for conditions observed on the day the river is to be run. The total number of points describes the general level of difficulty.

Once the basic difficulty rating is calculated for a river, however, how is it to be matched against the skill level of a prospective paddler? The American Whitewater Affiliation relates the point system for rivers back to the International Scale and to traditional paddler classifications.

Class	Total Points	Skill Required
I	0–7	Practiced Beginner
II	8–14	Intermediate
III	15–21	Experienced
IV	22–28	Highly Skilled
V	29–35	Team of Experts
VI	36–42	Team of Experts with every precaution

This helps, but only to the extent that the individual paddler understands the definitions of "Practiced Beginner," "Intermediate," "Experienced," and so on. If, like most of us, the paddler finds these traditional titles ambiguous and hard to differentiate, he or she will probably classify himself or herself according to self-image. When this occurs, we are back to where we started.

Correctly observing the need for increased objectivity in rating paddlers as well as in rating rivers, several paddling clubs have developed self-evaluation systems where paddlers are awarded points that correspond to the point scale of the river rating chart (table 1). Thus an individual can determine a point total through self-evaluation and compare his or her skill, in quantified terms, to any river rated through use of the chart. The individual paddler, for instance, may compile 18 points through self-evaluation and note that this rating compares favorably with the difficulty rating of 17 points and unfavorably with a difficulty rating of 23 points. It should be emphasized here, however, that river ratings via the river difficulty chart pertain to a river only on a given day and at a specific water level.

The most widely publicized of the *paddler* self-evaluations was created by the Keel-Haulers Canoe Club of Ohio. This system brings the problem of matching paddlers with rivers into perspective but seems to overemphasize nonpaddling skills. A canoe clinic student who is athletically inclined but almost totally without paddling skill once achieved a rating of 15 points using the Keel-Haulers system. His rating, based almost exclusively on general fitness and strength, incorrectly implied that he was capable of handling many Class II and Class III rivers. A second problem evident in the system is the lack of depth in skill category descriptions. Finally, confusion exists in several rating areas as to whether the evaluation applies to open canoes, decked boats, or both.

To remedy these perceived shortcomings and to bring added objectivity to paddler self-evaluation, Bob Sehlinger has attempted to refine the paddler rating system. The refined system is admittedly more complex and exhaustive, but not more so than warranted by the situation. Heavy emphasis is placed on paddling skills, with description adopted

Table 1. Rating the River*

	Secondary Factors — Factors Related Primarily to Success in Negotiating			Primary Factors — Factors Affecting Both Success and Safety			Secondary Factors — Factors Related Primarily to Safe Rescue				
Points	Obstacles, rocks and trees	Waves	Turbulence	Bends	Length (feet)	Gradient (ft/mile)	Resting or rescue spots	Water Velocity (mph)	Width and depth	Temp °(F)	Accessibility
0	None	Few inches high, avoidable	None	Few, very gradual	<100	<5, regular slope	Almost anywhere	<3	Narrow (<75 feet) and shallow (<3 feet)	>65	Road along river
1	Few, passage almost straight through	Low (up to 1 ft) regular, avoidable	Minor eddies	Many, gradual	100–700	5–15, regular slope		3–6	Wide (>75 feet) and shallow (<3 feet)	55–65	<1 hour travel by foot or water
2	Courses easily recognizable	Low to med. (up to 3 ft), regular, avoidable	Medium eddies	Few, sharp, blind; scouting necessary	700–5,000	15–40, ledges or steep drops		6–10	Narrow (<75 feet) and deep (>3 feet)	45–55	1 hour to 1 day travel by foot or water
3	Maneuvering course not easily recognizable	Med. to large (up to 5 ft), mostly regular, avoidable	Strong eddies and cross currents		>5000	>40, steep drops, small falls	A good one below every danger spot	>10 or flood	Wide (>75 feet) and deep (>3 feet)	<45	>1 day travel by foot or water
4	Intricate maneuvering; course hard to recognize	Large, irregular, avoidable; or med. to large, unavoidable	Very strong eddies, strong cross currents								
5	Course tortuous, frequent scouting	Large, irregular, unavoidable	Large scale eddies and crosscurrents, some up and down								
6	Very tortuous; always scout from shore	Very large (>5 ft), irregular, unavoidable, special equipment required					Almost none				

Source: Prepared by Guidebook Committee—AWA (from "American White Water," Winter 1957).
*To rate a river, match the characteristics of the river with descriptions in *each* column. Add the points from each column for a total river rating.

Table 2. Ratings Comparisons

International Rating	Approximate Difficulty	Total Points (from Table 1)	Approximate Skill Required
I	Easy	0–7	Practiced Beginner
II	Requires Care	8–14	Intermediate
III	Difficult	15–21	Experienced
IV	Very Difficult	22–28	Highly Skilled (Several years with organized group)
V	Exceedingly Difficult	29–35	Team of Experts
VI	Utmost Difficulty–Near Limit of Navigability		

from several different evaluation formats, including a non-numerical system proposed by Dick Schwind.*

Rating the Paddler

The paddler rating system that follows will provide a numerical point summary. The paddler can then use this information to gauge whether a river of a given ranking is within his or her capabilities.

Instructions: All items, except the first, carry points that may be added to obtain an overall rating. All items except "Rolling Ability" apply to both open and decked boats. Rate open and decked boat skills separately.

1. Prerequisite Skills Before paddling on moving current, the paddler should:
  a. Have some swimming ability.
  b. Be able to paddle instinctively on nonmoving water (lake). (This presumes knowledge of basic strokes.)
  c. Be able to guide and control the canoe from either side without changing paddling sides.
  d. Be able to guide and control the canoe (or kayak) while paddling backwards.
  e. Be able to move the canoe (or kayak) laterally.
  f. Understand the limitations of the boat.
  g. Be practiced in "wet exit" if in a decked boat.

2. Equipment Award points on the suitability of your equipment to whitewater. Whether you own, borrow, or rent the equipment makes no difference. *Do not* award points for both *Open Canoe* and *Decked Boat*.

Open Canoe

0 Points	Any canoe less than 15 feet for tandem; any canoe less than 14 feet for solo.
1 Point	Canoe with moderate rocker, full depth, and recurved bow; should be 15 feet or more in length for tandem and 14 feet or more in length for solo and have bow and stern painters.
2 Points	Whitewater canoe. Strong rocker design, full bow with recurve, full depth amidships, no keel; meets or exceeds minimum length requirements as described under "1 Point"; made of hand-laid fiberglass, Kevlar®, Marlex®, or ABS Royalex®; has bow and stern painters. Canoe as described under "1 Point" but with extra flotation.
3 Points	Canoe as described under "2 Points" but with extra flotation.

Decked Boat (K-1, K-2, C-1, C-2)

0 Points	Any decked boat lacking full flotation, spray skirt, or foot braces.
1 Point	Any fully equipped, decked boat with a wooden frame.
2 Points	Decked boat with full flotation, spray skirt and foot braces; has grab loops; made of hand-laid fiberglass, Marlex®, or Kevlar®.
3 Points	Decked boat with foam wall reinforcement and split flotation; Neoprene or latex spray skirt; boat has knee braces, foot braces, and grab loops; made of hand-laid fiberglass, Kevlar®, roto-molded or blow-molded cross-link polyethelene.

3. Experience Compute the following to determine *preliminary points*, then convert the preliminary points to *final* points according to the conversion table.

Number of days spent each year paddling:
  Class I rivers × 1 = _____
  Class II rivers × 2 = _____
  Class III rivers × 3 = _____
  Class IV rivers × 4 = _____
  Class V rivers × 5 = _____
Preliminary Points Subtotal _____
Number of years paddling experience × subtotal = Total Preliminary Points _____

Conversion Table	
Preliminary Points	Final Points
0–20	0
21–60	1
61–100	2
101–200	3
201–300	4
301–up	5

Note: This is the only evaluation item where it is possible to accrue more than 3 points.

4. Swimming

0 Points	Cannot swim
1 Point	Weak swimmer
2 Points	Average swimmer
3 Points	Strong swimmer (competition level or skin diver)

5. Stamina

0 Points	Cannot run mile in less than 10 minutes
1 Point	Can run a mile in 7 to 10 minutes
2 Points	Can run a mile in less than 7 minutes

---

*Schwind, Dick, "Rating System for Boating Difficulty," *American Whitewater Journal*, volume 20, number 3, May/June 1975. See also Sehlinger, Bob, *A Canoeing and Kayaking Guide to the Streams of Tennessee* (Menasha Ridge Press, 1983).

6. **Upper Body Strength**
   - 0 Points   Cannot do 15 push-ups
   - 1 Point   Can do 16 to 25 push-ups
   - 2 Points   Can do more than 25 push-ups

7. **Boat Control**
   - 0 Points   Can keep boat fairly straight
   - 1 Point   Can maneuver in moving water; can avoid big obstacles
   - 2 Points   Can maneuver in heavy water; knows how to work with the current
   - 3 Points   Finesse in boat placement in all types of water, uses current to maximum advantage

8. **Aggressiveness**
   - 0 Points   Does not play or work river at all
   - 1 Point   Timid; plays a little on familiar streams
   - 2 Points   Plays a lot; works most rivers hard
   - 3 Points   Plays in heavy water with grace and confidence

9. **Eddy Turns**
   - 0 Points   Has difficulty making eddy turns from moderate current
   - 1 Point   Can make eddy turns in either direction from moderate current; can enter moderate current from eddy
   - 2 Points   Can catch medium eddies in either direction from heavy current; can enter very swift current from eddy
   - 3 Points   Can catch small eddies in heavy current

10. **Ferrying**
    - 0 Points   Cannot ferry
    - 1 Point   Can ferry upstream and downstream in *moderate* current
    - 2 Points   Can ferry upstream in *heavy* current; can ferry downstream in *moderate* current
    - 3 Points   Can ferry upstream and downstream in *heavy* current

11. **Water Reading**
    - 0 Points   Often in error
    - 1 Point   Can plan route in short rapid with several well-spaced obstacles
    - 2 Points   Can confidently run lead in continuous Class II; can predict the effects of waves and holes on boat
    - 3 Points   Can confidently run lead in continuous Class III; has knowledge to predict and handle the effects of reversals, side currents, and turning drops

12. **Judgment**
    - 0 Points   Often in error
    - 1 Point   Has average ability to analyze difficulty of rapids
    - 2 Points   Has good ability to analyze difficulty of rapids and make independent judgments as to which should not be run
    - 3 Points   Has the ability to assist fellow paddlers in evaluating the difficulty of rapids; can explain subtleties to paddlers with less experience

13. **Bracing**
    - 0 Points   Has difficulty bracing in Class II rivers
    - 1 Point   Can correctly execute bracing strokes in Class II water
    - 2 Points   Can correctly brace in intermittent whitewater with medium waves and vertical drops of 3 feet or less
    - 3 Points   Can brace effectively in continuous whitewater with large waves and large vertical drops (4 feet and up)

14. **Rescue Ability**
    - 0 Points   Self-rescue in flatwater
    - 1 Point   Self-rescue in mild whitewater
    - 2 Points   Self-rescue in Class III; can assist others in mild whitewater
    - 3 Points   Can assist others in heavy whitewater

15. **Rolling Ability**
    - 0 Points   Can only roll in pool
    - 1 Point   Can roll 3 out of 4 times in moving current
    - 2 Points   Can roll 3 out of 4 times in Class II whitewater
    - 3 Points   Can roll 4 out of 5 times in Class III and IV whitewater

Add up your points from items 2 through 15. Then compare your score with the "Total Points" in table 2 to determine your skill level.

Hazards and Safety

Hazardous situations likely to be encountered on the river must be identified and understood for safe paddling. The lure of high adventure has in part explained why there are so many more paddlers these days. Unfortunately, an alarming number were not prepared for what they encountered and lost their lives.* They didn't use good judgment or just didn't understand the potential dangers.

American Whitewater Affiliation Safety Code

The American Whitewater Affiliation's safety code is perhaps the most useful overall safety guideline available.

I. **Personal Preparedness and Responsibility**
   A. **Be a competent swimmer** with ability to handle yourself underwater.
   B. **Wear a life jacket.**
   C. **Keep your craft under control.** Control must be good enough at all times to stop or reach shore before you reach any danger. Do not enter a rapid unless you are reasonably sure you can safely navigate it or swim the entire rapid in the event of capsize.
   D. **Be aware of river hazards and avoid them.**
      Following are the most frequent killers.
      1. **High Water.** The river's power and danger, and the difficulty of rescue, increase tremendously as the flow rate increases. It is often misleading to judge river level at the put-in. Look at a narrow, critical passage. Could a sudden rise in the water level from sun on a snow pack, rain, or a dam release occur on your trip?
      2. **Cold.** Cold quickly robs your strength, along with your will and ability to save yourself. Dress to protect yourself from cold water and weather extremes. When the water temperature is less than 50°F, a diver's wet suit is essential for safety in event of an upset. Next best is wool clothing under a windproof outer garment such as a splashproof nylon shell; in this case one should also carry matches and a complete change of clothes in a waterproof package. If, after prolonged exposure, a person experiences uncontrollable shaking or has difficulty talking and moving, he or she must be warmed immediately by whatever means available.
      3. **Strainers.** Brush, fallen trees, bridge pilings, or anything else that allows river current to sweep through but pins boat and boater against the obstacle. The water pressure on anything trapped this way is overwhelming, and there may be little or no whitewater to warn of danger.
      4. **Weirs, reversals, and souse holes.** Water drops over an obstacle, then curls back on itself in a stationary wave, as is often seen at weirs and dams. The surface water is actually going *upstream*, and this action will trap any floating object between the drop and the wave. Once trapped, a swimmer's only hope is to dive below the surface where current is flowing downstream or to try to swim out the end of the wave.
   E. **Boating alone is not recommended**—the preferred minimum is three craft.
   F. **Have a frank knowledge of your boating ability.** Don't attempt waters beyond this ability. Learn paddling skills and teamwork, if in a multiperson craft, to match the river you plan to boat.
   G. **Be in good physical condition** consistent with the difficulties that may be expected.
   H. **Be practiced in escape** from an overturned craft, in self-rescue, and in artificial respiration. Know first aid.
   I. **The Eskimo roll should be mastered** by kayakers and canoeists planning to run large rivers or rivers with continuous rapids where a swimmer would have trouble reaching shore.
   J. **Wear a crash helmet** where an upset is likely. This is essential in a kayak or covered canoe.
   K. **Be suitably equipped.** Wear shoes that will protect your feet during a bad swim or a walk for help, yet will not interfere with swimming (tennis shoes recommended). Carry a knife and waterproof matches. If you need eyeglasses, tie them on and carry a spare pair. Do not wear bulky clothing that will interfere with your swimming when water-logged.

II. **Boat and Equipment Preparedness**
   A. **Test new and unfamiliar equipment** before relying on it for difficult runs.
   B. **Be sure the craft is in good repair** before starting a trip. Eliminate sharp projections that could cause injury during a swim.
   C. **Inflatable craft should have multiple air chambers** and should be test inflated before starting a trip.
   D. **Have strong, adequately sized paddles or oars** for controlling the craft and carry sufficient spares for the length of the trip.
   E. **Install flotation devices** in noninflatable craft. These devices should be securely fixed and designed to displace as much water from the craft as possible.
   F. **Be certain there is absolutely nothing to cause entanglement** when coming free from an upset craft; e.g., a spray skirt that won't release or that tangles around the legs; life jacket buckles or clothing that might snag; canoe seats that lock on shoe heels; foot braces that fail or allow feet to jam under them; flexible decks that collapse on boaters' legs when trapped by water pressure; baggage that dangles in an upset; loose rope in the craft or badly secured bow and stern lines.
   G. **Provide ropes to allow you to hold on to your craft** in case of upset, and so that it may be rescued. Following are the recommended methods:
      1. **Kayaks and covered canoes** should have six-inch-diameter grab loops of one-fourth-inch rope attached to bow and stern. A stern painter seven or eight feet long is optional and may be used if properly secured to prevent entanglement.

---

*Paddling Fatality Facts: (1) Over three-quarters of the operators in canoe/kayak accidents have not had any formal instruction; (2) 86 percent of fatalities occurred within 90 minutes of departure on an outing; (3) approximately 74 percent of the victims encountered water temperatures less than 70°F. (From a presentation by the U.S. Coast Guard at the 1976 American Canoe Association instructors' conference in Chicago.)

2. **Open canoes** should have bow and stern lines (painters) securely attached consisting of eight to ten feet of one-fourth- or three-eighths-inch rope. These lines must be secured in such a way that they will not come loose accidentally and entangle the boaters during a swim, yet they must be ready for immediate use during an emergency. Attached balls, floats, and knots are not recommended.
3. **Rafts and dories** should have taut perimeter grab lines threaded through the loops usually provided on the craft.

H. **Respect rules for craft capacity** and know how these capacities should be reduced for whitewater use. (Life raft ratings must generally be halved.)

I. **Carry appropriate repair materials:** tape (heating-duct tape) for short trips, complete repair kit for wilderness trips.

J. **Cartop racks must be strong and positively attached** to the vehicle, and each boat must be tied to each rack. In addition, each end of each boat should be tied to the car bumpers. Suction cup racks are poor. The entire arrangement should be able to withstand all but the most violent accident.

III. **Leader's Preparedness and Responsibility**

A. **River conditions.** Have a reasonable knowledge of the difficult parts of the run, or, if an exploratory trip, examine maps to estimate the feasibility of the run. Be aware of possible rapid changes in river level and how these changes can affect the difficulty of the run. If important, determine approximate flow rate or level of the river. If the trip involves important tidal currents, secure tide information.

B. **Participants.** Inform participants of expected river conditions and determine whether the prospective boaters are qualified for the trip. All decisions should be based on group safety and comfort. Difficult decisions on the participation of marginal boaters must be based on group strength.

C. **Equipment.** Plan so that all necessary group equipment is present on the trip: 50- to 100-foot throwing rope, first aid kit with fresh and adequate supplies, extra paddles, repair materials, and survival equipment, if appropriate. Check equipment as necessary at the put-in, especially: life jackets, boat flotation, and any items that could prevent complete escape from the boat in case of an upset.

D. **Organization.** Remind each member of individual responsibility in keeping the group compact and intact between the leader and the sweep (a capable rear boater). If the group is too large, divide into smaller groups, each of appropriate boating strength, and designate group leaders and sweeps.

E. **Float plan.** If the trip is into a wilderness area, or for an extended period, your plans should be filed with appropriate authorities, or left with someone who will contact them after a certain time. Establishing of checkpoints along the way from which civilization could be contacted if necessary should be considered. Knowing the location of possible help could speed rescue in any case.

IV. **In Case of Upset**

A. **Evacuate your boat immediately** if there is imminent danger of being trapped against logs, brush, or any other form of strainer.

B. **Recover with an Eskimo roll** if possible.

C. **If you swim, hold on to your craft.** It has much flotation and is easy for rescuers to spot. Get to the upstream side of the craft so it cannot crush you against obstacles.

D. **Release your craft if this improves your safety.** If rescue is not imminent and water is numbingly cold, or if worse rapids follow, then strike out for the nearest shore.

E. **When swimming rocky rapids,** use backstroke with legs downstream and **feet near the surface.** If your foot wedges on the bottom, fast water will push you under and hold you there. **Get to slow or very shallow water before trying to stand or walk. Look ahead.** Avoid possible entrapment situations: rock wedges, fissures, strainers, brush, logs, weirs, reversals, and souse holes. Watch for eddies and slackwater so that you can be ready to use these when you approach. Use every opportunity to work your way to shore.

F. **If others spill, go after the boaters.** Rescue boats and equipment only if this can be done safely.

V. **International Scale of River Difficulty**
(If rapids on a river generally fit into one of the following classifications, but the water temperature is below 50°F, or if the trip is an extended one in a wilderness area, the river should be considered one class more difficult than normal.)

Class I Moving water with a few riffles and small waves; few or no obstructions.

Class II Easy rapids with waves up to three feet, and wide, clear channels that are obvious without scouting; some maneuvering is required.

Class III Rapids with high, irregular waves often capable of swamping an open canoe; narrow passages that often require complex maneuvering; may require scouting from shore.

Class IV Long, difficult rapids with constricted passages that often require precise maneuvering in very turbulent waters. Scouting from shore is often necessary, and conditions make rescue difficult. Generally not possible for open canoes; boaters in covered canoes and kayaks should be able to Eskimo roll.

Class V Extremely difficult, long, and very violent rapids with highly congested routes that nearly always must be scouted from shore. Rescue conditions are difficult and there is significant hazard to life in event of a mishap. Ability to Eskimo roll is essential for kayaks and canoes.

Class VI Difficulties of Class V carried to the extreme of navigability. Nearly impossible and very dangerous. For teams of experts only, after close study and with all precautions taken.

Injuries and Evacuations

Even allowing for careful preparation and attention to the rules of river safety, it remains a fact of life that people and boats are somewhat more fragile than rivers and rocks. Expressed differently, accidents do occur on paddling trips, and *all* boaters should understand that it can happen to them. Although virtually any disaster is possible on the river, there seems to be a small number of specific traumas and illnesses that occur more frequently than others. These include:

1. Hypothermia
2. Dislocated shoulder (especially common in decked boating)
3. Sprained or broken ankles (usually sustained while scouting or getting into or out of the boat)
4. Head injuries (sustained in falls on shore or during capsize)
5. Hypersensitivity to insect bite (anaphylactic shock)
6. Heat trauma (sunburn, heat stroke, heat prostration, dehydration, etc.)
7. Food poisoning (often resulting from sun spoilage of lunch foods on a hot day)
8. Badly strained muscles (particularly of the lower back, upper arm, and the trapezius)
9. Hand and wrist injuries
10. Lacerations

What happens when one of the above injuries occurs on the river? Many paddlers are well prepared to handle the first aid requirements but are unfortunately ill prepared to handle the residual problems of continued care and evacuation. The following is an excerpt from *Wilderness Emergencies and Evacuations* by Ed Benjamin, Associate Program Director at SAGE, School of the Outdoors in Louisville, Kentucky: "When a paddler is injured during a river trip he can usually be floated out in a canoe. Unfortunately, however, circumstances do sometimes arise when the victim is non-ambulatory, or when lack of open canoes or the nature of the river preclude floating the injured party out. In such a situation the trip leader would have to choose between sending for help or performing an overland evacuation."

When sending for help, send at least two people. Dispatch with them a marked map or drawing showing your location as exactly as possible. (Yes, that means pencil and paper should be part of every first aid kit). Also send a note giving directions for finding you plus information on the nature of your emergency and the type of assistance you require. Have your messengers call the proper agencies, such as local police, a rescue squad, the U.S. Forest Service, the state police, plus any unofficial parties such as professional river outfitters who could lend special expertise to the rescue. This having been done, the messengers should be instructed to report the situation simply and factually to the families of the persons involved.

Many paddlers, unfortunately, do not know where they are except in relation to the river, and all too few carry topographical maps. Rescuers need to know exactly where you are in terms of the land, roads, etc. A helicopter pilot will not make much sense of the information that your victim is on the left bank below Lunchstop Rapid. Establish shelter for yourselves and your victim; any rescue is going to take a long time. In the time it takes your messengers to walk out, organize help, and return to you, many hours or perhaps days will pass. Psychologically prepare yourself for a long wait. To expedite the rescue attempt, build a smoky fire to help your rescuers locate you.

Many people believe that if they are ever hurt in the wilderness, a helicopter will come fly them out. This is not necessarily so. Only if you are near a military air base or a civilian air rescue service do you have a good chance of getting a helicopter. Even if one is available, there are several serious limitations. A rescue helicopter will not fly in bad weather, over a certain altitude, or at night. A helicopter needs a clear area about 150 feet in diameter that is reasonably level to land. Moreover, the pilot will probably need some sort of wind indicator on the ground such as a wind sock or a smoky fire. All helicopters are not the same; most do not have cable on which to raise a victim, and all have limitations on where they may hover. If a helicopter is successful in landing near you, do not approach the craft until the crew signals you to do so, and then only as the crew directs. In most situations the availability or usefulness of a helicopter is doubtful. More likely you will be rescued by a group of volunteers who will drive to the nearest roadhead, reach you on foot, and carry the victim out on a litter. Be advised that volunteer rescue teams are usually slow and sometimes lack adequate training (particularly for a river or climbing rescue). Occasionally you may encounter a topnotch mountain rescue team, but this is rare.

If help cannot be obtained, or if you have a large, well-equipped group, it may be possible to carry the victim out yourself. A litter can be improvised from trees, paddles, packs, etc. Any litter used should be sufficiently strong to protect your victim from further injury. If you do attempt to evacuate the victim yourself, be advised that overland evacuations (even with the best equipment) are extremely difficult and exhausting and are best not attempted unless there are eight or more people to assist. When carrying a litter, a complement of six bearers is ideal. Not only does this spread the load, but, if one bearer loses footing, it is unlikely that the litter will be dropped. Bearers should be distributed so that there are two by the victim's head, two by the feet, and one on each side in the middle. Those carrying at the head of the victim must pay careful attention to the victim. An unconscious victim requires constant checking of vital signs. A conscious victim will be uncomfortable and frightened and will need reassurance. Bear in mind also that a day warm enough to make a litter carrier perspire may be cool enough to induce hypothermia in an unmoving victim. Always have one bearer set the pace and choose the safest and easiest route. Go slow and easy and be careful. Always use a rope to belay the litter from above when ascending or descending a slope—a dropped litter can slide a long way. Paddlers should insist that their partners learn first aid. First aid gear (including pencil and paper), extra topographical maps, and rope should be carried in the sweep boat.

Hypothermia

Hypothermia, the lowering of the body's core temperature, and death from drowning or cardiac arrest after sudden immersion in cold water are two serious hazards to the winter, early spring, and late fall paddler. Cold water robs the victim of the ability and desire to save him- or herself. When the body's temperature drops appreciably below the normal 98.6°F, sluggishness sets in, breathing is difficult, coordination is lost to even the most athletic person, pupils dilate, speech becomes slurred, and thinking irrational. Finally unconsciousness sets in, and then, death. Hypothermia can occur in a matter of minutes in water just a few degrees above freezing, but even 50° water is unbearably cold.

To make things worse, panic can set in when the paddler is faced with a long swim through rapids. Heat loss occurs much more quickly than believed. A drop in body temperature to 96°F makes swimming and pulling yourself to safety almost impossible, and tragically, the harder you struggle, the more heat your body loses. Body temperatures below 90°F lead to unconsciousness, and a further drop to about 77°F usually results in death. (But this same lowering of the body temperature slows metabolism and delays brain death in cases of drowning, therefore heroic rescue efforts have a higher chance of success.)

Paddlers subjected to spray and wetting from waves splashing into an open boat are in almost as much danger of hypothermia as a paddler completely immersed after a spill. The combination of cold air and water drains the body of precious heat at an alarming rate although it is the wetness that causes the major losses since water conducts heat away from the body 20 times faster than air. Clothes lose their insulating properties quickly when immersed in water, and skin temperatures will rapidly drop to within a few degrees of the water temperature. The body, hard pressed to conserve heat, will then reduce blood circulation to the extremities. This reduction in blood flowing to arms and legs makes movement and heavy work next to impossible. Muscular activity increases heat loss because blood forced to the extremities is quickly cooled by the cold water. It's a vicious, deadly cycle.

The best safeguards against cold weather hazards are: recognizing the symptoms of hypothermia, preventing exposure to cold by wearing proper clothing (wool and waterproof outerwear or wet suits), understanding and respecting cold weather, knowing how the body gains, loses, and conserves body heat, and knowing how to treat hypothermia when it is detected. Actually, cold weather deaths may be attributed to a number of factors: physical exhaustion, inadequate food intake, dehydration of the body, and psychological elements such as fear, panic, and despair. Factors such as body fat, the metabolic rate of an individual, and skin thickness are variables in a particular person's reaction and endurance when immersed in cold water. Since the rate of metabolism is actually the rate at which the body produces heat from "burning" fats, carbohydrates, and proteins, one person may have a higher tolerance for cold weather than another. Stored fatty tissues also help the body resist a lowering of its core temperature. Shivering is "involuntary exercise"—the body is calling on its energy resources to produce heat. Proper food intake and sufficient water to prevent dehydration are important in any cold weather strenuous exercise, especially paddling.

The key to successfully bringing someone out of hypothermia is understanding that their body must receive heat from an external source. In a field situation, strip off all wet clothes and get the victim into a sleeping bag with another person. Skin-to-skin transfer of body heat is by far the best method of getting the body's temperature up. By all means don't let the victim go to sleep, and feed him or her warm liquids. Build a campfire if possible. Mouth-to-mouth resuscitation or external cardiac massage may be necessary in extreme cases when breathing has stopped, but remember that a person in the grips of hypothermia has a significantly reduced metabolic rate, so the timing of artificial respiration should correspond to the victim's slowed breathing.

Knowing Your Rights on the River

A paddler's legal right to run a river is based on the concept of navigability. This is somewhat unfortunate since navigability as a legal concept has proven both obscure and somewhat confused over the years. The common law test of navigability specifies that only those streams affected by the ebb and flow of the sea tides are navigable. Obviously, if this were the only criterion, none of the streams in the Appalachians would be navigable. Fortunately, most states expressly repudiate the common law test and favor instead the so-called civil law test—thus a stream is considered navigable if it is capable of being navigated in the ordinary sense of that term, which relates essentially to commerce and transportation. But even if a stream is not navigable from a legal perspective according to the civil law test, it may still be navigable in fact. This means basically that its navigability does not depend on any legislative act but is based rather on the objective capability of the stream to support navigation. Thus a creek swollen by high waters may become navigable for a period of time.

If a stream is navigable in the legal sense (civil law test), ownership of the bed of the stream is public. In this case the public possesses all navigation rights as well as incidental rights to fish, swim, and wade. Property rights of those who own land along a navigable stream extend only to the ordinary low water mark. If the water later recedes or islands form in the bed of the stream, the property remains that of the state.

On the other hand, if a stream is only navigable sometimes (as in the case of a seasonal stream), the title of the land under the water belongs to the property owners over whose land the stream passes. However, the ownership is subject to a public easement for such navigation as the condition of the stream will permit.

Regardless of the question of navigability, the right of landowners to prohibit trespassing on their land along streams (if they so desire) is guaranteed. Therefore, access to rivers must be secured at highway rights-of-way or on publicly owned lands if permission to cross privately owned land cannot be secured. Landowners, in granting access to a river, are extending a privilege that should be appreciated and respected. Do not betray a landowner's trust if extended the privilege of camping, putting in, or taking out. Do not litter, drive on grass or planted fields, or forget to close gates. In some cases property owners may resent people driving for hundreds of miles to float through what the landowner may consider private domain. Indeed, it is not unusual for landowners to firmly believe that they "own" the river that passes through their land.

On the other hand, good manners, appreciation, and consideration go a long way in approaching a landowner for permission to camp or launch. The property owner may be interested in paddling and flattered that the paddler is interested in the countryside and so may be quite friendly and approachable. Cultivate and value this friendship and avoid giving cause to deny paddlers access to the river at some time in the future.

Legally, paddlers are trespassing when they portage, camp, or even stop for a lunch break if they disembark from their boats onto the land. If approached by a landowner while trespassing, by all means be cordial and explain your reason for being on the property (portage, lunch break, etc.). Never knowingly camp on private land without permission. If you do encounter a perturbed landowner, be respectful and keep tempers under control.

Landowners certainly have the right to keep you off of their land and the law will side with them unless they inflict harm on you, in which case they may be both civilly and criminally liable. If you threaten a landowner verbally and physically move with apparent will to do harm, the landowner has all the rights of self-defense and self-protection in accordance with the perceived danger that you impose. Likewise, if the landowner points a firearm at you, fires warning shots, assaults, injures, or wounds you or a boater in your group, you are certainly in the right to protect yourself. In Tennessee there is a statutory provision that permits a private citizen to arrest an individual for a misdemeanor (criminal trespassing) committed in the citizen's presence. If this unlikely situation arises, remain calm and avoid escalating the confrontation. Draw the landowner away from the group and explain the situation, apologizing for any transgression already committed. If you feel imperiled at the hands of the property owner, avoid detainment. A landowner's rights to use force to apprehend you for a misdemeanor are extremely limited, particularly if you are posing no real or perceived threat. If you elect for whatever reasons to accompany the landowner, do so in good faith but with all precautions having been taken. Insist on proper identification by some documentary source and find out what local law enforcement jurisdiction you are being taken to. If some of your party is allowed to continue, arrange for them to notify the same authority of the incident. Contact legal counsel as soon as you can. If you fear for your life at the hands of the landowner, you do have the right to protect yourself.

Without question, confrontations between belligerent paddlers and cantankerous landowners are to be avoided. Although the chance of such a meeting may be rare, paddlers nonetheless should know their rights, and the rights of the landowners. Remember, judges do not like trespassers any more than they like landowners who shoot trespassers.

Ecological Considerations

Presenting a set of ecological guidelines for all paddlers sounds like preaching, but with the number of persons using our creeks and rivers today, it is indeed a valid point. Many of the streams listed in this guide flow through national parks and forests, state-owned forests and wildlife management areas, and privately owned lands that in some cases are superior in quality and aesthetics to lands under public ownership. It is the paddling community's responsibility to uphold the integrity of these lands and their rivers by exercising ecologically sound guidelines. Litter, fire scars, pollution from human excrement, and the cutting of live trees is unsightly and affects the land in a way that threatens to ruin the outdoor experience for everyone.

Paddlers should pack out everything they packed in: all paper litter and such nonbiodegradable items as cartons, foil, plastic jugs, and cans. Help keep our waterways clean for those who follow. If you are canoe camping, leave your campsite in better shape than you found it. If you must build a fire, build it at an established site, and when you leave, dismantle rock fireplaces, thoroughly drown all flames and hot coals, and scatter the ashes. Never cut live trees for firewood (in addition to destroying a part of the environment, they don't burn well). Dump all dishwater in the woods away from watercourses, and emulate the cat—bury all excrement.

Stream Dynamics

Understanding hydrology—how rivers are formed and how they affect man's activities—is at the very heart of paddling. To aid the paddler, brief discussions of the effects on paddling of seasonal variations of rainfall, water temperature, and volume, velocity, gradient, and stream morphology will be presented.

The most basic concept about water that all paddlers must understand is, of course, the hydrologic or water cycle, which moves water from the earth to the atmosphere and back again. Several things happen to water that falls to the earth: it becomes surface runoff that drains directly into rivers or their tributaries, or it is retained by the soil and used by plants, or it may be returned directly to the atmosphere through evaporation, or else it becomes ground water by filtering down through subsoil and layers of rock.

Seasonal variations in the flow levels of watercourses are based on fluctuations in rainfall. About 40 percent of each year's rainfall runs either directly into the streams or through the ground and then into the streams.

Local soil conditions have a great deal to do with streamflow as do plant life, terrain slope, ground cover, and air temperature. In summer, during the peak growing season, water is used more readily by plants, and higher air temperatures encourage increased evaporation. The fall and winter low-water periods are caused by decreased precipitation, although since the ground is frozen and plant use of water is for the most part halted, abnormally high amounts of rain, or water from melting snow, can cause flash floods because surface runoff is high—there's no place for the water to go but into creeks and rivers. Though surface runoff is first to reach the river, it is ground water that keeps many larger streams flowing during rainless periods. Drought can lower the water table drastically. Soil erosion is related to the surface runoff—hilly land in intensive agricultural use is a prime target for loss of topsoil and flash flooding.

The Water Cycle

The water on and around the earth moves in a never-ending cycle from the atmosphere to the land and back to the atmosphere again. Atmospheric moisture flows constantly over the Appalachians, and the amount that falls on the region now is much the same as it was when only the Indians worried about dried-up springs and floods in their villages.

Beginning the cycle with the oceans, which cover some 75 percent of the earth's surface, the movement of the water follows these steps (see figure 1):

1. Water from the surface of the oceans (and from the lands between) evaporates into the atmosphere as vapor. This water vapor rises and moves with the winds.
2. Eventually, either over the ocean or over the land, this moisture is condensed by various processes and falls back to the earth as precipitation. Some falls on the ocean; some falls on the land where it becomes of particular concern to man.
3. Of the rain, snow, sleet, or hail that falls on the land, some runs off over the land, some soaks down into the ground to replenish the great ground-water reservoir, some is taken up by the roots of plants and is transpired as water vapor, and some is again evaporated directly into the atmosphere.
4. The water that flows over the land or soaks down to become ground water feeds the streams that eventually flow back into the oceans, completing the cycle.

The key steps in this great circulation of the earth's moisture are evaporation, precipitation, transpiration, and streamflow. All occur constantly and simultaneously over the earth. Over the Appalachian river basins the quantities in any part of the cycle vary widely from day to day or from season to season. Precipitation may be excessive or may stop entirely for days or weeks. Evaporation and transpiration

16 Stream Dynamics

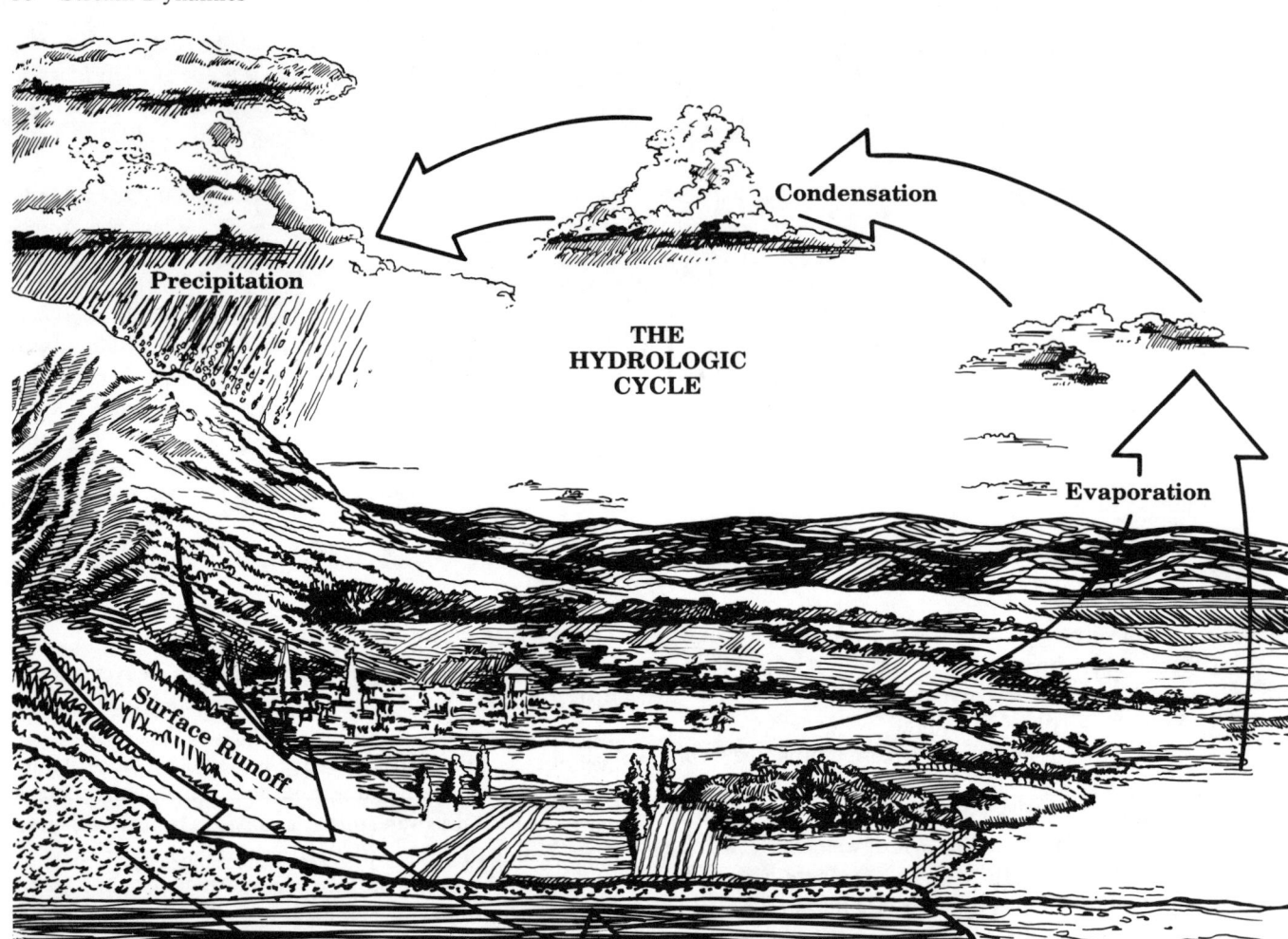

Figure 1. The Hydrologic Cycle

demands are low in winter but high in July and August. Streamflow depends on the interrelation of these processes.

Climate in the Appalachians

The mountains generally have cooler and wetter climates than neighboring low-lying elevations. This is apparent in the distribution of mean annual temperature and precipitation. The variation of mean temperature with surface elevation is approximately three degrees Fahrenheit per 1,000 feet. The effect of such conditions as shielding by mountain barriers, spillover of precipitation across mountain barriers, and channeling of air flow over rough terrain make the relation between elevation and precipitation a variable one. The dependence of temperature and precipitation on elevation plays an important role in determining the plant and animal life found in the area.

Water Temperature

Water temperature is another important factor to be considered by paddlers because of the obvious dangers of encountering cold water when you're not prepared for it.

Surface water temperatures tend to follow air temperatures. Generally, the shallower the stream or reservoir, the closer the water temperature will be to the air temperature.

Streams show a wide variation in temperature throughout the year, ranging from a low of 32°F in winter to a high of about 88°F on some days in July, August, and early September. Streams also show a daily variation: the smaller the stream, the greater the variation, with the least variation occurring in large rivers. The Tennessee River may change only one or two degrees in a day while changes in a small stream can be almost equal to the range in the day's air temperature.

Coal-burning steam plants and industrial users may influence the water temperature in some rivers through thermal discharges. Usually, the added heat is lost within 20 miles downstream from the entry point, but this heat loss depends on the amount of water used, the temperature of the waste water, the size of the stream, the air temperature, and other factors.

Stream Evolution and Morphology

Often, when teaching canoeing or paddling socially, someone will fix an inquisitive stare at a large boulder in midstream and ask, "How in the blazes did that thing get in the middle of the river?" The frequency of being asked this and similar questions about the river has prompted us to include in this book a brief look at river dynamics.

Basically river dynamics represent the relationship between geology and hydraulics, or, expressed differently, what effect flowing water has on the land surface and, conversely, how the land surface modifies the flow of water.

To begin at a rather obvious point, we all know that water flows downhill, moving from a higher elevation to a lower elevation and ultimately flowing into the sea. Contrary to what many people believe, however, the water on its downhill journey does not flow as smoothly as we sometimes imagine the water in our home plumbing flows. Instead, to varying degrees depending on the geology, it has to pound and fight every inch of the way. Squeezed around obstructions, ricocheted from rock to rock, and funneled from side to side, almost any river's course is tortuous at best. This is because the land was there first and is very reluctant to surrender its domain to the moving water, and therefore it does so very slowly and grudgingly. In other words, the water must literally carve out a place in the land through which to flow. It accomplishes this through erosion.

There are three types of moving water erosion: downward erosion, lateral erosion, and headward erosion. All three represent the wearing away of the land by the water. *Downward erosion* is at work continuously on all rivers and can be loosely defined as moving water wearing away the bottom of the river, eroding the geological strata that compose the river bottom, and descending deeper and deeper down into the ground. A graphic example of downward erosion in its purest form is a river that runs through a vertical-walled canyon or gorge. Here the density of the rock forming the canyon walls has limited erosion to the side and left most of the work for downward erosion. Down and down the river cuts without proportional expansion of its width. A gorge or canyon is formed this way.

Most of the time, however, two and usually three kinds of erosion are working simultaneously. When the water, through downward erosion, for example, cuts into the bottom of the river, it encounters geological substrata of varying density and composition. A layer of clay might overlay a shelf of sandstone, under which may be granite or limestone. Since the water is moving downhill at an angle, the flowing water at the top of a mountain might be working against a completely different type of geological substratum than the water halfway down or at the foot of the mountain. Thus, to carve its channel, the water has to work harder in some spots than in others.

Where current crosses a seam marking the boundary between geological substrata of differing resistance to erosion, an interesting phenomenon occurs. Imagine that upstream of this seam the water has been flowing over sandstone, which is worn away by the erosive action of the current at a rather slow rate. As the current crosses the seam, it encounters limestone, which erodes much faster. Downward erosion wears through the limestone relatively quickly while the sandstone on top remains little changed over the same period of time. The result is a waterfall (see figure 2). It may only be a foot high or it may be 100 feet high, depending on the thickness of the layer eaten away. The process is complete when the less resistant substratum is eroded and the water again encounters sandstone or another equally resistant formation. The evolution of a waterfall by downward erosion is similar to covering your wooden porch stairs with snow and then smoothing the snow so that from top to bottom the stairs resemble a nice snowy hill in the park, with the normal shape of the stairs being hidden. Wood (the stairs) and snow can both be eaten away by water. Obviously though, the water will melt the snow much faster than it will rot the wood. Thus, if a tiny stream of water is launched downhill from the top of the stairs, it will melt

Figure 2. Headward Erosion: Waterfalls

through the snow quickly, not stopping until it reaches the more resistant wood on the next stair down. This is how erosion forms a waterfall in nature.

Once a waterfall has formed, regardless of its size, *headward erosion* comes into play. Headward erosion is the wearing away of the base of the waterfall. This action erodes the substrata in an upstream direction toward the headwaters or source of the stream, thus it is called headward erosion. Water falling over the edge of the waterfall lands below with substantial force. As it hits the surface of the water under the falls, it causes a depression in the surface that water from downstream rushes to fill in. This is a hydraulic or what paddlers call a souse hole. Continuing through the surface water, the falling current hits the bottom of the stream. Some of the water is disbursed in an explosive manner, some deflected downstream, and some drawn back to the top where it is recirculated to refill the depression made by yet more falling current. A great deal of energy is expended in this process and the ensuing cyclical turbulence, which combines with bits of rock to make an abrasive mixture, carves slowly away at the rock base of the falls. If the falls are small, the turbulence may simply serve to smooth out the drop, turning a vertical drop into a slanting drop. If the falls are large, the base of the falls may be eroded, leaving the top of the falls substantially intact but precariously unsupported. After a period of time the overhang thus created will surrender to gravity and fall into the river. And that is one way that huge boulders happen to arrive in the middle of the river. Naturally the process is ongoing, and the altered façade of the waterfall is immediately attacked by the currents.

Lateral erosion is the wearing away of the sides of the river by the moving current. While occurring continuously on most rivers to a limited degree, lateral erosion is much more a function of volume and velocity (collectively known as discharge and expressed in cubic feet per second, cfs) than either downward or headward erosion. In other words, as more water is added to a river (beyond that simply required to cover its bottom), the increase in the volume and the speed of the current causes significant additional lateral erosion while headward and downward erosion remain comparatively constant. Thus, as a river swells with spring rain, the amount of water in the river increases. Since water is noncompressible, the current rises on the banks and through lateral erosion tries to enlarge the riverbed laterally to accommodate the extra volume. Effects of this activity can be observed every year following seasonal rains. Even small streams can widen their beds substantially by eroding large chunks of the banks and carrying them downstream. Boulders and trees in the river are often the result of lateral erosion undercutting the bank.

Through a combination of downward erosion, lateral erosion, and meandering, running water can carve broad valleys between mountains and deep canyons through solid rock. Downward and lateral erosion act on the terrain to determine the morphology (depth, width, shape, and course) of a river. Headward erosion serves to smooth out the rough spots that remain.

Curves in a river are formed much as waterfalls are formed; i.e., the water will follow the path of least resistance and its path will twist and turn as it is diverted by resistant substrata. Rivers constantly change and do not continue indefinitely in their courses once they are formed. Water is continuously seeking to decrease the energy required to move from the source to the mouth. This is the essence of all erosion.

As we have observed, headward erosion works *up*stream to smooth out the waterfalls and rapids. Lateral erosion works to make more room for increased volume, and downward erosion deepens the bed and levels obstructions and irregularities. When a river is young (in the geological sense), it cuts downward and is diverted into sharp turns by differing resistance from underlying rock layers. As a stream matures, it carves a valley, sinking even deeper relative to sea level and leaving behind, in many instances, a succession of terraces marking previous valley floors.

Moving water erodes the outside of river bends and deposits much of the eroded matter on the inside of the turn, thereby forming a sand or gravel bar. Jagged turns are changed to sweeping bends. The result in more mature streams is a meander, or the formation of a series of horseshoe-shaped and geometrically predictable loops in the river (see figure 3). A series of such undulating loops markedly widens the valley floor. Often, as time passes, the current erodes the neck of a loop and creates an island in midstream and eliminates a curve in the river.

In the theoretically mature stream, the bottom is smooth and undisturbed by obstructing boulders, rapids, or falls. Straight stretches in the river give way to serpentine meanders, and the water flows at a very moderate rate of descent from the source to the sea. Of course, there are no perfect examples of a mature stream, although rivers such as the Ohio and the Mississippi tend to approach the mature end of the spectrum. A stream exhibiting a high gradient and frequent rapids and sharp turns is described as a young stream in the evolutional sense of the word (stream maturity having more to do with the evolutional development of a stream than with actual age; see figure 4).

All streams carry a load that consists of all the particles, large and small, that are a result of the multiple forms of erosion we discussed. The load, then, is solid matter transported by the current. Rocky streams at high altitudes carry the smallest loads. Their banks and bottoms are more resistant to erosion and their tributary drainages are usually small. Scarcity of load is evident in the clarity of the water. Rivers such as the Mississippi and Ohio carry enormous loads collected from numerous tributaries as well as from their own banks and bottoms. Water in these and in similarly

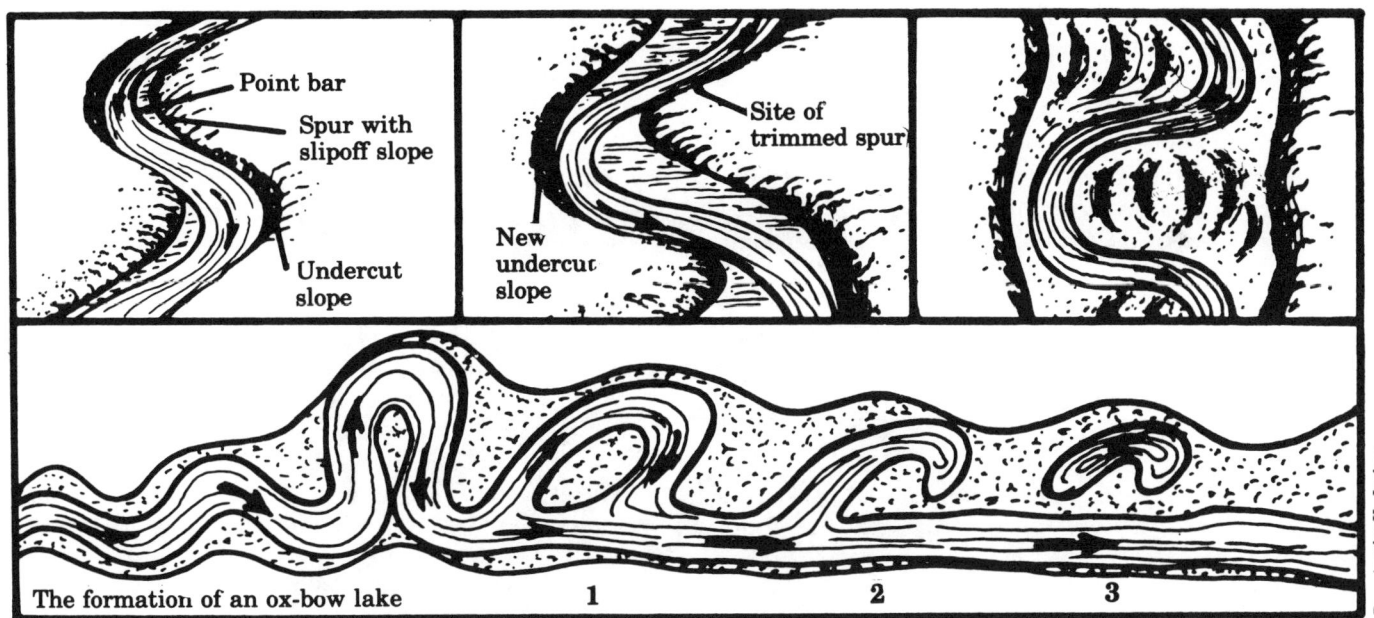

Figure 3. Floodplain Features

large rivers is almost always dark and murky with sediment. Since it takes a lot of energy to move a load, many rivers transport conspicuous (readily visible) loads only during rainy periods when they are high, fast, and powerful. When the high waters abate, there is insufficient energy to continue to transport the large load that then, for the most part, settles as silt or alluvium on the bottom of the stream.

Understanding stream dynamics gives any boater an added advantage in working successfully with the river. Knowledge of stream evolution and morphology tells a paddler where to find the strongest current and deepest channel, where rapids and falls are most likely to occur, and what to expect from a given river if the discharge increases or decreases. But more, understanding the river's evolution and continuing development contributes immeasurably to the paddler's aesthetic experience and allows for a communion and harmony with the river that otherwise might be superficial.

Components of Streamflow

Being able to recognize potential river hazards depends on a practical knowledge of river hydrology—why the water flows the way it does. Since river channels vary greatly in depth and width and the composition of streambeds and their gradients also enter into the river's character, the major components of streamflow bear explanation.

Discharge is the volume of water moving past a given point of the river at any one time. The river current, or *velocity*, is commonly expressed as the speed of water movement in feet per second (fps), and *stage* is the river's height in feet based on an arbitrary measurement gauge. These terms are interrelated; increased water levels mean increased volume and velocity.

Another factor in assessing stream difficulty is *gradient*, which is expressed in feet per mile. As gradient increases, so does velocity. The streams profiled in this book have gradients that range from about 1 foot per mile to an astounding 200 feet per mile. The gradient in any stream or section of a stream changes with the landforms, the geology of the basin. If a river flows over rock or soil with varying resistance to

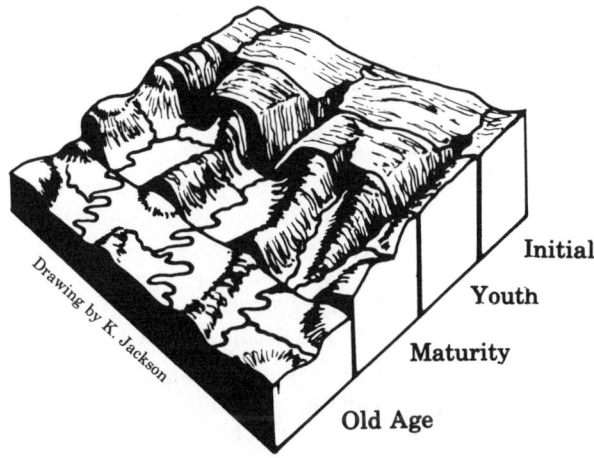

Figure 4. Stream Dissection Cycle: Evolution of a Landscape

20 Stream Dynamics

Whitney Shields running the last drop (the Spout) of the Virginia side of Great Falls of the Potomac (2.87 feet on the Little Falls gauge). Photo by Ed Grove.

erosion, then ledges, waterfalls, and rapids sometimes form and dramatically affect gradient.

Velocity is also affected by the width and depth of the streambed. Rapids form where streams are shallow and swift. Large obstructions in shallow streams of high velocity cause severe rapids. Within a given channel there are likely to be rapids with different levels of difficulty. The current on straight sections of river is usually fastest in the middle. The depth of water in river bends is determined by flow rates and soil types. Water tends to cut away the land and form deep holes on the outsides of bends where the current is the swiftest.

Pennsylvania

Lower Youghiogheny River

Confluence To Ohiopyle

The Yough in Pennsylvania is less demanding than its Maryland headwaters, being suitable for practiced intermediates. The ten mile run from Confluence to Ohiopyle passes through a beautiful winding gorge. You can put in on river left in Confluence; however, if there is not enough discharge from the dam, put in downstream beyond the mouth of the Casselman or at the Riversport Camp a mile or so downstream. For about two miles below the dam, there are only occasional riffles, with flat water predominating. About a mile below the outskirts of town, the river turns away from the broad valley and heads left into narrow confines. The first of several Class II rapids begins here. These are all easily read and delightful to run. Soon the rapids recede and the river broadens out considerably for three or four miles. If it is a windy day, this section can be painfully arduous (the wind always blows upstream for some reason). Soon, however, the canyon walls begin to squeeze the river and rapids reform for the last three miles of the trip. Aside from the railroad tracks on either side, the river flows through a roadless, peopleless setting.

When you see the first signs of Ohiopyle in the distance on the right bank, you should begin to plan your exit from the river; dangerous Ohiopyle Falls is just downstream. Conservative paddlers will want to hang to the left of the island above the Ohiopyle bridge and land on the rocky "beach" just below it. More experienced paddlers will want to run the more difficult passages to the right and take out at either side of the bridge. In water under two feet, an upset at this point is not serious; all one has to do is stand up and walk to shore. Nonetheless, a take-out in Ohiopyle should always be made with caution and with consideration for the inexperienced members of the group. Do not paddle beyond the abandoned railroad bridge, as this will commit you to running the falls.

Ohiopyle to Stewarton

The seven-mile Ohiopyle to Stewarton run on the Yough was for many years the single most popular whitewater paddling run in the eastern U. S. (slipping only recently into second place behind the Nantahala River in western North Carolina). With beautiful scenery, dependable year-round flow, and delightful Class III+ rapids, the Yough has it all. Rich in paddling history, the Ohiopyle to Stewarton run was the birthplace of commercial rafting in the eastern U. S. and the training ground for some of the nation's best paddlers. Popularity, however, is not without its costs; many are the boaters who have forsaken the Yough for less trafficked streams. And many are the summer Saturdays when you could seemingly walk from Ohiopyle to Stewarton by hopping from raft to raft and kayak to canoe in an endless river-choking flotilla of private and commercial craft. Neoprene and ABS were to the Yough what water hyacinths are to the Suwanee.

While crowds have diminished the enjoyment of some and created a circus-like spectacle for others, increased usage of the river has resulted in a management plan to limit use, and the construction of a convenient take-out to replace the previous climb up a mountainside and over a railroad track to the previous take-out. The Yough is still heavily used, but conditions are improved.

The first mile of the run, known as the Loop, is the most popular and contains a great deal of action. The paddler has everything thrown at him but the kitchen sink. For openers, after putting in below Ohiopyle Falls, the paddler must face

---

Section: Confluence to Ohiopyle

Counties: Somerset, Fayette (PA)

USGS Quads: Confluence, Ohiopyle

Suitable for: Day cruising, training

Skill Level: Novice

Months Runnable: All, when not frozen

Interest Highlights: Challenging rapids

Scenery: Excellent

Difficulty: Class I-II

Average Width: 300 feet

Velocity: Slow to fast

Gradient: 11 feet per mile

Runnable Water Levels: Ohiopyle gauge: Pittsburgh Weather Service (412) 644-2890
  Minimum: 0.5 feet at Ohiopyle; minimum enjoyable level is 2.0 feet.
  Maximum: 4.0 is high and fast; 8-9 feet is the maximum

Hazards: Falls just below the take-out

Scouting: None

Portages: None

Rescue Index: Accessible but difficult

Source of Additional Information: Ohiopyle State Park, Ohiopyle, PA 15470 (412) 329-8591

Access Points	River Miles	Shuttle Miles
A-B	11	13

Lower Youghiogheny River 23

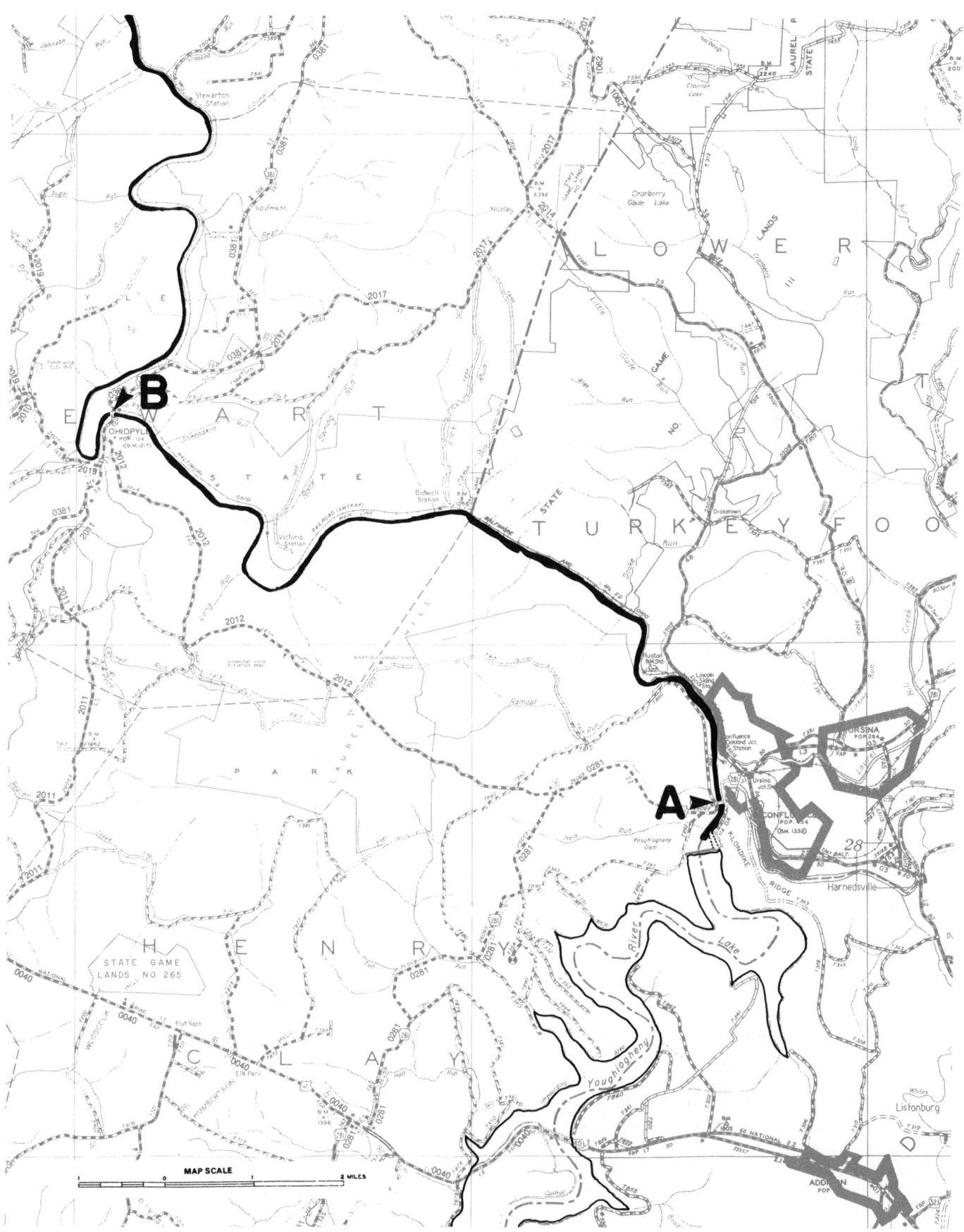

a series of ledges known as Entrance Rapids without any warm-up. It is a long, tortuous course into twisted currents. For indiscretions, a huge rock (Sugarloaf) stands in midriver as a sentinel to broach paddlerless boats or even paddled boats. Half of the upsets on the Loop take place here. Most paddlers stick to the left and regroup in an eddy below Entrance to mend boats, bandage bodies, retrieve paddles, and gather courage for the next rapid, Cucumber.

Here a long rock garden precedes an extremely vigorous drop through a narrow passage. Usually you should stick to the far left, carefully avoiding anything resembling a broaching situation, and gradually move to the right where huge boulders have forced the course of the river. The best advice from here is to hang on and keep your reflexive and anticipatory braces ready. Going through Cucumber with or without a boat is what it must be like to be flushed down the john.

The next rapid is merely a minor surfing hydraulic divided in mid-stream by a boulder, followed by an interesting drop into an S-shaped curler. After this there is a long, steep rock garden which can be run in a variety of ways. The far right is the most direct except for an extremely sharp left-hand turn that must be made precisely, to avoid running your boat several yards up onto shore. Another vigorous but straightforward rock garden known as Dartmouth Slalom Rapids follows.

The final Loop rapids, Railroad, is another infamous boat chewer. Several passages exist over the steep drop, the most vigorous of which is slightly left of center, but you won't recognize it until you are right on it. If you wind up too far to the right you will be in a particularly juicy hydraulic known as Charlie's Washing Machine and it will be all over very quickly. A flip will take a boat or paddler a considerable distance in high water. Immediately after dropping over the ledge, you may have several options, depending on water level. If the water is low, you will have to immediately make a sharp left to avoid the next set of boulders. In high water, you can paddle straight ahead over them. If you've had enough, you can take out up a very steep bank on the right and take a long trail up to the picnic area.

Generally, paddlers spend a lot of time playing around on the Loop and then go on to Stewarton. For those not up on handling such rough water, a put-in can be made below Railroad Rapids and, with a few judicious carries, the trip can be made to Stewarton in comparative safety. The first two miles below the Loop are open and easily read Class II descents with only one dropping sharply.

Soon the river narrows and appears to end, but a loud roar coming from the left warns the paddler of a special treat. A paddler who is on this section for the first time may want to scout this—Dimple's Rapids—considered by some to be the most difficult of the lower Yough. The current is choked down into a bulging filament, smashes directly into a large boulder, and veers off to the right. Immediately below this is a dazzling combination of reefs and boulders, and below these are a long field of haystacks and a riverwide, gaping hydraulic (Swimmers' Rapids), followed by more haystacks; hence goofing Dimple's can make a long day for the paddler. Don't try to miss the big boulder at the top; ride with the current and bounce off the pillow with the appropriate lean and brace. At medium water levels you can sneak this drop by running down the center.

Other gems before reaching the take-out are: Bottle of Wine, next below Swimmers; the Double Hydraulic, which is just what it says, and if you didn't drive through the first, forget the second; River's End, where huge boulders seemingly dam up the river but actually funnel it through a sharp left and steep drop; and Schoolhouse Rock, possibly so named because of the expensive tuitions it has collected in broached boats.

At the mouth of Bruner Run the trip ends. The Park Service has taken over shuttling, so you can just sit back and think about that day in the future when other rivers will be like the Yough. Tokens for the bus must be purchased at the put-in. Be sure to check for details as they may change after this writing.

Section: Ohiopyle to Stewarton

Counties: Fayette (PA)

USGS Quads: Ohiopyle, Mill Run, Ft. Necessity

Suitable for: Day cruising

Skill Level: Intermediate

Months Runnable: All, when not frozen

Interest Highlights: Ohiopyle Falls, Fallingwater by Frank Lloyd Wright, Ferncliff Peninsula

Scenery: Excellent

Difficulty: Class III+

Average Width: 300 feet

Velocity: Fast!

Gradient: 27 feet per mile (48 feet in the loop)

Runnable Water Levels:
 Minimum: 0.5 feet
 Enjoyable: 2.0
 Maximum: 4.0 is high and fast; 8–9 feet is the maximum

Hazards: None

Scouting: Dimple, Rivers End, and Railroad rapids

Portages: None

Rescue Index: Accessible but difficult

Source of Additional Information: Ohiopyle State Park, Ohiopyle, PA 15470 (412) 329-8591

Access Points	River Miles	Shuttle Miles
B–C	7	7 plus bus shuttle

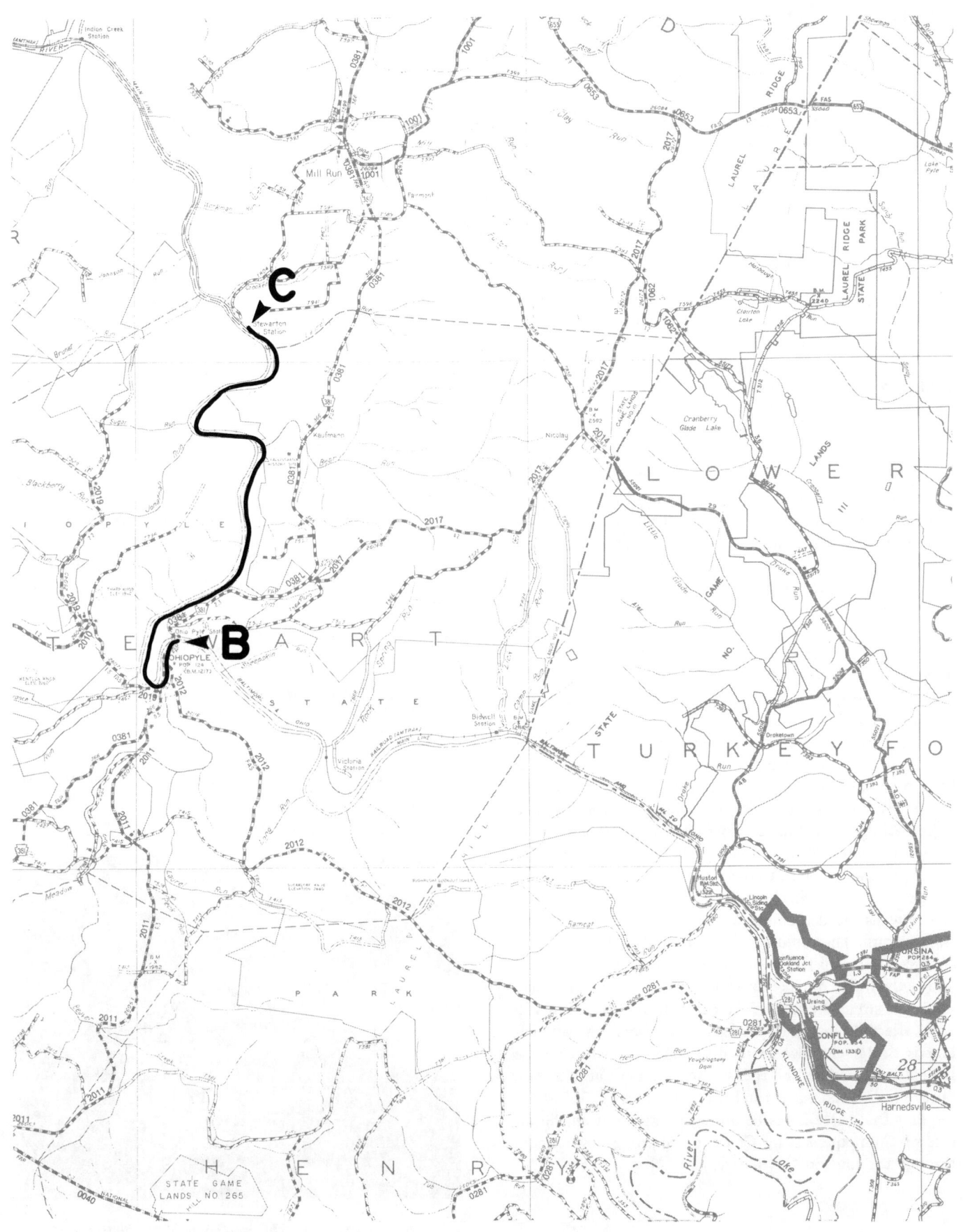

Slippery Rock Creek

The Slippery Rock Creek has long been a favorite of Pittsburgh and northern Ohio boaters, combining beauty, accessibility, and challenging whitewater. Although the best part of the run is protected within McConnells Mill State Park, all access points are on private land. The landowner relations at the Route 422 bridge at Rose Point (map point B) are strained at best; use the downstream left side and be sure your car is off the road but not on the grass. There is a private campground on the other side which permits access to their patrons. You can avoid all this hassle by putting in at the Route 19 bridge at Kennedy Mill, or by parking at the State Park offices on McConnells Mill Road and following a trail to the river. The creek has been run as far upstream as Route 173; this is a flatwater run, quite unspoiled, broken only by an occasional Class I riffle.

The first few miles below Kennedy Mill are not exciting, but the river begins to pick up below Route 422. The rapids are a series of S-shaped boulder gardens, with powerful twisting currents at high levels and tight maneuvers during dry periods. One of these, "Airport Rapids," has a vigorous eddyline pop-up spot. The river is deep, offering lots of opportunities for squirts. The last rapid dies in the backwash of a low dam at McConnells Mills. Carry on either side; the left appears to be easier. There is road access to this point, and trails parallel the river from here on. (See map point C.)

Below the dam is a mile of continuous rapids formed by huge sandstone boulders. The river is extremely constricted here. At low water, the maneuvering is tight and many drops are blind. High levels can exhibit extremely violent holes; the river should not be underrated. The Three Rivers Paddling Club of Pittsburgh runs an annual slalom race here in the fall, augmented by a release of water from Lake Arthur. Below this "mad mile" the river opens up a bit, and Eckert Bridge (Breakneck Bridge) is reached. The popular whitewater run ends here, and there is a gauge on the bridge which corresponds well to the Slippery Rock readings.

The river now begins to open up, and the river gets quieter as the walls recede. This is a popular novice-intermediate training run. The rapids, while easier, retain the "S-Turn" character seen upstream; an assortment of large boulders add to the fun and make for good teaching eddies and ferry sites. The stretch between Eckert and Harris Bridge is also a good alternate for weak parties at high water. A gauge at Harris Bridge can also be used to track water levels. The river can be paddled all the way to its mouth at Wurtemburg. This is a flat water run broken by Class I riffles, and it requires that three dams be portaged. Take out on the far side of Connoquenessing Creek, or continue downstream through the Elwood City Gorge.

Section: Kennedy Mill to Connoquenessing Creek
Counties: Lawrence (PA)
USGS Quads: Portersville, Zelienople, Beaver Falls
Suitable for: Cruising and training
Skill Level: Intermediate to advanced
Months Runnable: March through May, and after heavy rains
Interest Highlights: McConnells Mill State Park
Scenery: Pretty to beautiful
Difficulty: Class III-IV
Average Width: 90 feet
Velocity: Fast
Gradient: 23 feet per mile
Runnable Water Levels: Call Pittsburgh Weather Service (412) 644-2890. Listen for the Slippery Rock reading. The river can rise several feet after a good rain!
  Minimum: 0.0; minimum for fun is 0.5
  Optimum: 2.0
  Maximum: 3.0 is high water (Class IV); 5.0 is near floodstage (Class V)
Hazards: Dam at McConnells Mill State Park and three others on the last stretch, just above Connoquenessing Creek
Scouting: None
Portages: All dams
Rescue Index: Accessible
Source of Additional Information: McConnells Mill State Park (412) 368-8091. Pittsburgh Council, American Youth Hostels, 6300 5th Avenue, Pittsburgh, PA 15232. The latter has an excellent guidebook to western Pennsylvania.

Access Points	River Miles	Shuttle Miles
A-H	11.1	15.0

Western Pennsylvania Whitewater School on Slippery Rock Creek. Photo by Tom Irwin.

Slippery Rock Creek 27

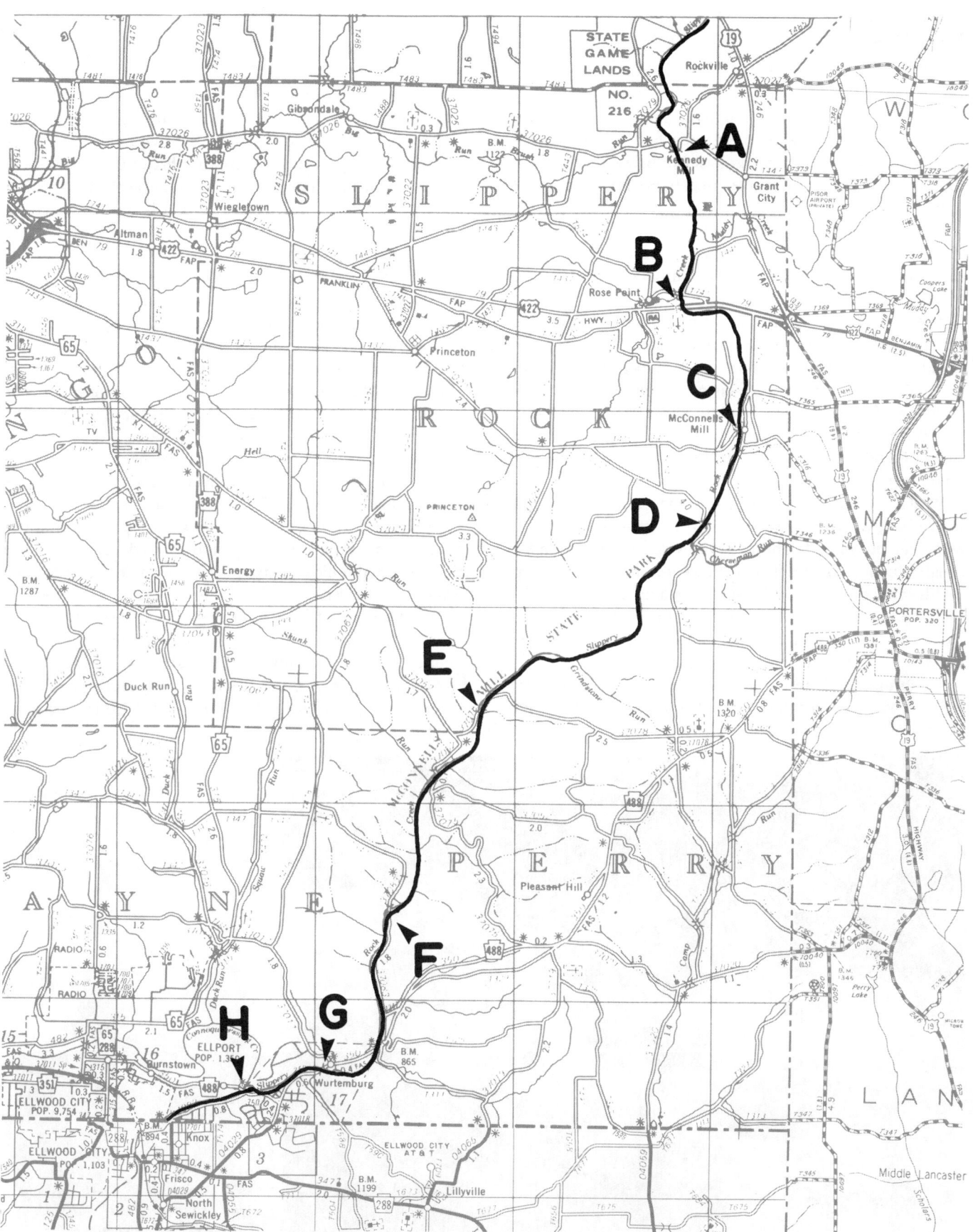

Wills Creek

For the advanced boater, this is an outstanding five-mile trip on a pistol of a river through a small scenic gorge just north of the Maryland/Pennsylvania border. The shuttle road parallels the river and crosses two bridges on the way to the put-in, so there is ample opportunity for scouting the tougher parts of the trip and taking out if there are problems. The only unfortunate part about this superb stretch is that it is not runnable more often. The best times to target this stretch are after heavy rains or during snowmelt in late winter and early spring.

The description below refers to Wills Creek after the summer flood of 1984 (which heavily damaged the town of Hyndman) and the heavy rain of November 1985. The severely damaged shuttle road has now been repaired. However, the aforementioned flooding and bulldozer work in the riverbed have rearranged some of the rapids. Paddlers should therefore carefully scout this river from the road to note these changes.

Basically, this Class III-IV run at moderate levels begins with a bang at an irregular Class III-IV four-foot ledge just below the put-in and continues with Class II-III action for roughly a mile. It reaches a crescendo at Class V Yoyo rapids (only runnable tight right at medium and high levels) followed shortly by a strong new Class IV just below. Wills Creek then slowly simmers down through Class III and then Class II stuff to the take-out at Hyndman.

The bridge at Fairhope is an easy bucolic put-in on river right. A vigorous surfing spot just upstream of the bridge provides a warm-up for the adventurous. All then is relatively calm until the paddler hits a sloping diagonal four-foot ledge (Class III-IV) 150 yards downstream. The ledge has a strong hydraulic and another hole just below in the center which backenders paddlers at high levels. First-timers should scout this ledge from the right bank or during the shuttle for primary and sneak routes. The carry is on river right.

Once all errant boats and bodies are picked up below the ledge, the action is Class II and III for about a mile at reasonable levels. This gives the paddler a fleeting opportunity to enjoy some of the old smelter stacks and rhododendron in the gorge. Also, while dodging rocks and riding waves, the quick of eye and paddle can wave at passing trains that cut through this scenic gorge and perhaps spot several kilns and an old coke oven high on the left bank.

After this bouncy mile, an ominous roar announces the approach to Yoyo Rapids. Pull over on the right well above the rapids and scout. The faint of heart should also carry right. Hopefully, you will have looked at Yoyo during the shuttle. This rapids was originally named because of the tenacious hydraulic lurking below its main drop that did not always let paddlers go easily.

However, past floods have changed this rapids from a Class IV to a Class V and altered the route to run it. Previously, paddlers usually ran the main drop in the center. However, the center slot now has logs and debris jammed in it and is undercut. This is also true of the left side. The right

YoYo Rapids, Wills Creek, after the flood and rains of 1984 and 1985. Photo by Mike Fetchero.

Wills Creek   29

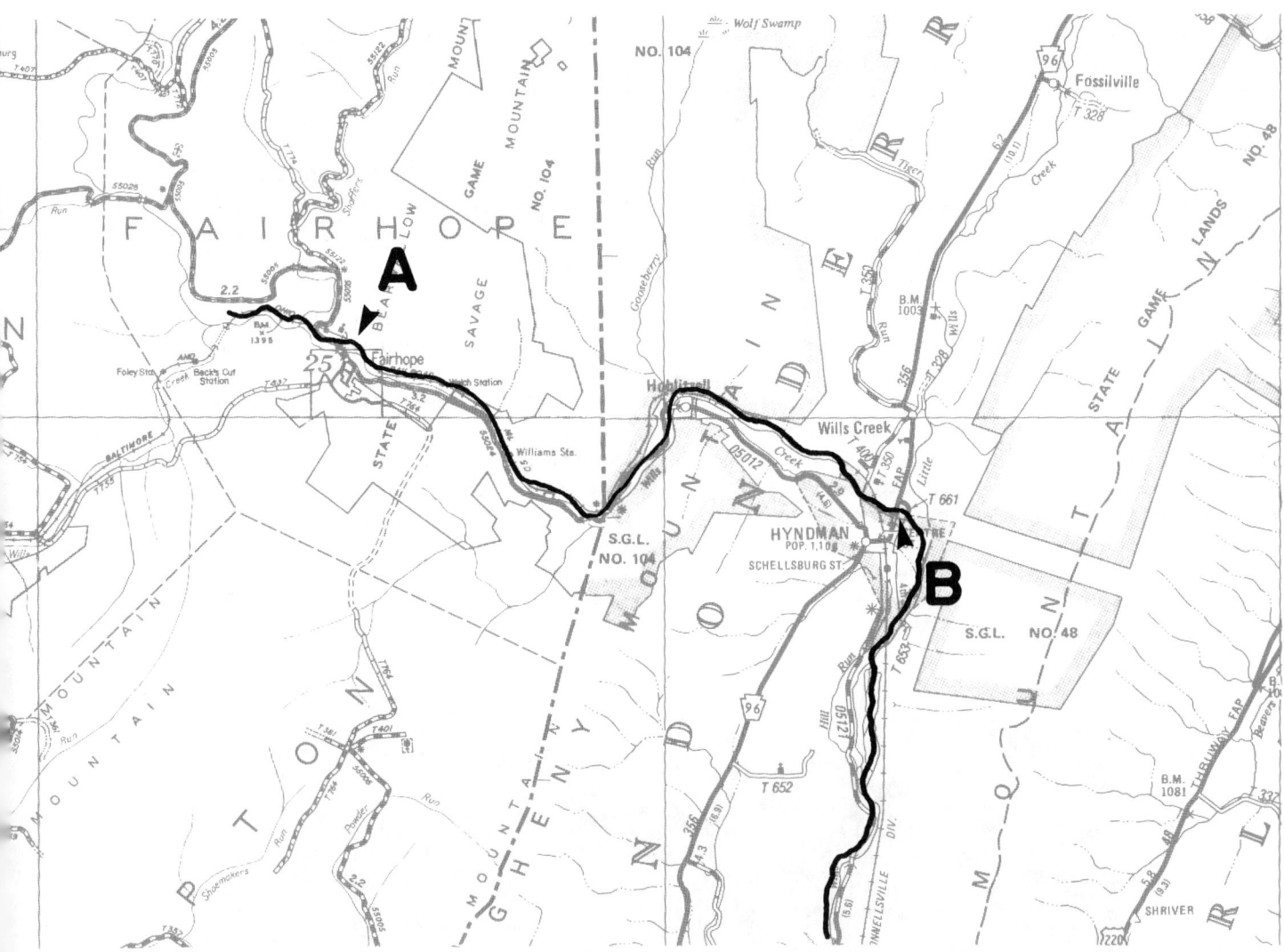

Section: Fairhope to Hyndman

Counties: Somerset, Bedford (PA)

USGS Quads: Fairhope, Hyndman

Suitable for: Day cruising

Skill Level: Advanced boaters (moderate levels) and expert boaters (high levels)

Months Runnable: Winter and spring after rains or snow melt

Interest Highlights: Small gorge

Scenery: Pretty to beautiful for most of the trip; good at the end

Difficulty: Class III-IV at low to medium levels; Class IV at medium to high levels; Class IV-V at high levels

Average Width: 20-35 feet

Velocity: Fast

Gradient: 72 feet per mile

Runnable Water Levels:
  Minimum: About 2.2 feet on the Hyndman gauge; 0.3 feet at Wills Creek (Cumberland) gauge; roughly 3.5-4.5 feet on Cumberland (Potomac) gauge or 4.5 feet on Kitzmiller gauge
  Maximum: About 3.5-4.0 feet on Hyndman gauge; 3.0 feet on Wills Creek (Cumberland) gauge; roughly 6-6.5 feet on the Cumberland (Potomac) gauge means very heavy water—decked boats only
  Note: The summer 1984 flood may have significantly changed the Hyndman gauge.

Hazards: Trees in river; huge holes and hydraulics at high levels; Yoyo Rapids.

Scouting: 4-foot ledge just below put-in (Class III-IV); Yoyo Rapids (Class V); rapids just below Yoyo (Class IV)

Portages: Yoyo Rapids at low levels and maybe at medium/high levels

Rescue Index: Accessible

Source of Additional Information: National Weather Service, Cumberland (Potomac) gauge, (301) 899-7378; USGS gauge Eckhart, MD—3 feet minimum

Access Points	River Miles	Shuttle Miles
A-B	5.5	6.0

side is now the only route, and it is unrunnable at low levels. At medium and high levels, the paddler must negotiate a pushy Class III entry and catch an eddy behind a boulder on the right. After leaving the eddy and staying tight right, the paddler must tweeze between a large boulder on the left and a pinning rock on the right. One then works to an eddy on the left to finish. Throw ropes should be set on river right.

After Yoyo, paddlers should remain alert. Just a couple of hundred yards below is a steep boulder clogged Class IV rapid. Scout this before running it.

Good strong Class III action continues for a mile below the first bridge after Yoyo. Then, the river slowly begins to quiet down. Upon reaching the second bridge, the stream bed widens and things calm down even further until you reach the take-out at Hyndman.

At low levels (see data sheet for gauges), Wills Creek is a Class III-IV bumpy rock slalom for experienced open and decked boaters. At medium levels it changes to a solid Class IV run—becoming powerful and pushy where the paddler must dodge boulders and holes. At high levels the run becomes an even tougher Class IV-V trip. The rocks are covered, the eddys have vanished, and the river is one long rapid of big waves and large nasty holes. This is decked boater territory. At high levels the major rapids (particularly Yoyo) should be carefully scouted for a way through before putting in.

The sections above Fairhope (Class III-IV with two waterfall portages) and below Hyndman (Class I-III) are also runnable. However, this center section remains the real whitewater heart of Wills Creek.

Wills Creek has two gauges that paddlers should check. Both are handpainted gauges. The first is reached from Cumberland. From downtown Cumberland follow Old Route 40 toward the "Narrows," a readily visible gap in Wills Mountain just north of downtown Cumberland. On the north side of the gap is a gauge on an old railroad abutment. This gauge on river right can be read while driving and saves the long drive to Hyndman if levels are marginally high or low. The gauge in Hyndman is near the take-out bridge there. For general reference before driving to Cumberland, a third gauge is helpful. The Cumberland gauge on the Potomac (checked by calling 301-899-7378) should be at least 3.5 to 4.5 feet. [E. G.]

New rapid below YoYo on Wills Creek. Photo by Mike Fetchero.

Dark Shade Creek, Shade Creek, and Stony Creek

Western Pennsylvania has a number of outstanding runs originating in the high central plateau. This run is unusual in that it connects three streams into a continuously difficult whitewater run. Starting with the steep, boulder-filled drops of Dark Shade Creek through the ledges of Shade Creek to the rolling power of the lower Stony, this run is one of the most interesting in the eastern U. S. when high water levels permit an attempt. At lower levels both Shade and Stony Creek offer exciting sport in an area not commonly known to paddlers.

The put-in for Dark Shade is at the Cairnbrook bridge. There is about a mile of fast flowing, riffly water for a warmup before the bottom falls out. The remainder of the run is a series of the steepest, tightest, blindest drops north of the Upper Youghiogheny. While the water and rocks are discolored by mine acid, the banks are unspoiled and the overall effect is one of wilderness. First-timers, however, will probably not notice the difference. And all too soon, it's over. You can walk about fifty yards from the mouth to Route 160, or continue on down the Shade.

Bernie Seth in the Beast Rapid on Stony Creek. Photo by Stan Dunn.

Dark Shade Creek

Section: Cairnbrook to mouth

Counties: Somerset (PA)

USGS Quads: Central City, Windber

Suitable for: Cruising

Skill Level: Advanced to expert

Months Runnable: February to March during high runoff or after heavy rains

Interest Highlights: Intense rapids!

Scenery: Beautiful

Difficulty: Class IV–V

Average Width: 30 feet

Velocity: Fast

Gradient: 90 feet per mile

Runnable Water Levels: There is no gauge, so walk down to the mouth along Clear Shade Creek from Rt. 160. If the last rapid looks runnable, the rest of the stream is o.k.

Hazards: Difficult rapids

Scouting: Advisable

Portages: None

Rescue Index: Accessible

Source of Additional Information: Edward Gertler, 503 Bonifant Street, Silver Spring, MD 20910. He publishes an excellent Pennsylvania guidebook which covers many small streams.

Access Points	River Miles	Shuttle Miles
A–C	1.9	2.1

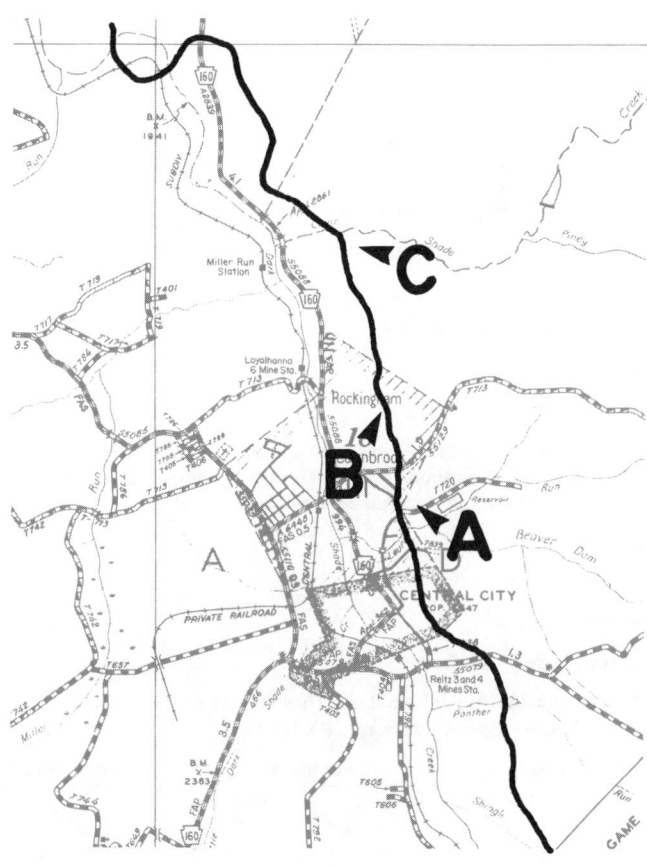

Shade Creek paddlers will walk downstream 50 yards along the banks of Clear Shade Creek from the Route 160 bridge. At one time this was a continuous Class III stream; the floods of 1977 changed it into a drop-pool run which reaches Class IV in a number of spots. The harder rapids are formed by rubble piles in combination with ledges. Many island passages are braided and strainers are not uncommon. As with Dark Shade Creek, the water is unattractive but the banks are beautiful. A late spring run amid the rhododendron and mountain laurel blooms will be quite memorable. There are three bridges on the run; at 4.2 miles, 6.3 miles, and at 9.3 miles in Seanor, just above the mouth of the Stony. The last rapid, a delightful series of ledges, is a favorite and is a great place to play.

Shade Creek empties into the Stony below Seanor. This river has more than twice the volume, and in its continuous rapids the contrast is quite exciting. Most drops are formed by sloping sandstone ledges which create unbeatable shallow-entry playing holes. At high water (over three-and-a-half feet) the river is extremely wide and powerful, with huge stoppers to be found in every rapid. Low levels can be pickier, but offer better playing opportunities. Difficulty is comparable to the Lower Youghiogheny. Three-quarters of the way downstream a steep rapid empties into a pool behind a dam. This should be carried. A short distance below a pipeline crosses, creating a nasty hydraulic. Portaging is recommended. There are easy riffles to the take-out, a bridge just upstream of the mouth of Paint Creek. This take-out is sometimes tricky to find; if you get lost continue under the Route 219 bridge to where numbered highways reach the river. The river can be run all the way into Johnstown, but it is neither attractive nor challenging to do so.

Shade Creek

Section: Junction of Clear Shade and Dark Shade Creeks to Stony Creek

Counties: Somerset (PA)

USGS Quads: Windber, Hooversville

Suitable for: Cruising

Skill Level: Intermediate to advanced

Months Runnable: March to April and after heavy rains

Interest Highlights: Excellent rapids

Scenery: Attractive to beautiful

Difficulty: Class III-IV

Average Width: 50 feet

Velocity: Fast

Gradient: 60 feet per mile

Runnable Water Levels: There is no gauge, so check the creek at the take-out. Casselman River at Markleton should be over 3.5 feet; call Pittsburgh Weather Service (412) 644-2890.

Hazards: None

Scouting: None

Portages: None

Rescue Index: Accessible

Source of Additional Information: Three Rivers Paddling Club, 115 Delaney Street, Pittsburgh, PA 15235

Access Points	River Miles	Shuttle Miles
C-F	9.6	15.0

Stony Creek

Section: Seanor (mouth of Shade Creek to LR55127 SW of Paint)

Counties: Somerset (PA)

USGS Quads: Hooversville, Johnstown

Suitable for: Cruising

Skill Level: Intermediate to advanced

Months Runnable: February to early May and after heavy rains

Interest Highlights: Whitewater

Scenery: Pretty in spots

Difficulty: Class III-IV

Average Width: 120 feet

Velocity: Fast

Gradient: 35 feet per mile

Runnable Water Levels: The gauge is at the Hollsopple bridge (two miles upstream of the put-in off Rt. 403)
  Minimum: 1.5 feet on Hollsopple (3.5 feet on the Markleton gauge on Cassleman River)
  Maximum: 3.0 feet at Holsopple is a good medium-high level, and probably a maximum for most open boaters. Watch out at 4.0 feet or more.

Hazards: Dam near end of run; pipeline crossing 100 yards below dam

Scouting: None

Portages: Dam must be carried. Pipeline carry is recommended, especially in high water

Rescue Index: Accessible but difficult

Source of Additional Information: Pittsburgh Council, American Youth Hostels, 6300 5th Avenue, Pittsburgh, PA 15232. They publish a guidebook to western Pennsylvania.

Access Points	River Miles	Shuttle Miles
F-G	4.3	6.5

Dark Shade, Shade, and Stony Creeks 33

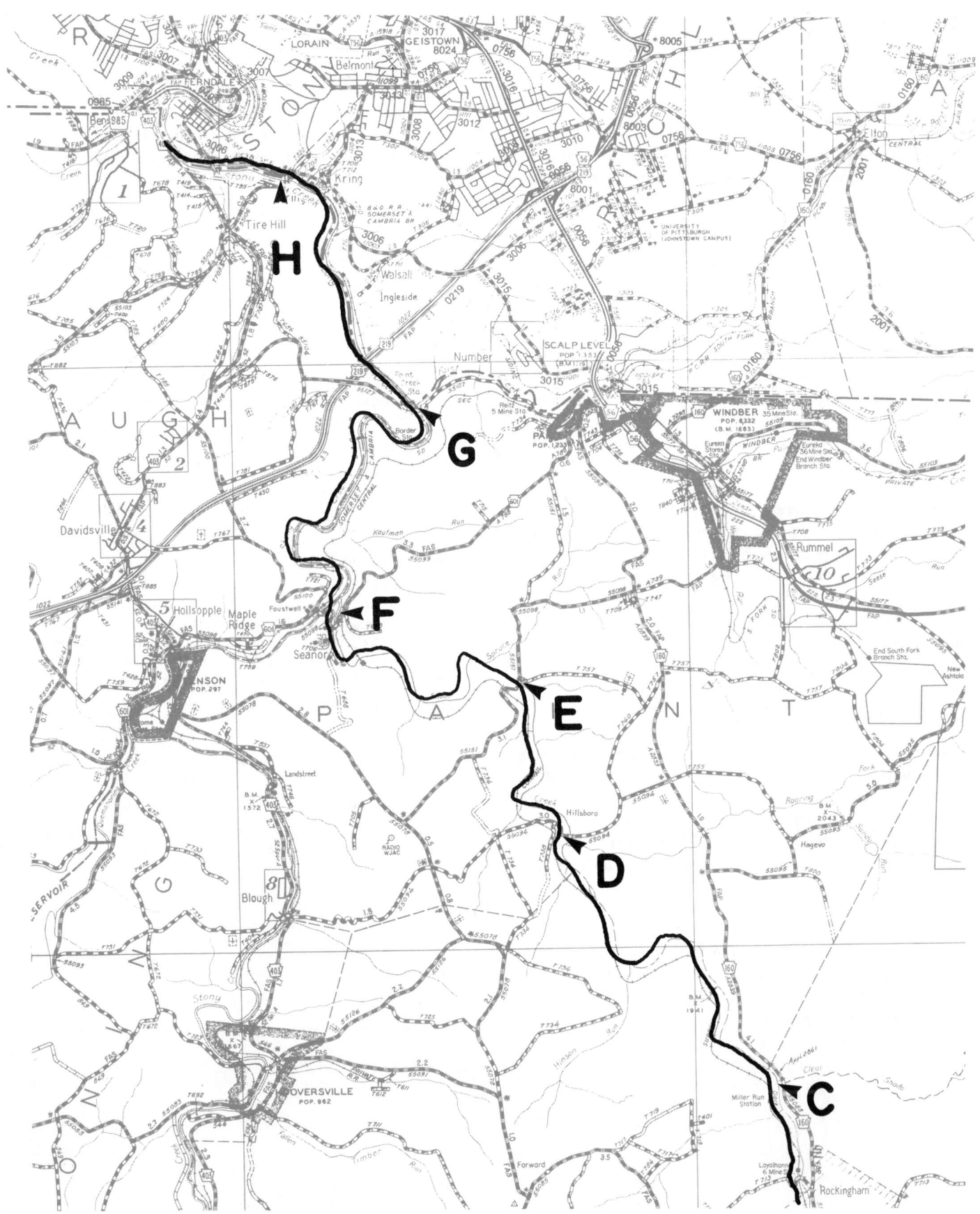

Pine Creek

Pine Creek is a beautiful, unspoiled stream which drains the wild plateau country of north-central Pennsylvania. The upper reaches in the Grand Canyon of Pennsylvania are near-wilderness; the lower stretch, paralleled by a road, is still attractive and rural. Both have easy access and camping facilities for the canoeist.

The "Grand Canyon" run starts at the Big Meadows Access area in Ansonia, where Route 6 crosses Little Pine Creek. There is a gauge on this bridge which allows a final check of water levels. The river quickly leaves the valley behind and enters the canyon, paralleled by a private dirt road on river right. The run is quite mild with one exception: Owassee Rapid, a Class II drop, which occurs on a left bend at the base of the first real cliffs seen in the canyon. The waves at higher levels can easily swamp an open boat; the sneak route is on the extreme left and should be scouted.

Below here the canyon becomes an uncomplicated float, with easy riffles alternating with fast-moving pools. The high green hills and the sparkling water makes for a memorable scene. There is road access at Tiadaghton nine miles downstream on the left; primitive camping can be found just upstream of this point; well water, sanitary facilities, and fireplaces are provided. Camping is not permitted in state park land or on posted private lands, but *is* permitted on state forest and game lands. Check the Pine Creek topographic map before you make camp. Since the railroad runs along the left bank throughout the canyon, the river is popular with fishermen. Wherever possible, pass behind them or across the river from where they are fishing.

There is a boater access area at Blackwell where Route 414 crosses the river. While more developed, the lower run is still quite attractive, with deep green pools joined together by Class I–II drops. Except for big waves at high levels there are no difficulties, leaving a paddler free to drift or fish. There is another access area at Slate Run and a camping area (Black Walnut Bottom) two miles downstream. Access to the camping area is by foot or boat only. The closeness of the road permits other unofficial access, but much of the land along the stream is private.

As you move down the stream the rapids become more widely spaced. Slate Run to Cammal is a popular run used by the Penn State Outing Club. We have ended the run at Waterville, but a trip could be made down the widening valley all the way to the Susquehanna, and thence downstream to Harrisburg and the Chesapeake Bay. The lower river has water throughout the summer except during a drought; however, you may have to drag your canoes across a few gravel bars.

Section: Ansonia to Blackwell

Counties: Tioga (PA)

USGS Quads: Tiadaghton, Cedar Run

Suitable for: Cruising; canoe camping

Skill Level: Novice

Months Runnable: March through May

Interest Highlights: Leonard Harrison State Park; Grand Canyon of Penn.; West Rim Trail

Scenery: Exceptionally beautiful

Difficulty: Class I

Average Width: 150 feet

Velocity: Moderate

Gradient: 16 feet per mile

Runnable Water Levels: The Cedar Run gauge is reported daily to the Williamsport Weather Service (717) 368-8744. Two feet is the minimum level; 2.5 feet gives solid Class II rapids at Owassee. There is also a gauge on the Rt. 6 bridge: 1.0 feet is a minimum enjoyable equivalent reading. With a foot more water, swamping becomes a problem for open canoes in a few rapids.

Hazards: Owassee Rapid, Class II–III

Scouting: Owassee Rapid

Portages: None, except that novices may want to carry Owassee on the left

Rescue Index: Remote

Source of Additional Information: Tioga State Forest, Box 94, Wellsboro, PA 16901, (717) 724-2866. Tiadaghton State Forest, 423 East Central Avenue, S. Williamsport, PA 17701 (717) 327-3450. The latter has a folder, "Canoeing Pine Creek," and a topographic map of the West Rim Trail that shows river access points and camping areas. For guided raft trips contact Pine Creek Outfitters, RD 4 Box 130B, Wellsboro, PA 16901 (717) 724-3003.

Access Points	River Miles	Shuttle Miles
A–C	17.0	27.0

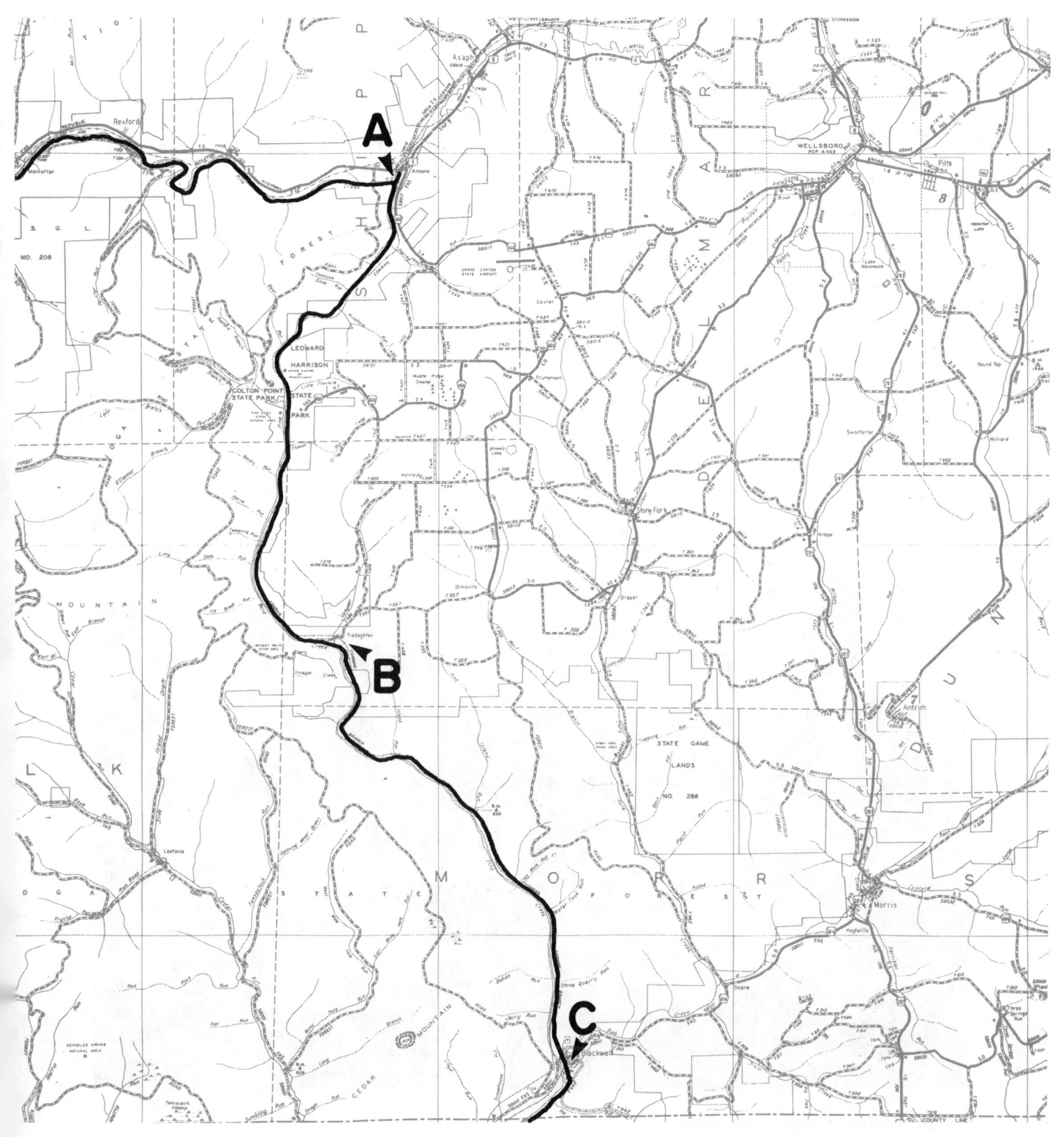

Pine Creek 35

36 Pine Creek

Section: Blackwell to Waterville

Counties: Tioga, Lycoming (PA)

USGS Quads: Cedar Run, Cammal, Slate Run, Jersey Mills

Suitable for: Cruising; canoe camping

Skill Level: Novice

Months Runnable: March through June

Scenery: Pretty

Difficulty: Class I

Average Width: 200 feet

Velocity: Slow to moderate

Gradient: 9 feet per mile

Runnable Water Levels: Check the Slate Run gauge at the Williamsport Weather Service (717) 368-8744.
Minimum: 1.75; minimum enjoyable level is 2.5

Hazards: Large waves at high water

Scouting: None

Portages: None, but there may be drag on gravel bars at low water

Rescue Index: Accessible

Source of Additional Information: Tioga and Tiadaghton State Forests (addresses above)

Access Points	River Miles	Shuttle Miles
C–G	27.0	28.0

Pine Creek Canyon. Photo by Tim Palmer.

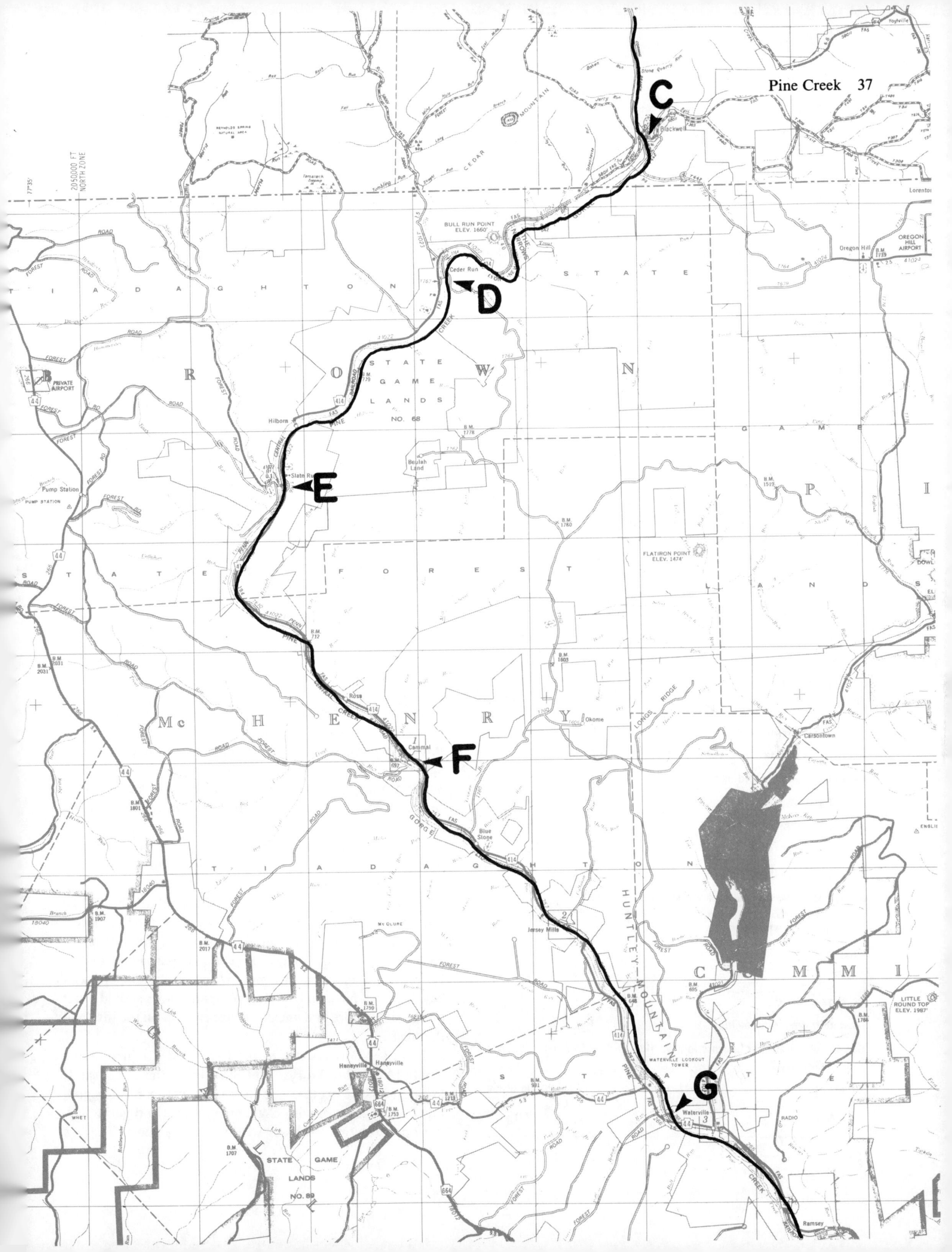
Pine Creek 37

Loyalsock Creek

The Loyalsock Creek drains the Endless Mountains of Sullivan County, an area famous for outstanding hunting, fishing, and hiking throughout the year. The river is outstandingly beautiful, with unspoiled banks and crystal-clear water making the exciting rapids even more enjoyable. On the downside, this is a cold weather river. It lies in mountains which are as far north as the Massachusetts line, and the river when runnable is comprised mostly of snowmelt. Once the snow has gone, it takes a lot of rain to bring the river back up. The river is also extremely popular among trout fishermen, and this requires the boater to take special care as he works his way downriver. It would be foolish and perhaps dangerous to attempt to run this stretch on the opening weekend of trout season. Dress warm and be on your best behavior when you canoe the 'Sock!

The Lopez to Route 220 stretch is quite small and rocky, and can only be done in times of high water. Put in at the Route 487 bridge at Lopez. The run starts easily and builds gradually to Class III, passing through hilly, unspoiled forest country. The rapids are continuous, but quite manageable in open canoes. Below Route 220, the river continues in

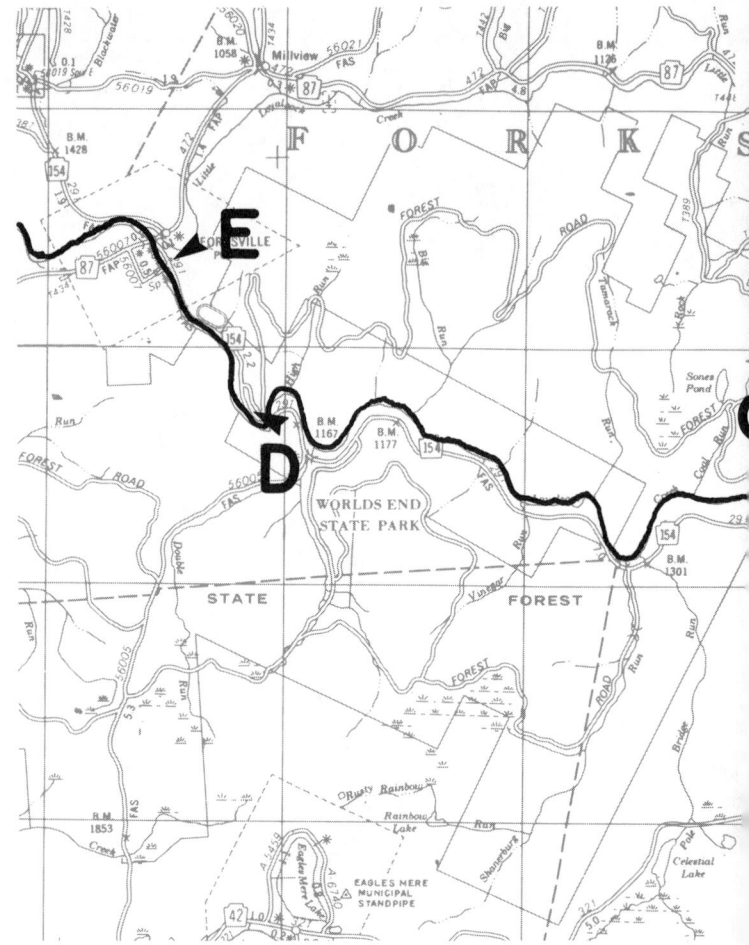

Section: Lopez to Rt. 220 bridge

Counties: Sullivan (PA)

USGS Quads: Laporte

Suitable for: Cruising

Skill Level: Novice to intermediate

Months Runnable: March to April

Interest Highlights: "Endless mountains" scenery

Scenery: Beautiful and unspoiled

Difficulty: Class II–III

Average Width: 65 feet

Velocity: Fast

Gradient: 30 feet per mile

Runnable Water Levels: Call Worlds End State Park (717) 924-3287. Gauge is on the Rt. 87 bridge in the Park.
   Minimum: 4.5 feet

Hazards: None

Scouting: None

Portages: None

Rescue Index: Accessible

Source of Additional Information: Worlds End State Park in season (717) 924-3287

Access Points	River Miles	Shuttle Miles
A–B	7.0	7.0

much the same fashion until a long pool and steep banks announce the presence of a greater challenge. "The Haystacks," named for the huge boulders deposited here ages ago, is rated Class IV+ to V depending on the water level. While runnable by experts in decked canoes or kayaks, most river runners carry along the right bank by a faint but passable trail.

Below the Haystacks the river increases in difficulty, alternating between easy and hard rapids. Four miles below the highway Sportsmans Park Bridge spans the creek. At lower water levels most people begin their trip here. The river bounces merrily down to the highway, then discretely curves away under a high bluff. This marks the start of the "S-Bend," a long and heavy rapid which approaches a Class IV rating at moderate to high water levels. Experienced kayakers will have no trouble, but open canoes should scout on the right shore and sneak the upper drop on the inside of the turn.

The river now returns to the road, and it is here along Route 154, within Worlds End State Park, that the greatest fishing pressure occurs. The river is here at its most beguiling. Exciting rapids with challenging routes and good playing opportunities alternate with sparkling pools. The low

Loyalsock Creek

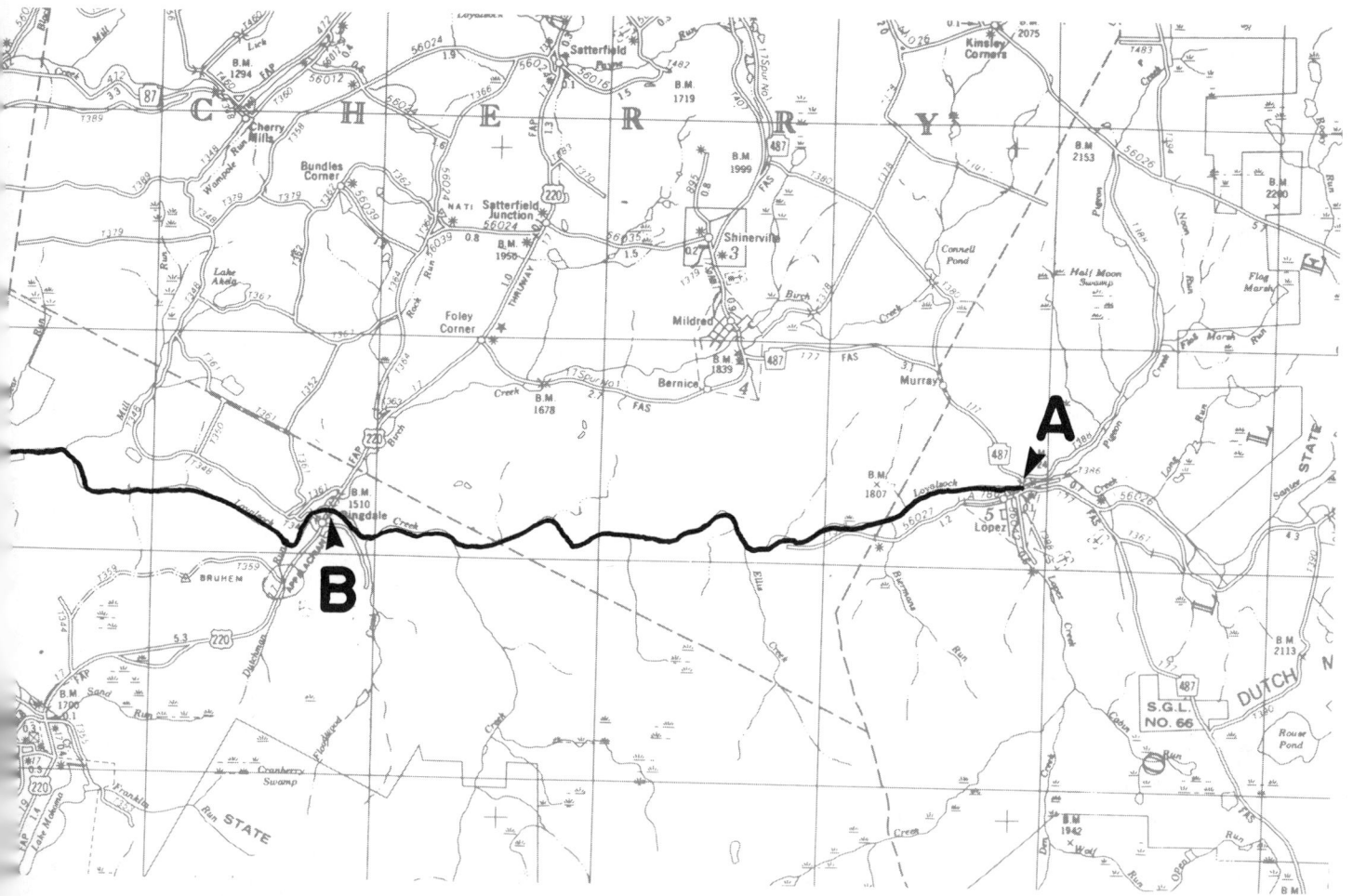

Section: Route 220 bridge to Forksville

Counties: Sullivan (PA)

USGS Quads: Laporte, Eagles Mere

Suitable for: Cruising

Skill Level: Intermediate to advanced

Months Runnable: Late March to early May

Interest Highlights: World's End State Park

Scenery: Beautiful and unspoiled

Difficulty: Class III (Class IV at high water)

Average Width: 80 feet

Velocity: Fast

Gradient: 40 feet per mile (one mile at 50 feet per mile)

Runnable Water Levels: For gauge information, call World's End State Park (717) 924-3287. The gauge is on the Rt. 87 bridge in the Park.
  Minimum: 4.0 feet is the minimum enjoyable level
  Medium: 5.0 feet
  Maximum: 6.0 feet is high, though this stretch has been run by experts at levels up to 7.0 feet.

Hazards: "Haystacks" falls, park dam

Scouting: "Haystacks," "S-curve," park dam

Portages: Optional at "Haystacks," park dam

Rescue Index: Accessible

Source of Additional Information: World's End State Park in season (717) 924-3287

Access Points	River Miles	Shuttle Miles
B–D	10.0	11.0

40 Loyalsock Creek

Section: Forksville to Loyalsockville

Counties: Sullivan, Lycoming (PA)

USGS Quads: Eagles Mere, Barbours, Huntersville, Loyalsockville

Suitable for: Cruising

Skill Level: Novice

Months Runnable: Late March to early June

Interest Highlights: Nothing outstanding

Scenery: Pleasant; considerable private land

Difficulty: Class I–II

Average Width: 150 feet

Velocity: Moderate

Gradient: 15 feet per mile

Runnable Water Levels: The gauge is at the Rt. 87 bridge in World's End State Park (717) 924-3287.
  Minimum: The lower stretch can be run at 3.5 feet if you don't mind dragging a bit; 4.0 feet is probably a better level.

Hazards: Low dam 3 miles below Forksville

Scouting: None at moderate levels

Portages: None

Rescue Index: Accessible

Source of Additional Information: World's End State Park in season (717) 924-3287

Access Points	River Miles	Shuttle Miles
D–I	30.0	32.0

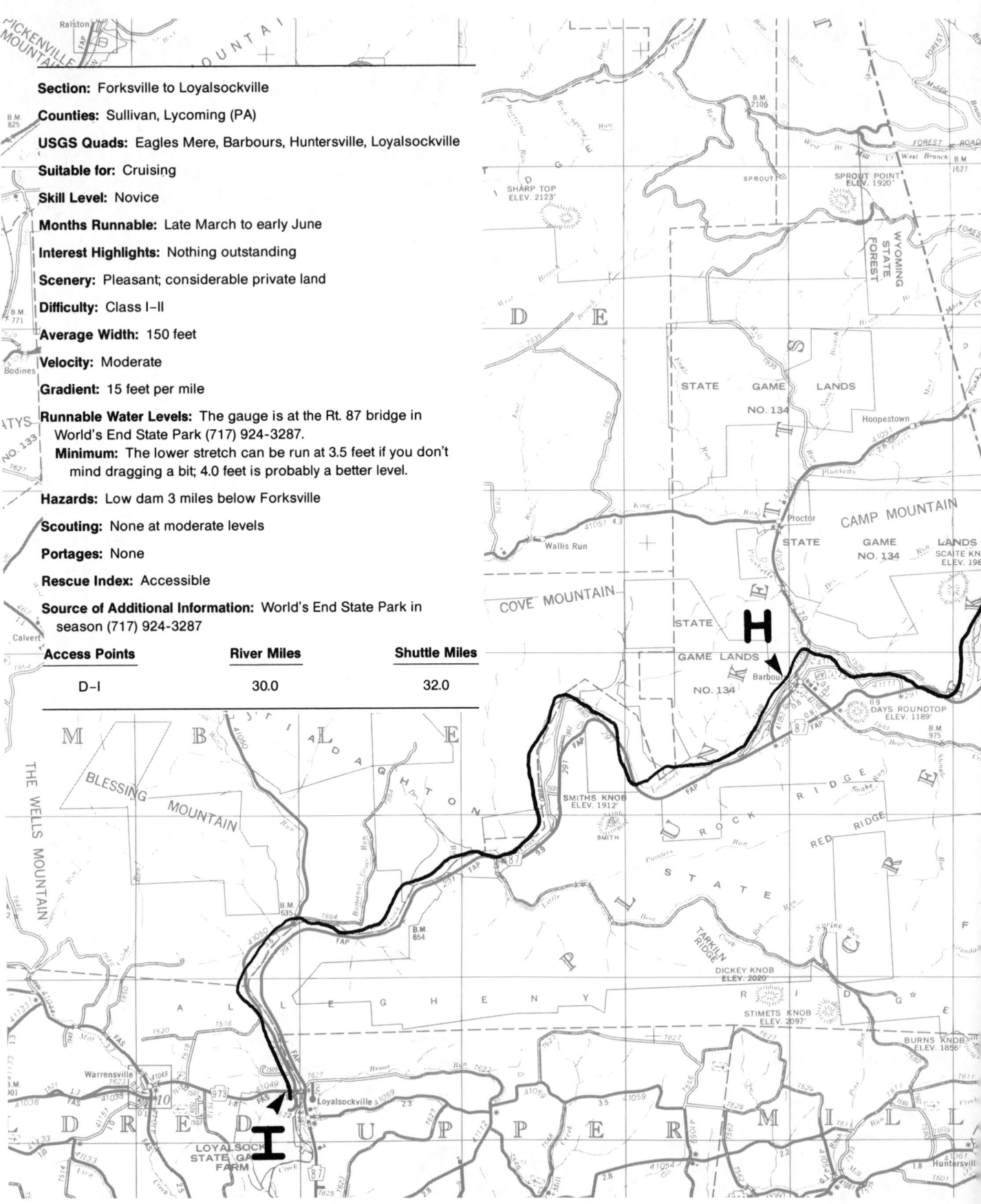

Loyalsock Creek 41

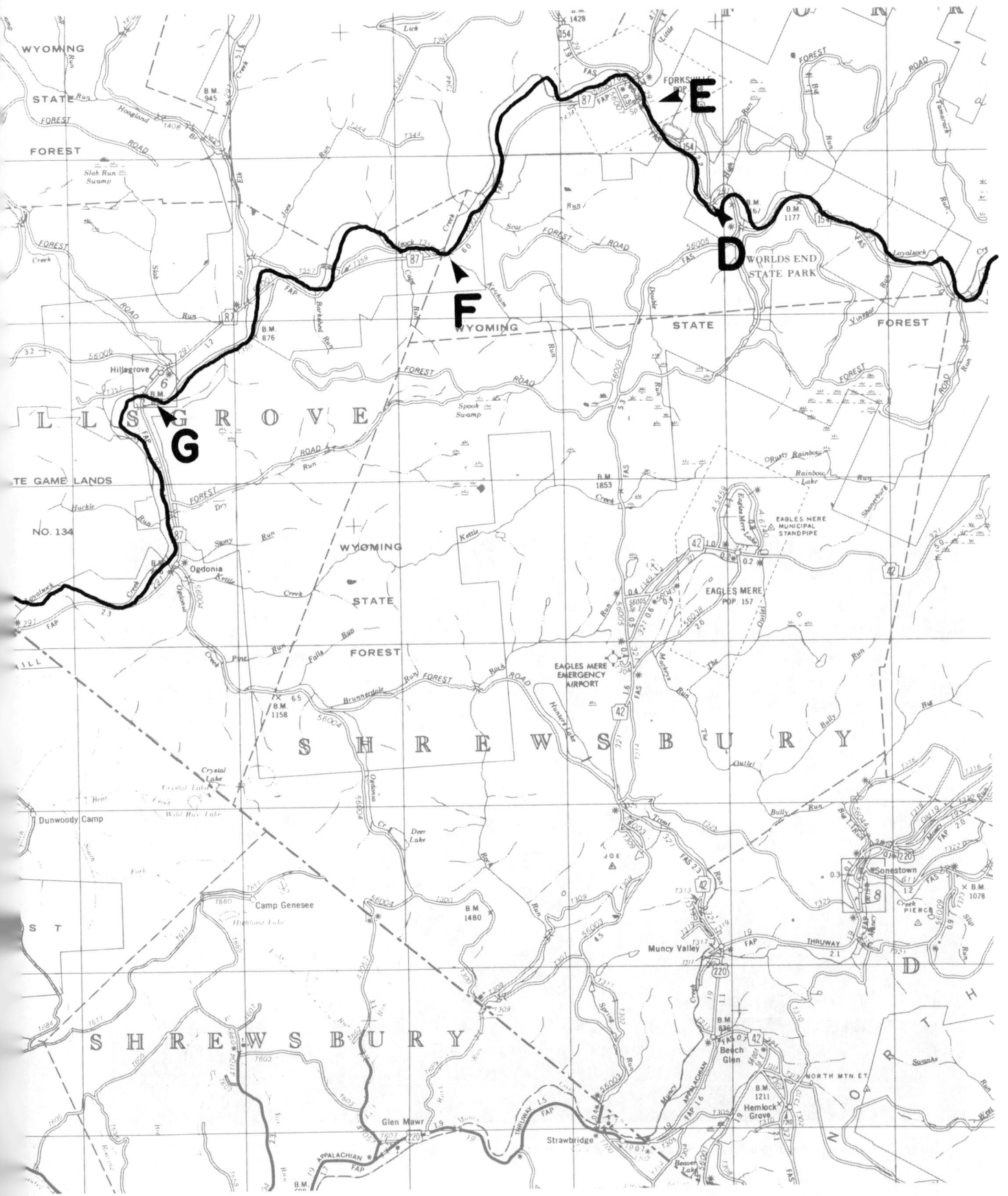

bridge within the park has been replaced and raised substantially, making this run more enjoyable in high water. But beware of the "Ice Canyons," sheer walls of ice up to six feet high which remain for a few weeks after winter releases her grip. These can make rescue and even stopping almost impossible. Just above the Route 87 bridge in the park the river runs along high shale cliffs overtopped by sparkling waterfalls. This is one of the prettiest places in the state; below the bridge the river pools before dropping through a narrow slot in a low dam. This is the site of the annual kayak slalom races put on by the Penn State Outing Club of State College, PA. Take out at the park, at the covered bridge a few miles downstream. There are campsites and cabins available for those who wish to stay overnight.

The lower river is considerably easier, and can be run all the way to the Susquehanna River below Montoursville. This section is flat and relatively unattractive, so most people prefer to take out at Loyalsockville. The upper part, from Forksville to Hillsgrove (ten miles), has the best continuous whitewater. The first part between the covered bridge at Forksville and the junction with the Little Loyalsock Creek a half-mile downstream is the most difficult, and inexperienced parties should put in one mile below, where the river first comes close to the road. Three miles below Forksville is a low dam which should be approached with caution; at low water, there is a chute on the right. Most rapids are open and straightforward, but can generate large waves at high levels which can swamp an open canoe. If unfamiliar with the river, stay to the inside of any turns.

Below Hillsgrove the rapids become more spaced out, but the river is still delightful. In high water, you can cover considerable ground in a single day. Sneaking through tight island passages in the warm sun of late spring and drifting through sparkling pools is central Pennsylvania paddling at its best. Route 87 parallels the river closely below Hillsgrove, offering innumerable access points. The river is wide enough that fishermen can be passed by keeping to the opposite side of the creek and drifting quietly. This stretch is often canoeable well into June, when the warm weather makes up for the occasional need to drag your boat through the shallows. Beware the late afternoon upstream wind, which makes solo canoeing almost impossible in the flat stretches. Take out at the Route 973 bridge or at any other suitable spot.

Janice Dunham and Fred Reinhall on the Loyalsock River. Photo by Robert Hall.

Loyalsock River. Photo by Tim Palmer.

Lehigh River

The Lehigh River is one of the most popular runs in eastern Pennsylvania, offering a long season and interesting rapids in a relatively unspoiled setting. Although the Lehigh Gorge is the most famous part of the run, interesting water for the less experienced paddler lies upstream and downstream. The river draws paddlers from the Philadelphia and New York metropolitan areas, and can be quite crowded on some weekends with private and commercial traffic. In addition, there is considerable fishing on Sections I and II.

Water flow on the Lehigh is regulated by the Francis Walter Dam, a flood control structure operated by the Corps of Engineers. Due to a number of design and operational problems, it is difficult to store water for whitewater recreation. In the past the dam has been operated capriciously, with little concern for downstream recreation among either paddlers or fishermen. It is not unusual to have the river run all week during the summer, then "dry up" on the weekend. Furthermore, we have often found flow projections by the Corps of Engineers to be unreliable. For this reason we suggest you contact White Water Challengers (White Haven, PA) or Pocono Whitewater (Jim Thorpe, PA) for river flow information. They also run rafting tours in the Gorge for those who are interested.

The Lehigh Gorge State Park, under discussion for well over a decade, is now in place. As it develops, some of the access information may become obsolete, and river management plans may affect private boating on the river. In addition, Pennsylvania Fish Commission Waterways patrolmen occasionally make an appearance to enforce life jacket and fishing rules. The man who currently holds the position is first-rate, and is also a good source of river information.

Lehigh River, Section I

Section: Francis Walter Dam to White Haven

Counties: Luzerne (PA)

USGS Quads: White Haven, Hickory Run, Pleasant View Summit

Suitable for: Cruising and training

Skill Level: Novice to intermediate

Months Runnable: March through June, plus special water release dates

Interest Highlights: F. Walter Dam

Scenery: Attractive and unspoiled

Difficulty: Class II

Average Width: 150 feet

Velocity: Fast

Gradient: 23 feet per mile

Runnable Water Levels: Call Lehigh Gorge State Park (717) 427-1861 (manned 8 to 3).
  Minimum: 500 cfs; 750 cfs is the minimum fun level
  Optimum: 1,500 cfs
  Maximum: 2,500 cfs or more is high water

Hazards: River-wide stopper halfway down

Scouting: None

Portages: None

Rescue Index: Accessible but difficult

Source of Additional Information: Lehigh Gorge State Park, RD #2, Box 56, Weatherly, PA 18255 (717) 427-8161; Whitewater Challengers, Star Rt. GA–1, White Haven, PA 18661 (717) 443-8345; Pocono Whitewater, Rt. 903, Jim Thorpe, PA 18229 (717) 325-3656.

Access Points	River Miles	Shuttle Miles
A–B	5.6	10.0

Lehigh River, Section II

Section: White Haven to Rockport

Counties: Luzerne, Carbon (PA)

USGS Quads: White Haven, Christmans, Weatherly, Hickory Run

Suitable for: Cruising and training

Skill Level: Intermediate

Months Runnable: March to June and on special water release dates

Interest Highlights: Old locks and canal remains

Scenery: Beautiful and unspoiled, except around White Haven

Difficulty: Class II–III at low to moderate levels

Average Width: 160 feet

Velocity: Fast, but with pools

Gradient: 26 feet per mile

Runnable Water Levels: Call Lehigh Gorge State Park (717) 427-1861 (manned 8 to 3).
  Minimum: 500 cfs; 750 cfs is minimum fun level
  Moderate: 1,000–2,000 cfs
  Maximum: Over 2,000 cfs is high; river is run regularly at high levels (5,000–10,000 cfs) by experienced Class IV boaters

Hazards: None

Scouting: None

Portages: None

Rescue Index: Accessible but difficult

Source of Additional Information: Lehigh Gorge State Park, RD #2, Box 56, Weatherly, PA 18255 (717) 427-8161; Whitewater Challengers, Star Rt. GA–1, White Haven, PA 18661 (717) 443-8345; Pocono Whitewater, Rt. 903, Jim Thorpe, PA 18229 (717) 325-3656.

Access Points	River Miles	Shuttle Miles
B–D	9.0	15.0

Lehigh River 45

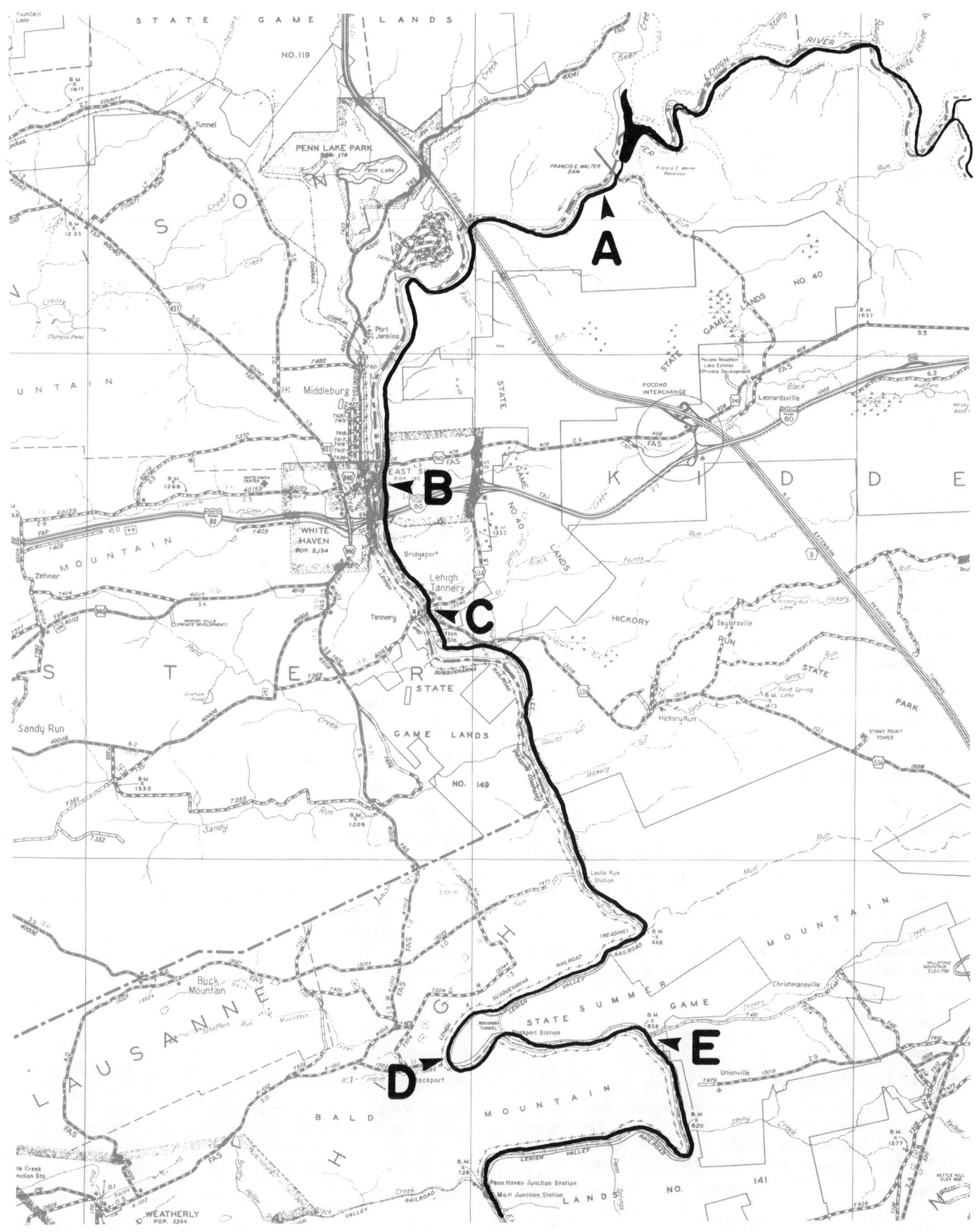

46 Lehigh River

Below the Francis Walter Dam the Lehigh runs over boulders and gravel bars, creating a delightful mixture of Class I–II rapids. This part of the river is not commonly run; it is closed to commercial raft trips, and is very popular among fishermen. To put in, you must carry your boat a quarter-mile down a steep dirt road on the right side of the dam. Take care not to disturb the fishermen at the base of the dam, as this is where most of them hang out. The upper part of the run is quite wild, running between low forested hills. The only feature of note is a river-wide stopper which is not difficult, but might cause trouble for beginners. It is an ideal run for those who are not quite ready for the "gorge sections" below, but please stay away on the opening day of trout season!

The float through White Haven is unattractive but short. At this time access can be found under the Route 80 bridge and a mile further downstream at Tannery bridge off Route 534. The former is the best bet: to get there, exit I-80 and follow 940 through White Haven. You will make a sharp right turn into town and head downhill. Just after you cross the railroad tracks, turn right into a shopping center and drive across the parking lot. There is a dirt road on the far side which follows the old railroad bed which paralleled the Lehigh on river right. About a half-mile downstream a steep trail leads to the river. There is plenty of parking, and several good eating spots for after the run.

Section II, the "Upper Gorge" from White Haven to Rockport, is one of the finest trips in the state. Interesting rapids and lazy pools alternate as the gorge deepens and the forests rise up along the side. It is also a good place to find derelict canoes, left by those foolish enough to attempt the run without extra flotation and sound whitewater skills. The stretch between White Haven and Tannery is popular among fishermen. It would pay to avoid this run early in trout season.

The run starts off quickly and with interest. There are nice surfing waves just above Tannery bridge which serve as a warmup. A mile below the bridge is "triple drop," marked by a large island which divides the current. Go left and you'll encounter a ledge with hole called "Volkswagon Bus Stopper." This can be rather stout at high water levels.

Lehigh River, Section III

Section: Rockport to Jim Thorpe

Counties: Carbon (PA)

USGS Quads: Christmans, Lehighton

Suitable for: Cruising and training

Skill Level: Intermediate

Months Runnable: March to June and special water release dates

Interest Highlights: The deepening gorge

Scenery: Outstanding

Difficulty: Class II–III at low to moderate flows

Average Width: 180 feet

Velocity: Fast, but with pools

Gradient: 24 feet per mile

Runnable Water Levels: Call Lehigh Gorge State Park (717) 427-1861 (manned 8 to 3). Release level from the dam will be augmented by tributary flows after heavy rains.
  Minimum: 600 cfs; 750 cfs is minimum enjoyable level
  Moderate: 1,000–2,000 cfs
  Maximum: Over 2,000 cfs is high water. The river is often run at very high levels (5,000–10,000 cfs) by experienced Class IV boaters

Hazards: None

Scouting: None

Portages: None

Rescue Index: Accessible but difficult

Source of Additional Information: Lehigh Gorge State Park, RD #2, Box 56, Weatherly, PA 18255 (717) 427-8161; Whitewater Challengers, Star Rt. GA-1, White Haven, PA 18661 (717) 443-8345; Pocono Whitewater, Rt. 903, Jim Thorpe, PA 18229 (717) 325-3656.

Access Points	River Miles	Shuttle Miles
D–G	14.5	19.0

Lehigh River, Section IV

Section: Jim Thorpe to Bowmanstown

Counties: Carbon (PA)

USGS Quads: Lehighton

Suitable for: Cruising

Skill Level: Beginner

Months Runnable: All year except for drought periods

Interest Highlights: Deep gorge; easy water

Scenery: Attractive to beautiful; water may be murky

Difficulty: Class I–II

Average Width: 250 feet

Velocity: Moderate

Gradient: 9 feet per mile

Runnable Water Levels: Call Lehigh Gorge State Park (717) 427-1861 (manned 8 to 3).
  Minimum: 100 cfs
  Maximum: The river is not run much at high levels; 2,000 cfs is a reasonable cut-off for novices.

Hazards: None

Scouting: None

Portages: None

Rescue Index: Accessible but difficult

Source of Additional Information: Lehigh Gorge State Park, RD #2, Box 56, Weatherly, PA 18255 (717) 427-8161; Whitewater Challengers, Star Rt. GA-1, White Haven, PA 18661 (717) 443-8345; Pocono Whitewater, Rt. 903, Jim Thorpe, PA 18229 (717) 325-3656.

Access Points	River Miles	Shuttle Miles
G–H	5.0	9.0

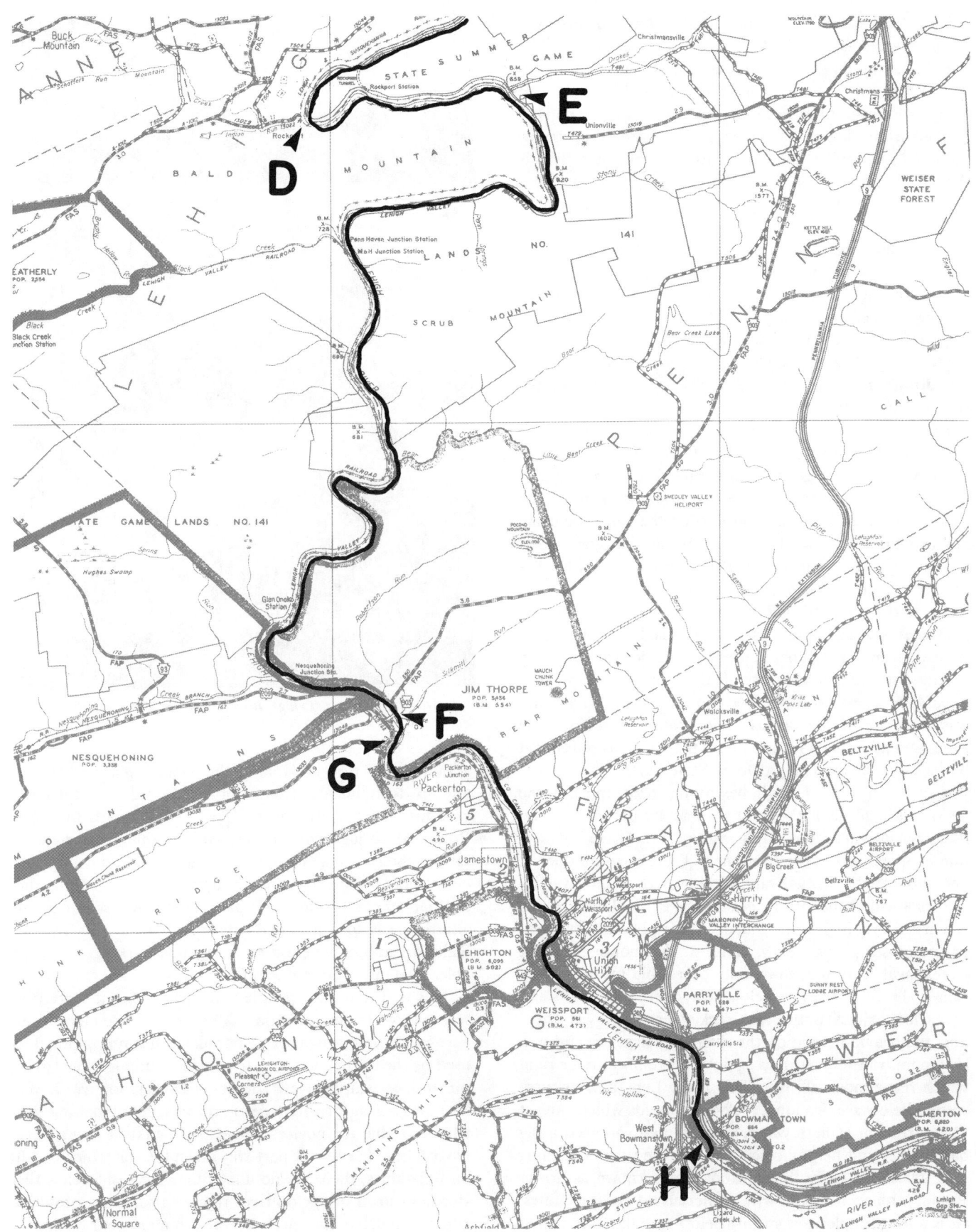

Lehigh River 47

"Lunch Rock," a Class II gravel bar, is hard to miss. On popular weekends hundreds of rafters and kayakers will be found relaxing on the warm rocks on river left. Below here "No Way," and "Staircase," both long Class III rapids with complex low water routes, lie waiting to separate the unwary paddler from his boat. There is an interesting drop below the mouth of Mud Run, which enters on river left. This is the home of the Beaver Hole, a popular play spot which has worn down the nose of many a kayaker trying for an ender. Wilhoyt's Rock, another Class III, lies just downstream. Named after a well-known canoeist of the 1950s who left a boat here, this rock is most dangerous at low water levels as its undercut upstream face pins rafts and canoes. At levels of over 1,000 cfs it is underwater and heavily pillowed, making it easy to avoid. Rockport, the intermediate access point for the gorge, lies just downstream. The take-out lies partway down a rapid, so you'll have to work hard to catch the eddy on river right.

Rockport was, at one time, a way station on a canal which ran from Jim Thorpe to White Haven. Twenty locks allowed the coal barges from the mines upstream to make the twenty-six mile trip in nine hours, about the time that well-conditioned boaters require to do the run. The canal ran profitably for twenty-seven years until a great flood swallowed up the waterworks. It was later replaced by Asa Packer's Lehigh Valley Railroad, and only remnants remain. In the early 1970s Rockport was the site of an access controversy when angry fishermen leased the river right railbed from the defunct Jersey Central Railroad, set up barricades, and ran paddlers off the river with guns. The impasse was broken when they ran off a scout leader who was a trustee of the railroad. He promptly modified the lease, and access was restored until the land was purchased by the state for the Lehigh Gorge State Park.

Section III of the Lehigh, beginning at Rockport, in the heart of the gorge, is the most spectacular part of the run. Also, because of accumulating mine acid drainage, this section is of less interest to fishermen. There are a number of uncomplicated Class III rapids below here as the river inscribes a wide bend from Rockport to Penn Haven, which is marked by a high stone wall on river right and a railroad bridge crossing just below. Here, at the mouth of Black Creek, was a mining town only accessible by railway or canal. The river eases up below here, alternating pools and long Class I riffles, until Bear Creek enters on the left. Pipeline, the heaviest rapid on the river, begins at the end of a long pool, running hard up against high cliffs at river right which rise almost 500 feet. This is the Lehigh at its most scenic. Below are two long, rock-filled rapids which can get very turbulent at high water. Open canoes will need a big bail bucket and helpful rescuers when the river is running at 1,500 cfs or more. Snaggletooth, also known as Tower Rapid, is an exciting run with numerous interesting chutes. (It is a long, unpleasant swim!) Below here the river makes

Mile Long Rapid, Lehigh River. Photo by Tim Palmer.

a sharp right turn at Hole in the Wall, a place where an attempt to build a railroad tunnel failed due to constant cave-ins. After a few mixed Class II–III rapids the high Route 903 bridge will appear. At this time boaters have several choices for a take-out. You can get out on river right, next to the bridge, and portage up the bank and along the railroad tracks to the A&P parking lot. A less strenuous alternative is to continue downstream to the Jim Thorpe Railroad station, where river access and parking are available. (See map points F and G.)

This is where most people end their trip, but there is a scenic Class I+ float (Section IV) of almost five miles from here to Bowmanstown. Long popular as a training run, it is used by the rafting outfitters to provide "summer float trips" for fresh-air-starved New Yorkers at levels as low as 100 cfs. The gorge is surprisingly deep and wild here, making this trip enjoyable for novices and experts alike. Except for a nasty Class II cribwork part-way down the run which is hell on inflatables, there are no difficulties. Take out below the Bowmanstown bridge on river right. Parking is a problem here and much of the land is private, so mind your manners.

Nescopeck Creek

The Nescopeck Creek is a longtime favorite of Philadelphia-area paddlers. Although not difficult, its rapids are lively and interesting even at low flows. The scenery is outstanding, with large flakes of rock, mountain laurel, and high cliffs vying for the paddler's attention. It is a popular early-season "icebreaker" and a later season training run among area canoe clubs. Philadelphia Canoe Club runs an annual training camp on a property at the end of the run.

There is a little-used Class I run from Honey Hole Road to the Route 93 bridge, but the lower run is so enjoyable that few paddlers use it. Most paddlers put in on the river left bank upstream of the bridge, where there is ample parking space. Although there is a gauge on the river downstream on river left, many paddlers "eyeball it" at the Route 93 bridge. What you see is what you get, and if you scrape your canoe here you'll do the same thing throughout the run.

While none of the rapids are exceptionally demanding, a few are memorable. Slide Rapid begins a few hundred yards past the second bridge; it is a long drop ending with a delicious slide into a roller. At higher levels there is excellent surfing here. This and the rapid below it get heavy and continuous at high water and narrow and picky at marginal flows; most of the other runs are easier. About a quarter mile past "Halfway Bridge" (the third bridge encountered on the run) there is a three-foot-high ledge drop with a huge flake of rock over 20 feet high downstream. This drop should be looked over by open boaters at high levels using the road which parallels the creek on river right.

The next significant drop is above a private campground on river left. It is long enough to swamp an open boat which strays into the waves at high water, but at lower water it's just tight and picky. Slalom Rapid is next; it is a series of interesting drops against a sheer right-hand bank. The Philadelphia Canoe Club holds its training camp here. The river pools before dropping into Eagle Rock Hole, a delightful mild playing hydraulic named for a huge overhanging flake on the left which looks like an eagle's profile. Below here lie a few minor riffles, then flatwater. It is a good time to enjoy the mountain laurel, which blooms in late April or early May. If there's water in the creek at this time, the run will be truly memorable.

The usual take-out is at the fourth bridge on the run, at river left. It is on private land, but the farmer who owns the field likes boaters (indeed, the whole area is extremely

Nescopeck Creek. Photo by Roger Corbett.

friendly). Don't do anything to change this situation. There is good road access downstream for quite some distance. The run down to Black Creek is easier and extremely pretty. Thickly forested slopes are broken by cliffs while the river provides a mixture of Class I–II drops separated by long pools. It is possible to continue your run downstream to the mouth of the river, an eight-mile trip over increasingly flat water. Except for I-80 which parallels the river in some places, the scenery is quite good.

50 Nescopeck Creek

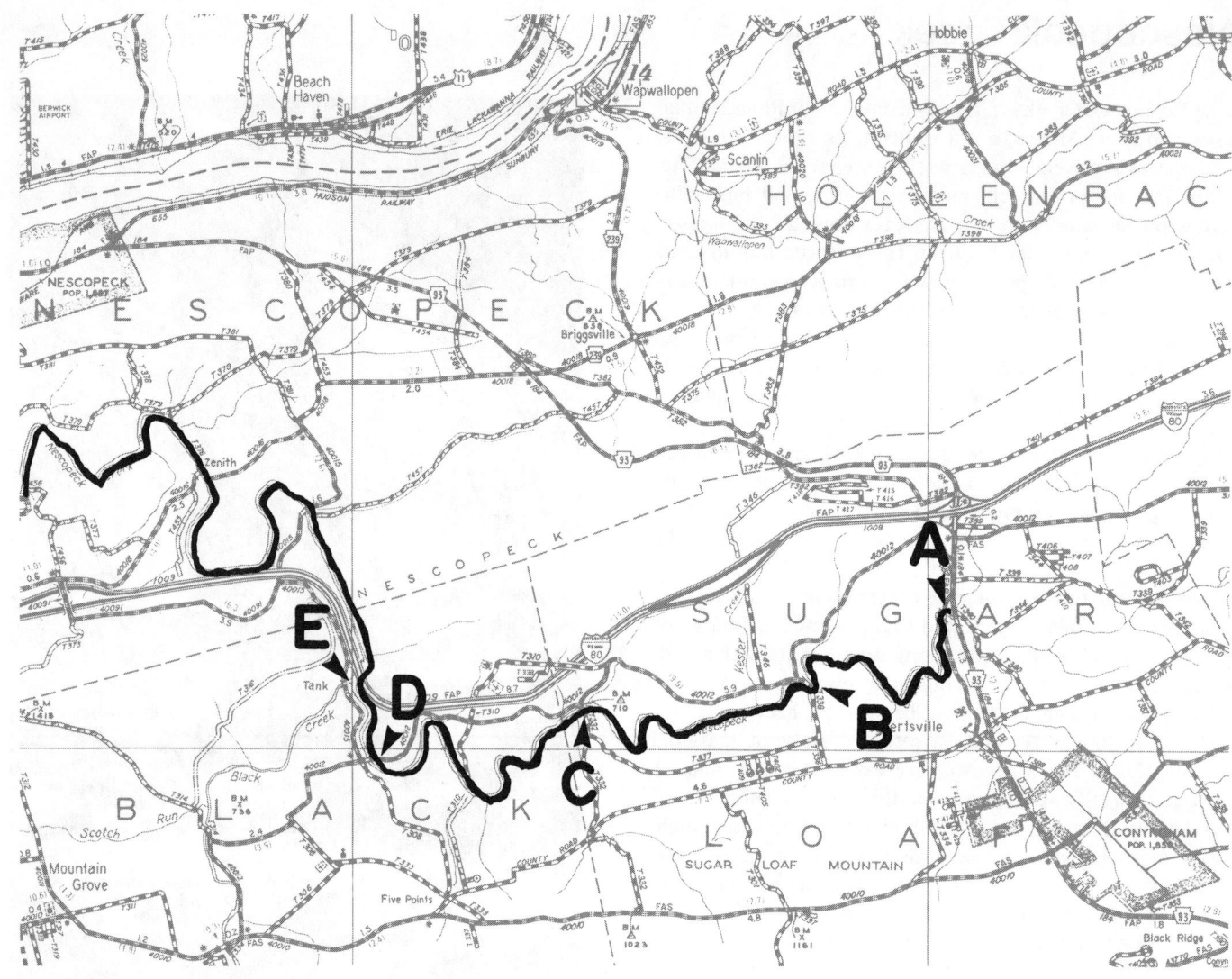

Section: Rt. 93 bridge to last bridge above I-80

Counties: Luzerne (PA)

USGS Quads: Seibertsville, Nurenburg, Berwick

Suitable for: Cruising and training

Skill Level: Novice to intermediate

Months Runnable: March to April and after heavy rains

Interest Highlights: River running

Scenery: Pretty to beautiful

Difficulty: Class II

Average Width: 50 feet

Velocity: Fast

Gradient: 27 feet per mile

Runnable Water Levels: The gauge is at the first bridge below the put-in, 100 yards downstream on river left.
  Minimum: 6 inches; 1 foot is enjoyable
  Moderate: 2.5 feet is a transition level from rock dodging to missing waves and holes.
  Maximum: 3 feet is high water, with the river continuous Class III; 4 feet is flood stage, with the river high and fast

Hazards: None

Scouting: None for qualified boaters

Portages: None

Rescue Index: Accessible

Source of Additional Information: Philadelphia Canoe Club, 4900 Ridge Avenue, Philadelphia, PA 19128

Access Points	River Miles	Shuttle Miles
A–C	8.4	9.5

Tohickon Creek

The Tohickon Creek is a small, fast runoff stream with headwaters in Lake Nockamixon, an artificial lake built for broadwater recreation. Once a close-kept secret among Pennsylvania boaters, its fame has spread with the event of the spring and fall releases and the running of several challenging races in Bucks County Park. These releases draw hundreds of paddlers each year, and the resulting traffic bottlenecks and parking problems bring out the worst in boaters. If you plan to use the river at this time, please follow directions and be prepared for crowded conditions.

The upper section of Tohickon Creek begins at the dam, but is most easily accessible below Route 611 north of Doylestown. The run consists of Class I–II riffles with easier going in between. Long sections are paralleled by a road, making access easy. There are two dams on the run which demand special care. The first comes shortly below Route 611 just below the junction of the Little Tohickon Creek. The portage is on Tohickon Valley Country Club land; no problems have been reported yet but mind your manners as you carry! The second dam is Meyers Dam in Stover Park. Carry on the right or avoid entirely by leaving your vehicle at the upper parking lot a short distance upstream. Both dams have been run by plastic kayaks at low to moderate flows, but this is not recommended. At high levels dangerous hydraulics form, and the pools above the drops are fast moving.

Below the park bridge is the classic Tohickon Creek run. It inscribes a huge loop, beginning with a gentle warmup under the bridge, then picks up slowly through small waves. There are plenty of good side-eddys on which to continue the warmup. The first major drop is "No Fish or Swim Ledge," named for some graffiti on a cliff on river right. The hole there is a vigorous playing hole at low to moderate levels and downright intimidating at high flows. There is a chute at center and a smaller hole at river left. The river then dances gracefully beneath the "High Rocks" climbing area in a delightful series of chutes and waves before gathering up above a sprightly four-foot drop best run in the center. At high levels there is a huge stopper on river right. The next spot of note is a river-wide drop of about three feet. There is a center passage, but the left chute is the most fun.

Below this ledge the gradient picks up noticeably. There are four distinct drops, each of which merits scouting by those not familiar with the river. The first ledge is a simple drop with a passage broken out on the right. Enjoy the play waves at the bottom before proceding to the second ledge, where the runout of a sharp drop is split by a midstream boulder. At the end of the pool below lies the Horserace, a long rapid studded with waves and holes. This drop can easily swamp a canoe, but there is a "sneak" chute on the far right which is not obvious from upstream. The third ledge is the most challenging of all, requiring a paddler to thread a careful path between four offset holes. The holes are very playable at moderate flows and incredibly nasty in high water. The river appears to calm down a bit here, but stay alert! After a short pool comes a drop which—if you are not careful—sends you towards a ships-prow rock. Play it safe by sneaking down the left.

Greg Doggett on Tohickon Creek. Photo by Paula Pardue.

52 Tohickon Creek

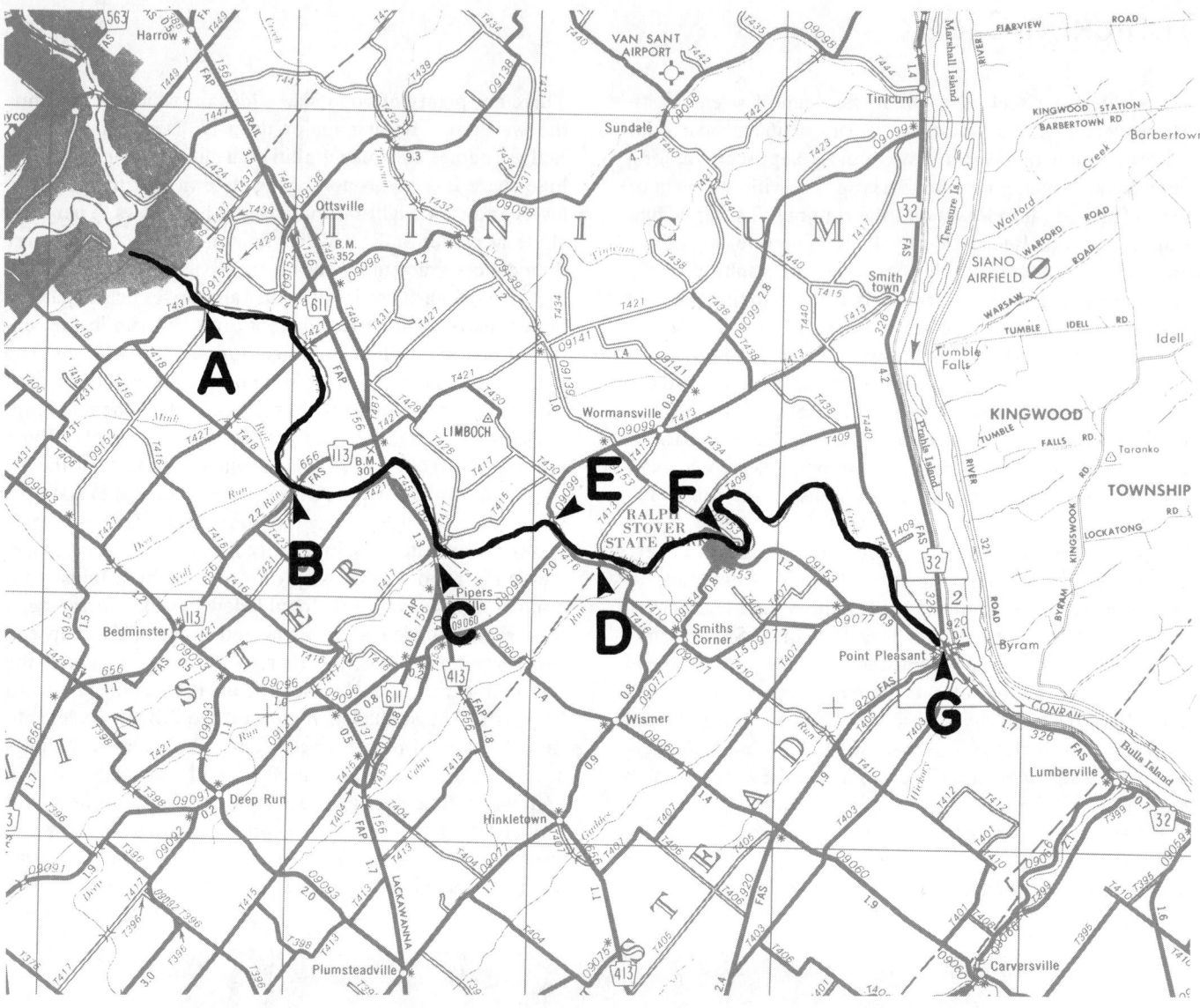

Section: South Park Road (L.R. 09152) to Ralph Stover State Park

Counties: Bucks (PA)

USGS Quads: Bedminster

Suitable for: Cruising and training

Skill Level: Novice to intermediate

Months Runnable: Releases are the last weekend of March and first weekend of November (except drought conditions) and after heavy rains of 2 inches or more.

Interest Highlights: Ralph Stover State Park

Scenery: Pretty

Difficulty: Class I–II

Average Width: 75 feet

Velocity: Fast

Gradient: 9 feet per mile

Runnable Water Levels: The gauge is at the Stover Park bridge. (Another gauge, at the Rt. 32 bridge in Point Pleasant, reads one foot lower than the Park gauge at most levels.)
Minimum: 0.0 is minimal and scrapy; 1.0 is a good running level.
Moderate: 2.5
Maximum: Over 3.0 is high water; beware the dam approaches!

Hazards: Dam at golf course; dam at Ralph Stover Park

Scouting: None

Portages: Dams

Rescue Index: Accessible

Source of Additional Information: Wildwater Designs, Penllyn, PA (215) 646-5034; Ralph Stover State Park (215) 297-5090. If you can get an answer at the Park, they can tell you the gauge reading.

Access Points	River Miles	Shuttle Miles
A–F	7.1	8.8

The take-out, especially on release weekends, demands special attention. Most people take out at a grassy cut just upstream of the Route 32 bridge in Point Pleasant. The town sees a lot of tubing activity on the Delaware, and is heavily posted against parking. During release weekends, a parking concession is operated by local firefighters. As this is a key to continued use of the river, it pays to patronize these folks. You can speed egress by carrying your boat across Route 32 to the lot rather than trying to get your vehicle into the limited loading space nearby. For off-season runs there are spaces at the Post Office and at several bars and restaurants. If no spot can be found, the next possibility is Bulls Island, a state park seven miles downstream on the Jersey side just off Route 29. Think about that when you get the urge to do something which might irritate the locals.

Section: Ralph Stover State Park to Point Pleasant

Counties: Bucks (PA)

USGS Quads: Lumberville

Suitable for: Cruising and training

Skill Level: Intermediate to advanced

Months Runnable: Scheduled releases the last weekend in March and the first weekend in November (except during drought periods) and after heavy rains of 2 inches or more

Interest Highlights: Ralph Stover State Park, High Rocks Climbing Area, Bucks County Park

Scenery: Beautiful

Difficulty: Class III–IV

Average Width: 75 feet

Velocity: Fast

Gradient: 40 feet per mile

Runnable Water Levels: Gauge is at the Stover Park bridge. (The Point Pleasant gauge on Rt. 32 reads one foot lower than the Park bridge.)
  Minimum: 0.0 is the absolute minimum; 1.0 is the minimum exciting level.
  Moderate: 2.5 is medium flow, with all major drops Class IV; open boats beware
  Maximum: 3.5 is high flow, with big waves and holes in a hot current; rescue is difficult in some places. Flood stage is 5.0, with huge holes and waves and few eddies; for expert decked boaters only! The river has been run at levels up to 8.0, but this is emphatically NOT recommended.

Hazards: None for experienced paddlers at normal flows

Scouting: Major drops for first-timers

Portages: None

Rescue Index: Accessible

Source of Additional Information: Wildwater Designs, Penllyn, PA (215) 646-5034; Ralph Stover State Park (215) 982-5560 (8 to 4). If someone is answering the phone at the Park, they can tell you the gauge reading.

Access Points	River Miles	Shuttle Miles
F–G	4.0	2.8

Tohickon Creek at release level (about 1.8 feet). Photo by Robert Hall.

Delaware River

The Delaware River marks the boundary between Pennsylvania, New York, and New Jersey. From the junction of the East and West Branches just below Hancock, New York to tidewater downstream of Trenton, New Jersey, the river flows free. Major highways seldom follow it for any distance, and except for Easton, Pennsylvania, and Trenton, New Jersey at its terminus there are no major cities to pollute its waters. It has been a popular canoe route for generations, and many people (including your author) got their first taste of river paddling here.

The Delaware is the major water supply for New York City and Philadelphia; the former gets their supply from reservoirs in the Catskills while the latter draws theirs from the Torresdale Intake near tidewater. During the droughts of the 1960s, New York refused to release water from its reservoirs. The entire upper river went almost dry, and the salt line crept upstream towards Philadelphia's intake. Pennsylvania sued New York, and a Supreme Court decision laid the groundwork for the Delaware River Basin Commission, which has the power to control all dams within the watershed to assure a reasonable flow in the river during low flow periods. Thus there is always enough water in the river to float a canoe even in periods of extreme drought.

The river's location close to metropolitan New York has brought about considerable recreational use. There are a number of large liveries which put thousands of canoes on the water each weekend, most of them piloted by inexperienced hands. With these numbers the patience of some residents has begun to wear thin. At one time you could camp almost anywhere, especially on privately-owned islands or railroad property. Increased use and complaints from landowners has brought this practice to an end. The river from Narrowsburg to Port Jervis is now the Upper Delaware National River. Except for established campgrounds, legal camping is hard to find, and the rangers patrol the river and force trespassers to move their camps or be fined.

The "middle river" lies within the Delaware Water Gap National Recreation Area and runs from Matamoras, Pennsylvania to Belvidere, New Jersey. This is the best stretch for canoe camping; there are a number of primitive campsites available, and the river, although quite attractive, is much less heavily used. The river below Easton is even less popular, except for a few short stretches used for tubing. Protected by railroad tracks and canals, the bank remains relatively undeveloped and attractive and the water quality is surprisingly good. There are a number of widely-spaced riffles and several major drops. The latter draw considerable day use from local whitewater paddlers for training.

The Upper Delaware stretch begins just upstream of Hancock, New York. You can start your trip on PA Route 191 on the West Branch or NY Route 97 on the East Branch, depending on the water levels left by reservoir operations upstream. The Hancock area can get pretty crowded during the summer, but you can avoid the crowds by using the Pennsylvania Fish Commission (PFC) access seven miles

Foul Rift, Delaware River. Photo by Roger Corbett.

56 Delaware River

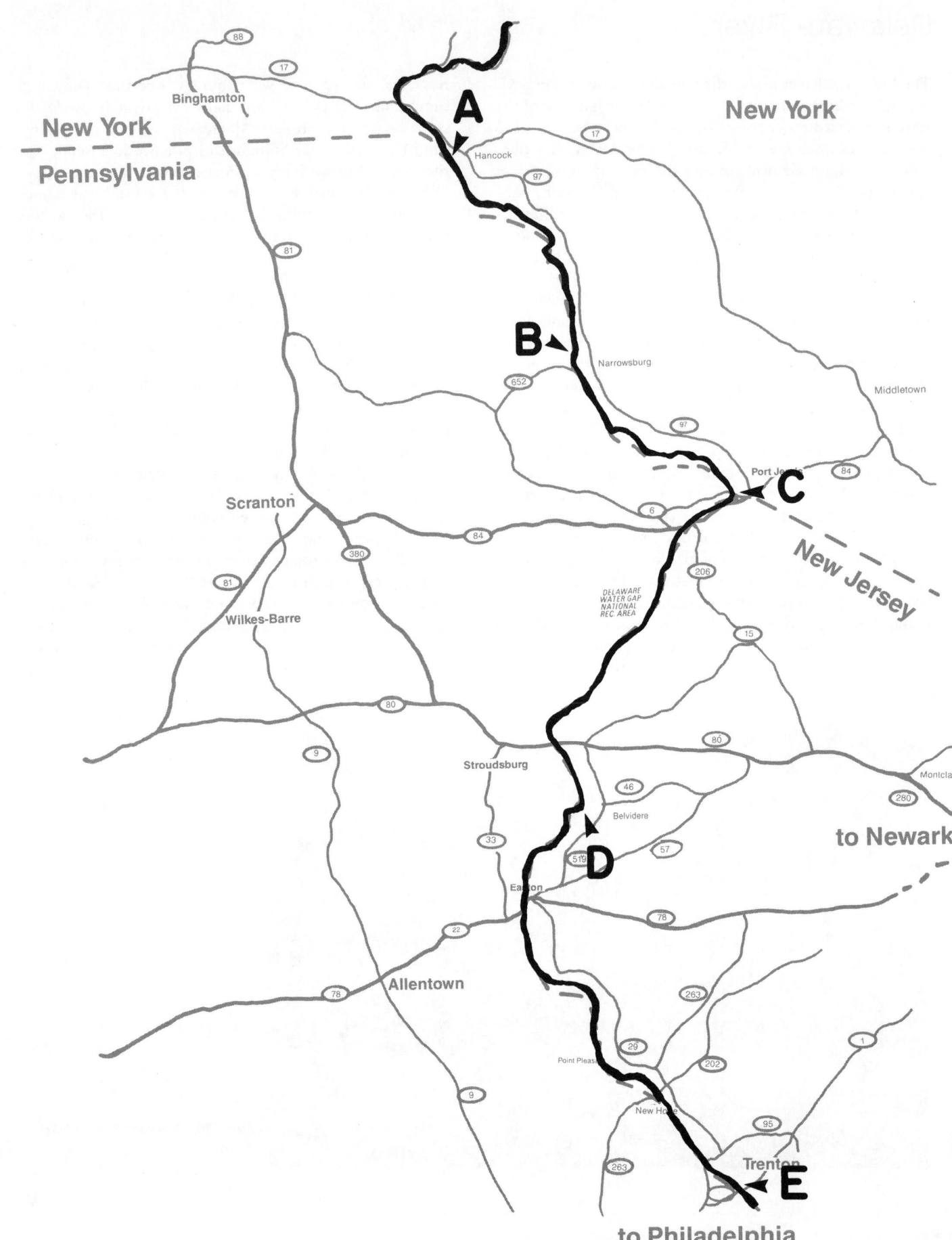

downstream. The upper river flows between high, green hills and flat, grassy banks. The area is surprisingly remote, and very attractive. Paddling in mid-summer is definitely a communal experience; canoe and tube traffic is very heavy and the roads and access points are crowded. But in late fall and early spring the river is all but deserted, offering surprising solitude for the hardy boater. Off-season paddlers should be aware of the dangers of capsizing on such a wide, cold river and protect themselves accordingly.

Access is not a problem. Dozens of places have been set aside by various state agencies for use of canoeists and fishermen. But parking may be difficult, so be careful where you leave your car. If one access is jammed, it may be wise to relocate to a less popular area. Bear in mind that the large number of paddlers have frayed the tempers of local residents. Do not land on posted property except in an emergency.

Most of the rapids on the Upper Delaware are straight shots over gravel bars, and are eminently suited for inexperienced paddlers. At high levels they may have large waves or wash out entirely; at low water you may have to get out and drag your canoe for a short ways. One rapid is not so easy. Skinner's Falls is located about five miles upstream of Narrowsburg, and is the most hyped-up drop on the river. It is not particularly difficult: a straightforward Class II+ rapid which at high water has good surfing waves and interesting hydraulics. But when the livery clientele gets there you can see innumerable capsizings, quantities of non-life-jacketed human debris, multi-boat pileups on "Killer Rock," unattended equipment floating downstream, and throngs of enthusiastic spectators taking it all in. A competent whitewater paddler will have no trouble; a skilled lake paddler should put on a life jacket and scout. Novices should consider carrying. If you want to witness this unique spectacle, the Park Service has an access point just upstream.

Below Narrowsburg the river continues to be attractive, with fine scenery and mild rapids. There are Class II rapids at the mouth of the Shohola River, just upstream of Barryville, and at the mouth of the Mongaup River a few miles upstream of Port Jervis. Both are popular training rapids for kayakers, but deserve respect by open boat paddlers, especially at high water. The deepest pool on the river, 113 feet deep, is just downstream of Narrowsburg. Fishing here in the heat of the summer is said to be excellent. The suspension bridge at Minisink Ford, built by John Roebling, used to carry the Delaware and Hudson Canal over the

---

Section: Hancock, NY to Narrowsburg, NY

Counties: Delaware, Sullivan (NY); Pike (PA)

USGS Quads: Hancock, Lake Como, Long Eddy, Calicoon, Damascus, Narrowsburg

Suitable for: Cruising, training, canoe camping

Skill Level: Novice

Months Runnable: All year

Interest Highlights: Pleasant, unspoiled scenery

Scenery: Attractive to beautiful

Difficulty: Class I–II

Average Width: 250 feet

Velocity: Slow to moderate

Gradient: 6 feet per mile

Runnable Water Levels: The USGS gauge at Barryville covers this section; call the National Park Service (914) 252-7100 for recorded information.
 Minimum: 2.9 feet
 Maximum: Over 5 feet means heavy waves at Skinner's Falls

Hazards: None for competent river paddlers

Scouting: Skinner's Falls

Portages: None

Rescue Index: Accessible

Source of Additional Information: National Park Service, P.O. Box C, River Road, Narrowsburg, NY 12764 (717) 559-7527 (manned number).

Access Points	River Miles	Shuttle Miles
A–B	31.0	36.0

Section: Narrowsburg, NY to Port Jervis, NY

Counties: Sullivan, Orange (NY); Pike (PA)

USGS Quads: Narrowsburg, Eldred, Shohola, Pond Eddy, Port Jervis North, Port Jervis South

Suitable for: Cruising, training, canoe camping

Skill Level: Novice

Months Runnable: All year

Interest Highlights: Roebling Bridge (at Lackawaxen)

Scenery: Pretty to beautiful

Difficulty: Class I–II

Average Width: 300 feet

Velocity: Slow to moderate

Gradient: 5 feet per mile

Runnable Water Levels: The USGS gauge at Barryville covers this section; call the National Park Service (914) 252-7100 for recorded information.
 Minimum: 2.9 feet is a low level.
 Maximum: Over 5 feet means big waves at Mongaup and Shohola rapids, which will swamp an open canoe.

Hazards: Mongaup and Shohola rapids

Scouting: None

Portages: None

Rescue Index: Accessible

Source of Additional Information: National Park Service, P.O. Box C, River Road, Narrowsburg, NY 12764 (717) 559-7527 (manned number).

Access Points	River Miles	Shuttle Miles
B–C	35.0	37.0

Lackawaxen. It was here that he perfected the designs he would later use to construct the Brooklyn Bridge.

At Port Jervis the river takes a hard turn to the west just below the mouth of the Neversink River. The pools on this section are longer, and the rapids shorter. The Delaware Water Gap National Recreation Area begins about four miles below Matamoras. It has its origins over a fight to dam this stretch with a huge structure at Tocks Island. The preservationists won out after a decade-long fight, but not until much of the land had been condemned and purchased by the Corps of Engineers. The banks are now returning to their original unspoiled state, and this makes for an unusually attractive canoe trip. This is also the best stretch of the river for canoe camping; there are a number of primitive sites available on a first-come, first-served basis. Contact the Park Service for a complete map showing all campsites. Running the entire section makes for a delightful multi-day trip. The Middle River ends at the Delaware Water Gap near Stroudsburg, Pennsylvania.

The Water Gap is magnificent, but it is crossed and paralleled by numerous highways. The close proximity of the Appalachian Trail means that good opportunities for hiking exist on both sides of the river. Downstream there are several power plants, large factories, and a large number of houses along the banks. This is the least attractive stretch of the Delaware. It is generally flat water with occasional riffles and a few good drops to provide interest. The scenery improves below Easton, and is surprisingly attractive as the river passes through Bucks County on the way to Trenton. Shielded by the Delaware Canal on the Pennsylvania side (now protected by Roosevelt State Park) and the Raritan Canal on the New Jersey side, the banks have remained undeveloped. Tubing is popular, especially on the stretch just north of Point Pleasant. You will not be alone if you run past here on a summer weekend, but the rest of the river is surprisingly quiet and peaceful.

There are several places which demand special attention. Foul Rift is located just below Belvidere, New Jersey, and is a strong Class II drop over jagged limestone ledges. The rapid is over a mile long and offers continuous action. It is a bad place to swim at low water, and the home of huge waves

---

Section: Port Jervis, NY to Belvidere, NJ

Counties: Pike, Monroe (PA); Sussex, Warrren (NJ)

USGS Quads: Port Jervis South, Milford, Culvers Gap, Lake Maskenzoha, Flatbrookville, Bushkill, Portland, Belvidere

Suitable for: Cruising, training, canoe camping

Skill Level: Novice

Months Runnable: All year

Interest Highlights: Delaware Water Gap

Scenery: Pretty to beautiful

Difficulty: Class I

Average Width: 300 feet

Velocity: Slow

Gradient: 4 feet per mile

Runnable Water Levels: Call the National Park Service (717) 588-6637. A level of 2.3 feet at Port Jervis is a good summer flow. The river should present no hazards except in flood.

Hazards: None

Scouting: None

Portages: None

Rescue Index: Accessible

Source of Additional Information: Delaware Water Gap National Recreation Area, Bushkill, PA 18324 (717) 588-6637

Access Points	River Miles	Shuttle Miles
C–D	60.0	64.0

Section: Belvidere, NJ to Trenton, NJ

Counties: Warren, Hunterdon, Mercer (NJ); Northampton, Bucks (PA)

USGS Quads: Belvidere, Bangor, Easton, Riegelsville, Frenchtown, Lumberville, Stockton, Lambertville, Pennington, Trenton West

Suitable for: Cruising and training

Skill Level: Novice except at major drops

Months Runnable: All year

Interest Highlights: City of Easton; major drops at Foul Rift, Lumberville, Lambertville, and Scudder's Falls

Scenery: Uninspiring to pretty

Difficulty: Class I; major drops are Class II–III depending on water level

Average Width: 500 feet

Velocity: Slow, except at major drops

Gradient: 4 feet per mile

Runnable Water Levels: The Trenton gauge covers this section; call the Philadelphia Weather Service (215) 627-5575.
  Minimum: 8.1 feet represents low flows
  Maximum: Beware of flood water, especially at major rapids!

Hazards: Major drops to untrained paddlers

Scouting: Major drops by untrained paddlers

Portages: Major drops by untrained paddlers

Rescue Index: Accessible

Source of Additional Information: Delaware River Basin Commission, P. O. Box 7360, Trenton, NJ 08628; they publish an excellent map of the entire river, available for $5.00.

Access Points	River Miles	Shuttle Miles
D–E	62.0	67.0

during the spring runoff. Scout from the Jersey side if in doubt and proceed cautiously.

Lumberville Wing Dam is located below Point Pleasant near Bulls Island State Park. The two half-dams at the shores were originally built to divert water into the Delaware and Raritan Canal, which begins here. The "wings" concentrate the flow of water at the center of the river. It is not difficult when run in the center, but do not blunder over the sides at high water, when dangerous hydraulics form to catch the unwary. Also remember that the river is quite wide, making off-season swims by unprotected paddlers potentially deadly.

Wells Falls, also known as Lambertville Rapids, lies just downstream of New Hope, a popular tourist and shopping destination. It has wing dam structures on the sides also, but the drop is considerably harder, reaching Class III at high water. Scout from the "wings" before running; if you want to simplify your run, lift over the "wing" on the Jersey side and run the rest of the drop. If the "wings" are underwater, the entire rapid may be too heavy for an open canoeist, and dangerous hydraulics will form along the sides. This spot is a popular hangout for local kayakers, and there is good "squirting" and "surfing" to be had here. There is also a mellow beginner's surfing hole on the right side of the river just below the wing dam. At high water it is a big "flush" with few playing opportunities.

The river now flows placidly past Washington's Crossing, where the rebel forces were ferried across the ice-choked river on their way to the Battle of Trenton. A state park commemorates this event. Scudder's Falls, the last major drop on the river, lies a few miles downstream, just above the I-95 bridge near Yardley. The main channel is a straightforward Class I riffle, but there is an interesting chute along the Jersey shore. Go to the left of the island; there is a strong wave at the bottom which promises excellent surfing at the right water level. There are plenty of good eddies, and kayakers congregate here when the Wells Falls wing dam is underwater, making it difficult to "play" that rapid. From here there are only a few easy riffles to tidewater just below the Route 1 bridge in Trenton. The mighty "fall line," where the Falls of Richmond and Great Falls of Washington are located, is only the smallest riffle here. It is possible to paddle downstream to Philadelphia and beyond, but you'll need to consult your tide tables and watch out for large merchant vessels.

The Delaware River at sunset. Photo by Robert Hall.

Muddy Creek

Located north of Baltimore and just a few miles into Pennsylvania, Muddy Creek is a superlative paddler's delight that flows through a small but spectacular gorge. There are two paradoxes, however, that characterize this wonderful stream. First, the name Muddy Creek is a misnomer; the water is usually crystal clear. Second, it is hard to believe that such a beautiful natural stream is not too distant from the controversial nuclear power plant at Three Mile Island on the Susquehanna River.

This Class II trip (with one Class III) of about six miles is especially suited for intermediates or shepherded novices when the put-in gauge is one foot or less. At higher levels the trip is somewhat more difficult. Several Class II rapids become heavier water, and hydraulics become more dangerous on the one Class III rapids as the river rises. The journey begins just above or below a seven-foot dam (depending on your nerve and water levels), and then continues into a striking little gorge which is highlighted by Class III Snap Falls. In the gorge there is one portage by a nasty boat-busting rock pile. Finally, the Muddy mellows out through several Class II rapids amidst spectacular scenery just before reaching the Susquehanna River.

The best put-in is not where Route 74 crosses Muddy Creek. Instead, it is just downstream on river left where a short road leads to a large parking area just below an old bridge and a seven-foot dam. After careful scouting, experienced boaters can run the dam at a couple of spots in the center. At moderate levels there's no menacing hydraulic at the bottom; indeed, in summer swimmers jump from carefully selected places on the dam into the pool below. The gauge for the river (courtesy of the Conewago Canoe Club) is on the river left side of the old bridge center abutment just below the seven-foot dam.

While passing under the bridge, look for fish in the deep, clear pools. They might be suckers instead of trout, but it's still nice to see them. A Class I–II riffle is located just below the bridge.

After a half mile of relatively calm water, the river splits. Take either channel if there is sufficient water. The paddler will notice that the bank here is covered by sycamores, river birches, and maples.

One and a half miles from the put-in lies the bridge at Paper Mill Road, which can also be used as a put-in. If you put in here and plan to park on river left just downstream of the bridge, please get permission from the landowner first. Inconsiderate folks have trashed his field, and he may not take kindly to strangers leaving vehicles without his blessing. Better yet, park on river right on the other side of the bridge where, as of this writing, permission is not necessary.

During the next half mile of paddling you encounter some Class I rapids, enter the gorge, and approach the first good rapids of the trip—a Class II double ledge at moderate levels. The first ledge is one foot, and the second is two feet. Don't be in a hurry to pass by these ledges because they can have challenging surfing possibilities, particularly below the second ledge with a foot of water on the put-in gauge. Experienced boaters can find some very interesting action here. About a half mile later, after a couple more one-foot drops, you arrive at the best rapids of the trip—Snap Falls. When

---

Section: Castle Fin to Susquehanna River

Counties: York (PA)

USGS Quads: Holtwood

Suitable for: Day cruising

Skill Level: Sheperded novices or intermediates (moderate levels); strong intermediates (high levels)

Months Runnable: Winter and spring most of the time; surprisingly often in summer

Interest Highlights: Beautiful gorge for most of the trip; hemlocks and rhododendrons

Scenery: Beautiful in the gorge for most of the trip

Difficulty: Class II (with one Class III section) up to 1.5 feet on put-in gauge; Class II–III at 2–4 feet on put-in gauge

Average Width: 20–40 feet

Velocity: Moderate to fast

Gradient: 15 feet per mile

Runnable Water Levels:
  Minimum: 0 feet on put-in gauge
  Maximum: 3–4 feet on put-in gauge

Hazards: One mile below Snap Falls is Muddy Creek Falls—a real boat buster with serious pinning possibilities; carry right. Occasional trees in river. Snap Falls has bad hydraulics on right/center at high levels.

Scouting: Snap Falls on river right

Portages: Muddy Creek Falls—portage 100–150 feet on right.

Rescue Index: Accessible with difficulty

Source of Additional Information: None

Access Points	River Miles	Shuttle Miles
A–B	5.0	5.0
A–C	6.0	4.0

Access points:
  A: Castle Fin—just below 7-foot dam by the old bridge near Rt. 74
  B: Boeckel Landing—on the Susquehanna upstream from the mouth of Muddy Creek
  C: Coal Cabin Beach—on the Susquehanna downstream from the mouth of Muddy Creek

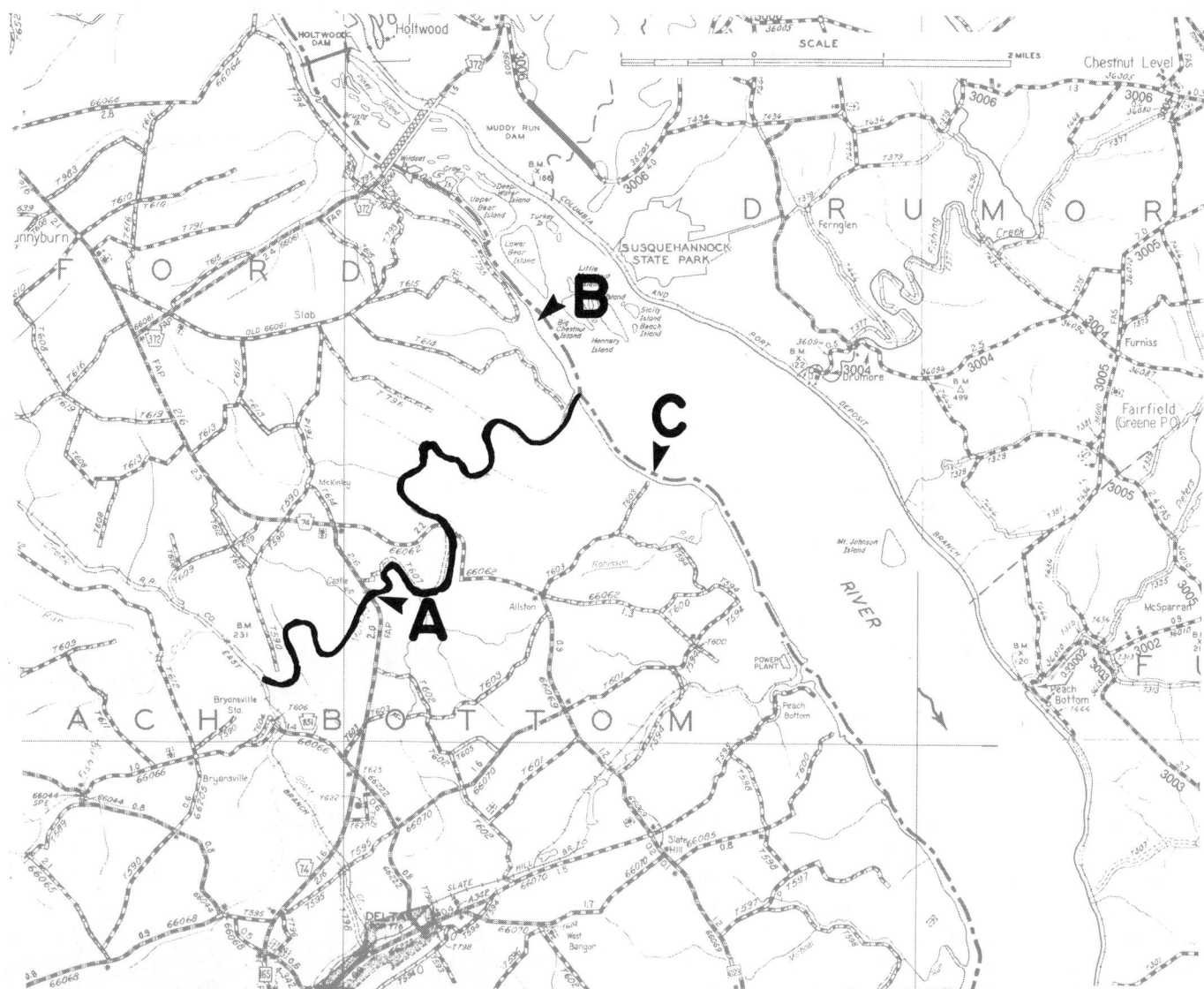

you hear a roar and see a horizon line, get over to river right and scout at all levels.

The river splits into right and left channels at Snap Falls. The right is a straight drop while the left is a rocky washboard. Paddlers should run the right side at moderate levels (Class III) because the left is too shallow. However, at higher levels (roughly one and a half to two feet on the put-in gauge) the hydraulics on the right side become quite nasty and the left side (still Class III) becomes padded enough to run. At really high levels (such as three feet on the gauge), the hydraulics on the right and center (now that there is enough water) have keeper characteristics and must be avoided at all costs. Throw ropes should be set below Snap Falls if the trip leader believes they are needed.

This respectable four-foot drop can be deceptively placid to first-timers. At low and medium levels it should be run very tight right on the fast-moving tongue next to the right bank. After hitting the tongue, paddlers should be immediately prepared to lean hard right because the curler at the bottom of this drop has a strong tendency to flip boaters to the left. In leaning right, left-handed paddlers should be ready for a very firm low brace and right-handers should be ready for a "rock brace." An appealing alternative is a notch roughly ten feet out from the right bank. However, there may not be sufficient water for the stern to pass over the edge of the drop without hanging up. If this happens, the paddler stops cold, the boat wobbles violently with a hung-up stern, and a flip often results.

During the next mile (which includes a couple of riffles), the paddler plunges deeper into the gorgeous gorge and can enjoy the large metamorphic rock formations (primarily schist), hemlocks, and rhododendron gracing its sides. At the end of the mile look for the river necking down to the left between some large rocks. Pull over to the right bank, and once your boat is well beached, go over and study this nasty drop which is called Muddy Creek Falls. The rocks in this cauldron are large and sharp and because of their location can create boat-busting and pinning situations. As the river gets higher Muddy Creek Falls gets worse. We emphatically recommend that this drop be portaged. In fact, we haven't given it a class rating because we do not want to tempt foolhardy paddlers into running it. The cheap thrill of attempting Muddy Creek Falls is not worth a broken boat or body and thus being a burden to fellow paddlers. Although the 100- to 150-foot portage on river right is bumpy and over large rocks, large groups can form a "boat brigade" whereby boats are slid from one group of hands to another across this rocky spot.

The portage at Muddy Creek Falls is clearly worth the effort because the beauty of the river continues to unfold. The ranks of rocks, rhododendron, and hemlocks pass by unbroken, and folks can revel in the scenery. Just below the portage lies a Class II tight right turn with an eddy on river left just above the turn for those with good boat control. A couple of minutes below the right turn is a tight Class II left turn; during a recent trip we had to duck under a tree that had fallen across the river at this turn. Less than half a mile below, a good two-foot drop is best run on the left at moderate levels. Just below the drop you'll see a 25-foot rock face on river left with spectacular little waterfalls cut into it. This provides a real photo opportunity and a super shower possibility in the summer! Plan to stop and enjoy this scenic wonder.

Shortly past the waterfalls lies the last rapid of significance—a strong Class II. Spanning most of the river from the left is a rock forming a two-foot drop and a vigorous surfing hole for the brave of heart and helmeted of head. The story is told of one poor experienced paddler who was surfing in the clutches of this hole. He tried all manner of maneuvers to get out and was getting thoroughly trashed. Finally, out of his kayak and beginning to panic, he felt his feet touch bottom. He then simply walked out.

Below this last rapid the gorge ends and the river widens and deepens. During the last mile to the Susquehanna, houses appear on the banks and civilization returns. Once you reach the mouth of the Muddy, you have about a mile to paddle upstream or downstream on the Susquehanna, depending on where you set your shuttle. While setting the shuttle, check the wind. If it is coming from the northwest down the Susquehanna, choose the downstream take-out at Coal Cabin Beach. If there is no wind or not a heavy current on the Susquehanna, pick the slightly shorter upstream take-out at Boeckel Landing.

In addition to the geologic and plant splendors on the river, there is also wildlife. Not only do kingfishers dart here and there, escorting paddlers down the river, but other birds such as red-tailed hawks abound. On an early spring trip, one author was fortunate enough to come upon three of these hawks, which had (apparently) come together to sort out their territories.

Another nice aspect of this river is that it holds its water well. It is normally very reliable in the winter and spring and suprisingly so in the summer. The only disadvantage is that there is no telephone gauge that correlates to the river. The only sure gauge is the one painted on the old bridge at the put-in.

[E. G.]

Greg Grove in Snap Falls, Muddy Creek. Photo by Ed Grove.

West Virginia

Upper Gauley

The Upper Gauley is a superlative and unique wildwater river, certainly one of the classic trips on the entire East Coast. It's big, long, inaccessible, tough, dangerous—and intoxicating. There are 100 rapids in the 25 miles between Summersville Dam and Swiss—most of them in the 15-mile section above Koontz Flume. However, while the rapids are very complex and challenging, the Upper Gauley is a river of alternating rapids and pools. The pools permit rescue and repair, providing an opportunity to marvel at the grandeur of this remote, vernal, steep-walled canyon.

In 1968 the Gauley was first paddled in whitewater boats by a group of the world's most experienced paddlers. During the 1970s, the Upper Gauley became known as the East's qualifying cruise for the title of expert paddler. However, this is no longer quite true. Although the Gauley hasn't changed, paddlers have gotten better; many now play their way down a river that used to push their skills to the limit. With improved paddling techniques and equipment, boaters are now running much more difficult rivers—such as the Lower Meadow which empties into the Gauley. Because numerous skilled paddlers now do the Gauley routinely, you should be prepared for heavy crowds of boaters and rafters on fall weekend releases.

Nevertheless, the Upper Gauley is still intense and has dangerous places. Do not attempt this river without the skill, confidence, and endurance that make the Cheat Canyon or New River Gorge seem easy. You should also be very comfortable on the Lower Gauley before attempting the substantially more difficult Upper section. Even then, undertake this trip only when accompanied by a trusted party who has previously experienced the "Upper." This is not a river for the first-timer to pick his way down; the Upper Gauley has a significant number of undercuts and traps to avoid. Indeed, before running the major rapids on this section, possible routes should be clearly discussed with trusted paddlers who know the river.

Assuming the standard release level of 2,500 cfs from Summersville Dam and minimal input from the Meadow River (just above Lost Paddle rapids), here are the primary rapids on the 15-mile section from Summersville Dam to Koontz Flume. After several minor rapids, Initiation (Class III-IV) is first. This drop is around the bend more than half a mile from the impressive put-in at the dam tubes. It looks like a clean drop that could be run anywhere, but be careful here! One kayaker has died and several others have been trapped in vertical pins by the invisible undercut rock sieve on the top right of Initiation, so run it left of center. The entrance is a wave train, the last "wave" being a large mound at the brink of the main drop. Go over the left center of this mound angled right. This will avoid the extremely dangerous invisible rock sieve at the top of the drop and the worst of the holes at the bottom right and left. The bottom right hole is quite stiff at lower levels (1,200 cfs). Below the drop, cut left of a large boulder and punch a few small holes to finish.

After a few minor rapids including a Class III wave train, Collison Creek or BFR (Big "Friendly" Rock) No. 1, comes Bud's Boner (a.k.a. Funnel). This Class III-IV rapid is

Mike Bush running Pillow Rock at 4,400 cfs. Photo by Bob Taylor.

recognized by the river squeezing to the right and plunging over two drops. Both drops have obstructing rocks at the bottom that mainly concern rafts. To avoid pins on these rocks, rafters should work quickly left after the first drop and run the second drop at a strong right angle.

About two miles into the trip a high sandstone wall looms ahead, signalling your approach to Insignificant (Class V), which is anything but. It is a long, open rapid with two particularly bad holes in the center usually marked by inverted boats and bobbing helmets. Scouting this rapid is difficult and time-consuming, but can be done from the right. Many paddlers start left of center, running just right (or left) of a large boulder with a log perched on top. As the river narrows and deepens, angle slightly right to reach the main current. Just downstream are two large, slightly offset holes that are hard to see until you are almost upon them. The left hole is grabbier, and its left side can really hold boats and rafts. The hole on the right is smaller and just upstream of the left hole. Hard boaters usually skirt these holes to the right or left while big rafts often tweeze left to right between the holes to insure avoiding the left part of the left hole. (Some hard boaters enter the complex top of this rapid on the right and work down to catch an eddy above the right hole before deciding to go right or left of the two holes.) Below these holes, make sure the main current does not push you against the right bank rocks (particularly a large sloping rock) and avoid the pourover on the left. Finish on an exciting wave train and eddy right or left for a surfing spot at the bottom.

After two lesser rapids, Iron Curtain (Class III+) appears three miles into the trip. Named for the iron oxide stains on the high sandstone wall on the right, this is an incredible wave train giving a great ride for rafts which should watch for a pinning rock below, easily skirted on the right or left. Then go right of Sperm Whale Rock, which is undercut. Kayaks can stay tight left to avoid the almost river-wide hole at the main drop. Iron Curtain indicates that Pillow Rock is around the next left bend less than a mile away.

Pillow Rock (Class V) is a 25-foot drop stretching over 50 yards of heavy turbulence and holes, piling up against a huge boulder on the left, and then slithering around and over Volkswagon Rock—a megachunk of Guyandotte sandstone. The Pillow is located where the river hits the wall extending from the left and puts many paddlers down for a damp rest. The main problem with the Pillow is that it consists of confused, highly aerated water that offers little support for a brace. Scout right or left. Carry on the right.

There are two reasonable routes to Pillow Rock. (See diagram.) The best kayak and canoe route starts in the center of the river. Enter just right of a boulder at the top; then hug the left sides of two successive rocks in the center of the river and be sure you go right of a small rooster tail between these two rocks. Then work slightly right, first skirting the right side of a large hole, and then carefully skirting the left side of a larger steep hole at the bottom

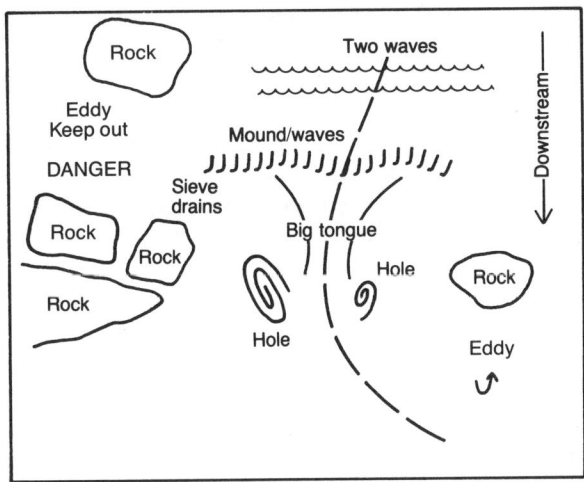

Diagram of Initiation Rapid.

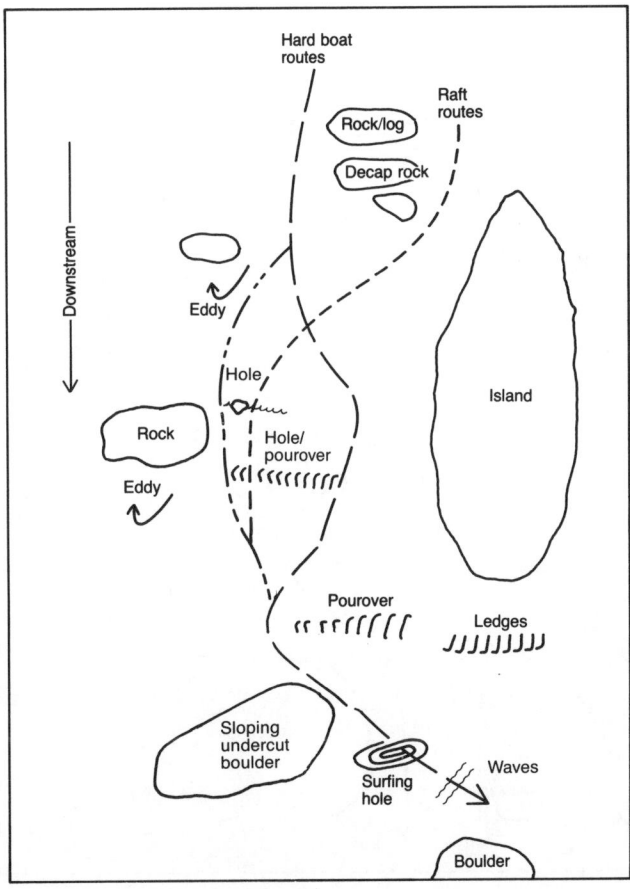

Diagram of Insignificant Rapid.

right. (If you must hit this last hole, do so on the left as the right side is shallow and obstructed.) If possible, use the foam pile behind the last hole on the right to turn you right —so you can avoid riding too high up on the Pillow. Catch the large eddy above and right of Volkswagon Rock. The best raft route is to enter on the far right, moving quickly left along a distinct wave train that terminates in the last steep hole on the right. Rafts punch the left side of this hole to slow their momentum, then slide off the left side of Volkswagon Rock below. Incidentally, Volkswagon Rock has a good (but turbulent) ender spot on its left eddy line.

Avoid running Pillow Rock too far left! Doing so will put you too high on the Pillow and slam you (upside down) against Pillow Rock. Even worse, you could get caught in the Room of Doom, a terminal box-shaped eddy just to the left of the Pillow. Many a hapless boater has spent anxious moments in the Room of Doom wondering what idiot told him to run this rapid on the left. A trail on the right bank leads up to the Carnifex Ferry overlooks (visible above on the right) for those who need an emergency take-out and have thoroughly strong legs.

Then comes a mile of several easier drops called Breather Rapids, which have such colorful names as Hungry Mother Hole (run right). After this, the Meadow River enters on river left, indicating your approach to Lost Paddle (Class V). When running the Upper Gauley, check the cfs of the Meadow River, because anything above a minimal input (200–300 cfs) from the Meadow can make a whale of a difference in Lost Paddle and other rapids below. (Indeed, there was one awesome time in 1978 when the Gauley was running 8,000 cfs but the Meadow was running 17,000 cfs!)

Rafters should be very careful of the last rapid before the Meadow enters. Known as Toothpaste or Flippers Folly, this Class II–III rapid is recognized by an island at the top

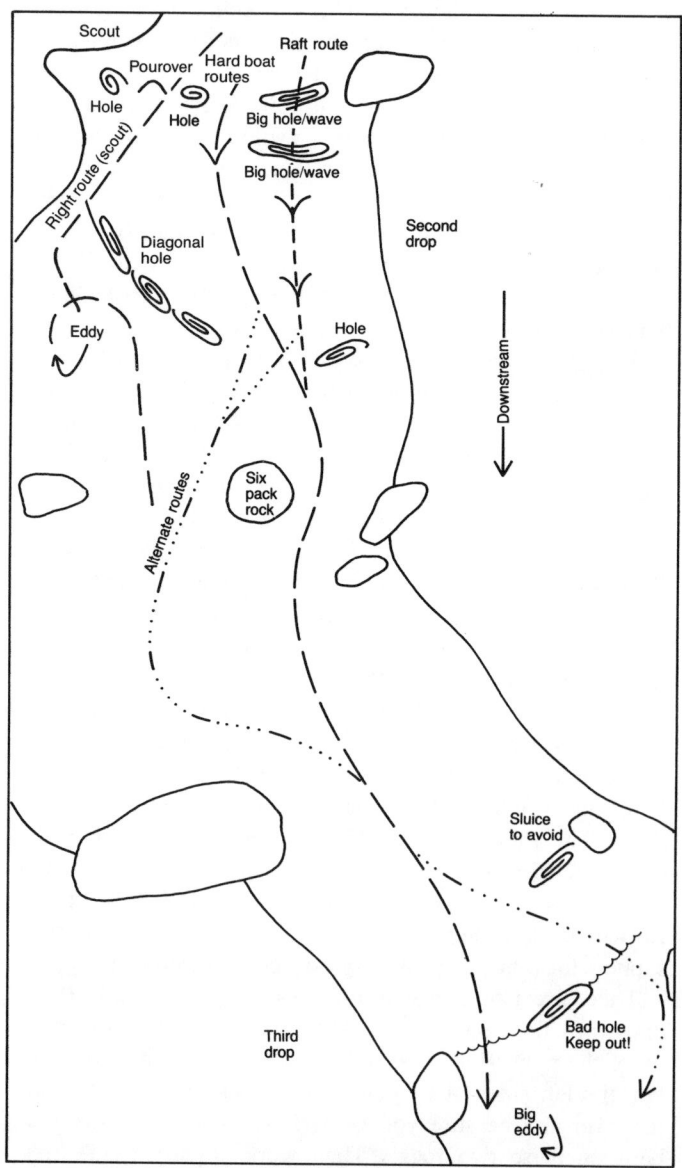

Diagram of Pillow Rock.

Diagram of Lost Paddle, Second and Third Drops.

and offers two pinning possibilities for rafts. The right side of the island funnels through Toothpaste Slot, which is too small for larger rafts to negotiate. Also, taking the right side of the left channel around the island almost always results in an embarrassing pin. Enter the left channel left of center and work right for a safe route.

Difficult to scout and murderous to carry, Lost Paddle is a third of a mile of pourovers, ledges, undercut rocks, holes and more holes. Lost Paddle has four parts. Paddlers should take special care to run this rapid upright—particularly Second Drop (part two) and Tumblehome (part four). The first part is 200 yards of rocks and ledges with an interesting hole near the bottom. Enter left of a pyramid-shaped rock at the top, work left of a pinning low table rock and split two holes as you go right, into the main flow. Stay just left of the wave train to avoid the bottom hole. Eddy left or right above the Second Drop.

The Second Drop is the steepest, shallowest part of Lost Paddle and can be boat scouted from the eddies above. The top of this drop is recognized by a large curling wave extending from the left shore to the middle of the river. This wave hides a large blind ledge. The best decked boat route is just to the right side of this curling wave—no more than two boat lengths from the left shore. (See diagram.) Entering here you will just miss or clip the big hole at the bottom of this ledge. Take the right side of the wave train below this drop. The rock in the left center near the bottom (called Decision or Six Pack Rock) can be run left or right with caution—it is undercut as are the rocks on the left shore. Rafts can run the middle of the wave at the top and punch the stiff hole below, then go between the left shore and Decision Rock. There is also a shallow rocky route on the right, which starts just left of a pourover. Scout this first, and be working hard right to miss a nasty diagonal hole at the bottom of the main drop.

Lost Paddle's third part is an easy chute with a hole at the bottom. Go right or left of the hole. Watch out for rafts in the big right eddy below. (All commercial rafters eddy out here!) Also, quickly pick up any swimmers in the calm but briskly moving water.

The fourth and last drop (Tumblehome) is just below—first-timers should scout it! The raft route begins by running right of the large trapezoid-shaped rock in the center of the river. Then, after punching or skirting the hole to the right of this rock, cut in behind it abruptly for the next good chute, which is over a rough irregular rocky ledge. Hard boaters with decent upstream ferrys can go left of the trapezoid rock, eddy out on the left, and then vigorously ferry river right above some nasty pinning rocks and undercuts to catch this chute. Work left below this chute to avoid being blown into boulders on the right. Continue working left towards the center of the river for the last chute—making sure you avoid a very dangerous narrow slot between two rocks to the right of this final drop. Bracketed by two big rocks, this last chute has a terrific ender spot.

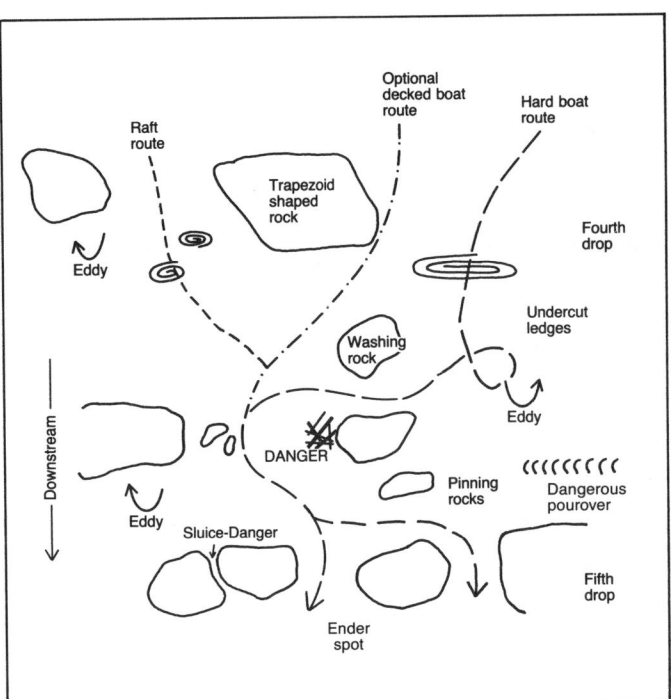

Diagram of Lost Paddle, Tumblehome (Fourth Drop).

Next is Conestoga Wagon rapids (Class III), which is a long S-turn and has a terminal hole (called Darrow's Doucher) to avoid in river center. Enter over a shallow ledge right of center, go right in the main wave train, and then go left through a chute between two boulders. If you don't go left to catch this chute, you will be on the brink of a steep slide into Darrow's Doucher—a bad hole whose backwash is backed by a rock. Very nasty. Having taken the proper left chute, rafts should work quickly right to avoid pinning rocks at the bottom of this rapid.

Table Rock (a.k.a. Shipwreck Rock) rapids follow, an easy Class III noteworthy only because of the significant hazard it poses for unwary boaters. Table Rock is a boxcar-sized rock in the center of the river with most of the river flowing UNDER it. Give this a wide berth to the far right after the left side approach. Also, beware of a razor-back rock lurking behind the largest wave in the left entrance. Go left of this wave. For those wanting an alternative, Table Rock can also be approached from the right.

Not far below Table Rock, the river bends right and the current is compressed along the right shore by a point of rocks. After seven miles of paddling, you have reached Iron Ring (Class V–VI), named for a huge iron ring set in the rocks on the left. The ring dates from an attempt to blast a log-floating passage here in the early 1900s. This dynamiting has created an irregular mid-channel obstruction. The river sharply constricts on the right and drops down a six-foot-high slide into a hole a boat length above the obstructing boulder (Woodstock Rock). The current welling up out of the hole mostly slips down the right side. Some splashes over the now smooth man-made block, and about a fourth

Upper Gauley River

Section: Summersville Dam to Koontz Flume

Counties: Nicholas and Fayette (WV)

USGS Quads: Summersville Dam and Ansted

Suitable for: Day trips

Skill Level: Experts only

Months Runnable: Dam releases, particularly in September and early October; runnable with natural flow occasionally during the rest of the year

Interest Highlights: Unique expert whitewater river; spectacular gorge and rock formations

Scenery: Beautiful!

Difficulty: Class IV–V, with one Class V–VI

Average Width: 75–100 feet

Velocity: Fast

Gradient: 28 feet per mile

Runnable Water Levels:
  Minimum: 2.4 feet on the Belva gauge; 800 cfs
  Maximum: 4.5 feet on Belva gauge; 5,000 cfs

Hazards: Undercut rocks; several long Class V–VI rapids; high water

Scouting: Insignificant (difficult); Pillow Rock; Second Drop and Tumblehome in Lost Paddle; Iron Ring; Sweet's Falls; Wood's Ferry

Portages: Probably Iron Ring; possibly Pillow Rock

Rescue Index: Remote

Source of Additional Information: National Weather Service in Charleston (304) 342-7771, Monday through Friday, 8:00 am to 4:30 pm for Belva gauge; Summersville Dam (dam release and Meadow River), (304) 872-5809

Access Points	River Miles	Shuttle Miles
A–B	8.5	10
A–C	15.0	16
A–D	17.5	14

Access Point Ratings:
A at Summersville Dam, excellent
B at Panther Creek, poor
C at Koontz Flume, fair (get permission first)
D at Peters Creek, poor

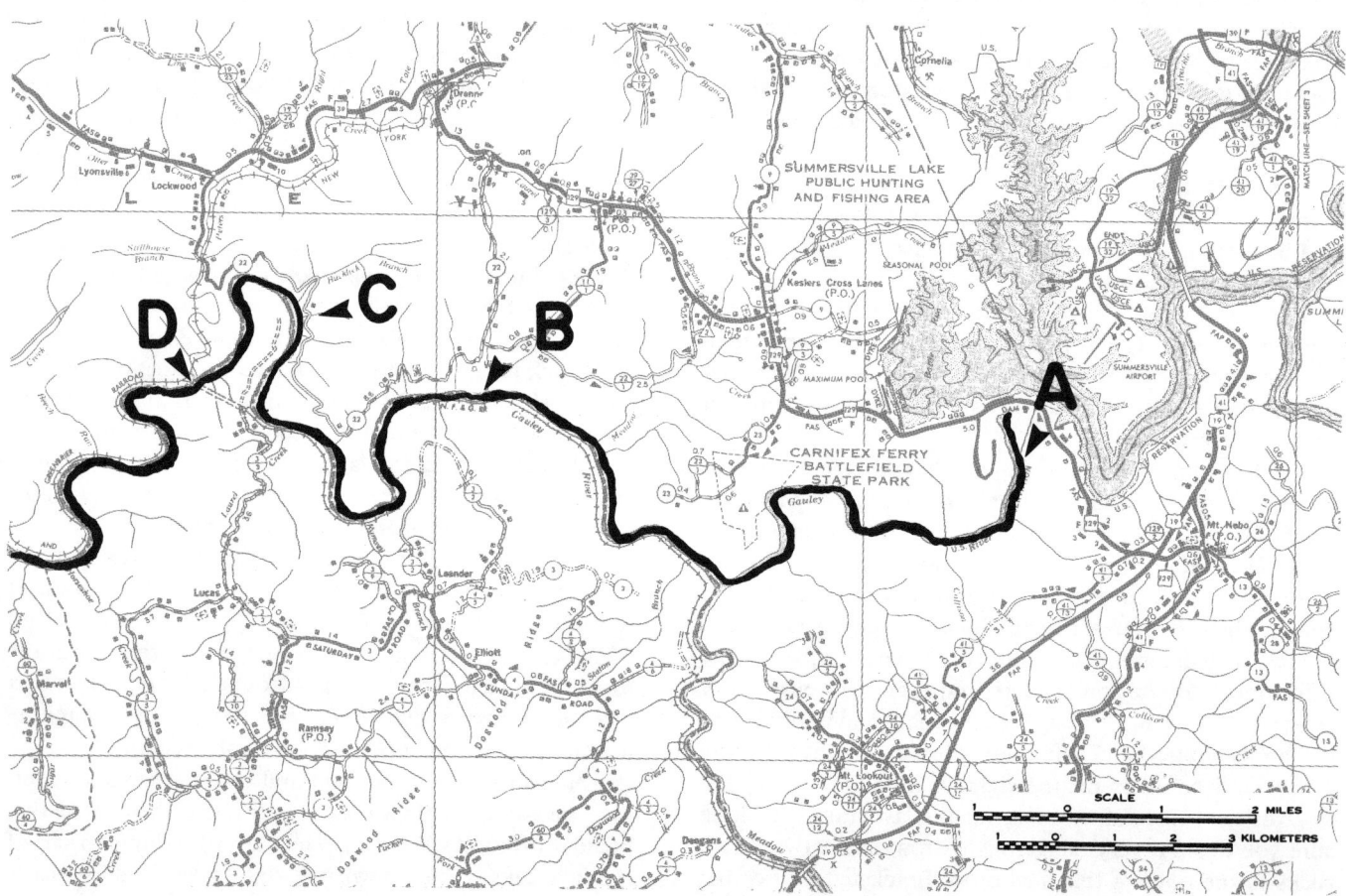

flushes under and around the left side of Woodstock Rock in a channel between it and its mother stone. The channel is crooked and turbulent without enough straightaway for a swamped boat and with enough force to fold an errant paddler and boat together. Carry on the left, or scout carefully and run from left to right and upright. The proper line leaves little margin for error. (See diagram.) You start from the left, skirting the right side of two hydraulics to line up for the main rapid. Then you work carefully from left to right on a large tongue to squeeze first between two holes and then between the Woodstock Rock obstruction on the left and Backender Hole on the right. Don't relax too soon at the bottom because a lot of current slams into rocks on the bottom right. Throw ropes should be set on the left below the holes. At lower levels, Iron Ring becomes meaner, and most paddlers walk this rapid below 1,500 cfs.

The next mile is easy except for a word of caution about Fingernail Rock Rapid (Class III), three-quarters of a mile below Iron Ring. The rock on the far left is badly undercut. Run right.

About eight miles into the trip you reach Sweet's Falls (Class V). Here the Welch sandstone, shale, and thin strata of Sewell coal rise straight up from the right side of the river. The river jogs right, then left, and drops over a cliff of

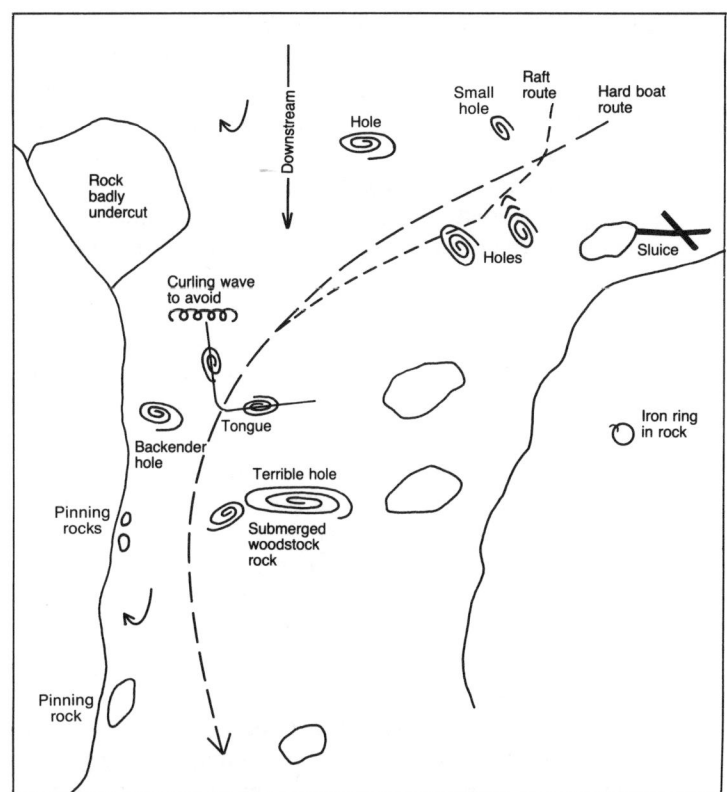

Diagram of Iron Ring.

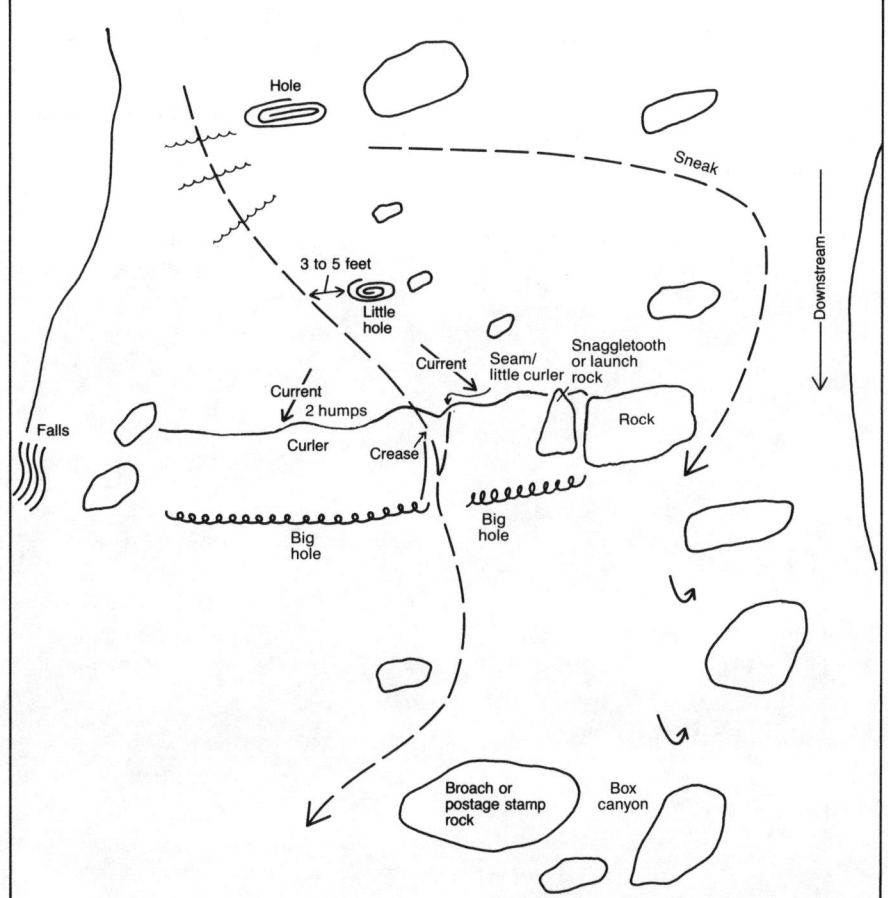

Diagram of Sweet's Falls.

this sandstone as heavy, steep, ten-foot falls. It was named for John Sweet who ran it on the initial Gauley trip in 1968.

The left side of the falls is a steep technical boat-crunching ledge-boulder garden with an obstructing rock at the bottom called Broach Rock or Postage Stamp Rock (because of the way rafts stick to it). This Class IV sneak should be scouted (or carried) on the left side. To run the falls proper, take out on the right well above the entrance for a difficult scout, or run carefully behind someone who knows this drop well. The entrance is three to five feet right of an easy little hole followed by a small wave train continuing to the lip of the drop just downstream. A large eddy is on the left. The main route to run the falls is very narrow. If you follow the wave train to the lip of the falls, you'll be too far right; here the drop is steepest with a terrible hole below. Running from the calm of the eddy will put you too far left with Snaggletooth Rock and another bad hole as a worse consequence. The correct line is a tongue or tube just below the seam or small depression where the wave train current and eddy current join. (See diagram.) Run the seam. Some paddlers angle right with a strong left brace. Others angle left. Talk to someone who has run this drop to determine your route. After the big plunge, recover quickly to avoid being swept into the rocks below. Rafters should move right to avoid being blown into Broach Rock or Box Canyon on the left. Catch swimmers quickly since the main current blasts diagonally left into the rocks on the left bank, which are undercut.

The river calms down for about two miles below Sweet's Falls. Here there are several minor rapids (including a nice play wave) and then a good ender spot on river left next to a ledge extending from river right. Shortly thereafter is Sleeper Shoals or Guide's Revenge (Class II–III), where most of the river necks down to a large sneaky diagonal hole on river left. Start working right at the top of the rapids to avoid this hole. Conversely, if you have some crabby rafters, this is a good place to give them an invigorating swim.

Next is Woods Ferry (a.k.a. Insignificant No. 2)—a Class IV drop. The river turns right as this rapid starts with a rock garden. However, two-thirds of the way down is a large hole extending from the left bank across half the river. Soon below and in the right center of the river is a large flat boulder (Julie's Juicer Rock) with a nasty hole (Julie's Juicer) just to its left. Rafts punch the wide hole above to ensure going left of Julie's Juicer. Hard boaters not wanting to punch this hole can make a vigorous right to left move between these two holes or sneak Julie's Juicer Rock on the right.

Just below is Ender Waves (Class III), a classic play spot. Enter left to catch the two large waves at the bottom for dynamic surfing. For the next two miles there are several minor rapids and then comes Backender (Class IV), which has a large rock on bottom right. Some hard boaters begin Backender right of center, avoid a hole on the top right, and then work left of Backender hole at the bottom which devours the right side of the river. Other boaters miss the hole on the bottom right by hugging the right bank. Rafts usually punch Backender hole with exciting results for paddlers in the bow. Be careful of Backender hole at 1,200 cfs because it has keeper tendencies. You are now just above Koontz Flume. See page 72 for additional put-in and take-out information.

*Diana Kendrick at Tumblehome/
Lost Paddle on the Upper Gauley.
Photo by Paul Marshall.*

Lower Gauley

The following description is for the standard release level of 2,500 cfs and covers the 10.5-mile section from Koontz Flume to the take-out at Omega Siding, near Swiss.

Koontz Flume (Class IV–V) is a demanding roller coaster ride with really BIG waves. The admission price to catch this roller coaster is high, though. Recognized by a huge undercut rock on river right, the flume is right of center but guarded at the top by a big hole which must be punched or skirted (usually on the right, but left is okay). Having gone right of the hole, work left to catch the main chute of the flume. However, working left can be difficult because a curler on the right edge of the hole kicks paddlers further right. Alternatively, some decked boaters carefully catch a tricky "last chance" eddy, right of the hole, before vigorously ferrying left to catch this flume, which is a long smooth slide into some big waves below. Whatever you do, don't get caught in the vertical drop at top right, which can flush you and your boat underneath Koontz Rock! At bottom left is Five Boat Hole, a great play spot (if you don't get run over by errant rafts and kayaks). Scout Koontz Flume on the left, and sneak it on the far left. The flume's long smooth slide is shallow, so decked boaters should take special care not to flip here.

Canyon Doors (Class III) is next, ornamented with beautiful sandstone cliffs on the right. Run far right, and then work left towards the bottom for a good surfing hole. Immediately downstream is Junkyard (Class III)—usually run on the left. There is a safe route on the far right marred by junk on the right bank.

After four minor rapids, the Peters Creek trestle (one alternate put-in) and 3.5 miles of paddling, you come to the Mash brothers, Upper and Lower. Upper Mash (Class III+) is a complex and tortuous bump and grind over and through a steep, shallow boulder garden. It is perhaps best entered in the center to the left or right of a large rock. In low water, to avoid a pinning rock below the two- to three-foot ledge on the left of this rock, stay well to the left of this ledge. After picking your way down the technical center channel, eddy right or left at the bottom. These eddies are your last chance to scout Lower Mash—a big downstream-pointing U-shaped ledge (Class IV) with some semi-friendly holes and waves below. The most conservative route starts left of center and ends right, in the eddy below the ledge. Beware of an undercut boulder sieve at the bottom left, well below the ledge. At high water levels, run right of center and watch out for big reaction waves crashing in from the left. Rescue flipped boaters quickly because the river continues fast and rocky for several hundred yards downstream.

After being "Mashed," the paddler reaches Diagonal Ledges (Class II–III) which has some good surfing holes. A chute between two rocks forms a semi-safe ender slot just to the right of the first drop. Even open boaters can get enders here, but a nose job on their bows may be the price. At high water watch for Maui Wave (a.k.a. Hawaii Five O Wave) at bottom left. A great surfing wave, it easily surfs (and flips) rafts.

Next is Heaven Help You (a.k.a. Gateway to Heaven), a long Class IV where the river constricts and finally squeezes between two big rocks (appropriately called the Pearly Gates) at the bottom. Enter center and quickly start working left to avoid a nasty ledge/hole covering the right half of the river halfway down. This ledge/hole is a notorious boat flipper. After skirting the hole, work right to catch a wave train in the center of the channel, which deposits you in a tricky hole between the Pearly Gates. Angle right in punching the hole and run right of a semi-undercut rock just below the Gates. Staying too far left will slam you against the left rock of the Pearly Gates, which is also slightly undercut. At high water, scout and stay right, right, right! The Pearly Gates Hole is now a monster and should be skirted far right. An alternate sneak is to hug the left shore and run left of the Gates; this works at all levels.

After Gateway to Heaven are three Class III rapids. The first is Rocky Top; run it on the right and look out for a hidden hole right of center near the bottom that gets larger as the river gets higher. To miss it work left in the lower part of the rapids. There is a good ender spot below Rocky Top on the left. Picture Rock (a.k.a. BFR No. 2) is next—a real sneaky rapids upstream of a large rock in mid-river. Here the current goes over a sloping ledge from right to left and can push you further left than you want to go. Just as you go over the bottom of the drop, water coming in suddenly from the left shoves you right—sideways into a hole that will flip you upstream unless you have a strong low brace ready on your left. Upper Stairsteps follows, a wave train roller coaster on river left. Look out for a large hole in the center halfway down, which gets bigger at higher levels.

Next is Riverwide Stopper (also known as Lower Stairsteps or THE HOLE). This is a larger Class III–IV wave train, run center with a large river-wide hole/curler midway down the rapids. Punch this hole squarely and with vigor to avoid a fisheye view of the river. You can sneak this hole right or left of center.

After a good Class II–III wave train called Rollercoaster, there are three more Class III rapids. The first is Cliffside: easy on the right, fun on the left. It is recognized by the cliffs on the left. If you run it on the left, angle right and brace left into a diagonal curler after you enter. Below is Rattlesnake—a long rapid with a rattler on the end, especially if started on the left. Enter left of the island; work right for the most conservative route. The last of the trio is Roostertail, which should be run left to avoid a pinning rock on the bottom right.

After a long pool (7.5 miles into the trip), you arrive at

the top of Pure Screaming Hell (Class IV–V), the last of the major Gauley rapids. This appropriately named rapid starts on a curve to the right and ends on a left turn which is far, far below. Scout this rapid on the right; sneak it far left. *Caution:* a potentially deadly sluice/strainer awaits swimmers at the bottom right. If you have had serious difficulties in the rapids upstream, this is the rapid to portage. Carry on the left. Start the top of Pure Screaming Hell center or right of center. After the initial holes and ledges, catch the wave train and watch for a large hole extending to the center of the river from river left. Kiss the right edge of this hole and work hard left to miss the huge hole (Hell Hole) just below. At moderate levels Hell Hole can be punched by good paddlers cranking hard. The big rock to the right of Hell Hole is undercut and creates the aforementioned sluice/strainer on the far right. Stay well to the left towards the bottom of Pure Screaming Hell! At high water, look out for High Water Hole upstream of Hell Hole. It flips paddlers working left to avoid Hell Hole and can be nastier than Hell Hole, which becomes more of a large crashing wave at high levels.

Following two little rapids, only Kevin's Folly (Class III) remains. Some big holes appear here at high water. A mile and a half below on river right is the take-out at Omega Siding. You pass an island just before this take-out.

Put-ins/Take-outs for the Upper and Lower Gauley

The put-in for the Upper Gauley is easy—the only easy thing about the trip. It is at the base of the Summersville Dam and is reached by going south and then west from Summersville. The huge torrents of water coming out of the dam tubes at standard release levels are humbling to see.

The first possible take-out is at the mouth of the Meadow, Carnifex Ferry—adjacent to a state battleground at the site of a Confederate rout. The access is one mile up a steep trail and is recommended only in an emergency. A jeep trail also goes near this ferry from Mount Lookout or from Hico to the south. This also is for emergency use only.

The next take-out from the Upper Gauley or first entry point for the Lower Gauley is from Panther Creek Road. One drives about two miles down this dirt road (Route 22) to a trail on the left. From here it is a half-mile carry on this trail (steep in places) to the Gauley. The put-in is about a

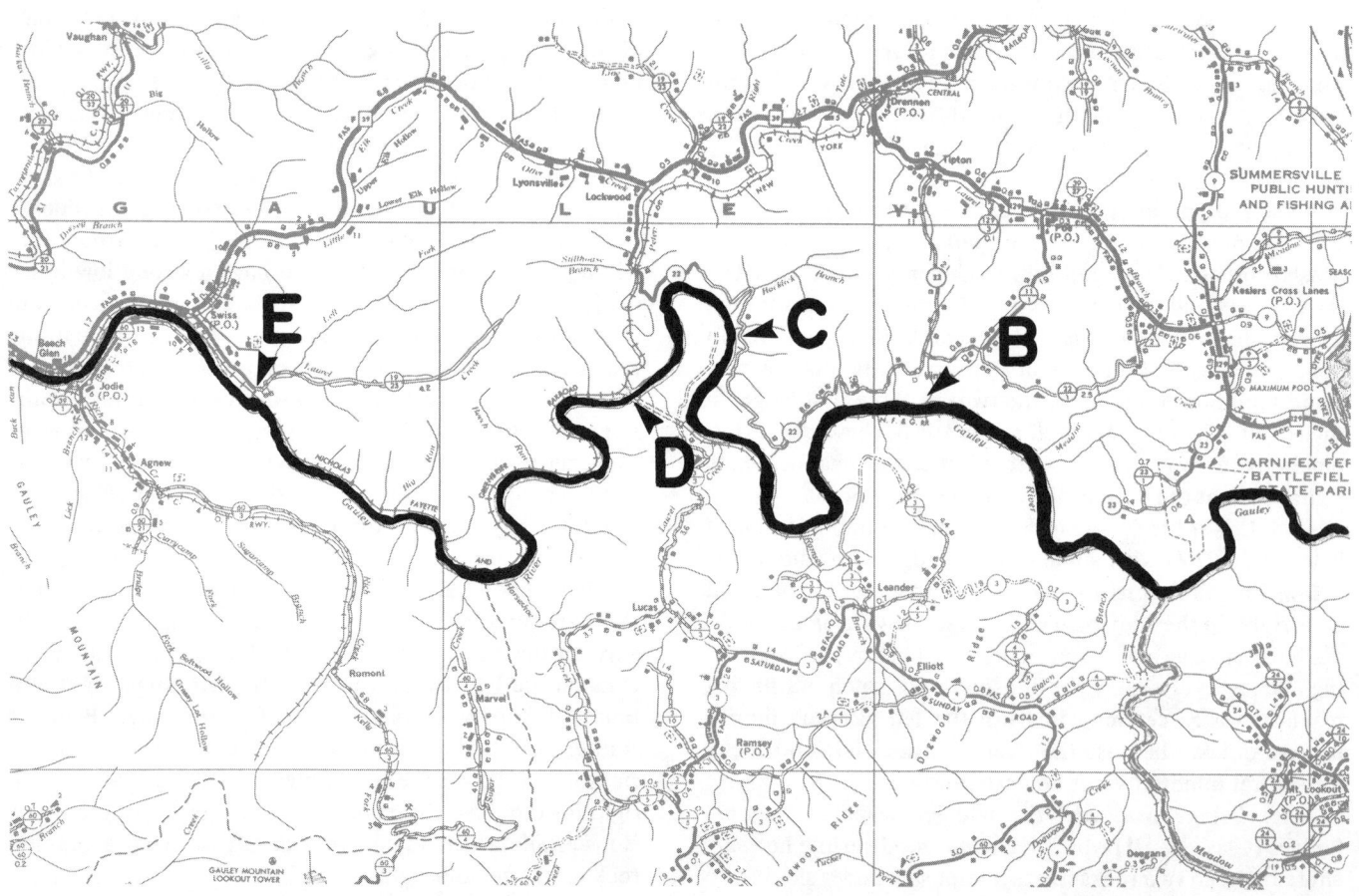

half mile below Sweet's Falls, about eight river miles from Summersville Dam. Because of the steepness of the trail, it is easier to put in than take out here. From Panther Creek to the Swiss take-out is 17 river miles. It is not wise to leave shuttle vehicles at Panther Creek because of possible vandalism.

At Woods Ferry, 12 miles into the Upper Gauley trip, a half-mile jeep trail from the Saturday Road to Leander leads to the river. There is also a put-in/take-out on river right just above Koontz Flume which gives a 15-mile Upper Gauley and 10-mile Lower Gauley trip. However, these access points are reserved for the use of commercial outfitters.

Finally, though far from an ideal access point, the Peters Creek put-in/take-out gives a 17-mile trip on the Upper Gauley and an 8-mile trip down the Lower Gauley. To reach this put-in, turn off WV 39 at Otter Creek School, west of Lockwood. After the blacktop ends, take the dirt road uphill to the first right fork. Drive down to a large field. The put-in is a one-mile portage down the railroad tracks, which reach the Gauley near the Peters Creek railroad bridge.

The final take-out is one mile up the river from Swiss along Route 19/25. This road parallels a railroad siding for several hundred yards, then swings away from the tracks up a creek. Stop here. The take-out is over the tracks on or just above a sandy peninsula. This siding is appropriately named Omega, the end of a classic trip.

To avoid shuttle hassles and possible vandalism, you may want to rely on non-paddling shuttle drivers. Alternatively, you may wish to call local rafting companies for shuttle advice or assistance. Check carefully, however, because shuttle possibilities and prices vary.

September and early October are the best times for a Gauley trip not only because of the splendid colors but because the water level is guaranteed by the letdown schedule for the Summersville Dam. The discharge can be obtained at the dam keeper's office at the put-in. The exact flow for the last half of the trip can be obtained from the Huntington Corps or National Weather Service as the Belva Gauge. This is at a discrepancy with the dam release if the Meadow is up. However, a recorded message at the dam (304) 872-5809 gives flows from the dam and the Meadow.

Gauley Conservation Efforts

The whitewater excitement of the Gauley River remains available today only because of the herculean efforts of a few private boaters, the commercial raft companies and the support they receive from the West Virginia congressional delegation.

To the U.S. Army Corps of Engineers, which operates the Summersville Dam, the project and the river held great potential for the construction of a hydroelectric power plant. During the early 1980s, the Corps made a big political push to build a "long tunnel" hydro project for taking water from Summersville Lake to a powerhouse to be constructed just above Pillow Rock. The project would have dried up several miles of the best whitewater on the Gauley. At the same time, the Corps claimed that whitewater releases from the Dam were not within the project's authorized purposes, which include flood control and pollution abatement. However, to gain support of river users for its proposal, the Corps promised that a hydroelectric power plant would enhance rather than detract from whitewater opportunities on the Gauley.

A group known as Citizens for Gauley River comprised of private and commercial whitewater boaters was quickly formed to fight the Corps hydro proposal and to work

---

Section: Koontz Flume to Swiss (see text for alternate put-ins)

Counties: Nicholas and Fayette (WV)

USGS Quads: Ansted

Suitable for: Day cruising

Skill Level: Advanced and expert

Months Runnable: Dam releases, particularly in September to early October; occasionally runnable with natural flow during the rest of the year

Interest Highlights: Classic trip through pristine gorge; cliffs at Canyon Doors

Scenery: Beautiful

Difficulty: Class III–V

Average Width: 100 feet

Velocity: Fast

Gradient: 26 feet per mile

Runnable Water Levels:
  Minimum: 2 feet on Belva gauge; 700 cfs
  Maximum: 9 feet on Belva gauge; 10,000 cfs

Hazards: Long rapids; high water; undercut rocks; strainers

Scouting: Koontz Flume; Lower Mash; Gateway to Heaven; The Hole; Pure Screaming Hell

Portages: None

Rescue Index: Remote to remote-but-accessible

Source of Additional Information: National Weather Service, Charleston, WV (304) 342-7771 Monday through Friday, 8:00 am to 4:30 pm for Belva gauge; Summersville Dam (dam release and Meadow River), (304) 872-5809

Access Points	River Miles	Shuttle Miles
B–E	17	14
C–E	10.5	11
D–E	8	9

Access Point Ratings:
  B at Panther Creek, poor
  C at Koontz Flume, fair (get permission first)
  D at Peters Creek, poor
  E at Swiss, good

for scheduled whitewater releases from Summersville Dam. David Brown of Knoxville, Tennessee forged this group into an effective and powerful political force, just as he had done in an earlier successful battle to save the Ocoee River in Tennessee. Under Brown's skillful leadership, the organization succeeded beyond all expectations.

In early 1984, U.S. Representative Nick J. Rahall of Beckley, West Virginia threatened to amend a funding bill for the Army Corps of Engineers with a provision prohibiting any further consideration of the proposed hydroelectric power project and vowed that the U.S. Congress would never authorize its construction. Almost immediately, the Corps withdrew the proposal and ceased further planning for Gauley hydroelectric developments. However, Rahall did proceed with legislation to authorize whitewater recreation as a project purpose of Summersville Dam. Enactment of this provision later that year was precedent setting because the Summersville Dam became the first, and to date only, U.S. Army Corps of Engineers water project to have whitewater recreation as one of its official purposes.

To further enhance whitewater recreation on the Gauley, Rahall also added a provision to the 1986 Omnibus Water Projects Authorization Bill which would guarantee whitewater releases from Summersville Dam at 2,500 cfs for a minimum of 20 days during the six-week period following Labor Day each year. This legislation was enacted by Congress and signed into law in November 1986.

John Wingfield at Iron Ring, Upper Gauley. Photo by Howard Kirkland.

New River

The New has a little something for everyone in its three most popular sections. The uppermost section of 15 miles from Sandstone to McCreery is the least paddled and consists of generally Class II rapids and some seemingly unending pools. It's a good run for open canoes and can be combined with the succeeding Prince to Thurmond run at moderate levels for canoe camping. This latter sports more continuous Class II and borderline Class III water than the section above and has been a long time favorite of novice and intermediate paddlers in both decked and open boats. Below Thurmond the bottom falls out in the celebrated Class III–V New River Gorge, one of the premier whitewater runs of the eastern U.S. Contrary to its name, the New is believed to be the oldest river in North America and is one of the few rivers in the world that flow north.

Sandstone to McCreery

The Sandstone to McCreery section is a very long run consisting of several nice impressive rapids, but, as with much of the New, these are interrupted by long expanses of flat water. It is a big powerful river, but very beautiful, always up in the summer, and it provides excellent fishing. Numerous campsites abound and it is perfect for overnight trips. The rapids are mainly long chutes dropping gently over ledges. Although the waves are large, not much maneuvering is required.

Open boaters and novices will encounter only two places that may cause trouble. The first of these occurs at the top of Horseshoe Bend seen from Grandview State Park. The entire river is necked down creating essentially heavy water which will swamp open canoes immediately. This is located about a half mile downstream from the obsolete concrete bridge piers at Glade. It is the second rapids from there. The river heads to the left and turns sharply back to the right. In this curve there is some very heavy water including a Class III stopper. After the rapids have pushed their way to the right, they straighten out and more very heavy turbulence may be seen in midstream. There is a mean hole in this turbulence large enough to fit the whole canoe. A lot of drive is required in order to get through this one. Open boaters or novices may avoid all of the heavy water by maintaining control and staying to the far right.

The second potential trouble spot is a delightfully long Class III rapids at Quinnimont just before reaching the railroad station. It is not difficult, but open canoes might swamp due to the length of it. Such canoeists might consider dumping excess water halfway down. Near the bottom, a huge drainpipe enters from the right. Just before this there is a powerful hydraulic in the middle of the river, followed by 20 yards of flat water, and then another very deceptive wave that camouflages a hole deep enough to set a C-2 in. Fun, but surprising!

Access at Sandstone is not ideal, but folks are neighborly and are normally happy to grant you access to the river. Then take WV 20 out of Sandstone to Meadow Bridge, turn left on CR 31 to Danese, and turn left again on WV 41 to McCreery. The take-out is easiest at a very large sandy beach located on the left, two rapids beyond the WV 41 bridge. It may be reached in a car by turning right off WV 41 onto a dirt road where 41 turns left to go up the mountain. This is McCreery.

Prince to Thurmond

The stretch from Prince (just below McCreery) to Thurmond is characterized by a slightly increased number of rapids and more long flatwater pools. In general the individual rapids are heavier than those in the upper river. The river is wide and powerful at 2.5 feet on the Hinton gauge, and it would be unwise for novices or open boaters without substantial experience and floatation to proceed at this or higher levels. Each rapids is a riverwide long stretch of big waves with very little obstruction. Occasionally a ledge is encountered at one side or the other, but is always eroded in the heaviest current. Consequently, although large stopper waves and an occasional hydraulic are encountered, very little maneuvering is required.

Intermediates with heavy water experience should encounter no difficulties or unexpected surprises, but this is no place for beginners. More than halfway along and after a particularly long flat stretch, four sand silos appear on the right bank of a left-hand turn. The sand in these silos is used for making glass. Just below this, very heavy water is encountered near the right bank. Very large Class III–IV-sized waves are present but are avoidable if desired. Another long flat stretch, two minor rapids, and a zesty chute over a ledge bring the paddler to the take-out.

You can put in at the McCreery beach mentioned above. There is also now a developed put-in across the bridge over McCreery Creek. The easiest take-out is on the sandy beach 200 yards above the bridge located a mile above Thurmond (the first bridge you will encounter). This take-out, located on the left side of the river, may be reached by a dirt road. It is pretty flat from this bridge to Thurmond itself, although there is a nice Class II rapids right under the Thurmond bridge. Even though there is a dirt road connecting Prince with Thurmond, we don't recommend using it in setting up the shuttle. Take WV 41 from Prince toward Beckley, turn right on WV 61 to Mount Hope, turn right onto WV 16 for about a mile, and then make one more right turn at CR 25 leading to Glen Jean and Thurmond.

For water information call the Bluestone Dam, at (304) 466-1234 or (304) 466-0156 to get the Hinton gauge reading, which takes into account the output of the Greenbrier. Call (304) 465-1722 for a computerized gauge reading at Hinton. The river seldom drops below 1.75 feet and is often at this level in the summer. Approach the entire river with great caution if over 2.5 feet.

76 New River

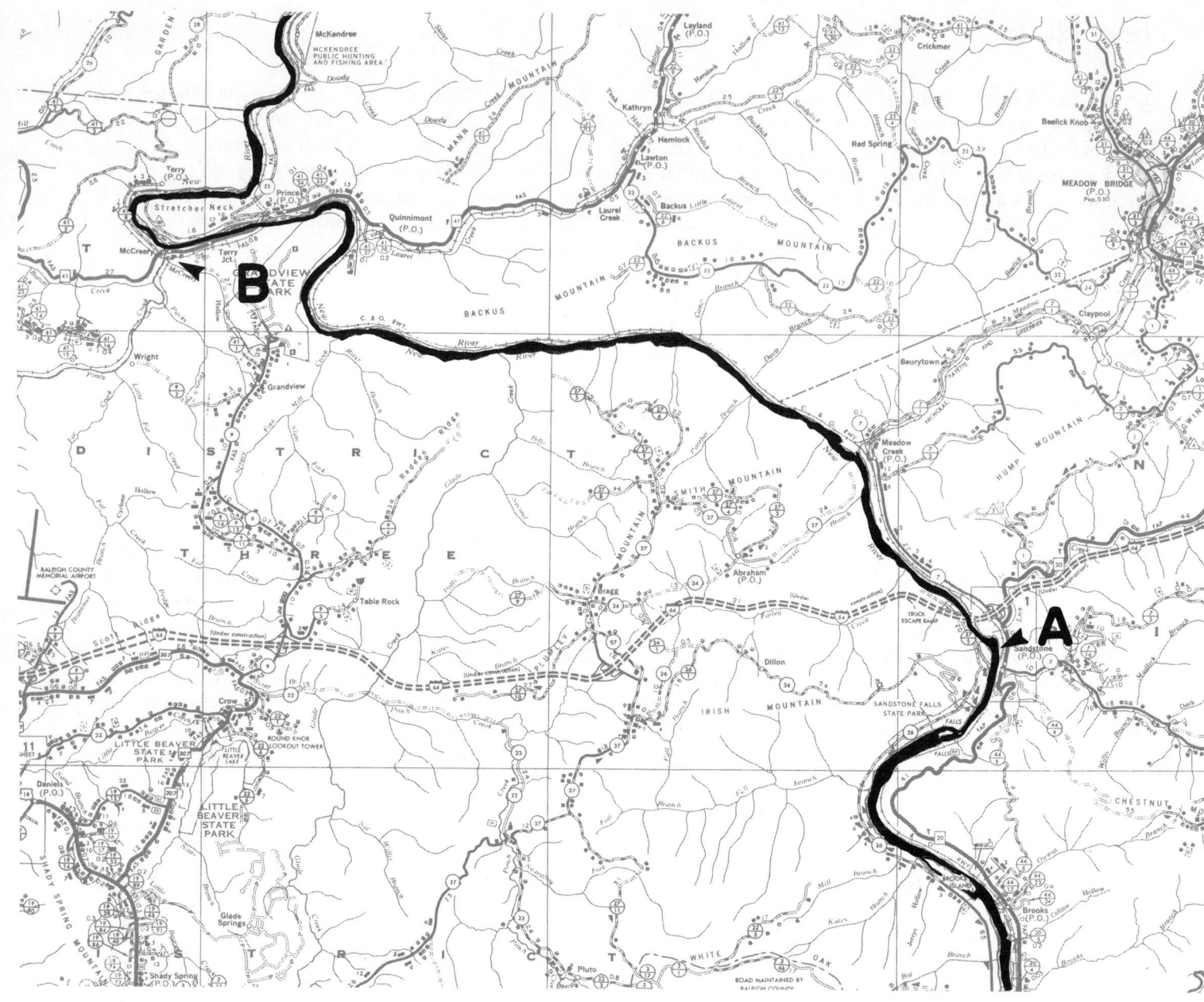

Section: Sandstone to McCreery

Counties: Summers, Fayette, and Raleigh (WV)

USGS Quads: Meadow Creek and Beckley (15')

Suitable for: Long day trips or camping

Skill Level: Shepherded novices, intermediates

Months Runnable: Virtually all year

Interest Highlights: Excellent fishing, camping

Scenery: Generally beautiful

Difficulty: Class I–III

Average Width: 125 feet

Velocity: Slow to moderate

Gradient: 8 feet per mile

Runnable Water Levels:
 Minimum: 1.75 feet on Hinton gauge
 Maximum: 2.50 feet on Hinton gauge

Hazards: None

Scouting: None

Portages: None

Rescue Index: Accessible to remote

Source of Additional Information: For Hinton gauge readings, call (304) 466-1234 or (304) 466-0156

Access Points	River Miles	Shuttle Miles
A–B	15	31

Access Point Ratings: Both put-in A and take-out B are good.

New River 77

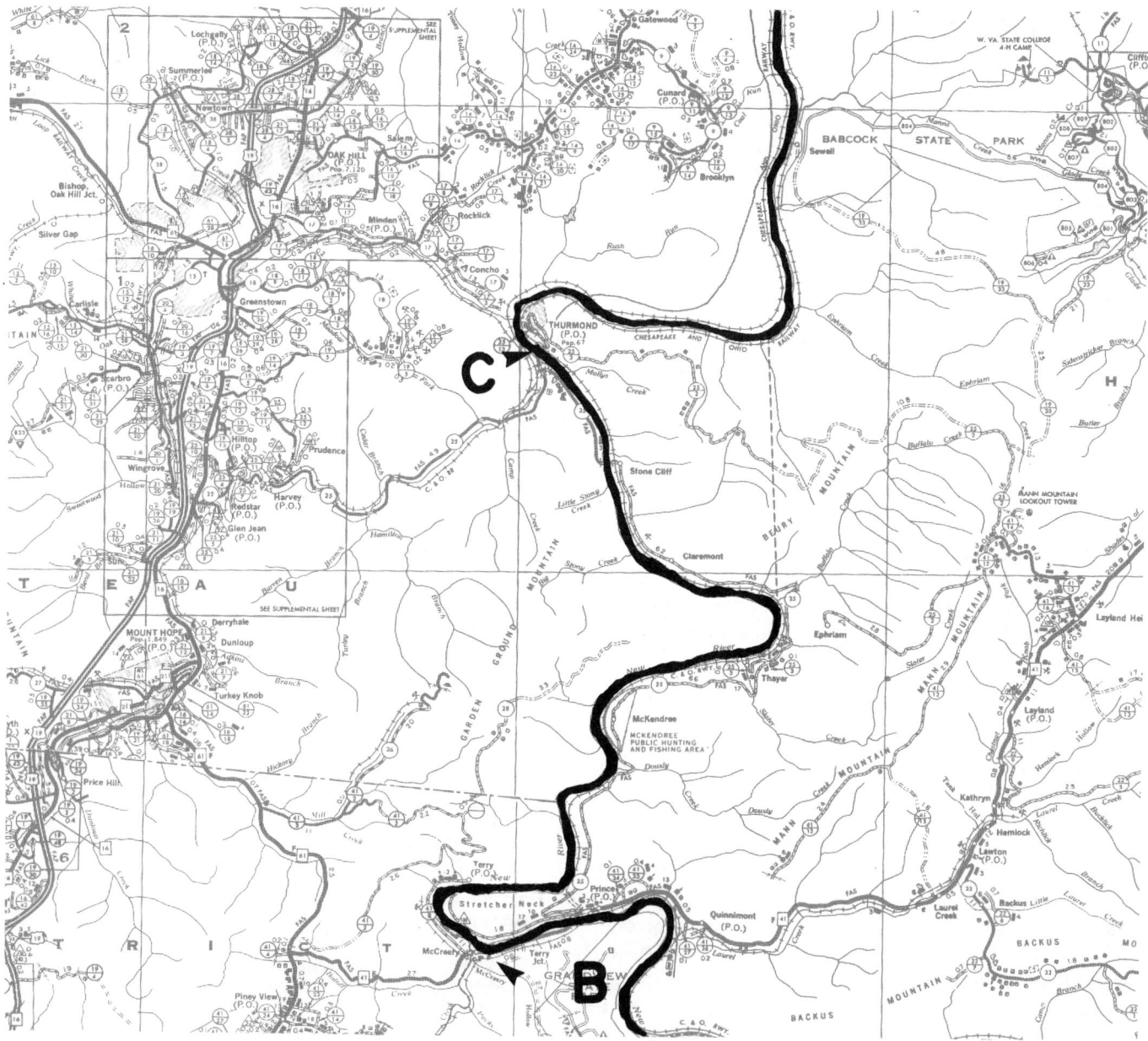

Section: McCreery/Prince to Thurmond

Counties: Fayette and Raleigh (WV)

USGS Quads: Beckley (15')

Suitable for: Day trips

Skill Level: Intermediates

Months Runnable: All year

Interest Highlights: Big river; rapids mainly waves, the biggest over halfway into trip below four sand silos

Scenery: Generally beautiful

Difficulty: Class II–III

Average Width: 150 feet

Velocity: Slow to moderate

Gradient: 10 feet per mile

Runnable Water Levels:
  Minimum: 1.75 feet on the Hinton gauge
  Maximum: 2.50 feet on the Hinton gauge

Hazards: None

Scouting: Large waves below four sand silos on river right; waves can be avoided on the left.

Portages: None

Rescue Index: Accessible

Source of Additional Information: For Hinton gauge information, call the Bluestone Dam at (304) 466-1234 or (304) 466-0156

Access Points	River Miles	Shuttle Miles
B–C	15	13 or 15

Access Point Ratings: Both put-in B and take-out C are good.

New River Gorge

The New River Gorge, from Thurmond to Fayette Station, is the biggest whitewater river in West Virginia. The long flat pools in the first half of this 14-mile run are the price for entrance, but once the gorge starts below the railroad bridge at seven miles into the trip, the surging waters are repayment with foaming dividends. The challenge in this type of water is remaining upright while bobbing among the six- to eight-foot waves and dodging souse holes, stoppers, and whirlpools. The entire river flows through an immense gorge with extremely rugged mountains and cliffs in view all of the way.

After putting in at Thurmond and passing the Class II rapids under the bridge there, you have several miles of relatively flat water with only a small rapid at Buzzards Bend to break the monotony. Your first clue as to what is in store for you occurs when you hit a small wave and discover how forceful it is. About four miles or so into the trip, look out for the first major rapids, which is appropriately named Surprise (Class III–IV). From the top it looks like a moderate wave train, but halfway through, the paddler realizes he is in a funnel and all of the water is converging toward a huge mountain of a double wave. There is a hole between the first regular wave and the second curler wave. Those attempting to punch the hole should hit it angled slightly left as the hole is slightly diagonal—pointing downstream to the right. At lower levels the hole can be skirted to the left or right, with the right being the more challenging route. Surprise at higher levels, with its pyramidal breaking wave, is too much and should be snuck on the left.

At the end of a long pool below Surprise is Plowshares rapid (Class II–III) in two parts. The first part is easily read. The second part warrants care. Either run the right side sneak or angle right about 20 feet from left shore. Plowshares Rock is the largest rock left of center. Just downstream and right of the rock is a steep nasty hole best avoided.

About three miles below Surprise, or about seven miles into the trip, look for a railroad trestle. Just above the trestle is Upper Railroad Rapids (Class III–IV), a steep drop over a shelf. It is best entered just to the right of a dry rock in the center of the river, and then the paddler should head left. The rapid has two parts. The first part is a huge hole on river right which is a keeper at levels from three to six feet on the Fayette Station gauge. At significantly lower levels, the hole has a tongue, but it's hard to see from upstream. Scout from the right. The second part is an exciting wave train on the left and a boulder garden on the right which should be avoided by swimmers. Ouch!

Just below is a horizon line which signals Lower Railroad (Class IV), a formidable cascade of water through a complicated barrage of boulders. It can be snuck on the far right with a good deal of maneuvering; it can be run (at levels above zero on the Fayette Station gauge) one-third of the way over from the left with careful scouting (from river left) and bravado. However, use extra care in running this rapid since an undercut rock just left of the left side route has trapped paddlers and boats. Run this left-of-center route over the big watery hump (which starts the tongue) by angling right and working right. Don't slide left.

After Lower Railroad are five rapids which offer no special problems and at high water provide a roller coaster ride over large waves. On the second of these rapids just left of a large rock in the middle, is a strong, boat-length hole called Stripper which can give a long rough surf. The fourth rapids

---

Section: Thurmond to Fayette Station

Counties: Fayette (WV)

USGS Quads: Thurmond, Fayetteville

Suitable for: Day trips

Skill Level: Advanced to expert

Months Runnable: Entire year

Interest Highlights: Biggest whitewater river in West Virginia; immense gorge

Scenery: Generally beautiful

Difficulty: Class III–V

Average Width: 150–200 feet

Velocity: Moderate to fast

Gradient: 15 feet per mile; the first 7 miles at 11 feet per mile and the last 7 miles at 19 feet per mile

Runnable Water Levels:
  Minimum: - 1.5 feet on the Fayette Station gauge, though it has been run at lower levels
  Maximum: 12 feet on Fayette Station gauge. For expert open boaters, the cut-off is 3–4 feet, although it has been run at 7-foot levels.

Hazards: Upper Railroad, big hole on river right; Lower Railroad, pinning rocks on left; Double Z, undercut rock at bottom left; Greyhound Bus Stopper, huge hole; Undercut Rock/Miller's Folly, undercut rock on top right; and "Bloody Nose" on lower left

Scouting: Lower Railroad; Middle and Lower Keeney; Double Z; Undercut Rock

Portages: None at lower levels

Rescue Index: Remote

Source of Additional Information: Call Bluestone Dam (304) 466-1234 for correlation to the Fayette Station gauge; better yet, call one of the local outfitters for the Fayette Station gauge reading.

Access Points	River Miles	Shuttle Miles
C–D	14	21

Access Point Ratings: Both put-in C and take-out D are good.

at minus one foot on the gauge and below has a pinning spot in the hole below the largest ledge left of center.

After nine miles of paddling, you are now ready to enter the big stuff, the Keeney Brothers. Regardless of how these rapids look, the best way is generally through the center no matter what the size of the waves. Upper Keeney (Class III) is recognized by a huge boulder the size and shape of a whale (Whale Rock) jutting out from river left. The current will generally take you to the right edge of Whale Rock. Angle left and eddy out behind Whale Rock so you can gather your spirits for Middle Keeney. (Use this eddy only at levels below four feet; at higher levels, the eddy line becomes a nasty eddy fence.)

Middle Keeney (Class IV) has three large holes in the center channel. Just left or right of these is generally the easier route. At up to two feet, rafts should head just left of a black rock near the bottom of the right center while open boats should head just right of a dry camel-back rock left of center near the top. Scout from the left. At higher levels Upper and Middle Keeney merge, hence a roll-less flip in the Upper makes for a long day. With higher water these rapids are difficult and flip many a paddler. At levels of four feet, waves here are eight feet and merge with the granddaddy of them all—Lower Keeney. Larger holes exist to the right and left, so don't try to sneak this long, high water rapid.

After this it is a good idea to get out and scout the next rapids from the left. Lower Keeney (Class IV-V) is often scouted, even by those very familiar with the river. It cannot be snuck, it cannot be lined, and it is one hell of a carry over

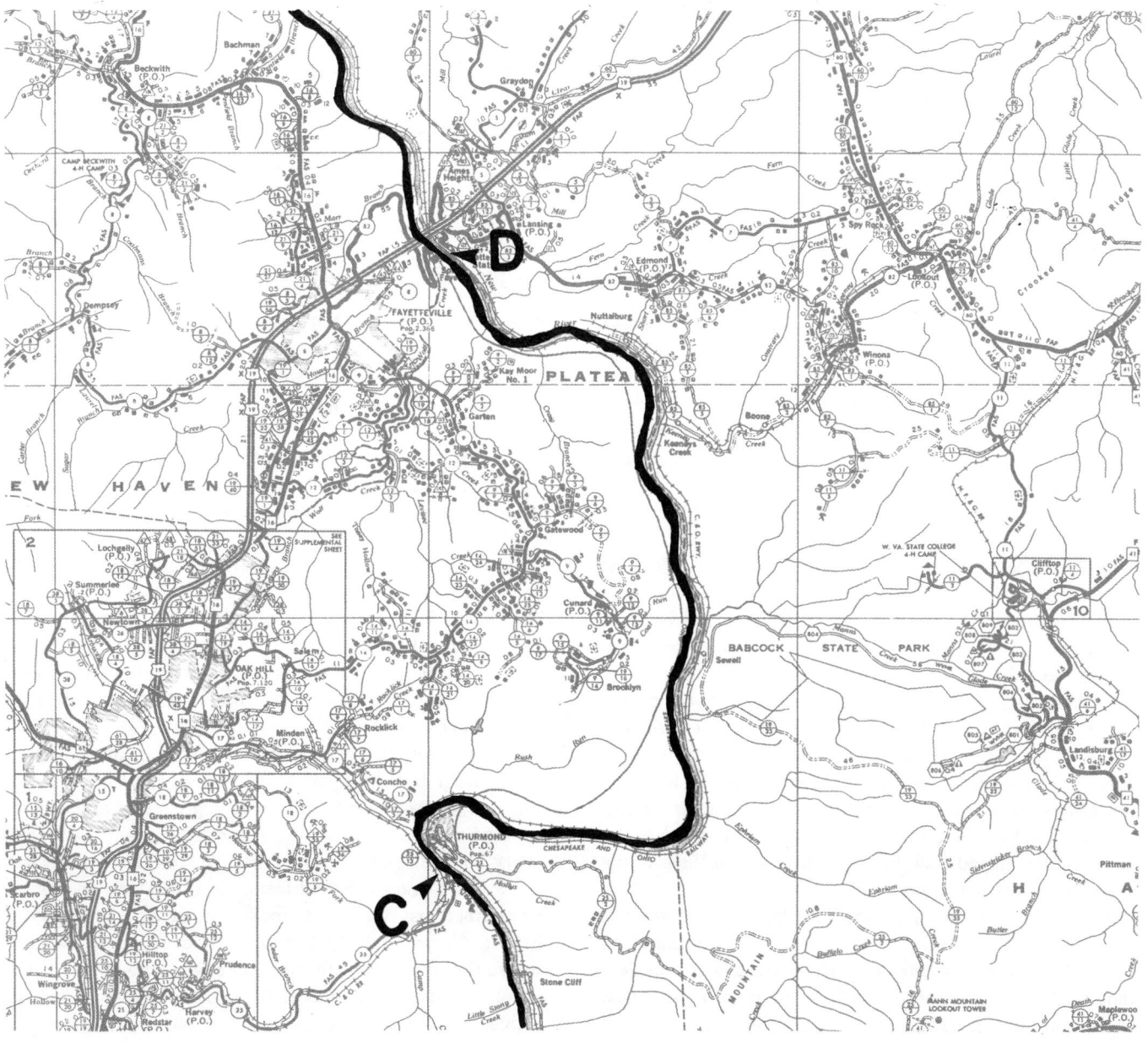

Diana Kendrick in Surprise Rapid of the New River Gorge. Photo by Paul Marshall.

the house-sized boulders, so you may as well make up your mind about how to run it. In general, the river has necked down to the size of a small trout stream, thus concentrating the action enormously. The current surges from the right to the left side, bombarding a huge boulder (Wash Up Rock) on the bottom left. If you are following someone closely, do not be disheartened when he drops suddenly from view into the first hole because you will look the same to the paddlers behind you. It is a short 50-yard rapids, but a flip (usually in the first hole) is long remembered. Generally you should enter left and angle to the right, paddling hard to avoid holes or reactionary waves on the lower left of the rapids. Be careful of a dangerous rock sieve 20 to 30 feet to the right of the left entry. The waves and holes are BIG, the closest thing to a natural rollercoaster. At one foot and above they are most dynamic; at two feet the waves begin to wash out; at three feet a big "V" forms halfway down the rapids and they wash out even more.

Dudley's Dip (Class III) follows. Above 0.5 feet on the gauge, begin this rapid left of center. As you enter look for a pourover rock and run just to the right of it. Below 0.5 feet, enter on the far right and work diagonally to the left. The route is easier to read from this angle. Go between the two pourover rocks on left and right of center. The large upside-down canoe-shaped rock on the right side and the slanting rock on the left side are undercut.

Next comes Sunset or Double Z (Class IV–V), which is the most technical rapids on the river. Over ten miles into the trip, it is a long rapids marked by a chain of rocks extending halfway across the river from the right. First-timers should pull over to the right above this chain of rocks and scout before entering the rapid. Enter the rapids and eddy out behind the rock chain in order to reach the extreme right channel and to avoid a nasty, complex V-ledge and hydraulic in the center. The right channel will take you diagonally to the left, but it tumbles steeply through a field of holes and boulders, ending with a mean pourover and powerful hole below at bottom center. At levels of up to two feet, try to run this rapids close to the right bank. Over three feet, it's best to run left of center down a big "V" which forms. At levels above four feet, watch for a nasty hole in the very middle of the rapid. At all levels, avoid the huge boulder towards bottom left which is undercut and has a powerful current under it.

The next rapids is Old 99 or Hook (Class III). This can be run left, middle or right. Left is straightest; middle is a backwards S-turn, and right gives a sliding board feeling. Just below is Bear's Rock or (to some paddlers) the second part of Old 99. Left of center is a smooth chute just to the right of a semi-dry rock. After running the chute, angle left to pass a large violent hole on your right.

Work far left or far right after running this rapids because Greyhound Bus Stopper is just below. This aptly named ledge really could stop a bus at high levels and can be avoided either to the far left or far right at any level. This nasty hole has heavy recirculation at even moderate levels. At levels of one and a half feet or less, dynamic enders can be attained just right of the rock forming Greyhound. Eddy behind Greyhound Rock and work back up to the spot where the river pours off the right edge. Enjoy!

Next comes Upper Kaymoor or Upper Tipple (Class II) which is easily read. At levels below zero the ledge on the

New River Gorge Water Level Conversion (correlation) Table

Information furnished by Dave Bassage

Fayette Station	cfs	Fayette Station	cfs
-3	544	5	9,550*
-2	1,072	6	11,400*
-1	1,704	7	14,100*
0	2,440	8	17,200**
1	3,352	9	20,200
2	4,436*	10	23,800
3	5,820*	11	26,800
4	7,550*	12	30,000

*Note: At these levels, the Fayette Station reading is approximately one-half of the cfs level, rounded to the nearest thousand. For example, 4,436 to 5,000 cfs equals 2 feet on the Fayette Station gauge; 5,820 to 6,000 cfs equals 3 feet; 14,000 to 14,100 equals 7 feet.

**Calling the Thurmond gauge at (304) 465-0493 gives a system of beeps, which can be converted to Fayette Station equivalents. First, translate the beeps into a reading: you will hear a series of four groups of beeps. A long first beep means zero; a short first beep means one, heavy water. Write down the numbers of each series of beeps, and put a decimal between the second and third numbers, for example, 03.62, or 3.62 feet at the Thurmond gauge.

To convert to Fayette Station equivalents, multiply the Thurmond reading by four-thirds (1.33), then subtract 4 2/3 (4.66) from the result. Your answer will show the equivalent reading at Fayette Station. Example: A Thurmond reading of 03.62 times 1.33 = 4.81 minus 4.66 gives 0.15 feet as the Fayette Station equivalent. This formula works for levels up to 7 or 8 feet at Fayette Station.

far right side creates a steep strong hole. Lower Kaymoor or Lower Tipple (Class III) can be run right (following a wave train) or left (more technical) of the large rectangular rock in the middle. If running left, watch out for the squirrelly curler just to the left of the big rock.

Miller's Folley or Undercut Rock (Class IV–V) follows, after twelve miles of paddling. Scout from the left. Avoid the temptation to begin at the far right, but instead begin in the center and paddle toward the left side of the big rock on the right (which is, of course, undercut). Stay in the left of the chute and then cut sharply left before you reach the rock, following the flow of this channel. Just below you will go through some enormous fun waves. At moderate levels, there are then large eddies on the left and right which you can use to scout the lower part of the rapids. The best route is just left of center. Watch for an L-shaped hole at the top, run just to the right of it, and then angle left to avoid hitting Invisible Rock and its accompanying steep, nasty hole. To sneak this lower part run right. The far left is appropriately called Bloody Nose and should generally be avoided.

Shortly after this you will see two bridges—one crossing the gorge high above. Soon, you will reach Fayette Station Bridge. Just below this bridge is Fayette Station Rapids (Class IV) which should not be missed. Run right of center. Since you have come this far, you might as well dig into it. It is a multiholed roller coaster with some deceptively vigorous drops hidden by big waves. Be ready to hit the waves squarely. You can scout from the left. Take out on river left

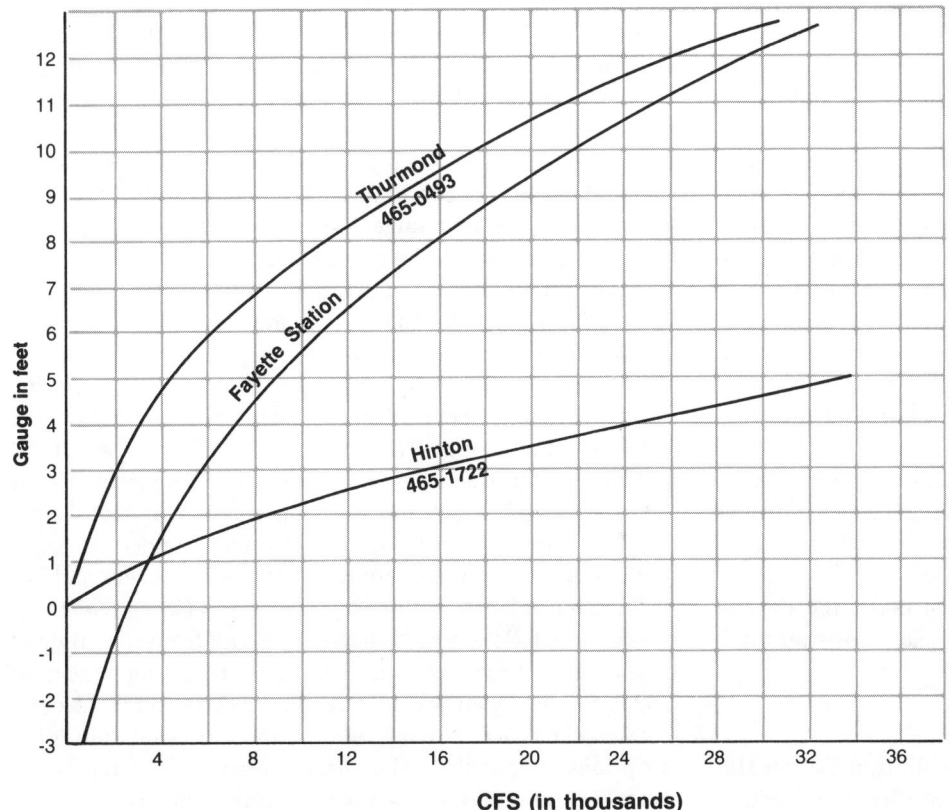

Don Bowman running Lower Keeney, New River. Photo by Ed Grove.

after running this rapids. Other than one or two minor rapids (the second one requiring care to avoid the pourover on the left side) the next four miles to Hawk's Nest Dam are mostly flatwater and seldom run. There is also a take-out a mile below Fayette Station at Teay's Landing on river right.

The shuttle amazingly is all on hard surface roads. Fayette Station can be reached from Fayetteville on WV 82. Put in behind the parking lot at the Thurmond store (reached by taking Rt. 25 from US 19). Use US 19 for the shuttle between these points.

An alternative put-in, which cuts off about seven miles of flatwater (except for Surprise), is just above Upper Railroad Rapids. It is reached by following signs out of Fayetteville to the sanitary landfill. The trip takes a half hour to reach the river (via Cunard) for a 7.0-mile run of two to three hours, but do not try it unless your vehicle can handle bad roads. Alternatively, you can have someone do the Cunard shuttle for you. Call Sleepy's Shuttle Service at (304) 574-3047. He covers shuttles from Prince to Thurmond on weekdays and from Cunard on weekends.

Take out below the Fayette Station rapids in the cove on the left. This is private property belonging to Wildwater Unlimited. A locked road leads back to the highway. Carry your boat a quarter mile back to your car.

A gauge is located on river left just under the Fayette Station Bridge. Refer to the graph for gauge correlations.

New River Dries

The New River Dries, a five-mile stretch from Cotton Hill to Gauley Bridge, is a little-known but much enjoyed section of whitewater through the tightest and most beautiful part of the New River Gorge.

The Dries only run when there is water spilling over Hawk's Nest Dam; this happens whenever the New is flowing above 9000 cfs or when the hydro plant at Gauley Bridge is not running at full capacity. At levels of 1,000–3,000 cfs it is Class II+ open boatable. From 3,000–10,000 cfs it is suitable for intermediate decked boats and advanced open boaters. From 10,000–20,000 cfs large holes and standing waves start to form and only paddlers comfortable with big water (like the New gorge at four to eight feet) should attempt the run. Above 20,000 cfs the sheer canyon walls constrict the flow into huge exploding waves and holes that should be attempted by experts only.

The rapids are long but readable with one exception. Entrance rapid is rocky on the right and sports "Broken paddle hole" at bottom left, but it is easily run down the middle. Then comes "Foreplay," a long stretch of smooth surfing waves at levels above 8,000 cfs. The river then bends to the left for "Preparation," a one-half mile series of Class II–III drops. After a short pool the river turns sharply left for "Mile Long," which has the biggest water at high levels. Watch out for "Multi-bender-bowl-hole" under the overhanging ledge at the bottom right at all levels and for "Hatch's hole" at bottom left above 18,000 cfs. Next is a long pool followed by "Landslide." Scout from river right at low water or river left at high levels. Enter through the right slot and pick your way through the squirrelly highly technical water below. Staying right all the way is safe but other options are possible. The Dries finishes with "Afterplay," a series of nice playable waves and holes at all levels.

Due to the unpredictability of water levels on the Dries, it is advisable to check with an outfitter or with Hawk's Nest Dam for the most current information before putting in.

New River Gorge High Water Information (between five feet and twelve feet on the gauge)

When the water gets really high, the New River Gorge changes dramatically. Huge holes, waves and other factors affect many of the rapids, dictating much more scouting and care in running the river. The river is substantially more pushy and tougher. The following two examples show how different the Gorge becomes.

A new rapids called the Halls of Karma (Class III) only exists beginning from seven to nine feet on the Fayette Station gauge. This is the short narrow section of the river between Double Z and Old 99 or Hook. The sudden extreme narrowing of the river creates some dynamic waves and currents with large waves that are pulsating and moving. Most of the time it's luck and quick reactions that get paddlers through.

Also, at higher levels Upper, Middle and Lower Keeney merge to become The Keeney (Class V–VI). At ten feet, Whale Rock at Upper Keeney becomes Whale Hole—awesome. Between eight and eleven feet (downstream of Whale Hole in the center of the river where Middle Keeney used to be), is a huge pulsating, crashing wave called The Mouth. It rises up, opens wide, and crashes down—even eating rafts on occasion. Below this (above seven feet), the rocks at the top right of Lower Keeney become Meatgrinder, a long nasty hole, and the rocks at the bottom left of Lower Keeney create another strong hole called Lollygag (which is worst between three and seven feet).

The expert paddler should first scout this rapids. Enter it far right so that Whale Hole does not swallow you. Then run to the right of The Mouth to avoid being eaten. Now start working left, but watch out for two very large breaking waves angled downstream towards the left. They can easily flip you if you have too much left angle. After this, the river seems to calm, but not much. Then set up for what used to be Lower Keeney. Meatgrinder, the long nasty hole extending from the right, begins fairly small in the center of the river. To avoid it and its downstream companion in mayhem, Lollygag, take the following route. Run just left or clip the left side of Meatgrinder (where the hole is still relatively small) and be angled right. Drive hard to the right so you can miss Lollygag which extends from the left side of the river. Then collapse from exhaustion and/or enjoy a king-sized adrenaline high in the calm area below.

At levels above eight feet the largest wave on the river is found on the left side of Fayette Station rapid; it shouldn't be missed. Enter in the left V at the top. Halfway through a huge, smooth wall of water blots out the sun. If you are good enough to have made it this far, you won't be flipped and the ride is only rivaled by Hermit rapid on the Colorado.

Back Fork of the Elk River: Three Falls Section

This section starts just below Skelt on Sugar Creek, a major tributary to the Back Fork. Action starts right away with a series of sloping ledges leading to an eight-foot falls. Sugar Creek is tight and interesting for the half mile to its junction with the Back Fork. The Back Fork then meanders along at a Class II pace until the "Three Falls" section is encountered. From here on, the river is pools or steep ledges to the take-out. A thrilling run through first-class scenery.

All of the ledges, starting with the first of the "Three Falls," should be scouted for the best passage. The "Three Falls" are big ledges about 100 yards apart, the first about eight feet, the second about four feet, and the third and most spectacular, about ten feet. Run the first left-center and the third off the far left. If you want to carry these there is an old log road on the right hidden by the rhododendron. Be prepared with a long rope to lower your boat back down to the river 25 feet below.

To run your shuttle take CR 24 from Webster Springs to the take-out up Back Fork Drive as far as you want or as far as you can go. CR 24 ends at the last big ledge. To get to the put-in, take WV 20 north out of Webster Springs to CR 18 then to Jumbo, Skelt, and eventually to Pickens if you go too far. This road follows the Right Fork of the Holley for several miles and then crosses a mountain to the Sugar Creek watershed. Put in where the road first parallels the creek.

Use the Webster Springs gauge for reference; the level should be around 6.0 feet, plus or minus 0.2 feet.

Section: Sugar Creek to Breece
Counties: Webster (WV)
USGS Quads: Webster Springs, Bergoo, and Skelt
Suitable for: Day trips
Skill Level: Strong intermediate and advanced
Months Runnable: Generally spring after rains
Interest Highlights: Spectacular trip with big ledges
Scenery: Beautiful
Difficulty: Class II–IV
Average Width: 30–50 feet
Velocity: Fast
Gradient: 64 feet per mile
Runnable Water Levels:
  Minimum: 5.8 feet on the Webster Springs gauge
  Maximum: 6.1 feet on the Webster Springs gauge
Hazards: Eight-foot falls; Three Falls section; trees down; high water
Scouting: Eight-foot falls; Three Falls section
Portages: One or more of the falls
Rescue Index: Accessible to remote
Source of Additional Information: National Weather Service, Charleston (304) 342-7771 for the Webster Springs gauge. Hours are Monday through Friday from 8:00 am to 4:30 pm.

Access Points	River Miles	Shuttle Miles
A–B	5.5	26.0

Access Point Ratings for both put-in A and take-out B are good.

Back Fork of the Elk River: Bottom falls of the "Three Falls" section. Photo by Ward Eister.

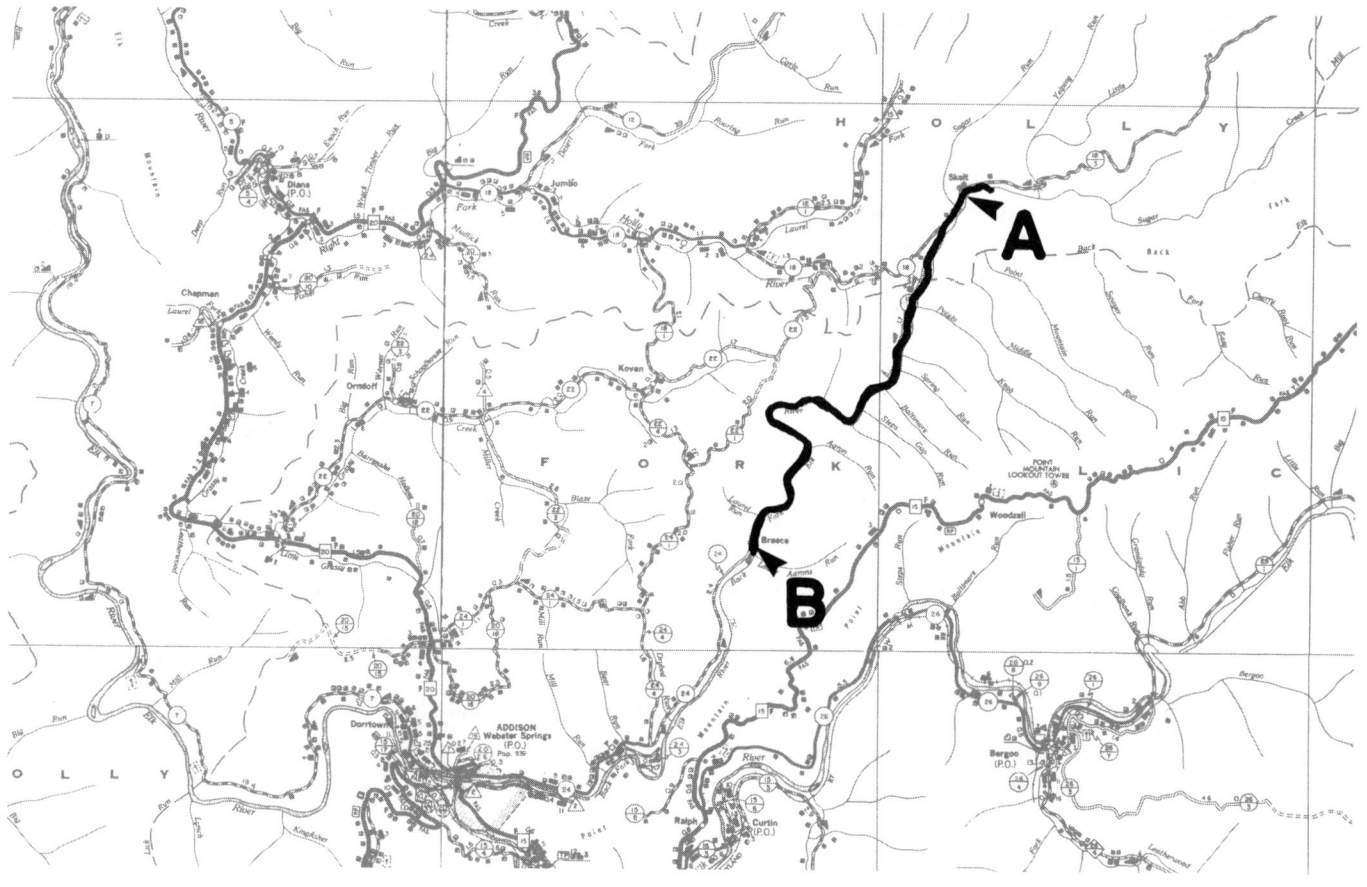

Little River, Forks of the Greenbrier, and the Greenbrier

The headwaters of the Greenbrier offer some of the best paddling in the system. The West Fork is runnable from Wildell or, more reasonably, from the mouth of Little River along FS 44 to Durbin. It is a fast-paced Class I–II stream with a few low, angled ledges. The best rapids may be seen from the US 250 bridge. The take-out is a half mile below US 250 at a bridge on the west side of Durbin. This is a beautiful stream passing through the Monongahela National Forest.

A second tributary is Little River. From the first road bridge (three miles above its mouth) to the West Fork of Greenbrier, it's a beautiful run down a tiny stream through dense forests and some glades. Very busy but easy, with only a few problems of the kind typically encountered on a little stream.

The East Fork is runnable from the Island Campground or from Camp Pocahontas, located at the junction of WV 28 and FS 14 to Durbin. This is a busier stream than the West Fork, passing through pastoral settings along the highway. Low-hanging branches and barbed wire present the greatest hazards. One can take out at the US 250 bridge at Bartow near the motel or two miles downstream at an iron bridge on the east side of Durbin. This latter section is heavily polluted and not as nice as the upper part.

There is a paddler's gauge on the Camp Pocahontas bridge, and you will need at least two feet on the Marlinton gauge or five feet on the Buckeye government gauge. For a reading of the Buckeye gauge, call (304) 529-5604.

Greenbrier River

The November 1985 flood hit the Greenbrier very hard. This was apparently the worst flood in the area in recorded history. However, unlike the Cheat River (also in this chapter), there is no indication of any really significant changes to the Greenbrier (at least on its lower sections).

Just below the confluence of the headwaters near Durbin, the Greenbrier is a beautiful, small trout stream that pours easily but steadily through rock gardens and eroded ledges. Stay in the middle at about a half mile from the junction of the East and West forks in order to avoid the concrete pier on the right side of a bridge. For three miles below this, the water is fairly calm, but soon the river narrows as the mountains squeeze in. The water in this area is Class II with some rock dodging required. The river flows fast through wilderness country. The bed remains narrow and three-foot haystacks are common at the ends of the rapids, but there are no boulders or souse holes to complicate the passages.

To run from Durbin, put in on the West Fork at the US 250 bridge near the edge of town. There are two ways to drive to Cass. CR 3 enters US 250 about a mile above the West Fork bridge and proceeds directly to Cass. A longer route over somewhat better roads is US 250 to WV 28 through Green Bank, turning right on secondary "7" to Cass.

The river below Cass has more volume but moves more slowly through uncomplicated rapids with no obstructions. The scenery remains beautiful, although some signs of civilization appear. Many wilderness campsites along the way make the whole trip from Durbin to Marlinton an ideal overnight camping trip in open canoes. In the spring, numerous small mountain streams supply fresh water, and trout or bass fishing may be done almost anywhere. A popular run is from Cass to the WV 39 bridge in Marlinton.

For water levels below Durbin down to Anthony look at the level of water under the bridge at Durbin. A depth of water there of about three feet will give a good run. Trips

---

Section: West Fork (Wildell to Durbin); Little River (first bridge to the West Fork); East Fork (Camp Pocahontas to Bartow)

Counties: Pocahontas (WV)

USGS Quads: Wildell, Durbin, Thornwood, Monongahela National Forest

Suitable for: Day trips

Skill Level: Shepherded novices and intermediates

Months Runnable: Primarily spring

Interest Highlights: West Fork, beautiful stream; East Fork, busy but easy; Little River, dense forests

Scenery: Usually beautiful

Difficulty: Class I–II

Average Width: 20–50 feet

Velocity: Moderate

Gradient: Up to about 20 feet per mile

Runnable Water Levels:
  Minimum: 0 feet on Camp Pocahontas gauge; 2 feet on Marlinton gauge; 5 feet on Buckeye gauge
  Maximum: Not available

Hazards: East Fork—low-hanging branches, barbed wire

Scouting: None

Portages: None

Rescue Index: Accessible

Source of Additional Information: Buckeye government gauge (304) 529-5604

Access Points	River Miles	Shuttle Miles
A–B' West Fork	8.0	8.0
B'–B West Fork	7.0	7.0
A'–B' Little River	3.0	3.0
AA–BB East Fork	5.0	5.0

Access Point Ratings: All put-ins and take-outs are very good.

Greenbrier River 87

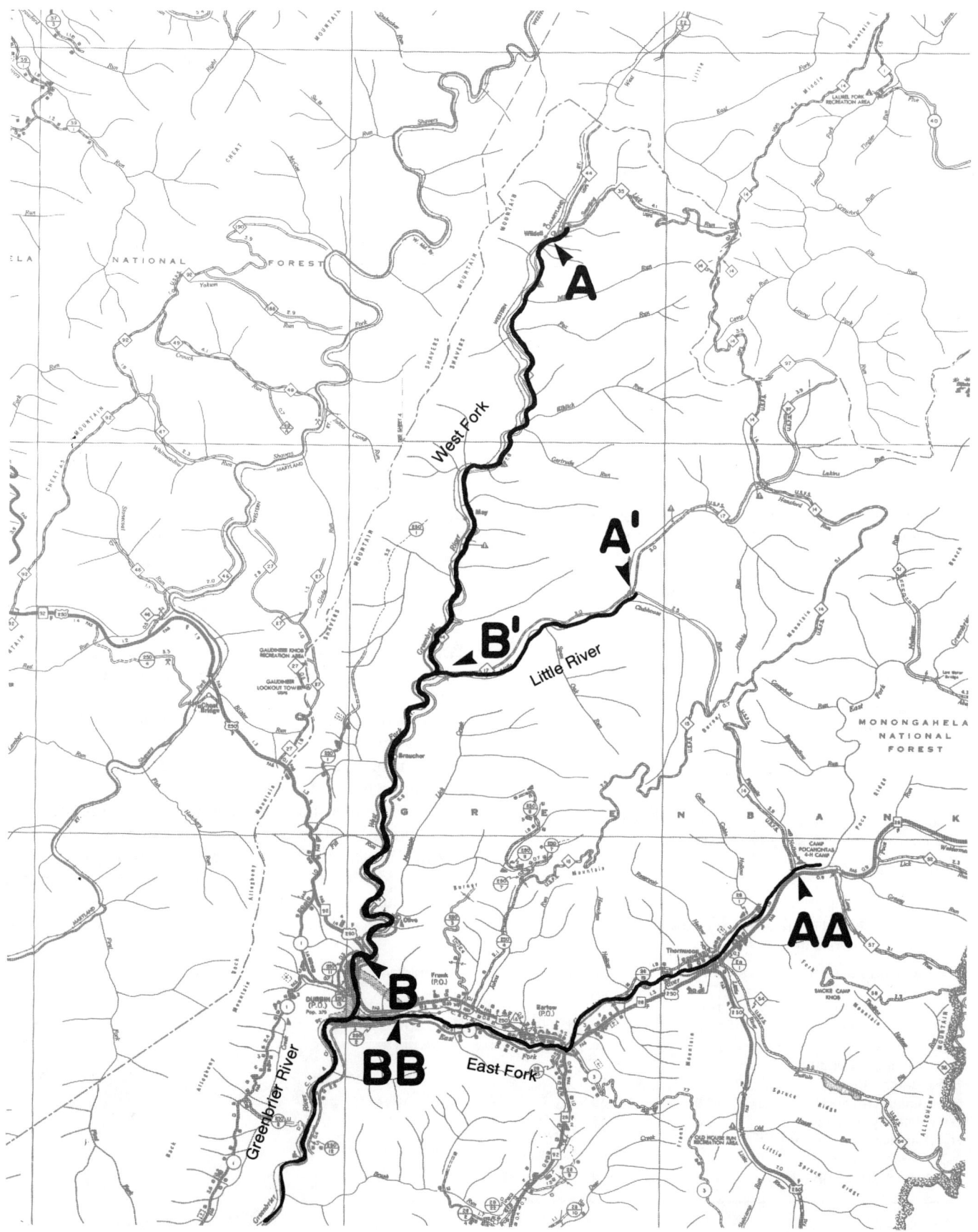

beginning at Cass could similarly be determined by examining water conditions under the bridge. There is a canoeing gauge on the Marlinton bridge which should read at least two feet for these upper runs. For non-on-the-spot planning, use the Buckeye gauge reading obtainable from the Corps of Engineers in Huntington, (304) 529-5604, or the National Weather Service in Charleston, (304) 342-7771.

The Greenbrier below Marlinton begins to take on the characteristics of a big river. With a large volume (having been added to appreciably by streams such as Knapp Creek and Deer Creek), in many places it may be quite wide and powerful. The rapids are usually formed at narrow places in the river or in curves. There are many long flat stretches between such rapids, and the gradient seldom exceeds eight feet per mile. It can be floated most of the year but is unrunnable in dry summers.

With few exposed rocks, the Marlinton-to-Denmar section is an easy run at all levels, with mostly Class I riffles. From Seebert on, the left bank is either state park or state forest. Seebert is at the second bridge from Marlinton.

There are few difficulties; a low-water bridge just below a new high one can be run through a breach in the middle. For this section, as well as any of the lower Greenbrier, novices should make decisions well before approaching any rapids as the water may be very swift. If in doubt, always stick to the inside bend of any curving rapids on this river (although this is not always a good rule to follow elsewhere).

To run from Marlinton to Denmar, shuttle from US 219 and take "27" into Seebert (the road to Watoga State Park) or "31" into Denmar. A new riverside campground exists on the left at Watoga State Forest. The river can be run down to 0.5 foot on the Marlinton gauge located on WV 39 bridge in Marlinton, lower right-bank bridge pier. Readings may be obtained from Brill's Exxon Station, (304) 799-9929. Referring to this gauge, an ideal level is about 1.5–2.0 feet, although runs up to 3.0 feet and higher have been made. At two feet or greater the current is swift, and long fields of large haystacks appear. At three feet the flat water is moving fast and very powerfully, most of the boulders have been covered up, and the waves, particularly on the outside of the curves, may reach five to six feet. Obviously at this level it is no place for inexperienced paddlers or undecked boats. In the Marlinton area, you will need about four feet on the government gauge at Buckeye. To be consistent, this is the reading we have listed.

Below Denmar the river continues winding its way into Greenbrier County picking up volume from numerous side streams, which can be appreciable during summer cloudbursts. Don't try to take out at Spice Run Station located about four and a half miles from Denmar. Apparently boaters aren't welcome by the locals. About a mile below

---

Section: Durbin to Bellepoint

Counties: Pocahontas, Greenbrier, and Summers (WV)

USGS Quads: Durbin, Cass, Clover Lick, Edray, Marlinton, Denmar, Droop, Anthony, White Sulphur Springs, Lewisburg, Ronceverte, Fort Spring, Alderson, Talcott, and Hinton

Suitable for: Camping or day trips

Skill Level: Mostly novice; intermediate on the last section

Months Runnable: Lower parts most of the year; upper parts less often

Interest Highlights: Trout fishing and wilderness camping on the upper sections; big river on the lower sections

Scenery: Pretty in spots to beautiful

Difficulty: Class I–II with one Class III and one Class IV section

Average Width: 40 to 200 feet

Velocity: Moderate to slow

Gradient: 3 to 18 feet per mile

Runnable Water Levels:
  Minimum: various; see narrative
  Maximum: various; see narrative

Hazards: Low water bridge with brush in middle (Marlinton-Denmar section)

Scouting: Class III rapids three miles above Anthony; rock dam at Ronceverte; Bacon Falls (Class IV); Linsey Slide

Portages: None

Rescue Index: Accessible to remote

Source of Additional Information: See sources of gauge information given in the text.

Access Points	River Miles	Shuttle Miles	Class	Gradient*
A–B Wildell–Durbin	16.0	16.0	I–II	20
B–C Durbin–Cass	17.0	16 or 21	II	18
C–D Cass–Marlinton	27.0	25.0	II	11
D–E Marlinton–Denmar	16.0	16.0	I	7
E–F Denmar–Renick	17.5	21.0	I	6
F–G Renick–Anthony	10.0	10.0	I–III	10
G–H Anthony–Ronceverte	18.0	18.0	I	4
H–I Ronceverte–Alderson	15.0	12.0	I–II	10
I–J Alderson–Talcott	14.0	12.0	I	3
J–K Talcott–Bellepoint	16.0	9.0	II–IV	5

*Feet per mile

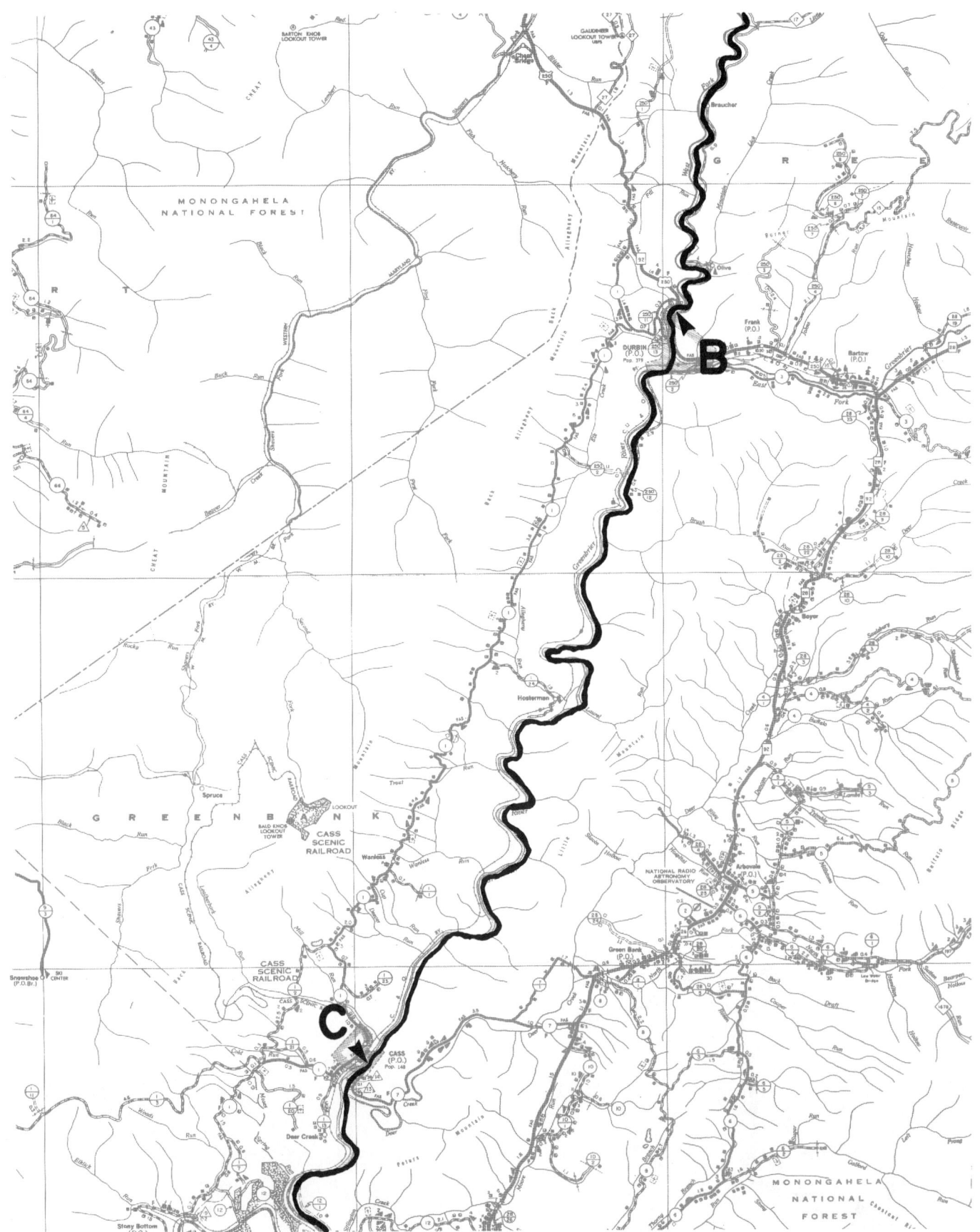

90 Greenbrier River

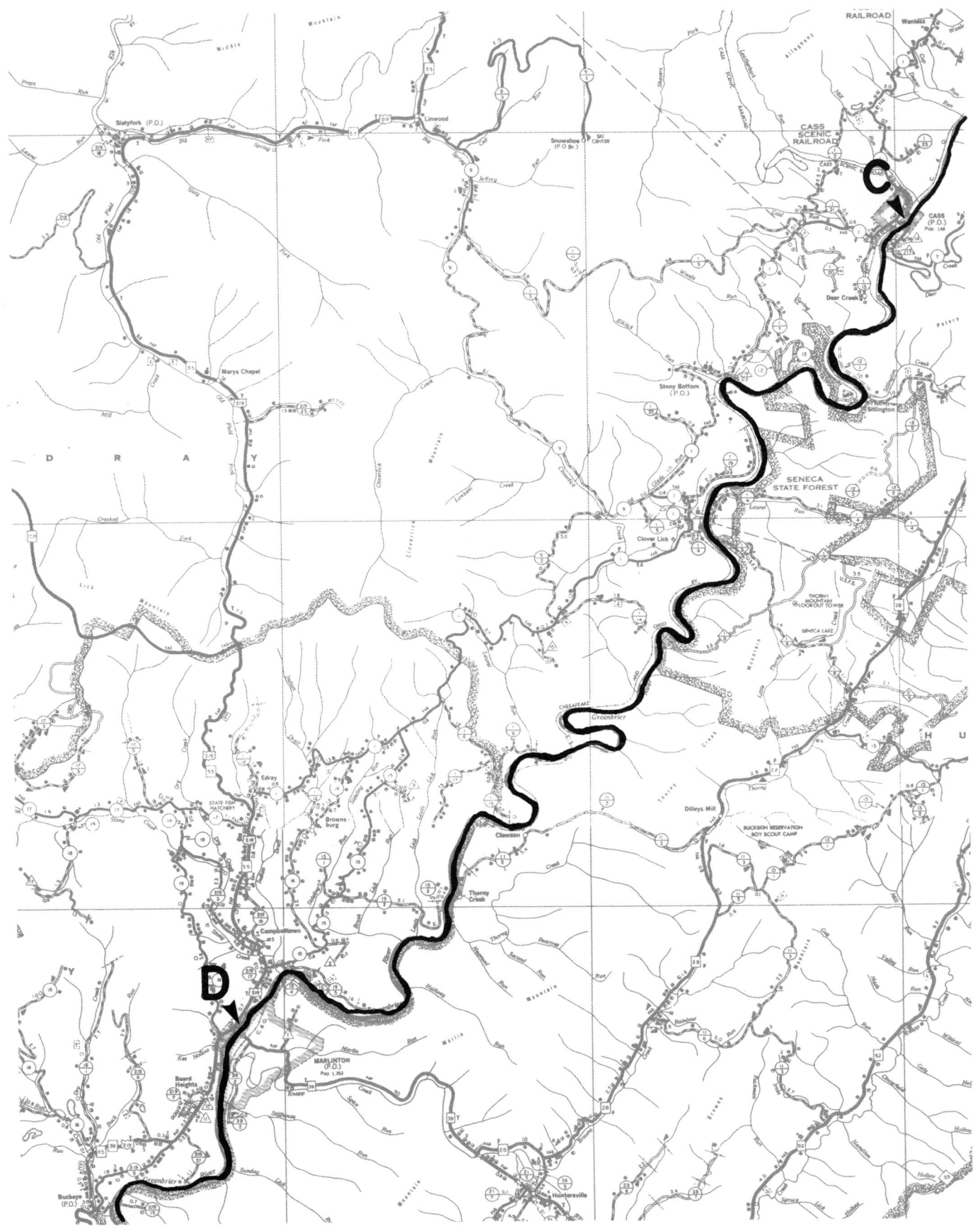

Greenbrier River 91

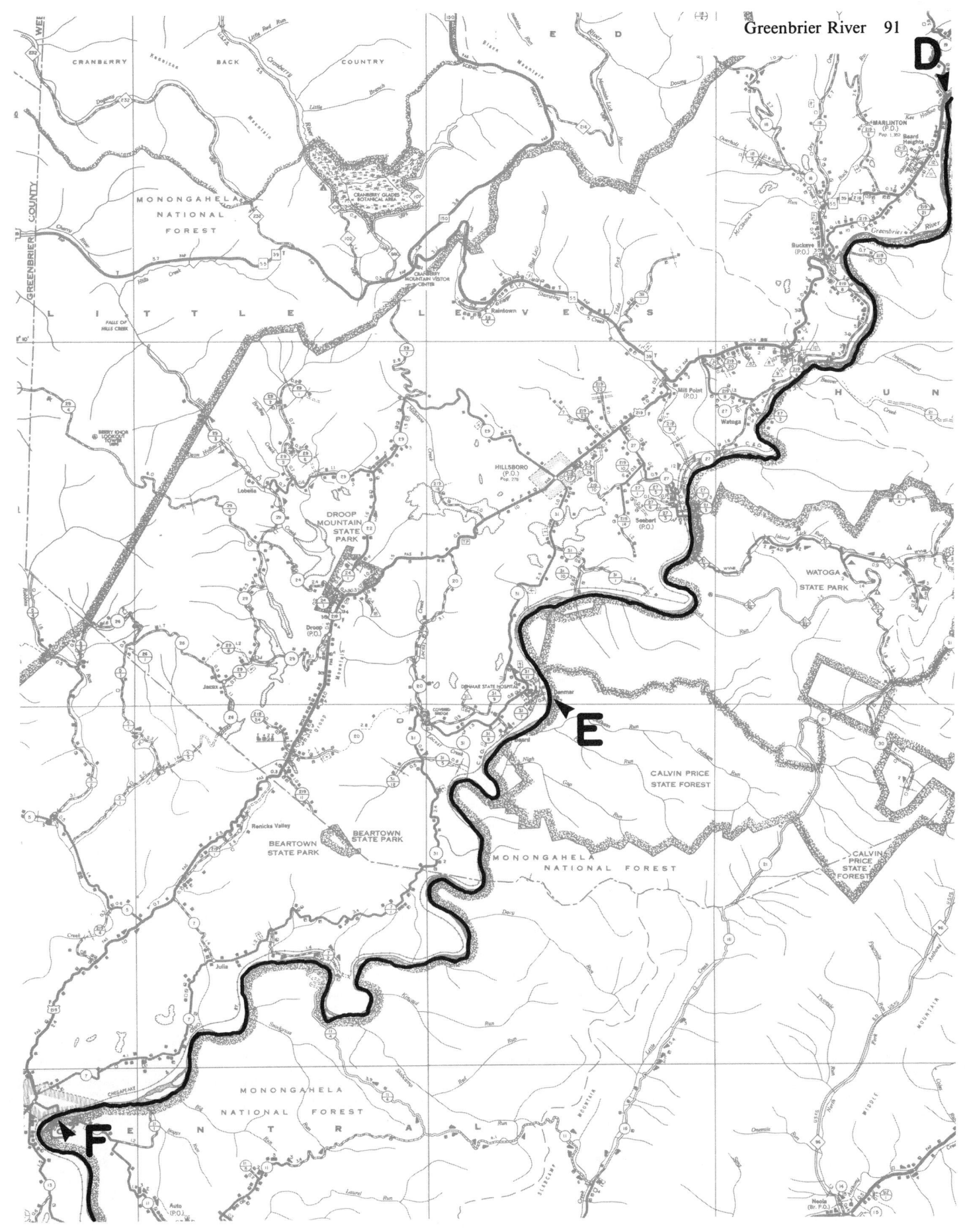

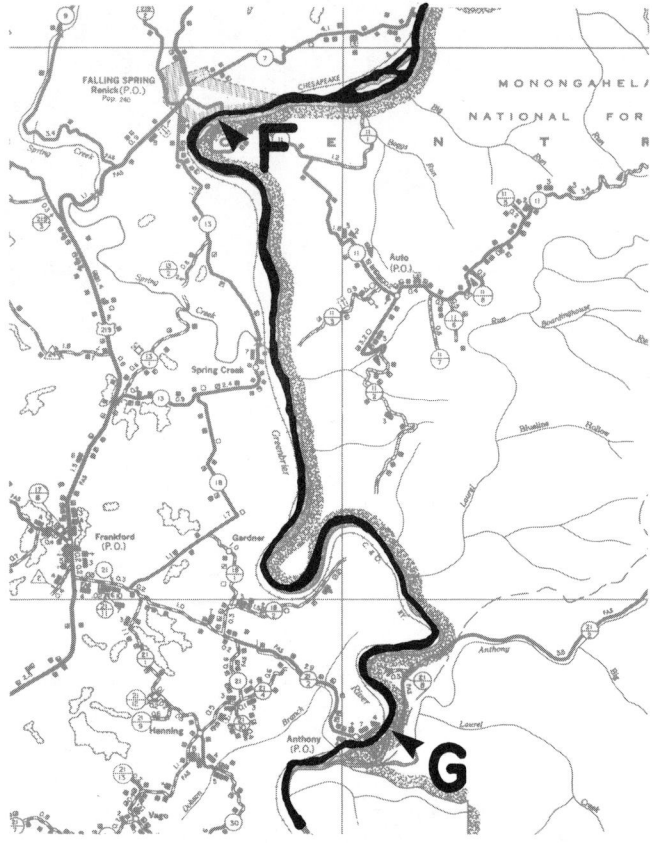

Spice Run after the river bends to the left, there are some big waves along the right bank which can get over five feet at high levels. For the 17.5 mile run from Denmar to Renick, get on WV 31 to reach Denmar, and to get to Renick, exit from US 219 onto WV 11. Check the Buckeye gauge for water conditions.

The Greenbrier has a much larger volume below Renick, being very broad and powerful in places. Rapids are usually formed at narrow places in the river. There are long flat pools between such rapids. It can be floated most of the year, but it is ideal to catch in high water when the current is swift and large haystacks appear for greater stretches. Danger consists of a rapid three miles above Anthony that open-boat paddlers should scout. Before the rapid begins, the river curves slightly to the right, toward the railroad tracks. There is a concrete post beside the tracks with a W on it. The rapid parallels the tracks for 100 yards and piles up against car-sized boulders before it curves to the left. The mouth of Anthony Creek may be seen on the left marking the Anthony take-out; this is a fine stream. The Buckeye gauge is the reference here, too.

Moving downstream toward Ronceverte the river flows rather slowly through occasional rapids. There is a rock dam at Ronceverte that sticks its head up every summer during the dry season. High water washes over it so there may be a passage. Scout if appropriate. For the 18-mile run from Anthony to Ronceverte, put in on the right bank below the "21" bridge at Anthony and take out on the right bank at Ronceverte City Park just before going under the bridge.

For the lower Greenbrier, the Alderson gauge is the reference of choice, with 3.5 feet being a minimal enjoyable level. Readings on the Alderson gauge and the Buckeye gauge normally correspond fairly well. Call (304) 529-5604 for readings.

On a historical note, Camp Greenbrier is just upstream of Ronceverte. This is the oldest continually operated camp for boys in the United States.

The current continues to pick up momentum below Ronceverte, and below Fort Spring the rapids become more numerous and interesting, consisting of nice runnable ledges up to two feet and boulder patches with waves up to three feet. Catching this section in high water is an exciting run. To paddle the 15-mile run from Ronceverte to Alderson, put in at Ronceverte City Park and take out on the right bank near the bridge in Alderson. For those who don't give a rap, the Federal Women's Reformatory is located just downstream on the left.

Below Alderson to Talcott the river is fairly flat, only offering a few rapids. This section is an excellent float-fishing part of the river for bass or just a beautiful place to indulge in general indolence.

The novice and inexperienced whitewater paddler should end his trip at Talcott because, from here on, the Greenbrier can get pretty nasty in medium to high water. The river is fairly flat for two and one-half miles below Talcott as it begins to transcribe a big loop, the famed Big Bend.

Bacon Falls, below Talcott, can be easily recognized upstream by the sheer rock cliff on the right bank. The correct approach is on the left side from which the falls can be scouted. This is unrunnable most of the summer due to the many exposed rocks in low water. When runnable, the easiest passage is on the left, while the right may be considered dangerous. Here the water piles furiously over the steep drop right into the cliffs and then over large boulders. About a mile below Bacon Falls is a tilted ledge known as Linsey Slide, and above this is a series of small ledges. The easiest passages are on the left. From Linsey Slide to the take-out, the river moves faster and there are several long rapids which are easily run. Consider Bacon Falls as Class IV. To shuttle this lower whitewater section put in at the "17" bridge in Talcott and take out on the left near the mouth on the New River below Bluestone Dam.

Greenbrier River 93

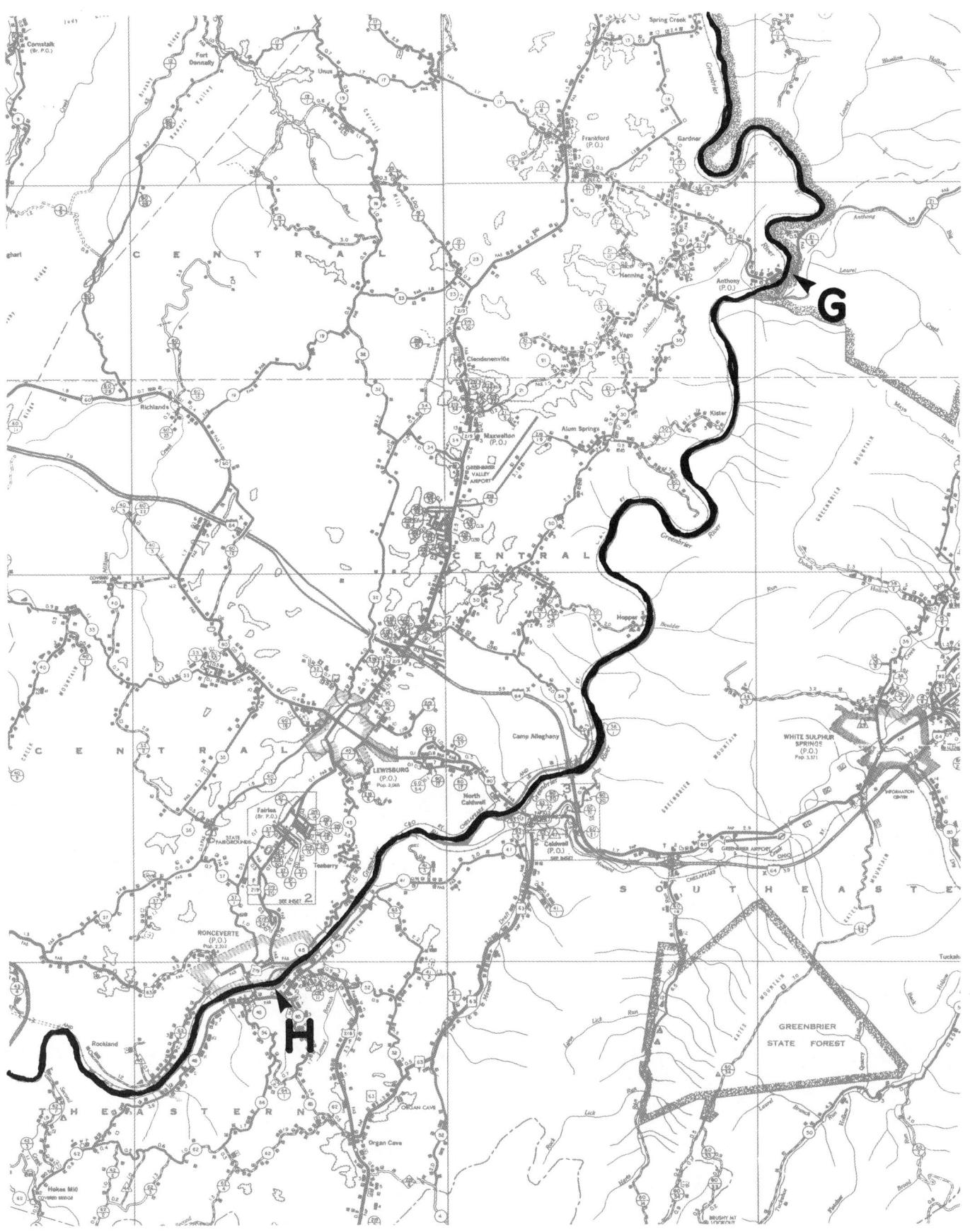

94 Greenbrier River

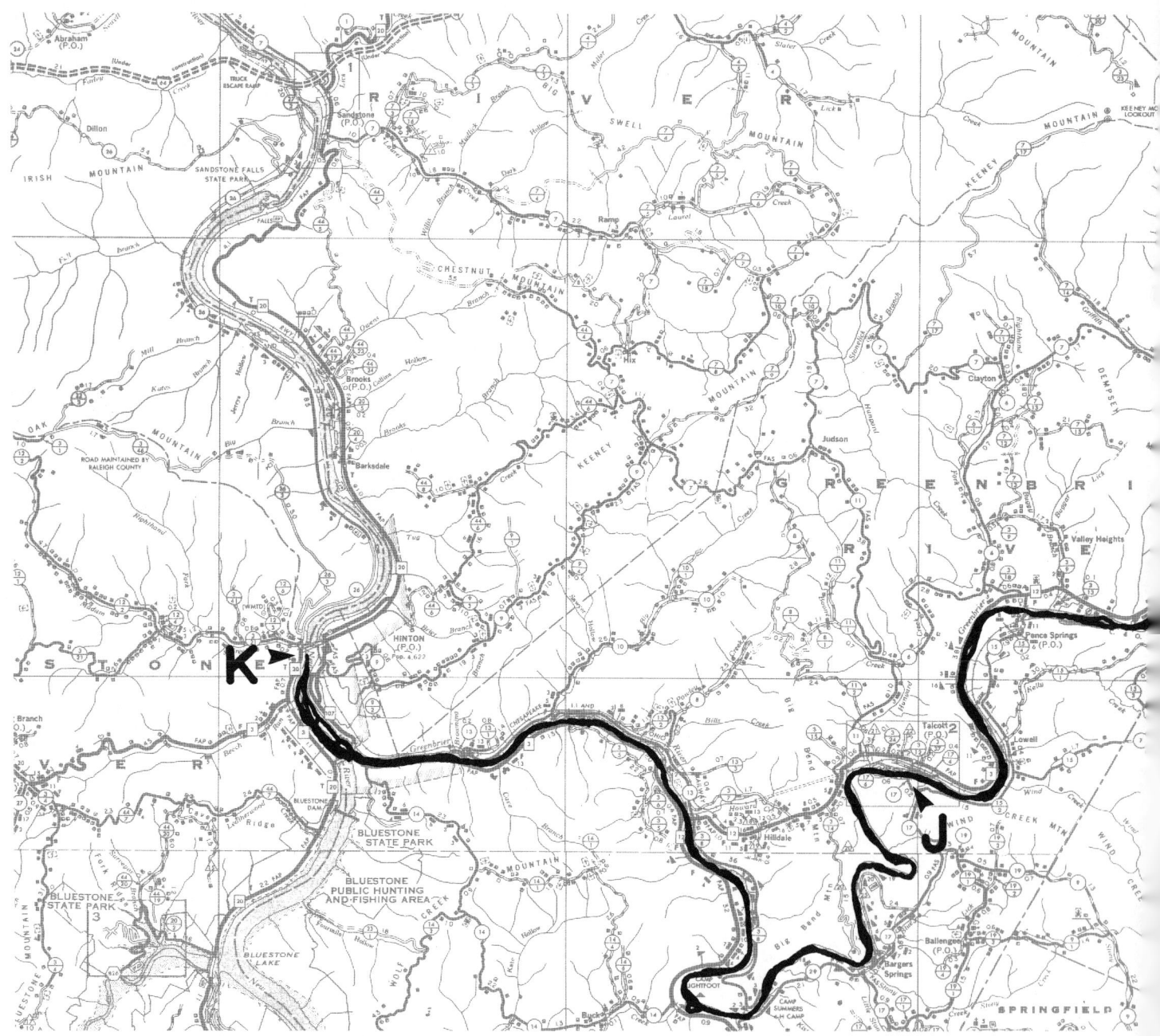

Greenbrier River

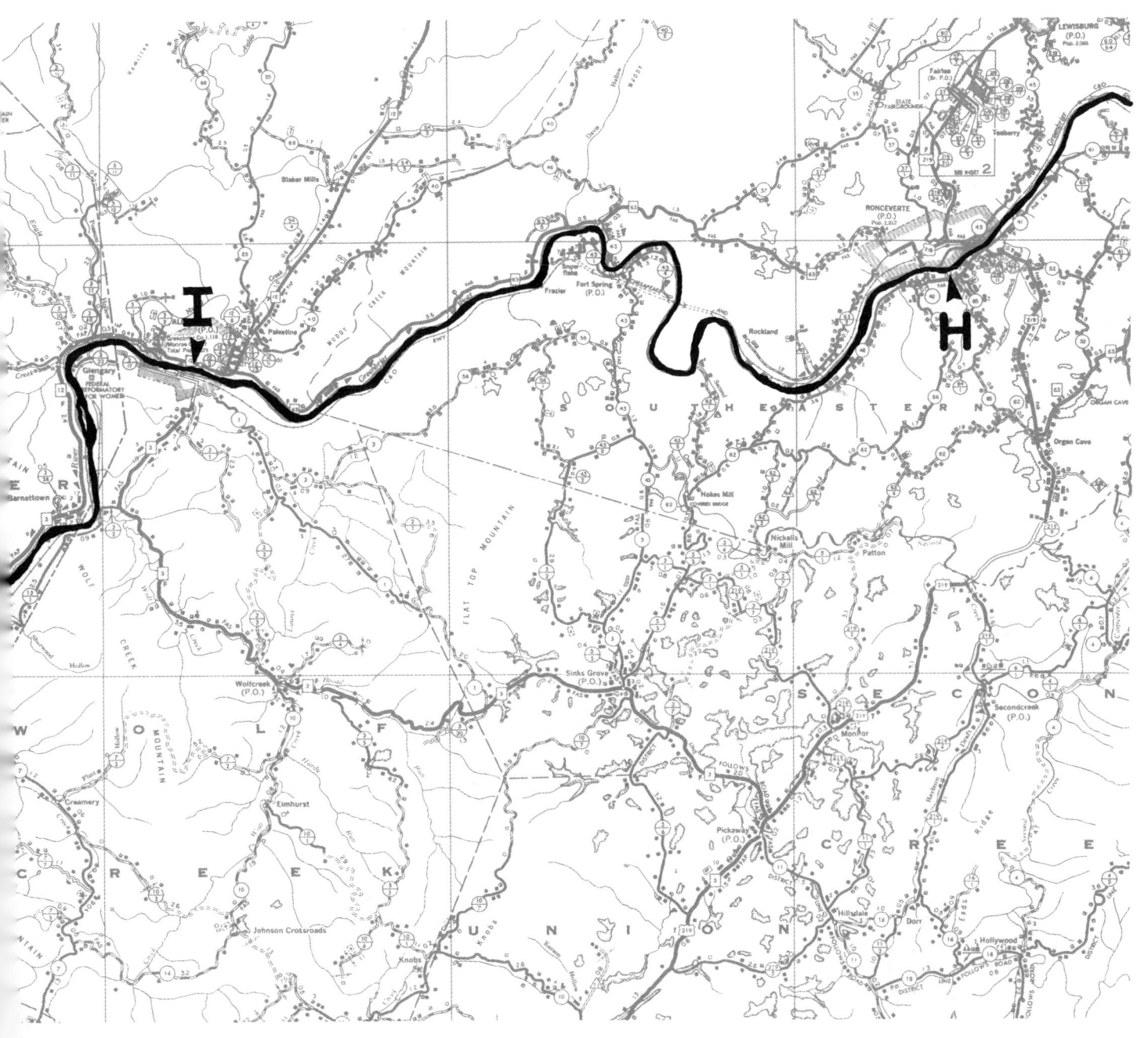

Middle Fork River

Look at the rapids under the bridge at Audra State Park, look at the lush sylvan surroundings, subtract the road, bridge, and bathhouse at the park, and then you'll know what to expect for the first 2.6 miles of this run. It's a beautiful, busy, boat buster. The rapids under the bridge can be run on the right side, heading straight for the retaining wall of the swimming area, and then slipping to the left down into the pool when the water is low. When it is high, it is more entertaining to fandango down through the center. Beyond the pool you'll have to carefully pick channels for the next 60 minutes to the first of three major rapids above the mouth of the Middle Fork.

The river empties into the Tygart Gorge at about its midpoint. The only way out is to paddle the remaining four miles to the mouth of the Buckhannon. This results in an interesting two trips for the price of one. First there is the steep, rocky, technical paddling of the lower Middle Fork and then the much heavier, pushy Tygart with its tripled volume.

About an hour into the trip a hemlock-bedecked isle looms midstream. It cannot be run on the left except in high water. The right side is an interesting slide rapids with a stopper that tends to shunt the unwary into a left-sided whirlpool. Several cycles are required before breakout. The big three rapids on the last half mile of the Middle Fork are next and will require scouting. The first is long and goes around a corner to the right after about 100 yards. The worst drop is before the turn. Enter in the middle and then paddle to the right. The next big rapids, recognized by a 50-foot boulder on the bottom left, looks bad on the right, but go there anyway because a broken ledge at bottom left is terrible. Go to the right over high, clean ledges. The third and last rapids before the mouth can be run on the left where the water smashes into a high bank wall.

Audra State Park may be reached by route "11" from either US 119 or 250. For the take-out, see the Tygart Gorge section. The ingeniously designed campgrounds at the state park offer the finest riverside camping of any place in West Virginia.

The government gauge just upstream from the bridge at Audra State Park has been partly washed away, but one can extrapolate to get a reading. The Belington gauge on the Tygart should be over about five feet as a minimum.

Jon Wright on the Middle Fork of the Tygart River. Photo by Charles Walbridge.

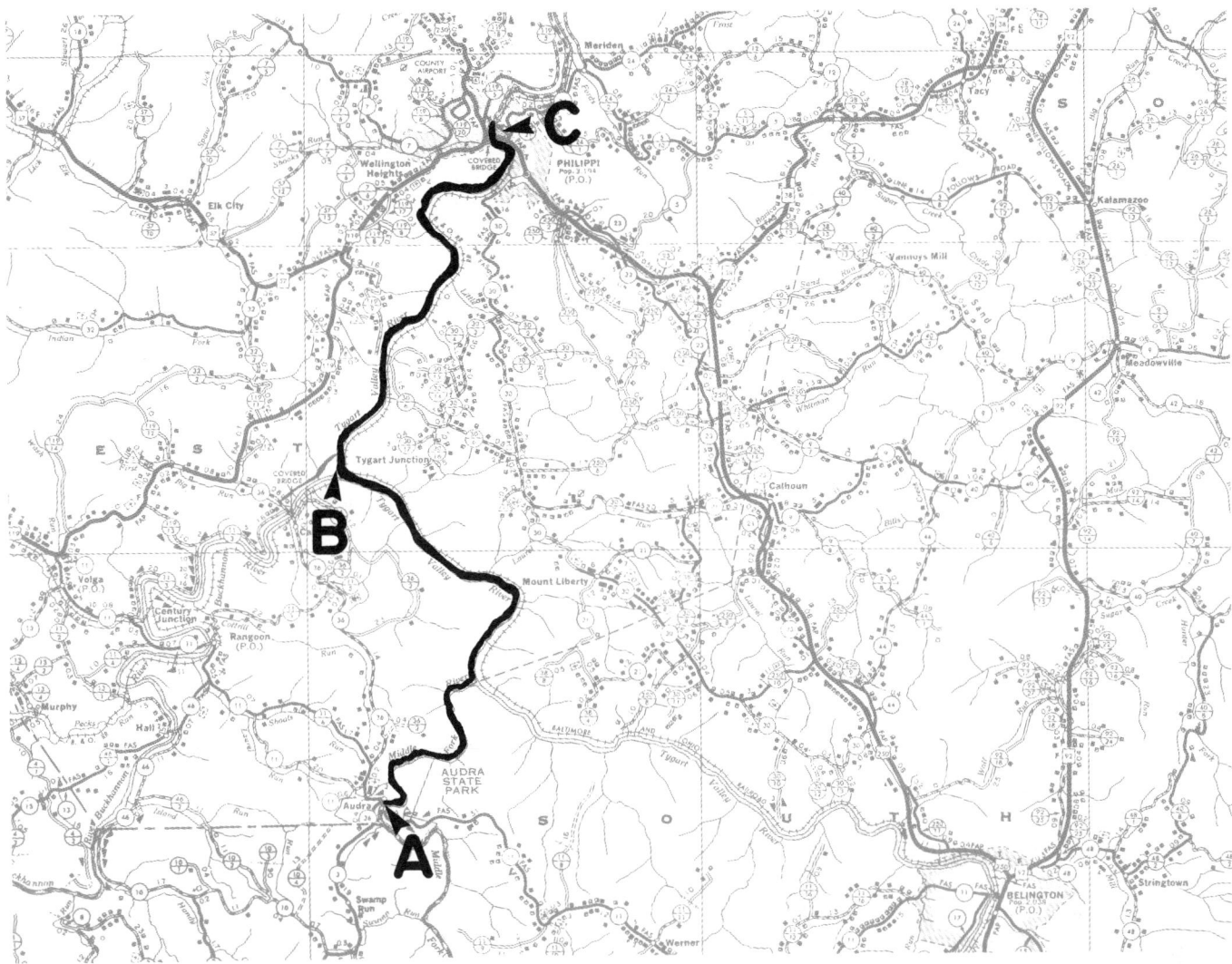

Section: Audra State Park to Tygart Junction

Counties: Barbour (WV)

USGS Quads: Audra

Suitable for: Day trips

Skill Level: Advanced and expert

Months Runnable: Generally in spring

Interest Highlights: Lush wooded surroundings

Scenery: Beautiful

Difficulty: Class IV

Average Width: 35 feet

Velocity: Fast

Gradient: 2.5 miles at 72 feet per mile

Runnable Water Levels:
  Minimum: 3.5 feet on the government gauge just upstream of the bridge at Audra State Park; the gauge has been partially washed away, so you must extrapolate.

Maximum: 5.0 feet on the government gauge (see above)

Hazards: Continuous rapids; rocky, steep, technical paddling

Scouting: Last half mile of Middle Fork (3 big rapids)

Portages: Possibly one or more of the 3 big rapids in the last half mile

Rescue Index: Remote

Source of Additional Information: National Weather Service (301) 899-7378; the Belington gauge should be a minimum of 5 feet

Access Points	River Miles	Shuttle Miles
A–B	6.6*	10.0

Access Point Ratings:
  A - Audra State Park, very good
  B - Buckhannon, poor (3/4 mile carry)
  C - Philippi, good

*2.6 river miles on Middle Fork plus four on the Tygart to mouth of Buckhannon, or nine river miles on the Tygart to Philippi

Tygart River

The Gorge

On this most rugged portion of the Tygart, the rapids are continuous, complex, and bodacious. The river tumbles through a spectacular gorge civilized only by the railroad tracks on the right bank. Incidentally, it is worth the slight disfigurement of those tracks to have an emergency walkway to safety available. The water, clear but acid-polluted, flows through second-growth deciduous and coniferous forests.

The trip starts out with a literal bang—three huge ledges must first be negotiated. Then it is one narrow, steep rapids after another for several miles. In most of these rapids vision is limited by huge boulders. The river then broadens somewhat, and the rapids gentle down to a Class II or III level before joining the Middle Fork.

The current is then noticeably more forceful and, although the gradient hasn't picked up (yet), the rapids are heavier. In about two miles the paddler arrives at the most interesting part of the river. It necks down and drops 80 feet in about 1.25 miles, which is terrific for a river of such volume. After this there are many interesting rapids with absolutely sinister countercurrents, boils, and assorted goodies. Finally the river broadens out considerably and welcomes its sister, the Buckhannon.

About 3.7 miles below Belington or just below the alternative put-in, the river begins tumbling over six- to eight-foot ledges between boxcar-sized boulders separated by three- to four-foot sluiceways. The first of these is Keyhole and consists of two very tiny passages that disappear between the huge boulders. Scout this rapids first. In low water, you may have to carry both as you may be slammed into undercut rocks guarding each slot. At levels above 4.5 feet you can take the one on your left (just a hair wider than your boat), making sure to hold your paddle in the vertical, rather than horizontal, position. You'll zoom down what looks like a gun barrel. At levels above 3.9 you can take the right chute. The next two ledges are blind and ought to be scouted to find the correct passage. Some will want to carry the fourth one, Hard Tongue Falls (Class V), which roars over the ledge and caroms off a boulder wall on the left into an incredible cauldron of boiling foam. Below this, look for the Gates, a row of boulders across the river forming three slots. Run the middle drop, please. The left is undercut. At high levels the section from Keyhole to Hard Tongue becomes substantially more difficult.

In the steep section two miles below the mouth of the Middle Fork, the river pools against a riverwide barrage of boulders and then disappears to the left, dropping 25 feet through a Z-shaped chute 75 yards long (Class IV at moderate levels, Class V at high levels). In general, run this the way most of the water does; start center, move left, then move right to avoid a left-side hole, and, finally finish left. (At high levels, you can sneak the Z by paddling down the right side to the bottom of the Z and dropping over a five-foot ledge of boulders.) The very next rapids is a carry for many paddlers (on the right). This is Shoulder Snapper Falls (Class IV), an eight-foot sheer drop into a pile of boulders. At low levels in particular, there are vertical pinning possibilities here. On one occasion when this falls was attempted, the boat got stuck in an almost vertical position behind boulders at the bottom. The unlucky paddler, who

---

Section: Belington to mouth of Buckhannon or Phillipi

Counties: Barbour (WV)

USGS Quads: Belington, Audra, and Monongahela National Forest

Suitable for: Day trips

Skill Level: Advanced; experts only at high levels

Months Runnable: Spring (but can be run in the summer after extended rains)

Interest Highlights: Big boulders, second growth mixed forest

Scenery: Pretty to beautiful in spots

Difficulty: Class III–V

Average Width: 100 feet

Velocity: Fast

Gradient: 37 feet per mile; 1-1/4 miles at 80 feet per mile

Runnable Water Levels:
  Minimum: 3.0–3.5 feet on the Belington gauge (3.5 cutoff for decked boaters)
  Maximum: 7.0 feet on the Belington gauge

Hazards: Vision limited by huge boulders; undercut rocks; Hard Tongue rapids; Shoulder Snapper has pinning possibilities.

Scouting: Hard Tongue, Z-turn, Shoulder Snapper

Portages: Usually Hard Tongue

Rescue Index: Remote

Source of Additional Information: For the Belington gauge, National Weather Service in Washington, D.C. (301) 899-7378 or Pittsburgh (412) 644-2890.

Access Points	River Miles	Shuttle Miles
A–B	11.0	20.0
A–C	12.0	10.0
A–D	16.0	13.0

Access Point Ratings: Access point B at the Buckhannon is rated poor; access point C one mile below Buckhannon is rated good; access point D five miles below Buckhannon at Philippi is rated as very good.

couldn't wiggle loose, dislocated his shoulder while attempting to leave his boat in the fast current. Another hit the rocks so hard he drove his foot brace into his shin and had to be hospitalized. On the other hand, plenty of water renders the right center a straight shot. In any event, scouting is advised. A half mile below Shoulder Snapper look for the Hook Drop (Class III–IV). This is a sharp left turn in heavy water. Scout it to determine a safe line! Just below is Instant Ender. Save time for playing in this area.

Put in at the bridge in Belington or, to avoid three miles of uninteresting flat water, shuttle via Philippi, turning right off US 250 at Mt. Pleasant Road, then left for 0.7 mile, and right one mile down over something imitating a road to the riverbank (Papa Weese's Paradise, a fishing camp). One take-out is reached from US 119 taking "36" to Carrollton. Park on the right side of the Buckhannon at the covered bridge. The carry from the river to your car is easy but long —a good three-quarters of a mile. From the river, you must paddle upstream upon reaching the mouth of the Buckhannon and land on the sandy bank 100 yards upstream on your left. Alternatively, there is a very complex shuttle which takes you a mile below the confluence with the Buckhannon on river right. (See diagram.)

A second alternative to carrying your boat up the railroad tracks to Carrollton is to paddle another 5.3 miles to Philippi in addition to the 11 miles you have already paddled.

The relevant gauge is operated by the Pittsburgh National Weather Service office, (412) 644-2890. Ask for the Belington reading, which is located on the left bank in Belington and can be read directly.

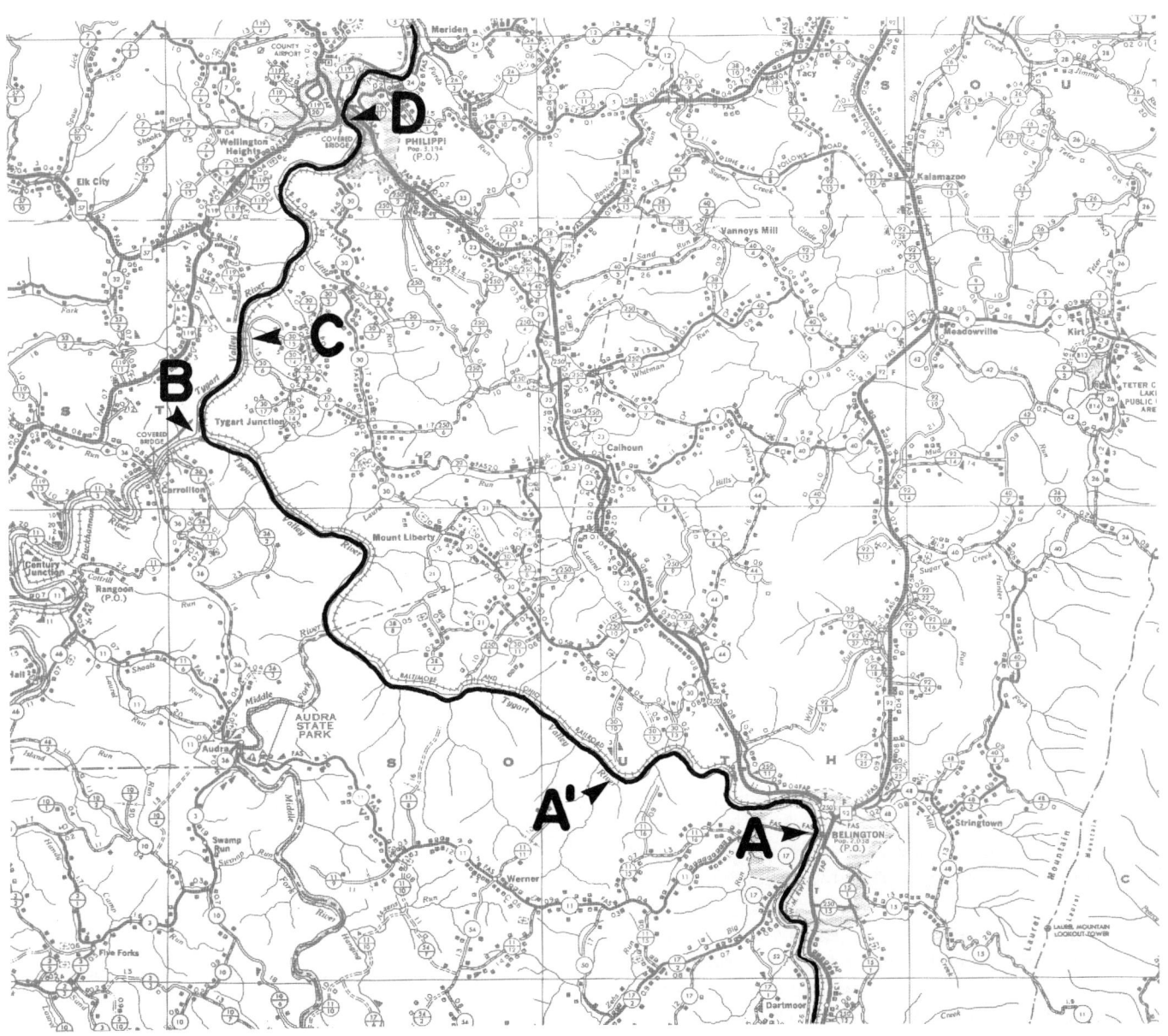

Below the mouth of the Buckhannon to Philippi is a pleasant short trip consisting of several rapids curving gently around large boulders. At low-to-medium-water levels (3.5–4.5 feet), the rapids are of Class I–II difficulty, but they could become more difficult in high water since all of the rapids are formed at narrow spots in the river. The scenery begins in a nice woodsy setting but soon breaks down when an extremely long strip mine is encountered on the left bank. This gives way to pastoral hillsides and then the small college town of Philippi. The first half of the trip contains most of the action while the latter is mostly flat. Contrary to what the Philippi topo map shows, there are no "falls" on this section and it is an excellent undecked boat run. There is one riverwide ledge (two feet in low water) just above the historic, doublelane covered bridge and in sight of Alderson-Broaddus College which is high on the hill in the background. Run at center. Below the bridge is a five and a half mile flat water paddle through mostly depressing scenery.

Arden Section

The Tygart is a big flat river for five and one-half miles below Philippi. Then, the first rapids of the eight-mile Arden Section are encountered. This section is strewn with huge boulders and drops over big rock ledges and reefs as the Tygart descends 170 feet before reaching the reservoir behind Grafton Dam. All but the last three miles of the run below Arden may be scouted from a secondary road on river right; this runs from Philippi downstream to the ancient concrete bridge at Teter Creek. (The November 1985 flood damaged this road, and it needed repair in early 1986.) However, don't take out at Teter Creek unless absolutely necessary because some of the best water is in the remaining three miles to the reservoir. At high levels (over 4.5 feet), this eight-mile section becomes expert decked boater country only.

About one mile below Arden there is a ledge channeled on the left. The current continues down the left side for 50 feet, dropping over a boulder and ending in two stoppers. This rapids is called Gallaway by local paddlers and can be scouted from the left. The larger upstream wave must be skirted to the right if one is to maintain the alignment and speed necessary to run a ledge and the second stopper. The second rapids downstream from Laurel Creek (which enters from the right under a steel bridge) is called Deception. Here the river narrows and piles over a rapid succession of three ledges with unavoidable five-foot standing waves. Three hundred yards below Deception, the river funnels over a ledge to the left and undercuts a shelf of rock on the left which has a one-foot clearance. This rapids is fittingly called Undercut (Class IV–V depending on levels) and should be scouted from the right. Be careful in running this rapids to guard against being blown to the left underneath the undercut rock shelf. Expert paddlers can get enjoyable

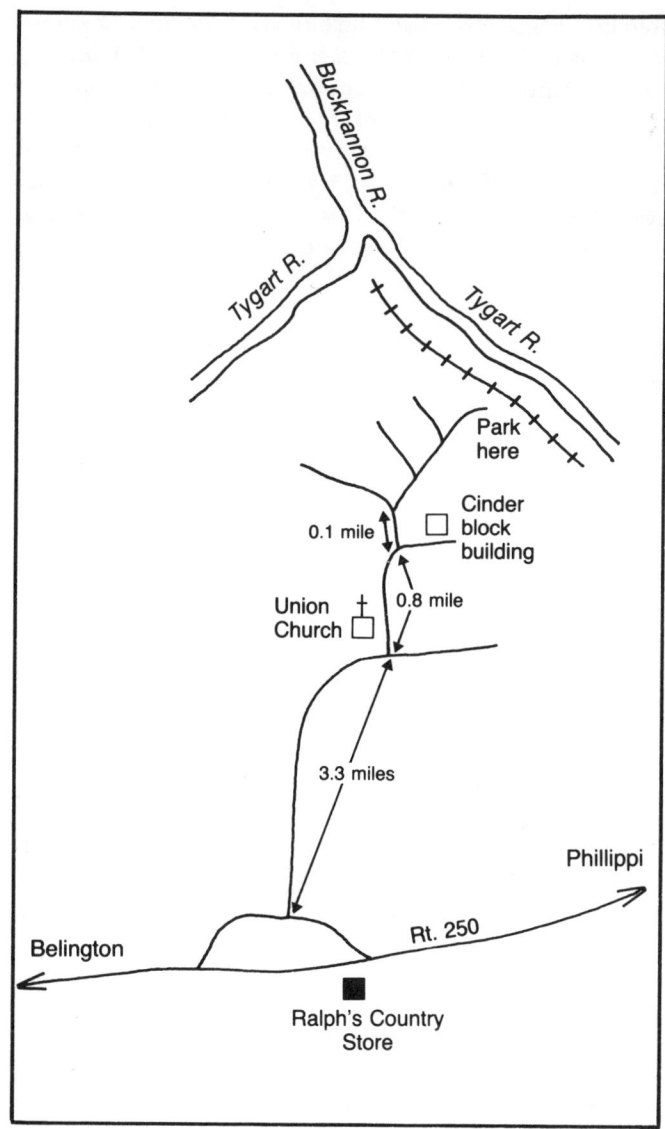

Alternate Take-Out for the Tygart River Gorge (one mile below the confluence with the Buckhannon)

Turn off Rt. 250 opposite Ralph's Country Store onto "Old Route Two Fifty." Take the first right and proceed about 3.3 miles to a sharp left turn. Just after the turn, the Union Church will be off to your left. Proceed about 0.8 miles to a point where the main road curves sharply to the right at a cinderblock building. Take the road to the left here and about 0.1 miles later, take a right and keep right down to the railroad tracks on the river bank. Proceed carefully; it's easy to get lost here.

Shoulder Snapper, Tygart River Gorge. Photo by Ed Grove.

enders here below four feet on the Philippi gauge. A couple of hundred yards below Undercut is a river-wide three- to four-foot ledge which should be scouted from the right before running it. The right side of this ledge (called Premonition by local paddlers) is a particularly dynamic drop with a curler which forces a quick left turn.

A hundred yards or so farther downstream, the river spills over a good 15-foot riverwide falls called Moats Falls. Very experienced paddlers are now carefully running this falls over the middle—a 15-foot drop into soft suds and a generally good-sized pool below. Those contemplating running the falls should first scout the launch and landing points carefully. For the squeamish and/or less advanced boater, an honorable option is to carry along the road on the right and put in just below the falls.

About 500 yards below Moats Falls is a rapids called Classic (Class IV–V at higher levels) by genteel paddlers and unprintable names by salty boaters. Get over on river left to scout this drop (which can be really nasty at higher levels) and carry it if you have any doubts. Here the river is narrow and split by a partially submerged, house-sized boulder in a powerful drop. After this rapids, the Tygart is fairly flat until the ancient Teter Creek bridge.

Below Teter Creek bridge is a nice wave train appropriately called Rodeo Rapids. After numerous other good rapids, the river pools behind a natural rock dam, turns left and then immediately right, all the time being necked down considerably. There are big diagonal stoppers pushing to the right in this turn, and as you regain alignment around the last corner, you are faced with a huge tongue of water called Wells Falls (Class IV at moderate levels; Class V at high levels), dropping ten feet over a slide into a formidable stopper. If you slide off the left side tongue to the right, you will slam into a four-foot wall of water. This is the most powerful, runnable rapids in the entire Monongahela Basin and should be scouted each time. The very next rapids is also mean; it is a sheer drop into another nasty hole. Both Wells Falls and the rapids below are runnable, but they are also easily carried on the right. However, one does have to contend with poison ivy on the portage. The remaining rapids below Teter Creek are nice Class III drops that offer no special problems in low water.

Regarding the shuttle, use the dirt road on river right from Arden once it has been repaired. Drive about two miles upstream to the first rapids for an easy put-in. Inexperienced paddlers should take out at Arden bridge. One can also take out at Teter Creek for an easy shuttle with a road alongside throughout. To reach the Cove Run take-out, turn right at Teter Creek and go out to the main highway, WV 92, and turn left. Take Cove Run Road "2" to the left, then take a right, another right and then a left at the succeeding forks. The last part takes you down a very steep unimproved road to the river. Be sure you recognize this point from the river. You will not find rapids on the lower part until the first of October. Peak drawdown is generally reached about the last of February. At such time there is another 1.8 miles of rapids dropping 30 feet per mile. You then have another two miles of flat water before taking out on the left side at Wildcat Hollow Boat Club.

102 Tygart River

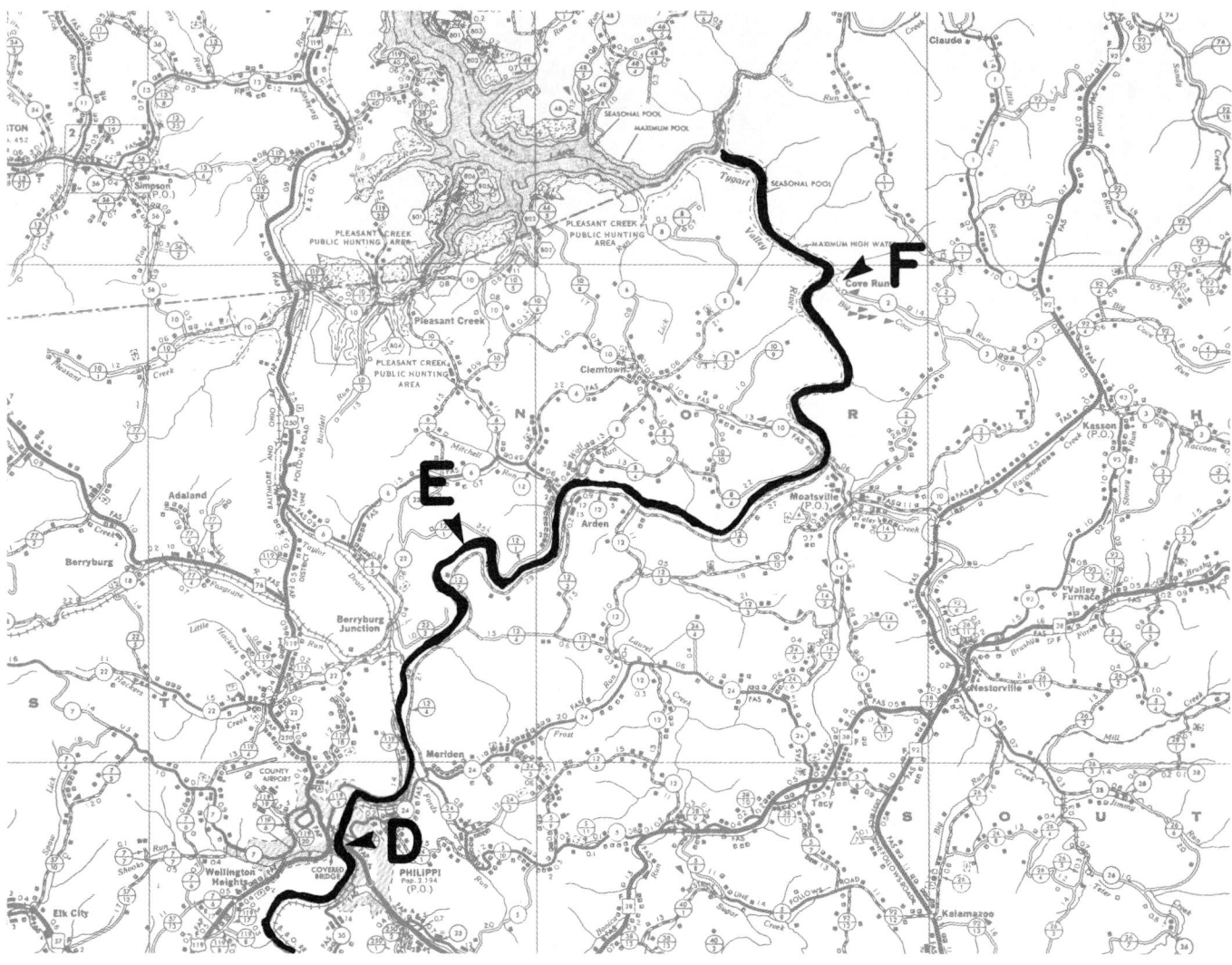

Section: Arden to Cove Run

Counties: Barbour (WV)

USGS Quads: Philippi, Nestorville

Suitable for: Day trips

Skill Level: Advanced; expert in high water

Months Runnable: Virtually all year, but can be very low in summer

Interest Highlights: Big ledges and large rapids, runnable Moat's Falls, big water at Wells Falls

Scenery: Pretty in spots; good to fair otherwise

Difficulty: Class III-V

Average Width: 125-150 feet

Velocity: Fast

Gradient: 27 feet per mile

Runnable Water Levels:
  Minimum: 2.5 feet on the Philippi gauge
  Maximum: 5.0 feet on the Philippi gauge

Hazards: Undercut Rock, Moat's Falls, Classic, Wells Falls; very difficult at high water

Scouting: Gallaway Beach, Undercut Rock, Moat's Falls, Classic, Wells Falls and rapids below

Portages: Depending on water levels and/or experience, Undercut Rock, Moat's Falls, Classic, and maybe Wells Falls

Rescue Index: Accessible for the most part

Source of Additional Information: National Weather Service, Pittsburgh, (412) 644-2890 for the Philippi gauge

Access Points	River Miles	Shuttle Miles
E-F	8.0	13.0

Access Point Ratings:
  E - two miles above Arden, very good
  F - Big Cove Run, very good

Valley Falls Section

This one-and-a-half mile section of the Tygart requires close scrutiny of the dam discharge from Grafton by highly experienced boaters. The major difficulty in addition to the 60-foot-per-mile gradient is the fact that this section of the river has been narrowed by 80 percent as it enters the steep gorge. This is a very heavy descent for such a large volume of water.

In this section there are several major drops. The first Valley Falls ledge is about ten miles downstream from Grafton and shortly into this trip. It is the site of an old mill, artifacts of which still remain. This is a riverwide ledge about eight feet high which has water coming over at least three chutes (at low water). The chute on the right is sloping and can be run with more water, although it does pile angrily into and off the shore rocks at its base. The chute on river left can be run after careful scouting.

The next Valley Falls ledge of twelve feet is sharp and appears unrunnable. However, at low water it can be run on the left of the right side. The third ledge is called Punk Rock. It is a Class III rapids with two runnable channels, both requiring right-angle turns to the left after running tight along the right bank.

The fourth ledge is clearly Class V–VI at even moderate water levels. Aptly called Hamburger Helper, the river here narrows to a single channel and drops eight feet over a boulder with a thin flow at the center and a boiling flume at each side. The fifth rapids (Twist 'n' Shout) is a series of three drops in rapid succession in a 20-foot channel. The last two have huge souse holes up against the undercut right shore. The remaining three ledges (colorfully called This, That, and It by local paddlers) are straightforward rapids, the last of which can be reached from the take-out.

Due to the discharge of the Grafton Dam, this section could conceivably be attempted anytime, but if several gates are open, the whole narrow valley is a nightmare of explosion waves, moving 12- to 15-foot waves, and terrible souse holes. It is an interesting sight from the railroad tracks, but no place for anyone's boat.

Valley Falls State Park is easily found by following the signs from either Fairmont or Grafton along WV 310 and CR 31/14 respectively. To reach the Hammond take-out, follow the yellow brick road (honest), "86," by turning off WV 310.

The Grafton Dam has a gauge, but readings are meaningless to the authors. Any decision to run the Valley Falls section can only be made after on-the-spot observations by very experienced boaters.

Section: Valley Falls to Hammond
Counties: Marion (WV)
USGS Quads: Fairmont East
Suitable for: Day trips
Skill Level: Advanced and expert boaters
Months Runnable: All year following dam releases
Interest Highlights: Steep gorge and huge drops
Scenery: Beautiful
Difficulty: Class II-VI
Average Width: 150 feet
Velocity: Fast
Gradient: 60 feet per mile
Runnable Water Levels: Since there is no gauge, levels have to be judged by inspection.
Hazards: Two Valley Falls ledges, Hamburger Helper
Scouting: Two Valley Falls ledges, Hamburger Helper, Twist 'n' Shout
Portages: Hamburger Helper
Rescue Index: Accessible generally
Source of Additional Information: None

Access Points	River Miles	Shuttle Miles
G-H	1.5	7.0

Access Point Ratings for both the put-in and take-out are very good.

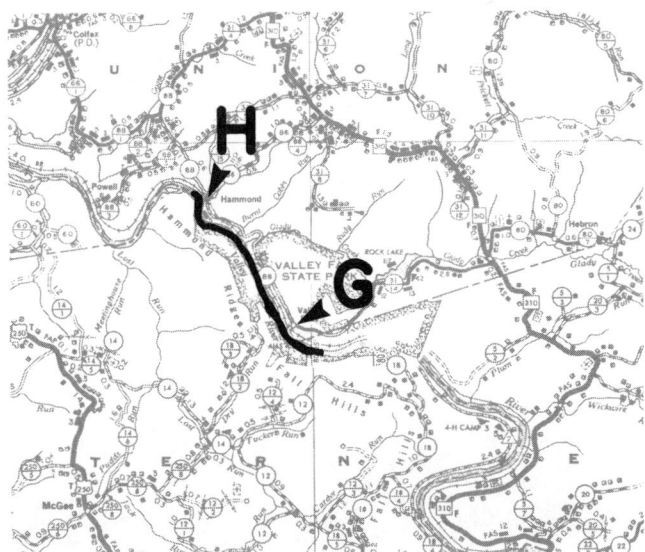

104 Tygart River

Moats Falls on the Arden section of the Tygart River. Photo by Ron Snow, WV Dept. of Commerce.

Ollie Fordham running the Valley Falls section of the Tygart River. Photo by Stephen Ensign.

Laurel Fork of the Cheat River

All things considered, this is unquestionably the best run of the Cheat basin. It is a long trip through uninhabited and virtually inaccessible country in the high valley between the Middle and Rich mountains. The remnants of an early logging railroad play tag with the meandering river for the first of a series of two- to four-foot ledges. These continue regularly for the next two miles to the grandaddy of them all, a twelve-foot runnable waterfall (demented experts only!) which you should portage on the left along the tramway bed. The November 1985 flood has eroded a big chunk of the left bank below this waterfall—making this portage more difficult. After lunch at the foot of the falls, be ready for seven miles of continuous Class III rapids to the mouth.

There are a total of eight bridge crossings on the run. None of the bridges remain but the abutments are readily spotted as landmarks. Between the seventh and eighth bridges there is a 50-yard tunnel from one limb of a half-mile loop to the other. The water visible at the mouth is typical of the entire river from the falls down. This is a very exhilarating run amidst the least spoiled scenery of West Virginia. After being flushed out into the Dry Fork, it is just a quarter mile to the Jenningston bridge.

Spotting the falls from upstream should be no problem. It takes about one and a half hours of paddling time to reach the falls. There are six bridge crossings to the falls; the sixth one is about a mile above the falls. The falls are just around a right turn. Fluorescent strips have been tied in the tree branches on the left above the falls. The only other difficulty is the fatigue of thirteen miles of wilderness travel, including nine miles of continuous maneuvering. Near the end is a cluster of several memorable hydraulics, not far from the Jenningston bridge. At high water, one needs to be extremely careful of this river. It has been a killer when the hydraulics below many of its ledges become keepers.

The put-in is at the US 33 bridge. The take-out is at the mouth downstream along the left side from the Jenningston bridge. The best way between the two points is west along US 33, four miles to Alpena, and north on "12" by the Glady Fork and Sully. There is a gauge painted on the right-side abutment of the US 33 bridge. It will not be high enough unless the Parsons gauge is over five feet.

Ron Honaker and David Whitley on Laurel Fork of the Cheat River. Photo by Stephen Ensign.

106 Laurel Fork of the Cheat River

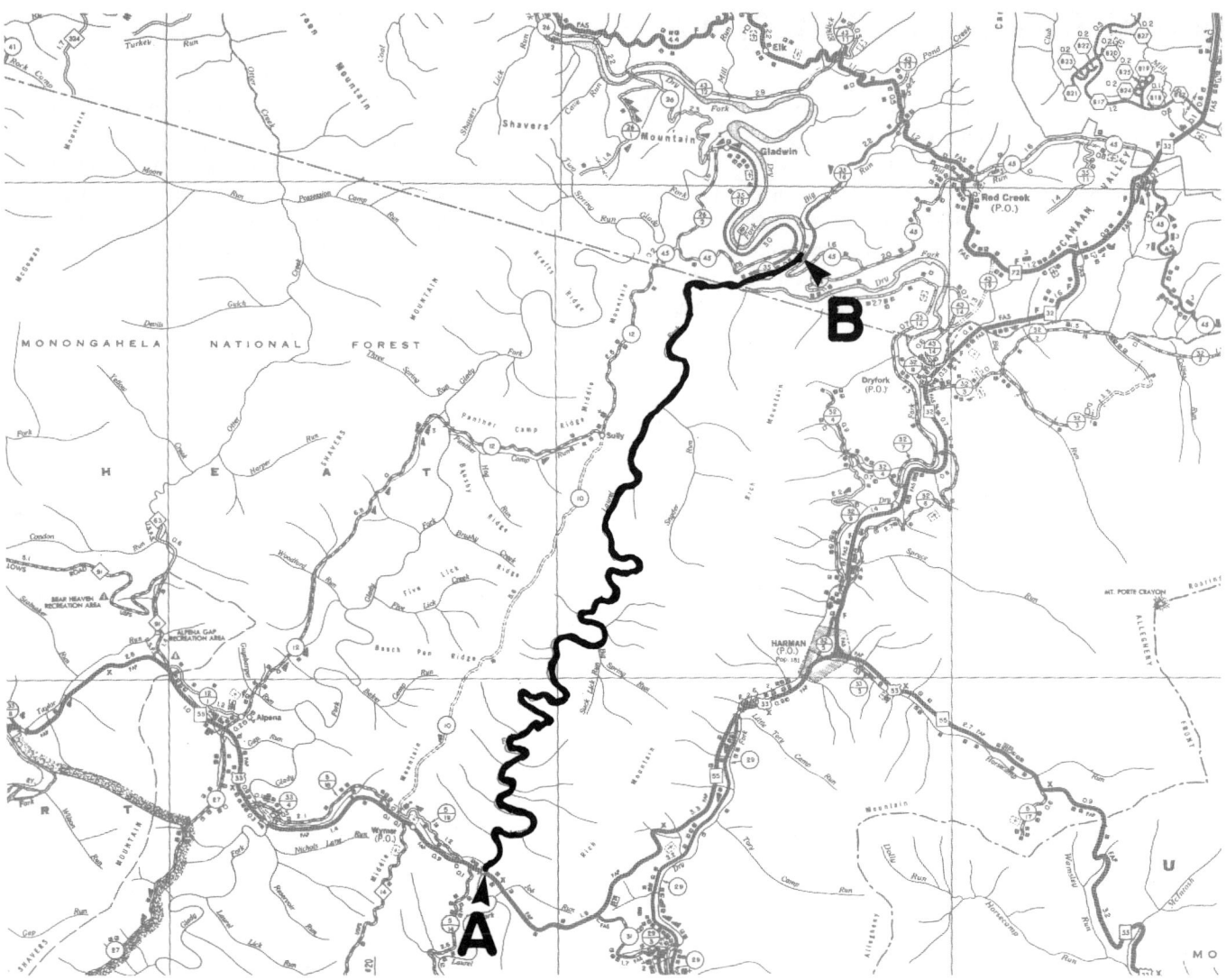

Section: U.S. 33 bridge to Jenningston

Counties: Randolph and Tucker (WV)

USGS Quads: Harman, Monongahela National Forest

Suitable for: Day trips

Skill Level: Advanced

Months Runnable: Generally spring

Interest Highlights: Scenic high valley; 12-foot falls

Scenery: Pretty to beautiful

Difficulty: Class III–IV

Average Width: 50 feet

Velocity: Fast

Gradient: 9 miles at 71 feet per mile

Runnable Water Levels: Gauge is on the right side of the Route 33 bridge abutment
Minimum: 0.3 feet
Maximum: 1.5 feet

Hazards: Keeper hydraulics in high water; 12-foot falls halfway through trip

Scouting: Several of the larger rapids

Portages: 12-foot waterfalls

Rescue Index: Remote

Source of Additional Information: National Weather Service (301) 899-7378; Parsons gauge should be at least 5 feet.

Access Points	River Miles	Shuttle Miles
A–B	13.0	15.0

Access Point Ratings:
A - US 33 bridge, very good
B - Jenningston bridge, very good

Blackwater River

The November 1985 flood has substantially changed the Blackwater and made it a significantly more difficult river. Before, it was a Class IV trip. Now it is a Class IV–V river with numerous rapids like the Upper Youghiogheny (discussed in the chapter on Maryland) and some even like the more difficult Lower Meadow in West Virginia (not described in this book). Although the individual drops are not as big, the continuous nature of this river makes it tougher than the Lower Big Sandy (also in this chapter). Since the 1985 flood many of the drops have become more complex with numerous pinning possibilities. Substantial rock slides from the flood and fallen trees make this a river for experts only who continually scout and take all safety precautions.

The Blackwater from North Fork Junction to Hendricks (seven miles) is West Virginia's longest rapids. It flows through a narrow, steep defile draining the Canaan Valley. The valley is a flat upland swamp on the west side of the Allegheny Front.

Multiple branches of the upper Blackwater funnel the 150-square-mile drainage basin into two main forks which respectively pass the former logging capitals of Davis and Thomas. Near these nineteenth-century towns, they suddenly leap off the mountain as two falls, 50 feet each, and begin their unrelenting rush to the Dry Fork eight miles and 1,000 feet below. The two main divisions of the river, the Blackwater and its North Fork, confluence about a mile below their initiation drops and slow their descent to a more "realistic" paddling gradient. Here the rhododendron towers 30 feet high along the river and 1,000 feet above are spruce-topped cliffs. Both falls, the one preserved by a state park and the other on the North Branch, should be viewed by the paddler.

From the recommended put-in at the junction and with only minimal veering from left or right, the river is one continuous blind bend—downwards. From the paddler's eye level one can never see more than 50 yards ahead before the river disappears over the edge of the world. It has a fantastic 112-feet-per-mile gradient for five miles to Lime Rock, an abandoned community two miles upstream from Hendricks. Fortunately, this descent is not broken into alternate stretches of rapids and pools but is generally evenly distributed. It is a gigantic sluiceway between mountains rising 2,000 feet on either side with almost no riverside beach.

Paddling the Blackwater is a constant challenge of reading and negotiating chutes over staircase ledges randomly strewn with five- to ten-foot boulders. The paddler is constantly maneuvering in the ever-pushing current. Moving side eddies are the only rest or rescue spots along the course. The waters of the river are a nonsilted brown covered with suds—a form of pollution that has been noted since the time of Thomas Lewis, a 1746 explorer who appropriately called this stream "the River Styx." The tannin color is attributed to organic acids from the upland swamps leaching iron oxides from the red shale that lines much of the riverbed.

Approximately 200 yards downstream from the put-in are two closely spaced drops that are Class VI at most water levels. The first has a horrible hole and the second a very tight channel into an undercut rock. Both may be carried at the same time down the left bank. The next several drops are blind from the top and have inconsiderately placed rocks at the bottom of the main drops, so scout if you cannot see from the boat. Particularly after the 1985 flood, there is the danger of tree strainers in these rapids.

In the first 1.5 miles, there is a unique rapids that serves as a landmark. The water races 75 yards over a flat, sloping red shale floor. With this minimum of friction, the current reaches horrendous speeds before abruptly dropping into a giant washing machine at the bottom. Shortly below this is Tub Run, a tributary on the right.

The next 3.5 miles are like the first 1.5 miles. About halfway through the trip, a shallow, wide eight- to ten-foot falls is found which may be carried or scraped over on the left. Paddle across the pool and look at the next rapids below as the river now funnels into a huge hole. Most people choose to carry this also. After the first horrendous five miles, the last two miles into Hendricks drop at an interesting 48 feet per mile, and the paddler can breathe a sigh of relief.

To single out any part of this trip as difficult is ludicrous. Everything about it, from getting to the put-in to the take-out, is difficult beyond the scope of all but the expert paddler. The incessant nature of the rapids without pools, the inevitable fatigue of constant maneuvering, and the complexity and pinning possibilities added since the 1985 flood make this a Class IV–V run. Another complication to consider is that the river runs in a southwesterly direction against the afternoon sun.

The Blackwater has been run from the base of Blackwater Falls to the North Fork, but that's a 2.5 mile trip only for demented experts heavily into self-punishment. The gradient for this short trip is a fantastic 230 feet per mile. Many rapids have to be carried, making the run really a test of rhododendron thicket versus kayaker. It is an understatement that we cannot recommend it.

The shuttle is easy, but the put-in is a bear. From the take-out under the WV 72 bridge in Hendricks, take US 219 to Thomas, and then right to Coketon, and on to Douglas via "27." Park where the road leaves the river, shoulder your boat, and walk one mile. That's right—one mile along the railroad track, then slide down about 300 vertical feet over a wooded 60-degree incline to the river. Incidentally, the railroad parallels the river some 300 feet above the water and serves as an avenue back to civilization in case of accidents.

For those who like sliding rather than hiking, there is now an alternative. Continue on the forest service road about a mile past Douglas until the road is clearly high above the river on the side of the gorge. At this point you are several hundred feet above the railroad tracks. Look for a sign painted "put-in" or some tape on a tree. Park and start sliding a third of a mile downhill (about 700 vertical feet—400 to the railroad track and 300 to the river).

The Canoe Cruisers' Association marked this new put-in during the summer of 1986.

There used to be a gauge at Hendricks, but the November 1985 flood sandblasted the paint right off the bridge abutment. The old rule of thumb previously reported apparently still works. If the river looks scrapy from the Hendricks bridge, it is probably adequate. If it looks adequate, it is probably too high. The Parsons gauge guide for the run should be between 4.0 and 5.5 feet before you go to Hendricks to check out the river.

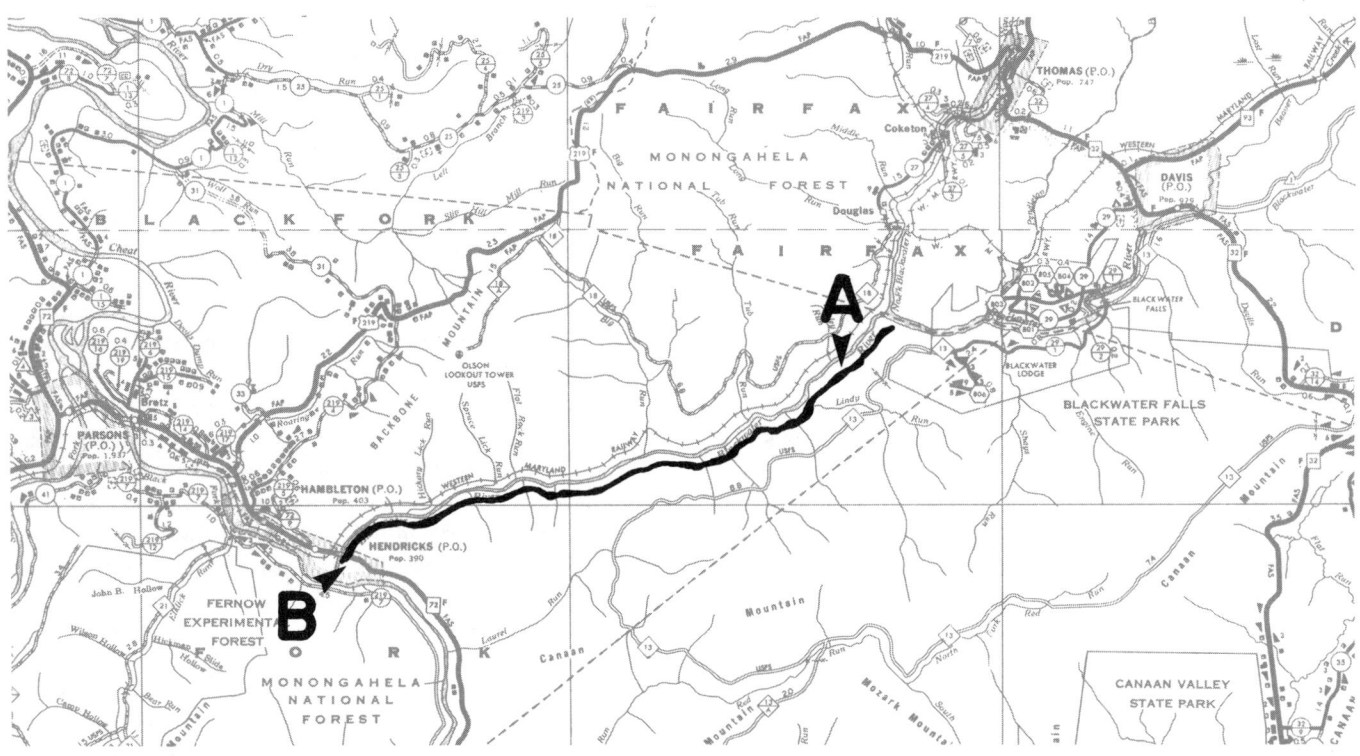

Section: North Fork Junction to Hendricks

Counties: Tucker (WV)

USGS Quads: Mozark Mountain, Monongahela National Forest

Suitable for: Day cruising

Skill Level: Expert

Months Runnable: Generally early spring

Interest Highlights: West Virginia's longest continuous rapids

Scenery: Beautiful

Difficulty: Class IV–V, VI

Average Width: 30–50 feet

Velocity: Fast

Gradient: 5 miles at 112 feet per mile; 2 miles at 48 feet per mile

Runnable Water Levels: The Parsons gauge should be between 4.0 and 5.5 feet before you go to Hendricks to check out the river.
  Minimum: If the river looks low from the Hendricks bridge, it is probably adequate.
  Maximum: If the river looks adequate from the Hendricks bridge, it is probably too high.

Hazards: Continuous heavy rapids; trees in chutes; many pinning possibilities

Scouting: Both boat and bank scouting are continuous

Portages: Several at least

Rescue Index: Remote

Source of Additional Information: National Weather Service (301) 899-7378; Parsons gauge

Access Points	River Miles	Shuttle Miles
A–B	7.0	16.0

Access Point Ratings: Put-in A is poor; take-out B is very good

Big Sandy Creek

Upper Section, Bruceton Mills to Rockville

As this little stream tips down beside Chestnut Ridge to the Cheat Gorge, it provides six miles of progressive slalom training starting at Class I and sequentially working up to Class IV. It is suitable for strong intermediate paddlers in open boats at lower water levels, but floatation is recommended. Automobile camping is provided at nearby Cooper's Rock State Park.

Hazel Run Rapids is the first problem and appears as an impassible barricade of boulders. Try the second passage from the right. Below the mouth of the Little Sandy (on the left), one will encounter a long slide rapids where the water zips quickly over very shallow rock tables and then terminates in several wide hydraulics. About 500 yards from the confluence with the Little Sandy is a six- to eight-foot falls. It can be recognized easily by the large shelf of rock jutting out from the left and forming a dam. The first shelf can be carefully run by cutting hard left below this ledge and then back across to near center for the main ledge. At higher levels run this straight over the left or far right.

A very long rapids or one rapids right after the other occurs just below the falls, and this is where the big action is found. Several steep drops over ledges around blind bends require quick decisions and paddle responses. This continues until the take-out. This area is usually a good Class IV run except in very low water. Paddlers in trouble may want to take out at the rustic cabin on the right just below the mouth of Sovereign Run and Corner Rapids. The approach to the bridge is tricky. At normal water levels, it's easiest to start in the center and then cut sharply to the right. At high levels the far left is no problem.

Put in below the dam at Bruceton Mills. Take out just under the Rockville bridge on the left. When parking, be careful not to block access to the cottages. Rockville can be reached from "73/73" crossing over Laurel Run. Take the left fork twice. The Big Sandy can also be run starting on Laurel Run at "73/73." For the gauge, see the end of the description of the Lower Big Sandy.

Lower Section, Rockville to Cheat River

The most stunning aspect of the Lower Big Sandy is that it has five of the most distinctive and most memorable Class IV–VI whitewater rapids on the entire East Coast. These are: Big Sandy Falls (Wonder Falls), Zoom Flume, Little Splat, Big Splat, and First Island. These rapids are truly unique compared to other rivers. Add to this a pristine mountain setting and expert boaters have a truly stupendous trip.

The Lower Big Sandy is an exciting, beautiful, piquant mistress who shows occasional flares of bad temper to even the most experienced paddlers. However, this five-and-a-half mile trip is perhaps the most scenic and most interesting whitewater in northern West Virginia. Possibly the "new" Blackwater which was changed by the November 1985 flood is more difficult because of its continuous nature.

Diana Kendrick running Wonder Falls of the Big Sandy. Photo by Paul Marshall.

110 Big Sandy Creek

Nevertheless, it does not have the huge vertical drops of the Lower Big Sandy.

Although the banks are choked with rhododendron, the necessary scouting and portaging are not difficult. If a walk-out is necessary, there is an old railroad bed on the right to within a mile of the Cheat River. Then you would have to figure how to get over to the left where the only road reaches the river at Jenkinsburg.

There are countless difficulties on this trip and numerous Class III–IV rapids not described here. Parts of the course are hazardous and require scouting and/or carrying. At 1.5 miles there is a rather difficult sequence terminating in 18-foot Big Sandy Falls, known also as Wonder Falls. The Class III–IV rapids approaching the falls has a fairly steep three-part drop on the left into a pool just above this falls. Scout and use safety measures. Carry the falls on the right. At most normal levels, Big Sandy Falls can be run on the left side of the main current, as the cover of this book indicates. If running the falls, it is critical that the vertical angle of your boat be 45 degrees as you drop over the falls. Too vertical an angle means you could dive too deep and crunch your bow on submerged rocks below the falls. Too horizontal an angle could mean a very flat landing at the bottom which could have serious consequences for your back.

The next series of rapids is busy for a quarter mile, followed by a broad ledge split by a large rock in midstream. This is known as Undercut Rock rapids (Class IV). Scout this rapids. The passage on the right ends in a big curler which throws even good boaters under an undercut rock. This is most dangerous at very low levels (around five feet on the gauge). At medium or high levels (when there is sufficient water), run more safely just left of the large undercut rock.

The next biggie is Zoom Flume, a steep eight- to ten-foot, Class IV drop which is easier than it looks and even more exciting. Scouting is again recommended to see the twisting flume. You can enter from river left to avoid being disoriented by the holes and ledges which interfere with a straight shot down the flume. Then work right to catch the flume properly. The cheese-grater rock shelf below has taken off a lot of elbow skin.

Get back out of your boat, if you are still in it, and scout the next rapids, Little Splat. This is one of the most complex and tricky Class IV–V rapids anywhere in West Virginia. The upper part can be boat scouted. It is safest to finish the lower part on the right (a relatively straight shot), because the lower left route has a reversal which has thrown boats into a nasty pinning slot. However, at lower levels (below six feet) the easier route on the right dries up and the left route becomes even more technical and complex.

Big Splat is next. Very aptly named, it is a complex double rapids dropping a total of over 25 feet. Although run by the most experienced boaters, this is clearly a Class VI rapids. If you find yourself wanting to run Big Splat, you should seriously question not only your skills but also your motives. The risks are significant and the margin for error is alarmingly small.

The eight- to ten-foot drop guarding the approach to Big

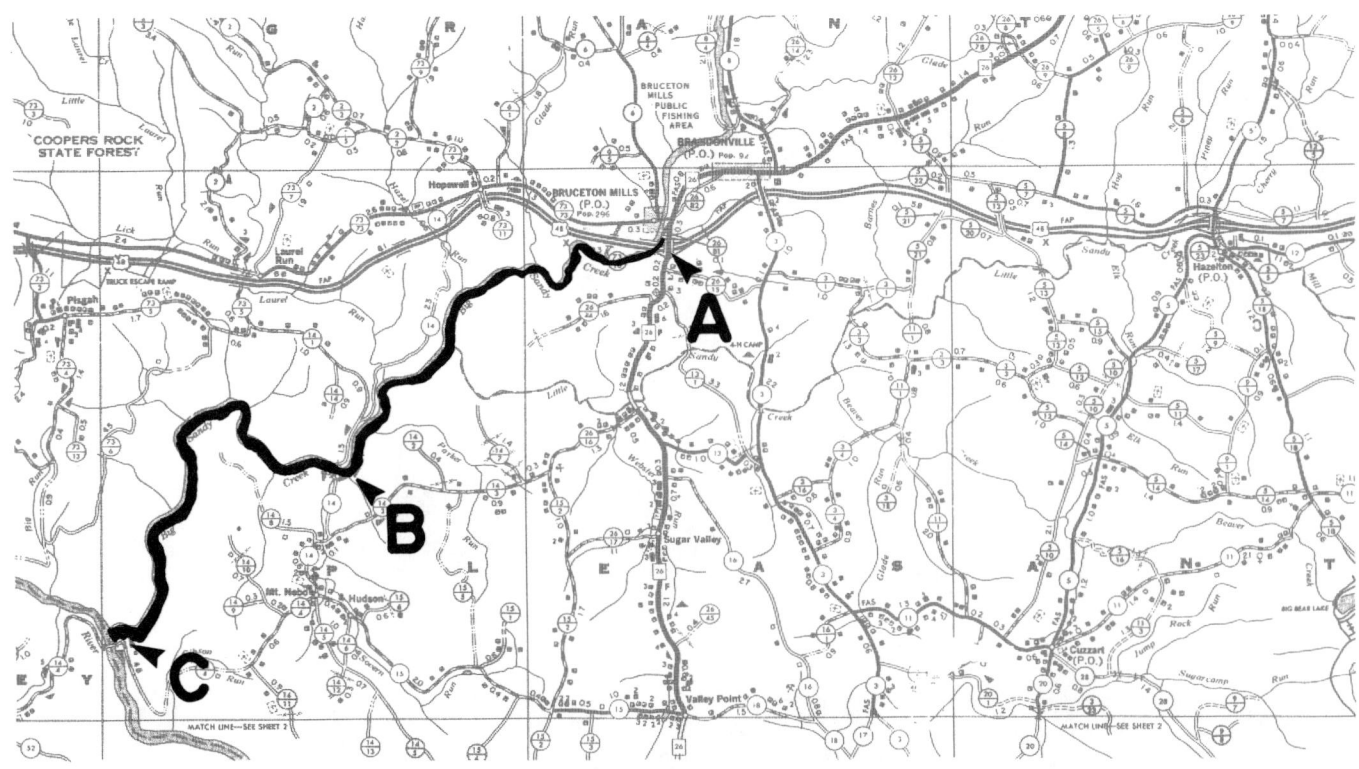

Splat falls below is perhaps the most dangerous feature. When scouting from the right bank, the dangers in this Class V+ approach rapids are well concealed. Beginning as a sloping ledge, the current drops directly towards an undercut, partially submerged slab rock. The right side of the chute ends under the downstream corner of another large undercut boulder. Almost all of the current then drops into a horseshoe-shaped hydraulic from which swimming would certainly be the only escape.

However, one glance at the base of Big Splat falls below should convince anyone that swimming here is simply unthinkable because after a short and very fast pool, the entire river drops 16 to 18 feet onto Splat Rock. Some of the water goes through sieves on the right, some underneath Splat Rock, and some pillows off Splat Rock—forming a frightening hole at the base of the falls. This area is fit for neither man nor boat. Fortunately, no one has been trapped in the approach rapids yet and most injuries have been limited to ankles bent by pitoning on Splat Rock. Portage both Big Splat drops on the right.

In the section below here, there is a long stretch of continuous Class III–IV rapids. Then you come to an island. Scout the rapids next to this island. Appropriately known as First Island, this is a Class V rapids with two drops. Take the first drop to land just to the right of a submerged rock below. Make sure you angle slightly right in going off the drop to miss this rock because it is a real boat buster. Then work quickly left to an eddy hidden behind a car-sized boulder where you run the second drop from left to right. These two drops are very technical and tight at low water levels with pinning and pitoning possibilities when the rocks at the bottom are not padded.

Soon below First Island there is a second island. Here there is a slalom boulder garden (Class III–IV) which should

---

Section: Bruceton Mills to Rockville

Counties: Preston (WV)

USGS Quads: Bruceton Mills, Valley Point

Suitable for: Day trips

Skill Level: Strong intermediate at lower levels; advanced at higher levels

Months Runnable: Winter/spring

Interest Highlights: Progressive slalom in wooded setting

Scenery: Pretty to beautiful

Difficulty: Class I-IV

Average Width: 60 feet

Velocity: Moderate to fast

Gradient: 4 miles at 9 feet per mile; 2 miles at 45 feet per mile

Runnable Water Levels:
  Minimum: Rockville gauge 5.8 feet; Bruceton Mills gauge 0 feet
  Maximum: Rockville gauge 7 feet; Bruceton Mills gauge 2.5 feet

Hazards: 6- to 8-foot falls and long rapids below Little Sandy; trees in river

Scouting: Falls and long rapids below Little Sandy

Portages: None

Rescue Index: Remote

Source of Additional Information: National Weather Service (301) 899-7378, Rockville gauge

Access Points	River Miles	Shuttle Miles
A–B	6.0	8.0

Access Point Ratings:
  A - Bruceton Mills, very good
  B - Rockville, good if you have a vehicle with clearance for the road

---

Section: Rockville to Cheat River

Counties: Preston (WV)

USGS Quads: Bruceton Mills, Valley Point

Suitable for: Day trips

Skill Level: Expert

Months Runnable: Winter, spring; occasionally summer

Interest Highlights: Five unusually distinctive rapids in a spectacular gorge

Scenery: Beautiful

Difficulty: Class IV-V with one Class VI

Average Width: 60 feet

Velocity: Fast

Gradient: 2 miles at 30 feet per mile; 4 miles at 80 feet per mile

Runnable Water Levels:
  Minimum: 0 feet on Bruceton Mills gauge; 5.2 to 5.8 on Rockville Gauge (5.2 feet can be very technical; open boaters and some decked boaters prefer a minimum of 5.8)
  Maximum: 2 feet on Bruceton Mills gauge; 6.5-7.0 on Rockville gauge

Hazards: Big Sandy Falls (Wonder Falls), Undercut Rock, Zoom Flume, Little Splat, Big Splat, and First Island rapids

Scouting: All six of the above rapids, at least

Portages: Possibly one or more of the six rapids

Rescue Index: Remote

Source of Additional Information: National Weather Service (301) 899-7378 for Rockville gauge

Access Points	River Miles	Shuttle Miles
B–C	5.5	5.0

Access Point Ratings:
  B - Rockville, good if your vehicle has clearance for the road
  C - Cheat River, good (but not a good road)

be run right. Three and a half miles and 272 feet (down) later, the paddler, who may be hiking by now, will reach the Cheat River near Jenkinsburg.

To get to the put-in at Rockville, see the description at the end of the Upper Big Sandy. The take-out is on the left at the mouth of the Big Sandy on the Cheat near the Cheat Canyon take-out. Take the steep trail up through the laurel thicket to the parking area. Jenkinsburg may be reached by continuing on the road from Rockville (from the left side of the river)—turn right at the top of the hill, then take a left at the next crossing and proceed to Mount Nebo School. At Mount Nebo bear hard right to Jenkinsburg. This is terrible driving and almost as rough as the paddling.

The gauge generally used is a government gauge on the bridge at Rockville which is now available on the phone via satellite. The National Weather Service telephone number is (301) 899-7378. There is also a paddler's gauge under the Bruceton Mills bridge. The correlation between the two is complex but good. Rockville = ¾ (Bruceton + 1) + 5. The recommended levels for Rockville at Bruceton are 0−2 feet. The painted gauge is very hard to read. The Lower Big Sandy is runnable many times in the spring.

Paul Marshall approaches Big Splat Falls on the Big Sandy. Photo by Joan Heldrith.

Cheat River

The "Narrows" Section

The Cheat leaves the town of Rowlesburg quietly and broadly. Soon, it becomes narrower and begins to pick up speed. The put-in for the "Narrows" is opposite a worked-out limestone mine approximately three miles below Rowlesburg. Here you encounter the first big waves below Rowlesburg called Cave Rapids. For the rest of this five-mile trip, the rapids become increasingly more difficult. There are good rescue spots after each rapids, but in high water (three to four feet) it's not so easy. After passing several Class II–III rapids, the paddler enters a long series of similar rapids, properly called the "Narrows."

In the first significant rapids, the entire river is necked down by the presence of an automobile-sized boulder (Calamity Rock) in midstream which makes passage at any level difficult. Those unfamilar with this Class III–IV rapids should scout it. Although this boulder is largely out of the water at roughly 1.5 feet on the "new" Albright bridge gauge, it is completely submerged when the reading is around 2.5 feet. This should give the paddler a healthy respect for what just a few inches increase in water level means on the Cheat. Usually this boulder should be run through the passage to the right. At very high levels, however, it's best to run along the left bank, whether in boat or afoot. Keep in mind that there are two problems—entering the passage correctly, which is not always easy due to the combination of waves immediately above it, and managing the powerful drop at the end of the chute. This passage will swamp an open canoe without floatation at any level and will flip a raft in high water.

There are three major rapids below this boulder that also pass through narrow confines. This creates a tremendous turbulence and results in powerful crosscurrents and eddies. In high water one simply blasts through the standing five-foot waves and tries to maintain stability, while at lower levels one must be more precise in maneuvering around the exposed boulders. The paddler inexperienced with big water might be fooled into thinking that he can "sneak" down the sides of these narrow rapids in the relatively calmer water, but usually he gets sucked over into the big stuff by the high velocity of the main channel (sort of like Bernoulli's Principle).

The first of these major rapids (Wind Rapids) is the most difficult in high water and consists of a wide hydraulic before one reaches the chute. This hydraulic is best taken on the far left. There is also a severe hydraulic about halfway down the chute on the left, always an interesting scene. The second rapids (Rocking Horse) is the longest narrow passage, 100 yards of turbulence. The last rapids is less severe but still interesting. There is not much left before the take-out at Lick Run after a hopefully enjoyable five-mile trip. Note that the land at the take-out is private property; landowners have been cooperative in the past, but get permission first.

The Cheat Canyon

The Cheat River has the largest undammed watershed east of the Mississippi. This fact became painfully clear on Monday, November 4, 1985. On that day, after four to six inches of rain in the previous 72 hours, a very strong low-pressure vortex swept through the Cheat headwaters. The 15-mile wide center of this storm left another eight inches of rain in 12 hours. The result was flooding not only of the Cheat tributaries (Shavers Fork, Glady Fork, Laurel Fork, Dry Fork, and the Blackwater), but also the watersheds of the South Branch of the Potomac, Greenbrier, Tygart, Maury, and James Rivers.

During the early morning hours of November 5, unsuspecting residents along the Cheat were awakened to water rising with alarming speed that gave them only brief moments to escape. The river crested at 7:30 that morning in Albright, completely covering the Route 26 bridge at the canyon put-in and taking with it the homes and possessions of those who had lived nearby. For example, near the Route 26 bridge, the gas station that paddlers used to call for gauge readings became a crater. The estimated flow of the Cheat was 250,000 cfs at least! The water's force substantially reshaped the banks and river bed as it descended the narrow 25-foot-per-mile canyon below Albright. This was a flood of geologic intensity, perhaps occurring only every one to two thousand years. Much of Albright was destroyed, and the Cheat will never be the same.

For those who remember the preflood Cheat, this eleven-mile trip through the changed canyon is now even more awe-inspiring and presents a rare opportunity to see how nature dramatically shapes rivers. Changes wrought by the 1985 flood are immediately seen—whether putting in at the Route 26 bridge in what is left of Albright or at the Cheat Canyon Campground nearly a mile downstream (now only half its previous size). The flood substantially rearranged the Cheat Canyon's channels and restructured its rapids. High water marks and a scouring line where trees were stripped and toppled are 30 feet above the river now. Much of the soil formerly along the banks is in Cheat Lake eight miles below Jenkinsburg.

The Cheat Canyon has traditionally been one of the more difficult and challenging runs in the East. If the Gauley and

114 Cheat River

other streams have stolen some of this reputation, then the new Cheat is here to reclaim a good measure of it! Low-water runs are technical boatbusters with more undercuts and pinning rocks than before. Higher water trades off some of the technical line picking and rock dodging for a pushy big water run full of boiling eddies, pillowed boulders, big wave trains, and, oh yes, BIG HOLES. At high water, the Cheat can be a killer, literally. All of this greets the paddler who follows the Cheat's new boulder-strewn course through a spectacular wilderness canyon.

Unprepared boaters should stay off this river. Sometimes rollers in decked boats and anyone who hasn't mastered good boat control and water reading skills had better go elsewhere. Massive boulders litter the riverbed, blocking the view through each rapids and contributing to the complexity of the run. The canyon is steep-walled and remote. Anyone undertaking this run should realize that it is far from any roads. A smashup with a lost paddle, broken boat or injury puts the paddler miles from any help in country that is extremely difficult to traverse by foot. To walk out of

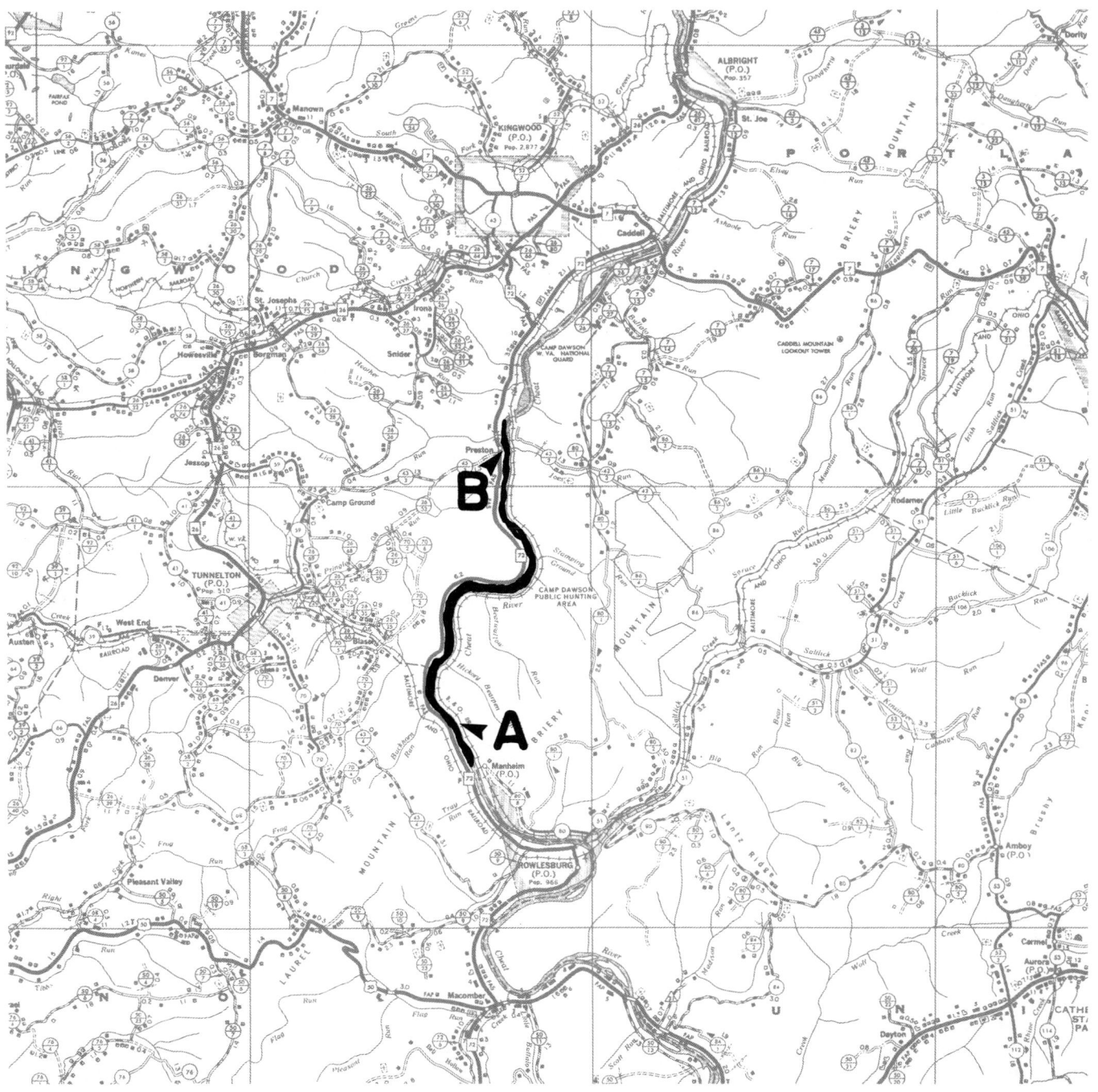

Bottom hole of Big Nasty, Cheat Canyon, flipping a raft at 3.5 feet. Photo by Greg Green.

Section: Narrows (below Rowlesburg to Lick Run)

Counties: Preston (WV)

USGS Quads: Rowlesburg and Kingwood

Suitable for: Day trips

Skill Level: Intermediate at moderate levels; advanced at high levels

Months Runnable: Virtually entire year

Interest Highlights: Limestone caves near put-in

Scenery: Fair to pretty in spots

Difficulty: Class II–IV

Average Width: 100–150 feet

Velocity: Fast

Gradient: 20 feet per mile

Runnable Water Levels:
  Minimum: 0.5 feet on Albright bridge, Route 26
  Maximum: 4.5 feet on Albright bridge, Route 26

Hazards: Big waves in high water (3–4 feet on the gauge)

Scouting: Calamity Rock

Portages: None

Rescue Index: Accessible

Source of Additional Information: National Weather Service, Pittsburgh (412) 644-2890; Cheat Canyon Campground (304) 329-1299

Access Points	River Miles	Shuttle Miles
A–B	5.0	5.0

Access Point Ratings at both put-in A and take-out B are good, but get permission to cross the property at Lick Run.

the canyon straight up takes two hours, and you still may be miles from the nearest farmhouse. There is a good trail on the right side of the river, but it is much higher than the river.

Some chutes of the canyon are very narrow, but the river gauge at the Albright bridge is located in a wide shallow spot. Hence, a two-inch difference on the gauge makes a whale of a difference downstream, translating into feet in many instances. This and the steep and close undammed drainage from many tributaries combine to form a situation not found on most eastern rivers. Snowmelt or heavy rains upstream can raise the gauge at a rate of feet per hour. This translates to even more sudden and dramatic changes in the constricted canyon below. The river has been known to rise two feet while a run was in progress!

The "new" Cheat gauge on Route 26 gives higher water levels compared to the "old" gauge until 5.0 feet is reached. Then, both gauges are about equal. The lower the level, the wider the spread between new and old gauges. For example, 3.0 feet on the new gauge equates to about 2.5 feet on the old gauge, while 2.0 feet on the new gauge is about 1.25 feet on the old gauge. Hence, anything below 2.0 feet on the new gauge will be extremely technical and in places scrapy. For decked boaters, some walking may be necessary below 1.5 feet. We estimate the bare minimum is perhaps a 1.0-foot level for open boaters wearing hiking boots. This compares with −0.5 feet on the old gauge as the absolute minimum.

The most challenging aspect of this trip is the number of complex rapids in an inaccessible setting. A detailed description of each rapids is impractical as there are still over 30 (count 'em) rapids rated Class III or more. Accordingly, scouting is not feasible in many cases. Also, several of the Class IV rapids are separated only by short pools or no pools in higher water. The remoteness of the canyon and the cold water in winter and spring make the Cheat a Class IV–V run in high water (over four feet).

The first rapids is Decision (Class III+). It is 1.5 miles below Albright where the Canyon begins. This rapids starts as a wide rubble bar and gradually narrows as it drops over smaller rocks and ledges forming several holes. Through this upper part, a left-of-center line works best, but move right toward a house-sized boulder during a short pool (or wave train at higher levels) before the river drops over a set of large eroded ledges. This rapids is similar to numerous others in the Canyon not described in this narrative and is certainly easier than many. If Decision is too much, please take the short carry out. Your body and boat will thank you.

After about another mile of pools and three significant smaller drops comes Beech Run (Class III–IV). Enter this long rapids on river right before moving left to dodge rocks or holes depending on water level. Connoisseurs of fine waves will groan when seeing how the 1985 flood has affected this run in higher water, but beware. About two thirds of the way through and just below the steepest section, a group of closely spaced rocks obstruct the main channel at levels below about 3.0 feet. At higher levels, one can go left of these rocks, but below 2.5 feet, technical moves are needed to miss them on the right. Be careful, there have been pins here.

The next big rapids, and the one to sway the minds of those who haven't seen any significant changes from the 1985 flood so far is Big Nasty (Class IV at medium levels and Class IV–V at higher levels). About a half-mile and two easier rapids below Beech Run, the river forms a large pool just before a right-hand bend. The left bank is a steep, high mountain here. Former canyon visitors will note the absence of Maui surfing wave on the top left at medium-high levels. (Too bad!) At levels above 3.0 feet, scout from the left bank. First-timers and those with foggy memories should scout in any case. Above Big Nasty (also called Old Nasty), flooding has deposited many small- to medium-sized boulders, building up the entire riverbed to raise the level of the pool there. The small rapids below Big Nasty has also been obstructed by more rubble, also raising the level of the pool there. In between these pools, the entire river has been channeled towards the right bank and over a ledge. The result is a steep fast rapids aiming all of the Cheat's water and anything on or in it into ONE BIG HOLE. Whoever named Big Nasty years ago must have had a premonition. At 2.0 feet the question "What Hole?" seems appropriate, but by 3.0 feet, the hole is hard for decked boats to punch and fully capable of holding or recirculating floating objects. Around 3.5 feet, it becomes most nasty, flipping and holding ten-man rafts and recirculating swimmers more than once. At 5.0 feet Big Nasty is a real circus. First, rafts and boaters must take a tight-rope line on the approach. Then, for those who slip off the tight-rope, the hole pulls repeated stunts like violently flipping and juggling up to three large rafts at once. Finally, the mega-hole pulls a real disappearing act with all swimmers—making them reappear up to 50 feet downstream. Above 5.0 feet, the hole is fortunately too violent to recirculate swimmers; it just gets BIGGER! Regardless of the water level, successful lines all aim to the extreme left. Still, it is necessary to negotiate several lateral waves or diagonal holes constantly pushing towards the hole. A portage on the left is an honorable option.

Even though Maui wave above Big Nasty is gone, a super surfing wave/hole still remains 200 yards downstream on river left. It is after you cross the cobble rapids forming the pool below Big Nasty. This usually benign hole is called Typewriter because you can easily move back and forth on it. Covering the left half of the river, it is most gentle on the right edge.

After one more rapids, the paddler reaches Even Nastier (Class III–IV). This long rapids is entered just right of center and propels all comers through a respectable wave train leading river left. From here it is either boiling eddies or ultra-quick boat scouting for the remaining 100 yards to avoid significant boulders or holes, depending on water level. At higher levels, this rapids can be entered on river left.

The middle third of the trip (a good three miles) is known as the Doldrums. Here you have Prudential Rock, a few playing waves and lovely scenery. This "flat" section with half a dozen significant lesser rapids ends as one enters the last third of the trip. This last section is the most demanding since it has several complex heavy rapids.

In place of Cue Ball (Class III, a rock boulder drop formerly on the right), the river has carved a whole new bed with dynamic wave and hole surfing opportunities on the left. A mirror of the Lower Yough's Swimmers Rapids (see the chapter on Pennsylvania), this new rapids at about 2.5 feet is one of the best playing spots in the state. Some folks now call this rapids Mis-Cue, because of the right-to-left change in the river bed.

Next comes Zoo rapids (also called Anticipation). It can be run straight on the far right. Or, enter this Class III rapid from river center through a hard-to-spot chute just behind Elephant Rock and then make a hard left turn. At low water it must be run down the far right.

The appearance of a high sandstone cliff on river left bisected by a 60-foot falls marks High Falls in the distance. However, Teardrop is first. In running it, do not key on an old familiar landmark here: Green's Hole (a hydraulic backed by a huge boulder) has been replaced by Green's Eddy.

Teardrop's 100-yard course begins with an easy boulder garden going from left to right. Then you reach the main drop. Enter this main drop close to the right and immediately work back to the left to avoid being pushed too far right into the pillows boiling off the ledge/hole strewn right bank. An alternate line starting and staying left through this heavy chute opens up in higher water, but watch out for a recently added mega-hole splitting the two lines at the top.

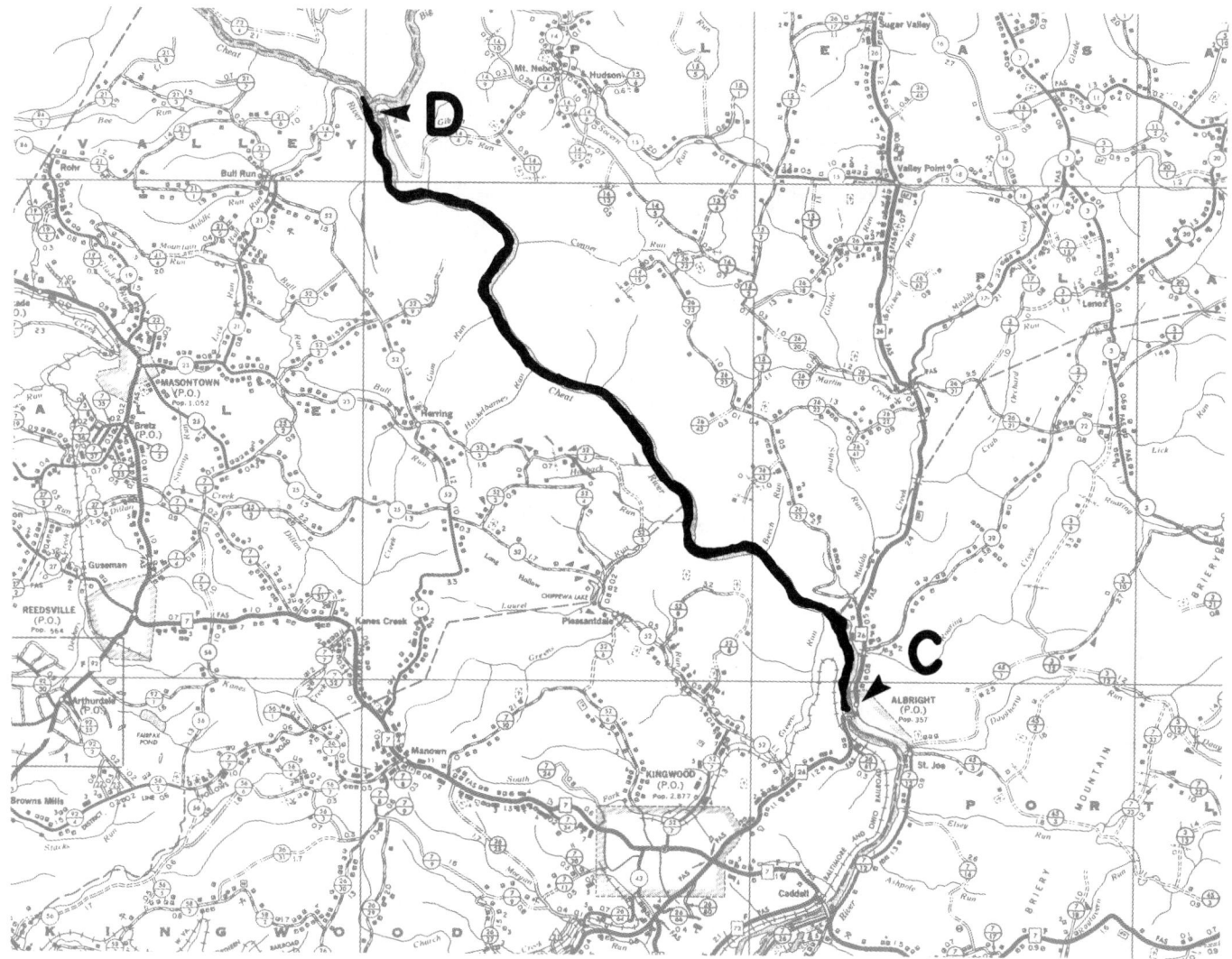

Section: Albright, WV 26 bridge to Jenkinsburg bridge

Counties: Preston (WV)

USGS Quads: Kingwood, Valley Point

Suitable for: Day trips

Skill Level: Advanced at moderate levels; expert at high levels

Months Runnable: Virtually entire year

Interest Highlights: Beautiful gorge marred by acid-stained tributaries near put-in, and the scouring of the November 1985 flood

Scenery: Pretty to beautiful

Difficulty: Class III–V

Average Width: 100–150 feet

Velocity: Fast

Gradient: 25 feet per mile

Runnable Water Levels:
  Minimum: 1.0 feet on Albright WV 26 bridge
  Maximum: 6.0 feet on Albright WV 26 bridge

Hazards: In low water: some undercut and pinning rocks. In high water, heavy water and big holes. The toughest rapids are Big Nasty, High Falls, and Upper Coliseum.

Scouting: At least Big Nasty (left), High Falls (right), Upper Coliseum (right), and Lower Coliseum (Pete Morgan's) at left

Portages: Possibly these same rapids at very high water levels

Rescue Index: Remote

Source of Additional Information: National Weather Service, Pittsburgh (412) 644-2890; Cheat Canyon Campground (304) 329-1299

Access Points	River Miles	Shuttle Miles
C–D	11.0	20 tough miles

Access Point Ratings: Put-in C is good. Though take-out D is good, the shuttle road is fair to poor; check before using this private property.

Entering the Cloud Chamber, Upper Coliseum, Cheat Canyon. Photo by Ed Grove.

By now it's obvious that the louder than usual roar is being echoed by those giant cliffs marking High Falls (Class IV at medium levels and Class IV–V at high levels). Reshaped into its present broken ledges by blasting to prevent log jams, this is a steep rapids studded with holes, and, at low water, shallow shelves and pinning rocks. Preferred canoe and kayak lines alternate from side to side with different water levels. Below 1.5 to 2.0 feet, this is a good place for decked boats in particular to start thinking of portaging (left or right). Low water lines on the left are better forfeited in favor of just right of center at levels around 2.5 feet. Above 3.5 feet, it's left of center again, and at 5.0 feet one goes a little further left through some enormous waves. Above 6.0 feet those waves become holes and the "sneak" on the right is something awesome. But don't memorize what you've read here. Scout this rapids first from the right and be careful, especially at low water.

If your adrenaline isn't pumping by now, you're not human. But wait. There's still a chance. Maze (Class III–IV) is proudly living up to its name with a brand new puzzle. Working from left to right through hard-to-spot lines is a must for missing deviously arranged and seemingly countless boulders (or holes in high water). It's more complex than before, and if you solve this puzzle, you win a chance at a trip through what's probably the most amazing adornment of the new Cheat: Coliseum is different!

Coliseum rapids (also known as Upper Coliseum) is THE place on the Cheat where an old fan will feel completely bewildered. Below Maze, eddy out on the right, upstream of a small tributary waterfall you will see on the right. Be sure to scout Coliseum (Class IV–V at medium levels and Class V at high levels). The best view is from a large rock on river right. Below 5.0 feet the entire river is channeled through a 50-foot wide section. The action begins with one of the most even natural hydraulics you'll ever see. It's aptly been dubbed Recyclotron. Almost covering the width of the channel below 3.5 feet, it can be missed on the left or skirted on the right. This hole offers some dynamic surfing or low-volume boat "blasting" for experts, but beware, it can be very dangerous at certain levels and recirculates with a long backwash. In any case, eddy out on the right below this hydraulic before making your next move.

Less than 50 feet below Recyclotron hydraulic, the entire river drops 6.0 feet over a sloping shelf which ends in a jagged diagonal ledge. The rapids/hole formed by this ledge is a notorious raft flipper and has been christened Cyclotron. To avoid Cyclotron, moderate water lines aim at a triangular rock (Mind Bender Rock) forming the extreme left edge of the river-wide chute which turns and accelerates a beam of water down into a strange and violent hole (called Cloud Chamber). Ferry over from the right eddy below Recyclotron to ride (as far left as possible) the pillow on Mind Bender Rock and to clip the hole below. Cloud Chamber gets nasty at 4.0 feet or so. Alternate lines open up with more water. At about 3.5 to 5.0 feet the right side can be run, but be ready for some challenging hole/wave action and have a bomb-proof roll ready. Above 5.0 feet think about sneaking left across a sloping boulder garden. At all levels be sure to set throw lines (on the right) and rescue boats to pick up errant accelerated particles of boats and bodies after they pass through the Cloud Chamber or Cyclotron. Portage on the right.

Cyclotron Rapid, Upper Coliseum, Cheat Canyon. Photo by Paul Marshall.

Move far left after Cyclotron and note the remains of Devil's Trap as you approach Pete Morgan's rapids (also called Lower Coliseum). When you reach Pete Morgan's, be sure to look for a house-sized boulder near river right. This is Picture Rock. Slightly rounded, it shows signs of being rolled by the 1985 flood for some distance. All its surfaces are new.

Pete Morgan's (Class III–IV) is named after a former Albright resident who took gauge readings and befriended paddlers for many years. It too has changed so please scout it. The old familiar line down the right below Picture Rock is now much nastier (Class IV–V). It is better to take a steep narrow chute down river left. At medium levels the two drops lead to a huge fun wave. Be careful of this rapid in low water, though, as the flow is almost equally divided and there are lots of shallow rocks in either passage. In the pool below, pause to marvel at the fluted columns carved into the base of the Greenbrier limestone.

After Pete Morgan's there is one long Class III generally run left. From here things calm down as the Cheat offers several fine but less challenging rapids in the remaining two miles to Jenkinsburg. Just after the ninth mile of this eleven-mile trip, there is a waterfall on the right. Here the slate outcrops are a good place to look for fossilized shells and catch some sun.

Anyone who gets to know the new Cheat will surely come to love this river. It's unique, but there is a problem. Preston County, West Virginia is classic coal country. About a dozen old strip mines in the Cheat drainage just above the canyon were never reclaimed. Consequently, the water is polluted and so acidic you could possibly use it to clean jewelry. The food chain has been completely destroyed. Fish entering these waters from upstream are caught later with only pebbles and bits of coal in their stomachs. If you can think of ways to help the Cheat, please try. If you hear of action to restore life to this magnificent river, do support it.

Another controversy stirring since the flood is the Rawlsburg Dam construction project upstream. Stay informed and be active to help protect this wonderful river.

For the shuttle, put in at the Albright bridge or, to avoid some flat, uninteresting water, at one of two campgrounds a mile downstream on Route 26. The take-out on river right at Jenkinsburg is hard to find. Take Route 26 south to Kingwood and go right on Route 7 to Masontown. Turn right at the drugstore on Main and Depot Streets and take this road to the fork. Turn left and continue on to Bull Run and a second fork. Take this to the right down the extremely steep, narrow road to Jenkinsburg. This is a Class IV road when it's dry! A shorter but rougher shuttle is via Valley Point and Mount Nebo on the right side of the river. (See the Big Sandy shuttle and map in this chapter.) From the river, paddle on down below the bridge almost to the mouth of the Big Sandy. An easy trail leads up to the parking area. You can avoid doing this horrendous shuttle yourself. A very likeable chap named Glenn Miller will take you out of the canyon to Albright for a fee. Just give him a call at (304) 379-3404. Call early though—he has a small truck and it's a 45-minute trip one way from the take-out to Albright.

Lost River

This section of the Lost River, called the Dry Gorge section, is the most unique and best-named river in West Virginia because it doesn't always exist! In low water the river actually disappears into the ground just beyond the bridge above Wardensville, thus leaving it indeed dry for most of the year. The river apparently traverses some unknown Stygian course only to emerge several miles away, seemingly *de novo*, to form the Cacapon River.

The Lost River Dry Gorge can only be run in high water when the underground river can't handle all of the flow and the river spills over into the flood channel cut around the mountain. This is truly a fantastic situation made even better because of the beautiful gorge surrounding the Lost River on this section. This three- to six-mile trip starts calmly, builds up to some tough Class III–IV rapids, and then calms down again for the last three miles. The paddler can take out after the first three miles at a utility road, or continue down the remaining three miles of milder water to the Route 259 bridge. The rock formations, hemlocks and sycamores lining the bank add to the beauty of this trip.

For the first half mile one warms up with a couple of riffles and two Class II rapids, the second of which passes a rock face on the right. The first good Class II–III action is about a quarter mile below where there are some gorgeous high cliffs on the left. Then, after more than a mile of paddling, one comes to a long strong Class III which is a series of large waves with some holes at higher water.

Just after this and as the river turns left, paddlers will come to an almost river-wide two-foot ledge/hydraulic. Get out on river right above this hydraulic and scout since a Class III–IV rapids is just below. The rapids goes through some congestion before dropping over a three-foot ledge through a narrow passage at the end. Scout the bottom passage which is sometimes choked with a log. At lower levels, make a hard right turn at the bottom of the ledge to avoid a rock several yards downstream. At higher levels, you can avoid the worst of the first ledge/hydraulic on the extreme left and work toward the center to finish the rapids, making sure to avoid a nasty curler which develops on the right side of the final narrow drop.

Below this rapids is a Class II–III drop followed by a great Class III wave train next to a sloping rock face on the left. This latter rapids is a great ride on the left at two feet on the Route 55 put-in gauge. About a quarter-mile later, the paddler goes left or right of some rocks in the center of the river.

At this point, the paddler should become quickly alert, particularly at higher water. Just below is a Class III–IV series of ledges. At low water there are seven of these large and small ledges (count 'em) with accompanying hydraulics. At high water, the smaller ledges are washed out and the big ledges form nasty holes, making this a very steep and really mean rapids. Generally, these should be run just to the right of center. Get out and scout if you are unsure of your route; there is a four-foot low-water bridge just below these ledges which forms a nasty hydraulic to snare errant boats and boaters. Portage this low-water bridge on the right.

Having made this portage, look carefully at the boulder-studded strong Class III rapids just below. Generally, this is run left of center. At two feet on the Route 55 gauge, how-

Cathy Lowry in Landslide Rapids after the November 1985 flood. Photo by Ed Grove.

ever, there are some significant holes to punch/avoid, particularly at the end of the rapids on the left. Scout this rapids if you can't see a clear path.

About a quarter mile below this, the river turns left, and the Cacapon River reaches the surface again. Here the underwater river miraculously reappears from a series of small springs and the volume of the river fascinatingly doubles. Not far below is the heaviest rapids of the trip, Landslide Rapids (Class III–IV).

Prior to the November 1985 flood, Landslide Rapids divided around an island. The left channel was a much tamer passage. However, the flood has choked the left side with rocks, making all the water go down the right side. This rapid should be scouted and approached very cautiously —the channel has many rocks from a landslide created years ago. Approach the rapids close to the left bank of the former island and scout from the left. At lower levels, one can maneuver either to the right or left after the first drop, proceed down the respective channels and take narrow passages through the final drops until the old left side passageway connects with the main river. At higher levels, one should enter the constricted first drop left of center and work to the left to finish.

About 50 yards below Landslide is a wonderful low-risk surfing spot at most levels. This is followed several hundred yards later by a good Class III which is a great rollercoaster at about two feet on the put-in gauge.

Now the river splits around an island. If you are using the shorter take-out on the maintenance road off Route 55, go to the right of this island or you will miss that take-out. After a couple of minor drops on the right-hand channel, you will be at the take-out.

If you go left around the island, you will see the remains of another low-water bridge which was washed downstream by the 1985 flood. From here it is about three miles of relatively uneventful water to the Route 259 take-out just beyond a sewage treatment plant.

Because of the water volume required, this is generally a spring trip after rainy weather or during snowmelt. Generally, 4.0 feet of water on the Great Cacapon River gauge at Capon Bridge or nearly 4.0 feet on the Cootes Store gauge is required before the Route 55 bridge west of Wardensville will read 0.0 for paddling. If the Lost is too low, the gentler Cacapon (from Capon Bridge to Forks of Cacapon) with its exceptional scenery is an alternative.

Section: WV 55 bridge above Wardensville to WV 259 bridge below Wardensville

Counties: Hardy (WV)

USGS Quads: Wardensville

Suitable for: Day trips

Skill Level: Intermediate at lower levels; advanced at higher levels

Months Runnable: November through April

Interest Highlights: Pretty gorge with striking rock formations near the beginning of the trip

Scenery: Generally pretty to beautiful

Difficulty: Class II–IV

Average Width: 75 feet

Velocity: Fast

Gradient: 40 feet per mile

Runnable Water Levels: Call the National Weather Service (see below); the Great Cacapon River gauge should be at least 4 feet.
  Minimum: 0 feet on Rt. 55 bridge west of Wardensville
  Maximum: 3 to 4 feet on Rt. 55 bridge west of Wardensville

Hazards: Ledges just above the low-water bridge; low water bridge; Landslide Rapids

Scouting: Constricted rapids over 1 mile into the trip; ledges above and rapids below low-water bridge; Landslide Rapids

Portages: Low-water bridge (carry on river right)

Rescue Index: Accessible to remote but accessible

Source of Additional Information: Call the National Weather Service (301) 899-7378; the Cootes Store gauge should be nearly 4 feet. See water level information, above.

Access Points	River Miles	Shuttle Miles
A–B	3.0	3.0
A–C	6.0	5.0

Access Point Ratings:
  A - Rt. 55 bridge, excellent
  B - utility road near Wardensville, good
  C - Rt. 259 bridge, good

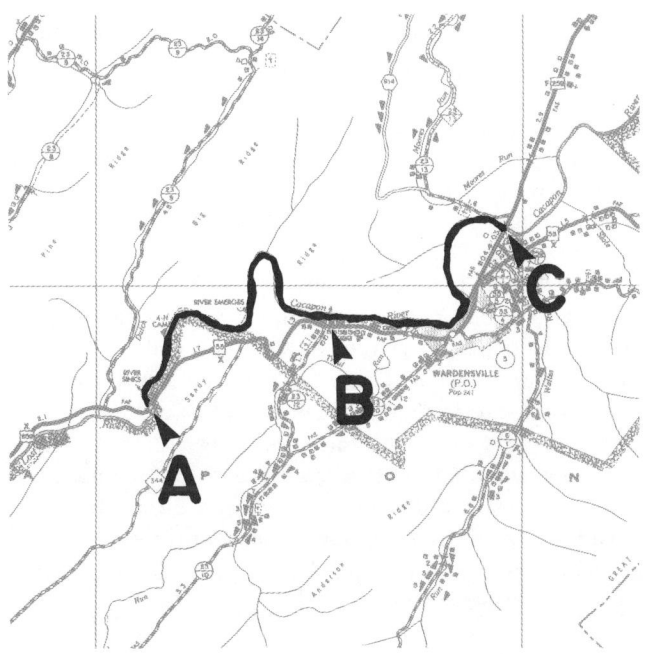

Cacapon River

This very popular river in eastern West Virginia has exquisite scenery and challenging whitewater for the intermediate paddler. This twelve-mile section is a good float-fishing stream for open boats, but at medium and high levels requires skills well beyond those of the novice to negotiate safely. It has drowned foolish, inexperienced paddlers. The Cacapon is often up in the winter, and the snow-covered banks combined with the unusual rock formations make this a highly recommended run for the experienced paddler. At lower levels on warmer days, carefully shepherded novices can make this run.

The trip from the Capon Bridge begins with flat water and a few riffles flowing through open farmland. After about three miles, the river heads to the left past some gorgeous high rocky cliffs on the right, and things begin to get more interesting. Soon after this bend, there are a couple of Class II rapids. Approaching four miles into the trip there is an alternate river left put-in on a secondary road (thereby shortening this section by almost a third).

Soon thereafter, the river turns right, and immediately after a couple of mild Class II rapids, you will see a large rock on the left and a horizon line in front of you. This is Darby's Nose Ledge (Class II–III). Novices should run this two-foot ledge on the extreme right or pull over to the right bank to scout for an alternate route over this drop. Below the ledge are nice surfing spots for the adventurous and a beach on river right for lunch.

For the next three miles the trip is gentle with a few Class I–II rapids to add interest. One then comes to Fairy Falls, a delightful spot on river left where water gently cascades into the river over a lush rocky face. It is indeed a nice shower stop in hot weather and a photo opportunity in all weather.

Not far below Fairy Falls, the paddler will notice a very interesting rock formation on the left which appears to be a triangular anticline. This is Chapel Rock which signals the second significant ledge of the trip. This two- to three-foot drop (Class II–III) is always runnable on the far left, but novices should scout it from the left bank to ascertain the correct passage. With sufficient water, the right side is easier, but novices should look at it first.

Roughly a half-mile below Chapel Rock is the biggest drop of the trip. A large rock on the right bank and a horizon line warn you that Caudy's Castle Ledge is just ahead. Novices and intermediates not familiar with this ledge should scout this drop of a good three feet; it is a Class II–III in low water and a Class III in high water. In low water, the passage is on the right, but there is a risk of banging your stern pretty hard. With nine inches or more of water on the gauge, the best passage is just left of center, but it requires more skill in maneuvering.

Castle rock, Cacapon River. Photo by Roger Corbett.

As you paddle beyond this ledge, be sure to admire Caudy's Castle on the left. This spectacular rock formation is worth a hike to the top for those who have the time and inclination. The remaining couple of miles or so to the takeout on river right at Route 127 are primarily flat water.

Although the put-in and take-out bridges have canoeing gauges, one cannot improve on the advice of veteran paddlers Roger Corbett and Louis Matacia who warn against scraping on the first riffle below the US 50 bridge (which can be estimated by inspection). The Cacapon can be boring if the water is too low. At such levels taking a hike is more rewarding. Gauge readings may be obtained from the National Weather Service, (301) 899-7378. The Great Cacapon gauge should be at least two feet.

Section: Capon Bridge to WV Rt. 127 bridge

Counties: Hampshire (WV)

USGS Quads: Capon Bridge

Suitable for: Day trips

Skill Level: Shepherded novices at low levels; intermediates at higher levels

Months Runnable: Primarily winter and spring; after a good rain in the summer

Interest Highlights: Beautiful rock formations; Chapel Rock, Caudy's Castle

Scenery: Beautiful

Difficulty: Class I–III

Average Width: 40–70 feet

Velocity: Moderate

Gradient: 14 feet per mile

Runnable Water Levels: See narrative for visual inspection description.
  Minimum: 0 feet at Capon Bridge; 2 feet Great Cacapon gauge
  Maximum: 3–4 feet at Capon Bridge; 5 feet Great Cacapon gauge

Hazards: Three ledges with hydraulics at high water

Scouting: For novices, the three ledges

Portages: None

Rescue Index: Remote but accessible

Source of Additional Information: National Weather Service (301) 899-7378; Great Cacapon gauge

Access Points	River Miles	Shuttle Miles
A–B	12.0	13.0

Access Point Ratings:
  A - Capon Bridge (U.S. Rt. 59), very good
  B - WV Rt. 127 bridge, very good

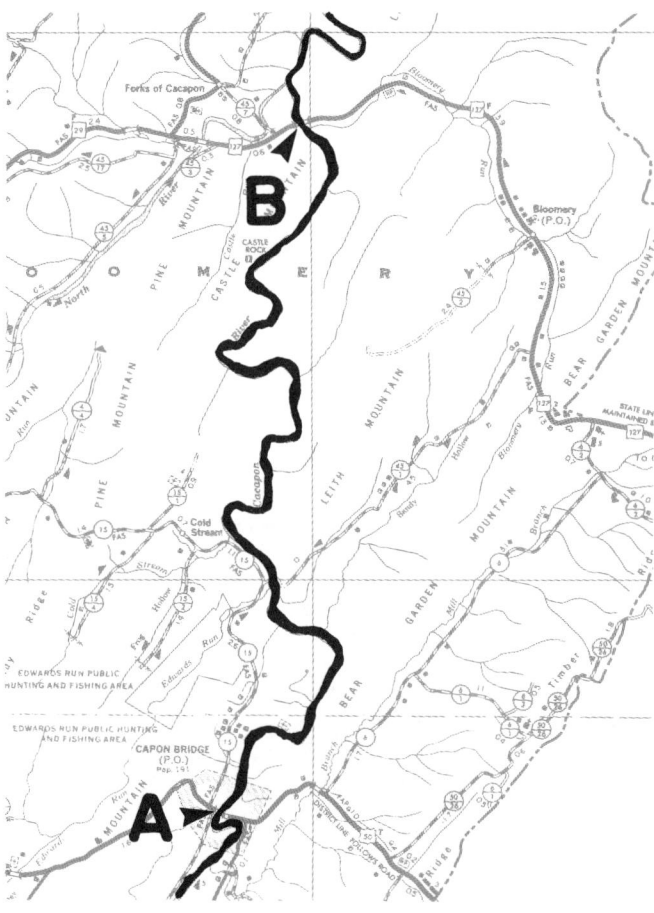

Put-in at Summersville Dam for the Upper Gauley. Photo by Ed Grove.

Maryland and Delaware

Youghiogheny River

The Youghiogheny River in western Maryland's Garrett County is the premier whitewater experience among Maryland rivers. The pristine scenery (including the exquisitely beautiful Swallow Falls State Park), the miles of continuous whitewater, the unique play spots, the accessibility to large metropolitan areas (Pittsburgh, Baltimore, and Washington), and the dam-released flows—all combine to make this river a classic expert whitewater run.

The Youghiogheny, affectionately known as the "Yough" (pronounced "Yock"), originates on Backbone Mountain, Maryland's highest. Runoff gathers in Silver Lake, West Virginia, from which the Youghiogheny flows into Maryland. The serious whitewater begins at Swallow Falls State Park north of Oakland. There are two standard runs. The Top Yough is a short but exciting stretch from Swallow Falls State Park to Sang Run Bridge (six miles) or to the power plant at Hoyes Run Road (two and a half miles). The better-known Upper Yough is a run from Sang Run Bridge to Friendsville (nine and a half miles). The Top Yough is described below; a description of the Upper Yough can be found on pages 129–33.

Top Youghiogheny River

The Top Yough begins with about two miles of premium whitewater, followed by roughly a half mile of flatwater to the power plant at Hoyes Run and nearly three and a half more miles of flatwater to Sang Run Bridge. Adding the 9.5 miles to Friendsville, a combined run on the Top and Upper Yough would be over 15 miles long. Over five miles of this, however, is the flatwater from Hoyes Run on the Top Yough to Warm Up Riffle on the Upper Yough.

The Top Yough can be run to Hoyes Run in anything from one and a half hours to more than three hours, depending on the group involved. Add one more hour of flatwater paddling to reach Sang Run.

The six-mile trip to Sang Run has a total gradient of 280 feet, most of which occurs at Swallow Falls and the drops immediately below. The gauge for the Top Yough is located on the downstream east bridge piling at Sang Run. This gauge can be correlated to the Pittsburgh Weather Service phone gauge reading for Friendsville (412) 644-2890. If the phone reading for Friendsville is 3.4, the reading on the bridge at Sang Run should be approximately 2.1. By adding or subtracting one tenth of a foot on the Sang Run gauge for each tenth of a foot on the phone gauge, you can determine with reasonable accuracy the level at Sang Run without leaving home. In addition to the gauge, local paddlers and raft guides can often give you a very accurate reading by looking at landmarks in the river near Friendsville. The minimum runnable level for the Top Yough is 1.6 feet on the gauge at Sang Run. You'll wind up walking if you catch

John Regan at Swallow Falls on the Top Yough. Photo by C. M. Laffey.

it any lower. Normal runs are in the 1.7- to approximately 2.5-foot range. Above 2.5 feet, extra caution would be in order. Of course, as with any river of this type, the maximum level will be significantly higher for a skilled paddler who is intimately familiar with the river, or for anyone else with paid-up premiums on his life insurance policy.

The take-out that eliminates most of the flatwater is located at the power plant near Hoyes Run. Take Route 42 south from Friendsville to Route 219. Bear right on Old Route 219 (also known as Deep Creek Drive) just past this junction; then very shortly thereafter take a sharp right down Sang Run Road. After less than a mile, turn left onto Hoyes Run Road which takes you to the power plant. (For important shuttle and parking information, see discussion of politics on page 130.)

The put-in for the Top Yough is located at Swallow Falls State Park. This can be reached from Route 219 by taking Mayhew Inn Road west to Sang Run Road. Take a right on Sang Run Road and a left on Swallow Falls Road, following the sign to the park. Using the map in this book, you can also reach the park from the power plant take-out.

Top Youghiogheny River

Section: Swallow Falls to Sang Run

Counties: Garrett (MD)

USGS Quads: Sang Run, Oakland

Suitable for: Day cruising

Skill Level: Experts only in top shape; this run is only slightly less difficult than the Upper Yough section (below)

Months Runnable: Winter/spring after rain or snowmelt; Top Yough first 3 miles are natural flow; hydroelectric release begins at Hoyes Run after a heavy rapids section

Interest Highlights: Beautiful wilderness gorge

Scenery: Beautiful in many places

Difficulty: Class II–V with 2 miles being steady Class IV–V

Average Width: 30–50 feet

Velocity: Fast

Gradient: 45 feet per mile; 2 miles at 100 feet per mile

Runnable Water Levels:
  Minimum: 1.6 feet on Sang Run gauge; 2.9 feet on Friendsville gauge
  Maximum: 3.6 feet on Sang Run gauge; 4.9 feet on Friendsville gauge

Hazards: Swallow Falls (100 yards below Swallow Falls Road bridge) and the first ledge just below it (Swallowtail Falls); Class V Suckhole rapids 1.5 miles below this; many Class IV rapids in the first 2 miles

Scouting: Suckhole; boat scouting of other rapids recommended when possible

Portages: Swallow Falls and the first ledge just below it (Swallowtail Falls); perhaps Suckhole rapids

Rescue Index: Remote

Source of Additional Information: Friendsville gauge (301) 899-7378 or (412) 644-2890; raft guides in Friendsville

Access Points	River Miles	Shuttle Miles
A–B	6.0	7.0

Access Point Ratings: Put-in excellent; take-out not good (see politics)

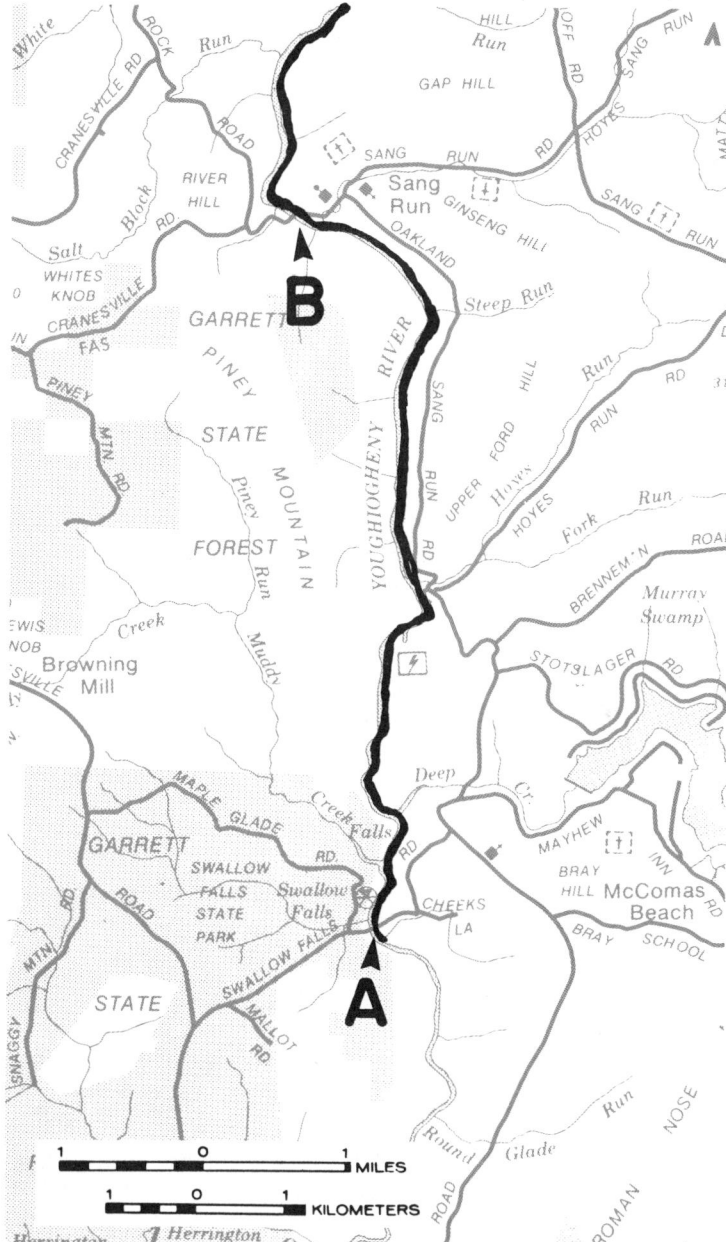

Swallow Falls is the initial rapid on the Top Yough. This spectacular spot needs no description. You can see it all from excellent vantage spots in the park. The vast majority of boaters who carefully examine the 15-foot Swallow Falls and its nearby smaller sister 8-foot Swallowtail Falls (a big ledge with a large nasty hydraulic) at runnable levels will elect to put in on river left just below these two large drops to enjoy the tamer pleasures of a second ledge and whitewater that follows. Just downstream to the left look up at 70-foot Muddy Falls, Maryland's highest waterfall.

Good technical whitewater continues from the falls almost without a let-up for the first mile or so. Easily the most notorious rapid on this section is the infamous Suckhole (Class V) located about 45 minutes (or one and a half miles) into the trip. It can be recognized by the high boulder at mid-river with nasty-looking timber and trash trapped menacingly in the pulsating gap between the high boulder and another boulder to its right. An exciting (and possibly apocryphal) tale is told of the hapless paddler who went for a swim above Suckhole only to find himself trapped under the debris in this nasty little spot. The story has a happy ending, but it would be a hair-raising swim under the Suckhole rocks and strainers.

To avoid this ugly mess, come down midstream over a series of holes, rocks, and waves which try to push you to the right. Work left against this tendency as you approach the high boulder. There is a rock on the left bank just before you reach the high boulder in midstream, a small hole just to the right of this rock, and a good eddy just beyond the rock. You may want to stop in this eddy, but don't drive so close to the rock on the left that you drop in the hole next to it and get disoriented. On the other hand, you can continue without stopping in the eddy, going left of the high boulder in midstream and staying in the center of the chute. Continuing on this route, you descend over some boulder-studded ledges with holes and waves, including a sizable hole at the bottom (Suckhole). These waves and holes (especially the bottom one) should be punched hard. A sharp rock divides the channel just above the bottom hydraulic. If you go to the right of this rock, you won't have to punch the large bottom hole. (See diagram.)

If you make it smoothly through Suckhole, it's unlikely that you'll have problems with the remaining whitewater. Take out on river right just below the power plant or for the flatwater trip continue on and take out on Appalachian Wildwaters property above Sang Run Bridge.

Most of the Top Yough rapids can be scouted from the boat. Suckhole is the exception. Those unfamiliar with the approach to Suckhole would be wise to step out and take a good look. Rescue ropes can be set up at various spots where foul-ups might occur. Keep in mind that the nearest hospital emergency room is in Cumberland, more than an hour away by road from the take-out.

[P. B.]

Figure 1. Critical portion of "Suckhole" rapids on the Top Youghiogheny.

Jon Lugbill and Dutch Downey at National Falls on the Upper Yough. Photo by C. M. Laffey.

Upper Youghiogheny River

The Upper Yough is the ultimate whitewater run for expert paddlers in Maryland. It is one of the premier streams in the entire Eastern United States. Longer and tougher than the Top Yough, it should be attempted only by expert boaters who are accompanied by someone who knows the river.

The total gradient on the Upper Yough for the entire 9.5 mile run from Sang Run to Friendsville is about 500 feet. From Gap Falls to Friendsville, the gradient is roughly 65 feet per mile, but for the section between Bastard and Heinzerling rapids the gradient is in excess of 100 feet per mile.

A normal run from Sang Run Bridge to Friendsville can take anywhere from three to six hours, depending on the levels and the group involved. Local boaters blast down at a much faster pace. If you are dependent on flows released at the power plant (see below), it would be risky to loiter for more than three hours even if you catch the initial flow just right. The duration of these flows can be very brief. Even a three-hour trip could run out of water.

The Upper Yough is runnable on natural flows throughout the spring and at other times with adequate local rainfall. It also is likely to be runnable during any season on weekdays and occasional weekends due to the flows released from the Pennsylvania Electric Project at Deep Creek Lake. The hydropower releases depend upon peak demands in the Pittsburgh area and on stream flows into Deep Creek Lake. Generating turbine starting and stopping times vary from day to day. Consequently, releases are not predictable ahead of time. Local knowledge is essential to get the scoop on the releases for a given day.

To catch the Penn Elec weekday releases you should get into Friendsville in the morning and ask raft guides at Precision Rafting what to expect for release timing and levels on that day. You can usually catch a release unless rainfall has been nonexistent for several weeks in the Deep Creek Lake watershed.

The gauge for the Upper Yough is located on the downstream east bridge piling at Sang Run. (See gauge information for Top Youghiogheny, page 126.) Normal runnable levels range generally from a minimum of 1.6 feet to somewhere around 2.5 feet on this gauge. From 2.5 feet on up, the steeper sections get noticeably more heavy-duty. As in the case of the Top Yough, the maximum runnable level is an individual matter of expertise, bravado, and life insurance.

The Upper Yough does not have the stupendous individual Class V falls and drops that characterize the Upper Gauley or the Big Sandy in West Virginia, but it generally does have a more narrowly channelized and technical character. Consequently, it is usually accorded an overall Class IV to V rating and is regarded as more difficult to paddle than either of those rivers. Unfortunately, accidents are becoming increasingly frequent; lost boats, damaged boats, broken paddles, bruises, and cuts are common. Even broken noses and legs are not unheard of. Exercise good judgment regarding your boating skills and those of the other boaters in your party. If anyone croaks on this river, the county government will be clamoring to ban all boating.

The political situation (discussed below) and the pattern of private land ownership make access to the Upper Yough a problem. Although the water belongs to the state, the banks are privately owned. (The status of lands under the river is uncertain.) Consequently, there is no legal public put-in in the Sang Run area, and the state road right-of-way adjacent to the bridge at Sang Run is off-limits. One boater has been prosecuted for trespass in attempting to use

Steve Park running Heinzerling, Upper Yough. Photo by Bill Millard.

the right-of-way adjacent to the bridge. There is even a county ordinance which prohibits dropping boats or rafts off the bridge. The farmer who owns the west bank of the river at the put-in has a lease with outfitters in Friendsville, but this arrangement does not cover private boaters. There are some private landowners in the area who have been cooperative in the past, but it is essential that you get permission first. Before 1985, parking anywhere in the put-in area was risky. Tires were slashed and other vehicle damage was inflicted. (See the discussion of politics below.) By 1985, however, the vehicle damage problem subsided.

The preferred method of handling the shuttle situation is to have a driver shuttle your car back to Friendsville from Sang Run. If no one on your trip is available, a shuttle can be set up for a reasonable price through one of the gas stations or stores in Friendsville, through one of the local rafting companies, or just by asking boaters in Friendsville.

If you are doing your own shuttle, see the map on page 131. Take Route 42 south from Friendsville to Bishof Road and go right on Bishof Road to its intersection with Sang Run Road. Then turn right on Sang Run Road.

No one should paddle the Upper Yough without being aware of one big problem: POLITICS.

Strip mining is common in western Maryland. One of the largest coal seams in the region underlies the river corridor.

Jeff Snyder, Triple Drop, Upper Yough. Photo by C. M. Laffey.

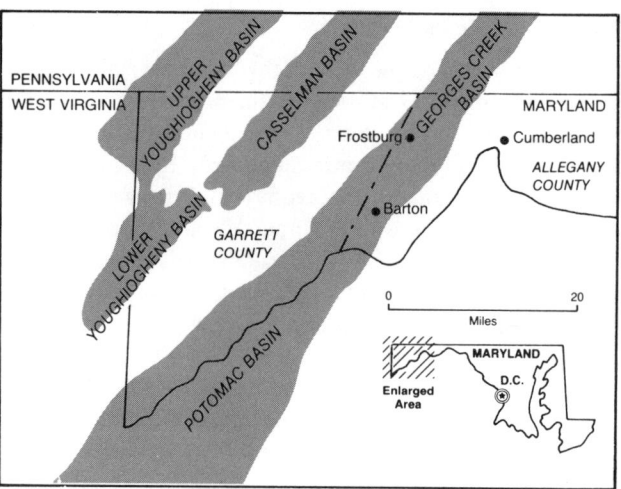

Figure 1. River basin areas in northwestern Maryland.

(See the map on this page.) Clear-cut timbering has occurred in some areas despite efforts by the state to control it, and second home development is the dream of every real-estate agent in the county. To protect the unique qualities of the Youghiogheny from these perceived threats, it has been designated as Maryland's only wild river and controversial restrictions have been imposed on land use in the river corridor.

A small group of disgruntled landowners, allied with local politicians, have waged an off-and-on battle in the state legislature to lift these land-use restrictions. The fallout from this controversy could continue indefinitely. Whenever the issue heats up, private and commercial boaters are subject to trespass lawsuits, vehicle damage, and other forms of harassment, including gunfire.

If you want to keep the Upper Yough in wild-river status and open to boating, send $15 to join the American Whitewater Affiliation, 146 N. Brockway, Palatine IL 60067. When things heat up on the Upper Yough, this group works to keep the politicians from doing a number on the boating community.

The political mess is the bad news. The good news is the miles of challenging whitewater amidst a pristine mountain setting. The river is clear, the shoreline is timbered and covered with rhododendron, and the rapids are superb. The whitewater ranges up to Class V with at least 13 or more spots that have been given affectionate names, such as Meat Cleaver or Eddy of Death.

A word of caution: this book won't get you down the Upper Yough. The descriptions provided here can only give you a rough impression of what to expect. If you have doubts about your ability to handle difficult, steep, or technical whitewater, you should go elsewhere or at least take your first trip with someone who knows the river well.

If there is one rapid that requires a special warning it would probably be Meat Cleaver. A blind drop that cannot be scouted entirely from a boat, it contains some wierd currents with the possibility of a broach on sharp rocks in midstream. More paddlers screw up here than anywhere else. Meat Cleaver is worth a few doses of adrenaline, but you will have lots of good stuff before you get there.

The rapids described below are generally Class IV unless otherwise noted when the Sang Run gauge is two feet. They are a shade easier at lower levels and tougher at higher levels.

About two to three miles down from the Sang Run Bridge you encounter Warm Up Riffle, a Class II rapid aptly named because it's a good place to goof off and warm up or picnic while getting your trip together. Not far downstream from Warm Up Riffle is Gap Falls, a sizable slide rapid with waves and holes on the way down. Enter from river left and just before hitting the bigger waves at the bottom, eddy out to your right toward midstream. As you become more familiar with Gap Falls, at lower levels you may want to try for the Eddy of Death next to the left bank about three quarters of the way down the drop. It derives its colorful name from the undercut rock guarding its downstream end.

Once past Gap Falls things mellow out for less than a mile before an intense three- to four-mile section begins. Bastard is first. Located on river left, it requires a tight right

Section: Sang Run Bridge to Friendsville

Counties: Garrett (MD)

USGS Quads: Sang Run, Friendsville

Suitable for: Day cruising

Skill Level: Experts only who are in top shape. Continuous technical rapids make this tougher overall than the Upper Gauley in West Virginia

Months Runnable: Winter/spring after rain or snowmelt; summer/fall on weekdays when water is released from Hoyes Run hydroelectric station

Interest Highlights: Wilderness gorge

Scenery: Beautiful in many places

Difficulty: Class II–V with 4.5 miles mostly steady Class IV–V

Average Width: 30–50 feet

Velocity: Fast

Gradient: 53 feet per mile; 3 miles at 100 feet per mile

Runnable Water Levels:
 Minimum: 1.6 feet on Sang Run gauge; 2.9 feet on Friendsville gauge
 Maximum: 2.5 feet on Sang Run gauge; 3.8 feet on Friendsville gauge

Hazards: Class V rapids (National Falls, Heinzerling, Meat Cleaver, Lost and Found); many Class IV rapids; there may be rattlesnakes on the rocks in the summer

Scouting: Above-mentioned Class V rapids; boat scouting of others is recommended when possible

Portages: Paddlers thinking of many portages should not run this river

Rescue Index: Remote

Source of Additional Information: Friendsville gauge (301) 899-7378 or (412) 644-2890; raft guides in Friendsville

Access Points	River Miles	Shuttle Miles
B–C	9.5	10.0

Access Point Ratings: Put-in, not good (see politics); take-out, excellent

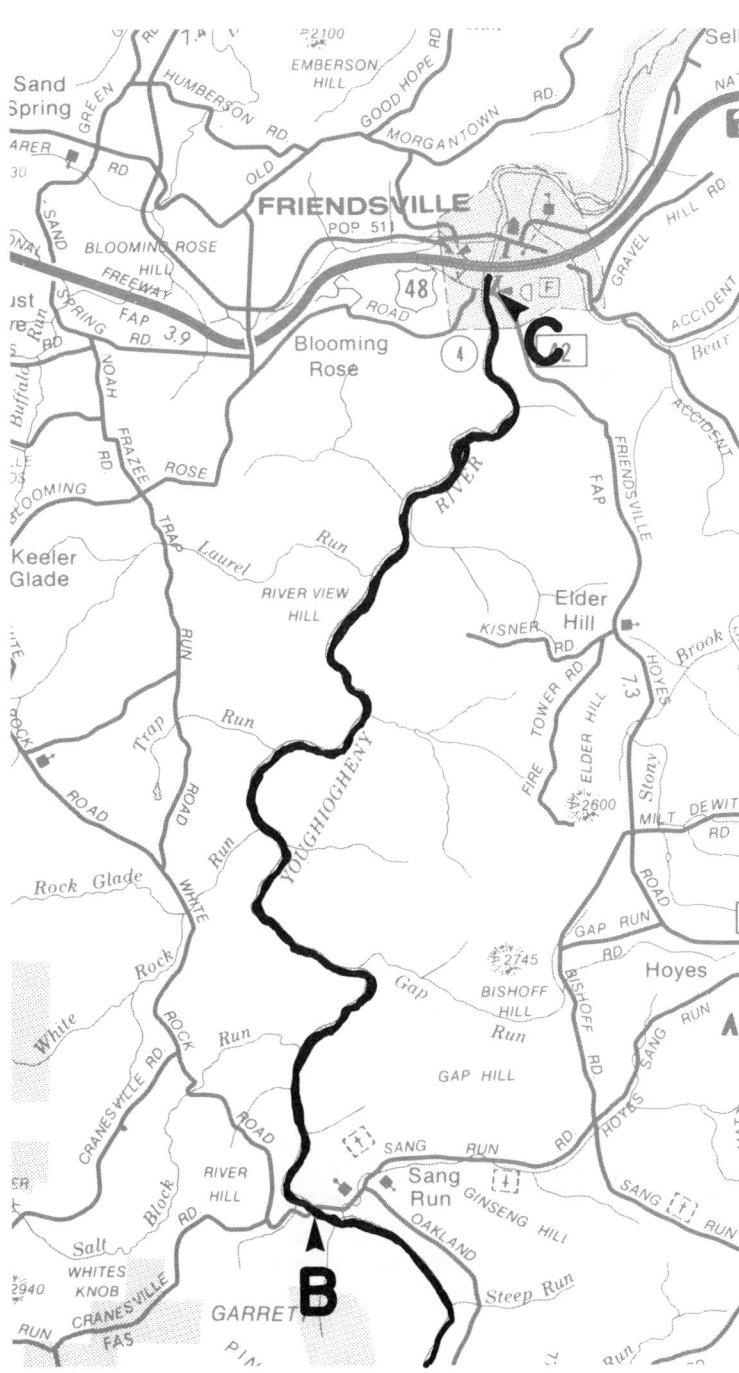

turn to pop lightly into a big eddy on the right behind the boulder that forms the right side of the drop. Avoid the hole in mid-channel by hugging this boulder.

Bastard is followed by Charlie's Choice which can be run in numerous ways. There are two tight moves between rocks at the top of two drops, both of which have a pillowed boulder at the bottom. The first one can be quite abrasive at low levels, but the second one has more of a pillow. A less exciting sneak for one or both of these choices exists on river left.

The next interesting spot the paddler encounters is Triple Drop (Class III–V). The first drop is a hole-ledge combination (Snaggle Tooth) which can be run down river right, entering from the big eddy upstream on river left. There are three boulders on river right as you go downstream, and for an uneventful descent, you should stay close to these boulders as you go down. There is a good eddy on river left just before you reach the second phase of Triple Drop, which is nothing more than some Class II ledges. The third part of Triple Drop contains National Falls. The easiest way to run this is from the eddy just above the main drop on river left, turning left as you ride the curler down. The other route (from river right over Class V National Falls) is not for the faint-hearted. Crank hard if you go this route, and expect to be trashed by the hole at the bottom.

Beyond Triple Drop lies Tommy's Hole. Located on river left, this hole is tightly packed between an upstream and a downstream boulder. As of 1986, there was a log blocking the left exit from the hole, so exit to the right (if you can exit at all). Some small boats with no edges have trouble getting out. A good sneak route exists to the right of Tommy's Hole near the middle of the river, but you should work your way back quickly to river left just past Tommy's Hole.

Not far downstream from Tommy's Hole the paddler confronts Zinger, a diagonal wave-hole combination. Enter from the top eddy on river left. There are two routes. You can stay far left as you exit the eddy, heading about two o'clock (cocking your bow 60 degrees to the right of downstream) and go straight, punching the diagonal curler-hole. To take the other route, first go right towards the large boulder which forms the right side of the drop, then surf the diagonal curler from right to left as you pass the large boulder to your right. Sanctuary can be sought in a good-sized eddy next to the left bank below the large boulder. The exit from this eddy is obvious (to the right if you opt not to catch the eddy). Zinger is not a notorious trouble-maker as Upper Yough rapids go, but it did manage to break the nose and leg of one kayaker in 1982.

After Zinger, and some Class III-type stuff, look for the right-side entrance to Heinzerling, a Class IV–V rapids. If you miss the hard-to-find approach on river right, you will be forced to take a much tougher route down the center and river left. In 1986, this involved a large strainer (downed tree) among other problems. To catch the recommended

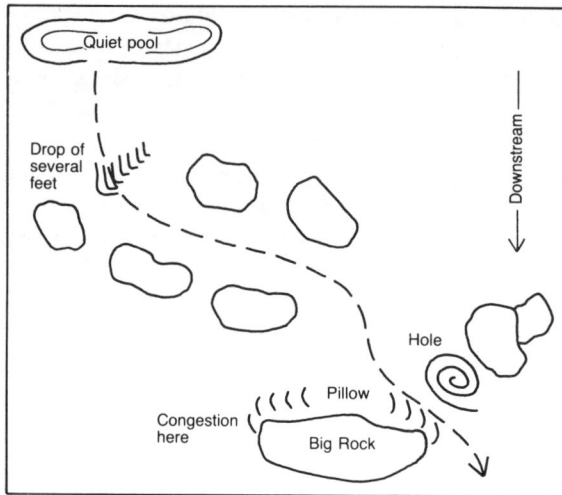

Figure 2. Lower right side of Heinzerling rapids on the Upper Youghiogheny.

approach, you need to cross a shallow rocky area on river right to reach a shady pool upstream and to the right of the initial drop of Heinzerling. The first phase of Heinzerling can be boat scouted from the bottom of this pool, and it truly is a classic whitewater spot. From the eddy at the top, it looks much steeper and complex than it really is. First you drop several feet over the first ledge, turn sharp left and eddy out to look over the bottom drop. From this eddy you head directly downstream toward the big pillowed boulder visible at the bottom. Ride the pillow on the boulder, bracing right and sliding off it to the left. If you ride high enough on the pillow, you will avoid the nastier parts of the holes just to the left of the big boulder. Going to the right of the boulder is a no-no (see chart above).

Meat Cleaver (a genuine Class V) follows Heinzerling. Start from river right, going over a small drop and turning left behind some big boulders. You can then see the final drop with two shark-teeth rocks more or less in the center of the drop. Thread your way between (or to one side of) these sharp rocks. (The route between the two rocks is preferable.) If you eddy out on the left above the shark teeth, your trip will become more exciting because it is more difficult to thread the proper course without broaching. Broaching on the Meat Cleaver rocks is not recommended (see chart, page 133).

Beyond Meat Cleaver the paddler encounters Powerful Popper, a Class III–IV rapids marked by three boulders in midstream. A pop-up and squirt stop is in order here.

The next major rapid is one of the more technical drops on the river, Lost and Found (Class V). Some choice surfing holes are immediately upstream, so enjoy them while you can. Lost and Found consists of a maze of congested offset rocks. As with almost everything on the Upper Yough, it can be run in different ways. The various possibilities can be boat scouted to some degree from an eddy just above the

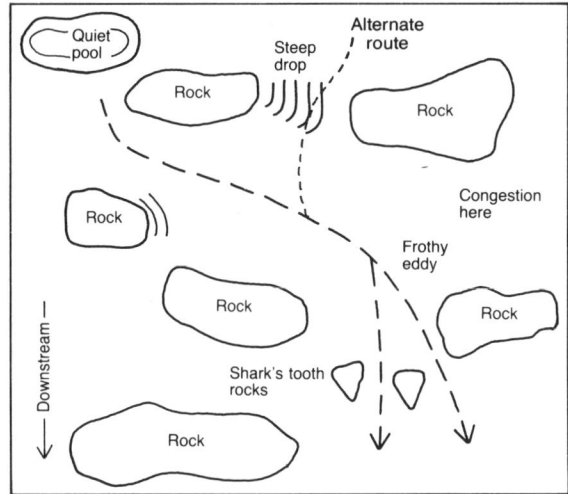

Figure 3. "Meat Cleaver" rapids on the Upper Youghiogheny.

rapid. The cautious boater on an initial run may want to look it over from the island on the right side of the main drop. There is a sneak route from the eddy way around on far river right. This involves dropping off a four-foot ledge into the pool below all the messy stuff. There are several routes through the messy stuff if you elect to try that. If enough water is available, the easiest route is to squeeze between the round rock on the upper river right at the beginning of the rapid and the adjacent midstream rocks just downstream. This approach offers a reasonably straight shot downstream leaving these midstream rocks to your left. With this approach you will be less likely to get lost slaloming right and left around the rocks in midstream. You also will not go so far left as to get tangled up in "F___ Up Hole" at the bottom.

If you have made it this far without incident, you'll probably have few problems with the remaining Class III–IV biggies: Cheeseburger Falls, Wright's Hole, and Double Pencil Sharpener. Except for Cheeseburger Falls (a blind drop on the river right), these can all be scouted from the boat. Try to run the main drop at Cheeseburger at least one boat length out from the right bank to avoid a submerged rock at the bottom of the ledge which forms Cheeseburger Falls. This submerged rock has broken several paddles. You can sweep into the eddy on river right just past this hole. Wright's Hole can be punched at the usual summer-release water levels by driving hard through the left portion of the hole. The hole can also be circumvented on river right by surfing down some diagonal waves.

After Cheeseburger, Wright's Hole, and Double Pencil Sharpener, three to four miles of less distinguished small stuff and flatwater remain until the cheeseburger you will be buying on Main Street in Friendsville.

There is one final item of interest about this spectacular river. Starting in 1981, there has been an annual downriver race on the Upper Yough by expert paddlers who know the river intimately. The 1986 race drew about 30 boaters who were on the cutting edge of paddling. National Falls is one of the best places to view the race. Contact Precision Rafting in Friendsville for details (Roger Zbel of this raft company has won the race five out of six times).

[P. B.]

Bill Warren running Meat Cleaver, Upper Yough. Photo by Bill Millard.

Savage River

The Savage is a little brawling river that certainly lives up to its name. Here you have four miles of jam-packed continuous whitewater for the advanced paddler. At very low levels (below three feet on the put-in gauge), perhaps carefully shepherded strong intermediate paddlers can try the last two miles of this section to see if they are ready for the tougher upper half. However, be warned: There are very few eddies on the relentless downhill scramble to the North Branch of the Potomac. Also, because of the cold dam-released water averaging 46 degrees Fahrenheit, wet suits should always be used—even in summer months at this elevation of 1,300 feet. One important safety feature is that the Savage River Road closely follows the river. It provides first-timers with the chance to see what they are up against, and a take-out is relatively easy if problems develop. However, some of the major rapids can't be seen from the road, so these will need to be scouted from the river. At moderate levels (800 to 900 cfs or 3.2 to 3.4 feet on the put-in gauge) the river is a continuous heavy Class III with a couple of Class IV's thrown in for added excitement. This is the level described below. However, at higher levels, the run gets much tougher because of the relentless 75-foot-per-mile gradient.

The best action and scenery are found within the first two miles of the trip. Here the clear, clean river drops through a small, pretty gorge, and the riverbanks are festooned with rhododendron, maples, mountain ashes, tulip poplars, and hemlocks. During the second two miles the rapids calm down to an easier steady Class III dull roar, and the scenery beyond the riverbanks slowly gets worse as one nears the take-out. Trash increasingly is scattered near the riverbank on the right, and big excavations scar the land beyond the riverbank on the left.

Nevertheless, this river is a whitewater gem of brilliance. The easiest put-in is just over four miles up Savage River Road. It is on river right from a very short dirt road spur about 100 yards upstream of a white concrete bridge. Or you can put in on river left half a mile farther upstream from a dirt road that leaves the camping area just downstream from the same bridge. The description that follows covers the trip from the put-in by the white concrete bridge.

About 20 to 30 yards downstream from the river right road spur put-in is a good 25-yard Class III rapids over two ledge-like drops. This will wake you up immediately—even if the cold dam-released water does not. You may want to peek at this rapid before running it. A river gauging station is found right below this rapid, on river left and about 30 yards upstream from the white concrete bridge. Unfortunately, this gauge goes into the ground at 4.5 feet—so you will have to extrapolate downward. Generally, it's better to rely on the recorded message at (301) 899-7378 with one exception. On race days you should check with race officials to determine the timing and level of cfs released.

Next to this gauge and immediately before passing under the bridge, the paddler will encounter a two-foot ledge. A half mile of continuous Class II and III waves and boulder-garden action follows, until the paddler reaches a pool 100 yards or so long—the only such sizable pool that will be encountered before the paddler is disgorged at the take-out on the North Branch of the Potomac. This pool is formed by the five-foot Piedmont Dam.

The dam can be run via a man-made flume on the far left (safest and interesting), by a two-yard notch in the dam a few yards to the right of the flume (exciting), or over a horrible jumble of rocks on the extreme right (runnable only

Savage River at 3,000 cfs. Photo by Bill Kirby.

Section: Below the Savage River Dam to confluence with the North Branch of the Potomac

Counties: Garrett (MD)

USGS Quads: Westernport, Barton, Bittinger

Suitable for: Day cruising and competent racers

Skill Level: Advanced boaters with helmets, wet suits, and floatation (moderate levels); expert decked boaters (higher levels)

Months Runnable: Generally a dam release for races and in winter and spring after hard rains and snowmelt

Interest Highlights: Beautiful small gorge for most of the trip

Scenery: Pretty to beautiful at the put-in; slowly changes to fair at the take-out

Difficulty: Class III–IV up to 800 cfs (up to 3.4 feet on gauge); Class IV from 800 to 1,200 cfs (from 3.4 to 3.8 feet on gauge); Class IV–V above 1,200 cfs

Average Width: 20–40 feet

Velocity: Fast

Gradient: 75 feet per mile

Runnable Water Levels:
  Minimum: 350 cfs or 2.5 feet on the Savage gauge
  Maximum: 1,200 cfs or 3.8 feet on the Savage gauge (open boat experts); 1,400 cfs or 4 feet on the Savage gauge (decked boat experts)

Hazards: Trees down in river; large holes at high levels; few eddies

Scouting: Advisable for Class III–IV Triple Drop and Class IV Memorial Rock

Portages: None

Rescue Index: Accessible

Source of Additional Information: National Weather Service, Savage River gauge (301) 899-7378

Access Points	River Miles	Shuttle Miles
A–B	4 to 4.5	4 to 4.5

Access Point Ratings: Put-in, excellent; take-out, good

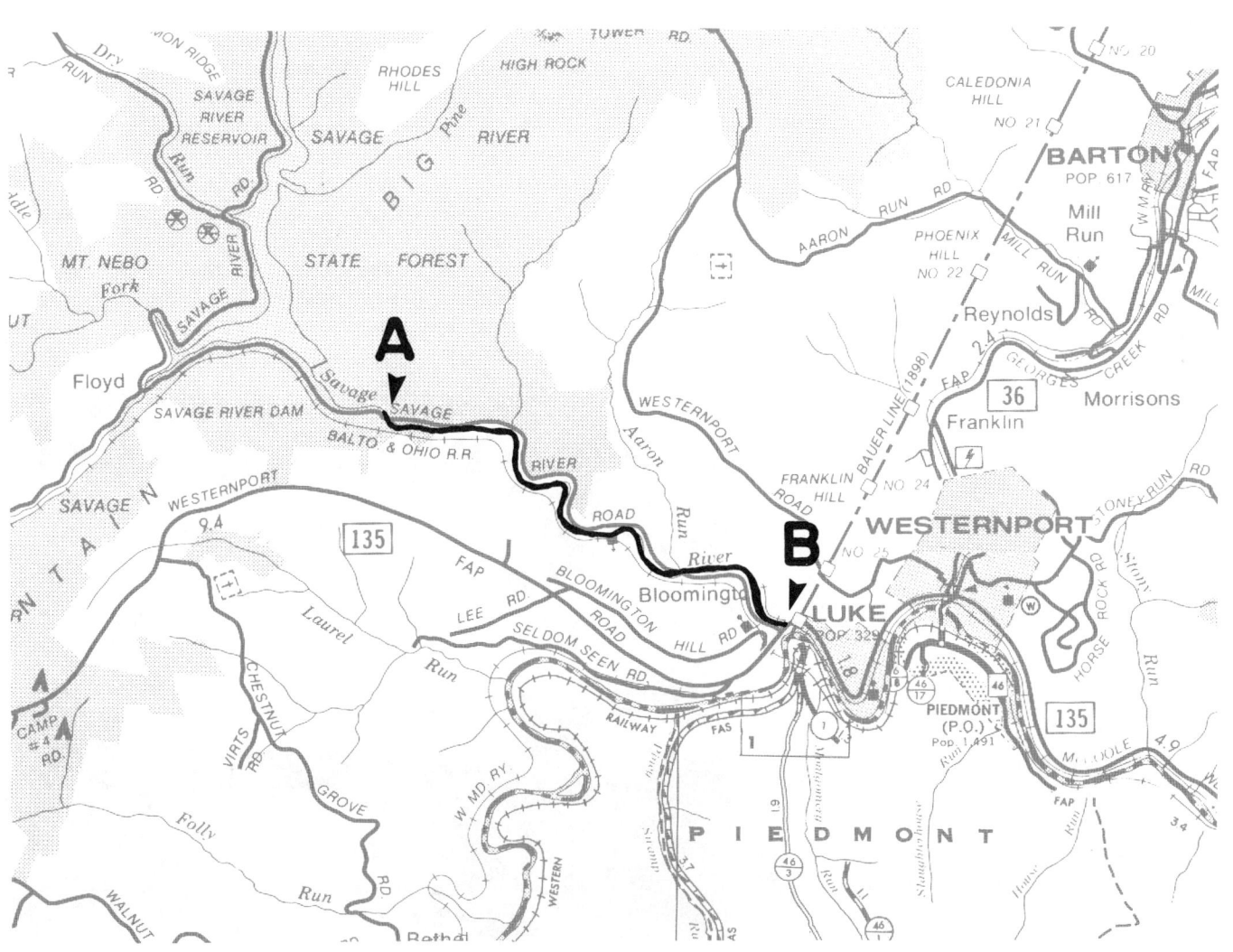

by very experienced boaters with great care and attentive scouting). At low levels (500 cfs or 2.8 feet on the put-in gauge) there is not enough water in the flume. At 1,000 cfs a nasty hydraulic develops below the runnable notch just to the right of the flume. Nervous nellies can carry on the left. Just below the dam (and where the whitewater slalom course is usually set up for regional and national competition) continuous Class III wave and boulder-garden action continues for another good half mile, then the river flows toward the road, which has a nice white stone face on its other side. As the Savage turns right and away from the road, get ready for Triple Drop, also known as Crisscross.

At moderate levels this rapid is a low Class IV consisting of three drops. Scout from the left. The first can be run next to a rock on the right side; the second has a nice tongue in the center; and the last drop, which can develop a strong hole, is best run on the right. Here it should be mentioned that trees occasionally fall across this small river. On one trip a tree blocked the third drop, and one boater (who had fallen out of his boat upstream) briefly suffered a body pin on the trunk of this tree.

Following Triple Drop, the paddler confronts the toughest single drop on the river, fittingly called Memorial Rock. At moderate levels this low Class IV can be recognized by a large pointed boulder sticking out of the water about ten feet off the left bank. Generally, one should run just to the right of the rock angled left to avoid a submerged rock and a mean hole covering the river on the right. Be ready to punch a couple of holes just below. Or, if there is enough water, one can sneak on the extreme left on the other side of Memorial Rock. No wonder things are so busy during this part of the trip; here the descent is 100 feet per mile!

Below Memorial Rock, go left of an island for the best

Savage River Water Level Conversion (Correlation) Table

Savage River Gauge (0.7 miles below Savage River Dam)

Ht.	(cfs)	Ht.	(cfs)
0.6	2.0	3.8	1,214
0.8	6.8	4.0	1,401
1.0	15.3	4.2	1,605
1.2	28.0	4.4	1,827
1.4	61.0	4.6	2,066
1.6	93.9	4.8	2,323
1.8	135.9	5.0	2,600
2.0	187.8	5.2	2,895
2.2	250.4	5.4	3,211
2.4	324.3	5.6	3,546
2.6	410.2	5.8	3,902
2.8	508.8	6.0	4,279
3.0	620.8	6.2	4,678
3.2	746.6	6.4	5,099
3.4	887.0	6.6	5,542
3.6	1,043	6.8	6,008

The above data, obtained from the Maryland District Office of the USGS, are based on 1984–86 measurements.

rapids. There are a couple of good holes to avoid or punch as the river closely follows the road again. Then, two miles into the trip, you reach a white clapboard church, which, as of this writing, was called the Full Gospel Church. Just before the church at lower levels, a super surfing hydraulic extends over three quarters of the river from the left and has a nice small recovery pool in which to pick up pieces of errant surfers.

This used to be the take-out for those only wanting to run the tougher upper part of the Savage and the put-in for more nervous souls who did not want to challenge the upper

Bob and Sylvia Grabus running the flume on Piedmont Dam, Savage River. Photo by Ed Grove.

section. As of this writing, however, a fence blocked the access and the riverbank was posted against trespassing. So put in or take out about 100 yards below the church, which was unposted as of this writing. Do ask permission first.

For the last two miles the Savage continues at a calmer pace. The main items of note on this lower section include a two-foot diagonal ledge just upstream of a bridge a mile below the church, followed about three quarters of a mile later by a pool in which paddlers can regain composure before the final quarter mile to the North Branch. Once on the North Branch, paddle upstream 100 yards for a river left take-out or across the river for an easier river right take-out.

The Savage is not a river for the inexperienced or unwary. Kayakers should have a bombproof roll under rocky conditions and open boaters should have full floatation, helmets, and wet suits—even in summer months. Swims generally are long and cold despite the small size of this river. Boat recovery is difficult because of the ceaseless nature of the rapids.

As mentioned earlier, this description reflects 800 cfs or 3.2 feet on the put-in gauge. As the level goes from 800 to 1,200 cfs the river becomes much pushier. Although the rocks are now covered and padded, the hydraulics become grabbier and the waves much more powerful. It gets more difficult to catch the few eddies available along the shore since by this time the river is running through the rhododendron on the banks. Consider this a solid Class IV run. At 1,200 cfs and above the river becomes very nasty with very dangerous hydraulics and should be considered a Class IV–V trip for expert decked boaters only.

Unfortunately, running this river is dependent on getting releases from the Savage River Dam through the cooperation of the Upper Potomac River Commission. These releases are scheduled sporadically in the spring and summer, particularly if races are scheduled, but sometimes heavy rains will allow the dam keepers to release unspecified amounts in an unscheduled manner.

On the other hand, exciting things are happening to the Savage. It has been chosen for the 1989 International Canoe Federation World Championships in Slalom and Whitewater. This international event for decked boats is currently scheduled for June 1989. To warm up U.S. and foreign paddlers, a Pre-World Championship is also scheduled for June 1988, and international races were planned for 1986 and 1987.

Incidentally, the Savage River Dam is worth a peek if you have the time and don't mind listening to the noisy pumping station. Only three quarters of a mile upstream from the white concrete bridge near the put-in, this earth and rockfill dam is over 1,000 feet wide and nearly 200 feet tall. Its capacity is six and a half billion gallons of water. Fishermen enjoy the lake formed by the dam and can often be seen casting from the dam's rocky face. Bass, crappies, and brown and rainbow trout can be caught here. Fish are also stocked downstream in the spring for the fishing season.

Eric and Carmony Thorp at Memorial Rock, Savage River, during the 1979 National competition. Photo by Barbara S. McKee.

North Branch of the Potomac

Gormania to Kitzmiller (Steyer to Shallmar)

The run from Gormania to Kitzmiller is the classic section of the North Branch of the Potomac River and is for advanced to expert paddlers only. Be warned that the length and continuous nature of this trip give it an expedition-like quality. Here the North Branch drops at a giddy gradient of over 50 feet per mile, which is quite a drop for a reasonably sized river. There are no midway take-outs, and the only solace is a set of railroad tracks next to the river, which can be used for emergency walkouts (with or without boats). For the first third of the trip, the tracks are on river left; for the remainder, they are on the right.

Do not venture on this river unless you are very competent and in good physical and mental shape. The whole run is long and strenuous, and a full day should be allowed to complete it by those running this section the first time. Even highly experienced boaters who know the river well should allow six hours of daylight on the river. Except at the very beginning and the very end you will be working continuously. Throughout most of the trip quiet stretches of water are not more than 50 yards long. Each decked boater should have a strong roll, and each open boater should be capable of self-rescue in continuous Class III rapids. Naturally helmets and floatation are mandatory for all boats. Rescue is very difficult, particularly at upper levels, and you're on your own because of the relentless nature of this run. There have been documented hairy experiences for intermediate paddlers who have found this river too much to handle. Advanced and expert paddlers have also had real trouble when the river was too high.

To avoid an excessive case of white knuckles or a long walk on a railroad track, pay careful attention to the gauge at Kitzmiller. The absolute scrapy minimum is about four and a half feet. An extra foot of water on this gauge (say, moving from five to six feet), can change this from a demanding Class III–IV trip to an extremely difficult Class IV– V run. A level of five and a half feet on the Kitzmiller gauge would be approaching the limit of expert open boaters with full floatation. Expert decked boaters should think of six and a half feet as an upper limit, primarily because of the countless hydraulics and the relentless gradient. Clearly, when the water gets higher, the hydraulics gets grabbier, with many becoming absolute keepers at levels over seven feet.

Besides checking the Kitzmiller gauge at the take-out, paddlers should also check Stony River where it crosses Route 50 to determine the volume of water from this river. The Stony joins the North Branch a third of the way into the trip and nearly doubles the volume of the North Branch.

To cut out 4 miles of less scenic flatwater from this trip of potentially 15 miles, the paddler should do two things. First, put in at Steyer, on White Church-Steyer Road. This is two miles downstream from Gormania on river left by an old building just as the road leaves the river. Second, take out in the town of Shallmar, which is two miles upstream from Kitzmiller on river left. These two adjustments give the paddler the best 11 miles of this stretch with minimal extra trouble.

About a half mile downstream from the put-in at Steyer, look for a Steyer river gauge on river left. It should be between 2.9 (very scrapy) and 4.2 feet. Unless you are really into rocks, however, this gauge probably should be a good three feet. On the other hand, if the gauge is underwater, perhaps you shouldn't be here at all.

Section: Gormania, WV (Steyer) to Kitzmiller, MD (Shallmar)

Counties: Garrett (MD); Mineral and Grant (WV)

USGS Quads: Gorman, Kitzmiller, Mount Storm

Suitable for: Long day-trip cruising for paddlers in good physical shape

Skill Level: Advanced boaters (moderate levels) and expert boaters (high levels)

Months Runnable: Generally winter and spring after a hard rain or during snowmelt

Interest Highlights: Heavy continuous whitewater through reasonably scenic gorge

Scenery: Pretty or beautiful in spots

Difficulty: Class III-IV (Kitzmiller 4.5–5.2 feet); Class IV (Kitzmiller 5.2–5.5 feet); Class IV–V (Kitzmiller 5.5–6.5 feet)

Average Width: 30–70 feet

Velocity: Fast

Gradient: 55 feet per mile

Runnable Water Levels:
  Minimum: 4.5 feet Kitzmiller; 2.9 feet Steyer
  Maximum: 6.5 feet Kitzmiller; 4.2 feet Steyer (heavy water for experts)

Hazards: Occasional trees in river; three large ledges; old bridge pier and "Maytag" rapids near the end of the trip; continual hydraulics and heavy water at high levels

Scouting: Corkscrew rapids below confluence with the Stony (Class III-IV); three big ledges (Class III-IV) at moderate levels; "Maytag" rapids (Class IV)

Portages: None

Rescue Index: Remote

Source of Additional Information: National Weather Service for Kitzmiller gauge (301) 899-7378

Access Points	River Miles	Shuttle Miles
A–B	11 (Steyer to Shallmar)	25

Access Point Ratings: Put-in, good; take-out, excellent

North Branch of the Potomac 139

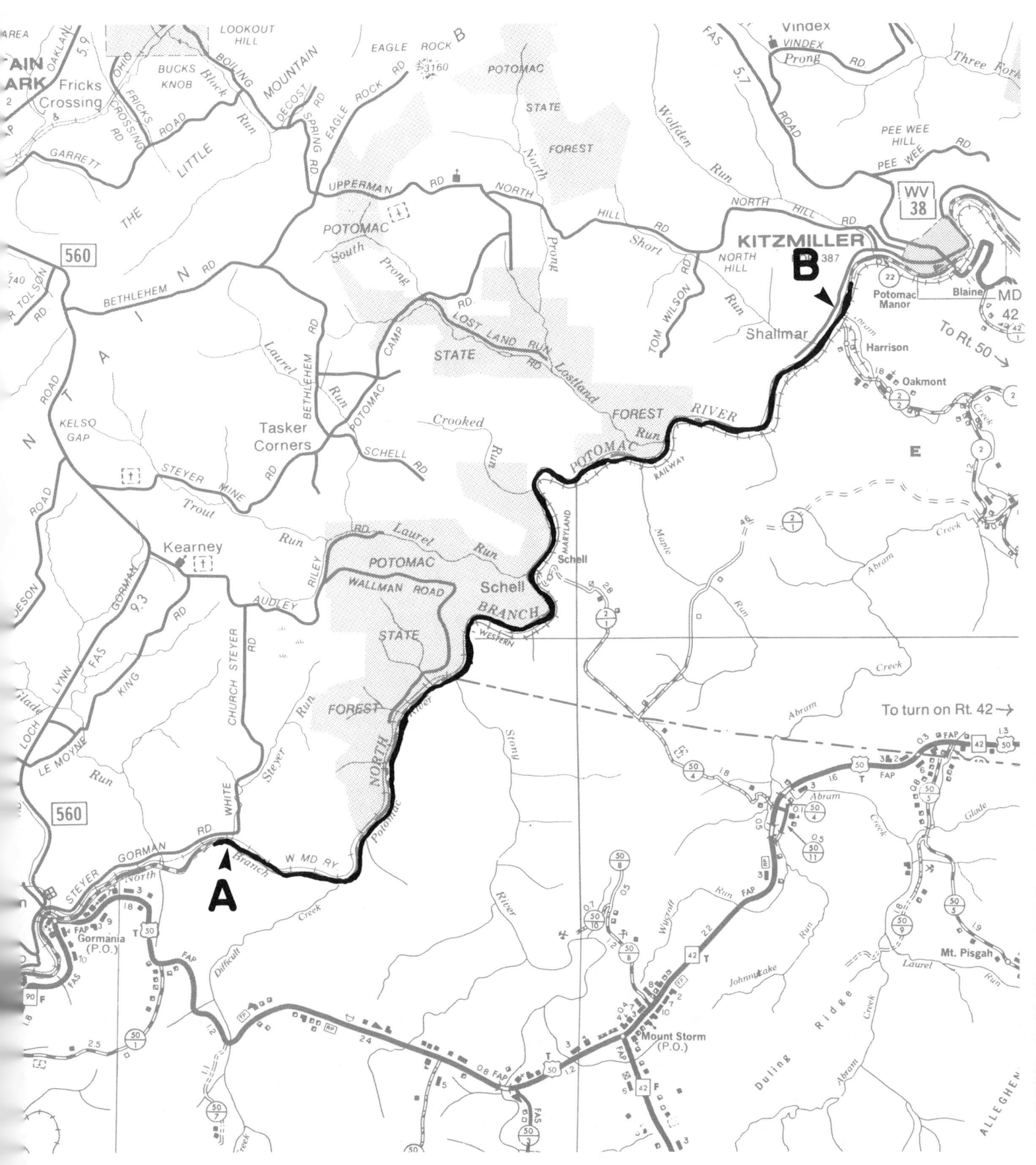

Corkscrew Ledge, North Branch of the Potomac above Kitzmiller. Photo by Hoyt Reel.

After a mile or two of placid Class I–II rock garden rapids (quite scrapy if the river is low), the drops become more abrupt and interesting. The first island below Steyer should be run to the right and has a good drop into a hole.

When you reach the second island, get out on the left bank, climb up to the railroad tracks, and scout Corkscrew —an aptly named Class III–IV rapids. Basically Corkscrew is a four foot horseshoe ledge (prongs downstream) and is best entered left of center, headed towards the right. This rapid previously had two nasty holes below the ledge, but two 1985 floods eliminated them. Also, at lower levels, most of the water is now channeled to the right of this second island, which provides an exciting alternative to Corkscrew. Here a fairly steep drop climaxes in a large but punchable hydraulic. If you have any real problems to this point, strongly consider the three-mile carry back to the put-in on the river left railroad tracks. A seemingly interminable walk *with* a boat is vastly preferable to a seemingly interminable flush down the river *without* it.

From here to its junction with the Stony, the narrow and rocky North Branch continues falling away at a steep and respectful pace. If you haven't noticed by now, this is probably the ledgiest river you have ever paddled. Surf away if you wish, but make sure you save enough energy to complete this long, demanding run. A half mile before the North Branch joins the Stony, look out for a steep rapids that features two powerful offset diagonal holes.

When the Stony joins the North Branch four miles below Steyer, not only does the water volume nearly double but the water color generally changes for the better, too. The brown foamy North Branch, usually muddy from strip mines, is diluted by the clearer waters of the Stony. Unfortunately, both rivers are sterile and polluted with mine acids. Once the Stony merges with the North Branch, the river also becomes more powerful and pushier. About a half mile below the confluence of these rivers you will pass under a railroad bridge. Get ready because just below lies the biggest action of this trip—three large ledges located fairly close together.

The first and perhaps most difficult ledge is a Class IV at moderate levels. It has been given a very salty name by old-time paddlers; "MF" is their abbreviation for this name. Get out and scout this rapids on the left. It is a large, complex sloping ledge of roughly six feet. Enter left of center and move farther left to skirt an impressive roostertail, then punch or miss (to the left) a deceptively nasty suckhole at the very bottom. Many a paddler has concentrated his attention on the roostertail and breathed a sigh of relief when safely past it, only to be nailed by the suckhole whose viciousness can escape a casual glance. This hole is appropriately called "Lady Kenmore" by local paddlers for obvious reasons.

Fortunately, at moderate levels there is a nice pool in which to pick up the pieces. Set throw ropes and rescue boats just below this large ledge and Lady Kenmore on river left. At about 4.8 feet on the Kitzmiller gauge a passage opens on the right that is probably best bridged by open boaters.

Although your attention will be focused totally on the river at this point, do look out for timber rattlesnakes here and elsewhere along the banks, particularly on warm, sunny days. A paddler who was once walking on the bank by this ledge thought the timer in his camera was buzzing, but it turned out to be a three-and-a-half-foot rattlesnake lying in front of him sounding its own built-in buzzer. Indeed, less salty paddlers call this first large drop "Rattlesnake Ledge."

Not too far downstream is the second big ledge, the steepest of the three and perhaps the most fun. At reasonable levels, this sharply sloping six-foot ledge is a Class III–IV rapids. It is a straightforward drop best run with good speed down the center of the ledge into a generally forgiving mass of foam and water.

The third ledge (Class III–IV) of over five feet also appears very shortly. It should generally be run on the right—a sloping and jagged complex drop with some scraping. At low levels this last ledge has been run on the far left with a turn to the right.

First-timers should scout all three ledges and even experienced paddlers who know the river should look them over—particularly at higher levels such as five and a half feet on the Kitzmiller gauge. Above six and a half feet on this gauge some of the holes below these three ledges become absolute keepers.

Following these drops the river broadens, and for a short distance the rapids become straightforward wave trains. Then the river narrows and again takes on a serious nature with a seemingly endless series of Class II and III ledges, boulder gardens, and crosscurrents at moderate levels. Surfing freaks can go bonkers again. Constant maneuvering, however, now becomes the order of the day. At higher levels, say, five and a half feet on Kitzmiller, this turns into Class IV stuff. At six feet and above, one rockets along through big waves and has to avoid some keeper holes.

Roughly three quarters of the way through the run, be alert for two dangers: first, a toppled concrete bridge pier, which should be run far left; and second, an innocent-looking rapid that contains several powerful holes and a series of sizable offset waves, appropriately called "Maytag." More paddlers seem to swim here than anyplace else, perhaps due to fatigue and the fact that Maytag resembles an approach to several other upstream rapids that are much easier. There are two ways to know when Maytag is imminent. First, it is located on the third left turn as the river winds close to the railroad tracks on the right. Second, look for a tall sheer rock cliff on river left reminiscent of the wall above "High Falls" on the Cheat River in West Virginia. This cliff has a man-made stone wall in the center that distinguishes it from other cliffs on this trip. Maytag is the next rapids downstream from this cliff. It begins as a gentle left bend that looks easy but soon becomes a monster. Approaching six feet on the gauge, this rapids is several large holes in the first half of a long train of big waves. Paddling on the extreme left is generally the way to miss the worst of the holes, but you will still have to keep your balance through some powerful offset waves. Maytag is Class IV at five feet on the gauge and tougher at higher levels. Scout it.

After you have paddled about 11 miles and are panting from maneuvering and playing (if you still have any energy), look for the take-out at the not-so-picturesque town of Shallmar on river left. Near the take-out, Abram Creek joins the North Branch on river right. By taking out at Shallmar you can avoid two miles of less interesting rapids (dredged chan-

First big ledge below the railroad bridge on the North Branch of the Potomac above Kitzmiller. Photo by Hoyt Reel.

nel) and scenery (strip mines) before you get to the Route 42 bridge in Kitzmiller. Also, at five feet and below on the Kitzmiller gauge parts of the last two miles become almost too shallow and picky to paddle.

Except for the water quality and railroad tracks, this is a very scenic trip when you can get your head out of the rapidly unfolding rapids and look around. There are pretty cliffs, hemlocks, rhododendrons, and forested canyon walls to make you forget your increasingly aching muscles.

For more experienced paddlers really in shape, a tougher trip can be had by putting in on the Stony River (with its gradient of 75 feet per mile) at Route 50. This makes the trip two miles and perhaps two hours longer and considerably more demanding. The Stony is significantly more difficult than the North Branch and consists of many sharp, blind drops throughout its boulder-choked descent. Downed trees are also a particular risk on this narrow stream. Several years ago an experienced paddler was trapped and killed underneath a log hidden just below water level. Paddlers who brave the Stony (a solid Class IV river at even moderate levels) will usually welcome the relatively open and larger nature of the North Branch.

The main negative aspect of this trip is that the North Branch is not up very often. The prime times are during winter and spring two to four days after a hard rain. But, keep the faith: It has been run on Labor Day after a humongous rain a couple of days earlier.

Barnum to Bloomington

The six-mile section of the North Branch of the Potomac River from Barnum to Bloomington is a solid intermediate run. It is basically composed of long, strong Class II wave action and rock gardens interspersed with long pools. At 1,000 cfs, a few of these wave trains approach Class III. To break this delightful monotony, however, a short but strong Class III double ledge appears midway through the trip. It should be scouted the first time. For those who like to play, surfing spots galore during the first third of the trip provide many opportunities.

This section of the North Branch is much gentler than the smaller Savage River which joins the North Branch at the Bloomington take-out. It is also easier than the tougher big-brother section of the North Branch from Gormania to Kitzmiller which ends about ten miles upstream from the Barnum put-in. However, the steady gradient and general feeling of going downhill often remind one of these other two sections.

The trip is a very scenic one. The North Branch flows through a beautiful gorge broken only by the occasional appearance of railroad tracks and, near the end, large industrial buildings and logging trucks. The hardwood forest generally extends right down to the river—maples, sycamores, and sometimes oaks are found near the banks, and evergreens, such as hemlocks, are also seen here and there. Unfortunately the clear waters are sterile. Acidity from earlier mining operations upstream has killed fish and other life in the river.

To reach the put-in at the remains of the Barnum bridge, proceed for about five and a half miles, making several careful turns, on WV 46, a Class IV dirt road (Class V when it's raining). Look for a right turn by three churches, which will take you about two and a half miles down to the river. After putting in don't hurry downstream. There are two small surfing spots about 50 yards upstream on river left for the wide awake and adventurous to warm up on.

Just below the Barnum bridge abutments you will encounter a 50-yard Class II rapids with a two-foot ledge, followed shortly by a 100-yard-long Class II rapids and a railroad bridge. This bridge is followed by a pool, 100 yards of good Class II–III standing waves, another pool, and then another spot of standing waves. The relaxing monotony of the run continues with yet another pool and still another 100 yards of Class II–III standing waves. However, here there is a difference. At the end of these last waves two major surfing ledges appear with several minor surfing places adjacent or downstream. At 1,000 cfs, one of these

---

Section: Barnum (WV) to Bloomington (MD)

Counties: Garrett (MD)

USGS Quads: Kitzmiller, Westernport

Suitable for: One-day cruising

Skill Level: Solid intermediates

Months Runnable: Late summer and early fall dam releases

Interest Highlights: Beautiful gorge

Scenery: Beautiful at start; pretty in spots at end

Difficulty: Class II–III with one solid Class III

Average Width: 40–70 feet

Velocity: Fast

Gradient: 35 feet per mile

Runnable Water Levels:
  Minimum: 600 cfs
  Maximum: 1,250 cfs (maximum release)

Hazards: None

Scouting: Class III double ledge

Portages: None

Rescue Index: Remote

Source of Additional Information: None

Access Points	River Miles	Shuttle Miles
C–D	6	8

Access Point Ratings: Put-in, excellent; take-out, good

ledges brings to mind Swimmer's Ledge on the Lower Youghiogheny in Pennsylvania except that the runout here is not nearly as clean if one flips. At higher levels these two ledges can create stopper hydraulics.

A couple of minutes and another set of standing waves later take note of the rock face on river left; as of this writing a pretty evergreen tree on this rock face had a rope swing attached. Ahead, when the river splits take the larger right channel and you'll find yourself dropping down a Class II rapids with a cobble bar on the left and a smooth concrete rock face on the right supporting the railroad tracks above. Two nice surfing spots are encountered at the end of this rapids. At 1,000 cfs, the second of these is a particularly enjoyable kayak-sized hole in the middle of the river. A kind but firm teacher, it does not discriminate against open boats. The cobble bar here also makes a nice lunch stop.

Past the cobble bar the long sections of standing waves and pools alternate again. One of these Class II standing-wave fields is about 300 yards long. After a few more rock gardens and pools the river splits again around an island and you should take the much larger main channel to the right. About a quarter mile later when the first island ends and another small river channel on the left creates a second island, continue on the right, but be alert because the one strong Class III rapids of the trip is approaching.

After a short wave patch, the river bends left into a horizon line and a major-sounding rapid. Quickly catch the last-chance eddy on the left. Get out on the island and scout this rapids, which consists of two ledges about 25 yards apart. The first ledge should be run center or left of center because at 1,000 cfs the hole formed by the ledge gets nasty toward the right. This will also set you up to run the second larger ledge center or left of center. At 600 cfs good tongues mark the routes over these two ledges, but at 1,000 cfs the routes are less obvious. The second island ends shortly after the rapids.

This spicy change of pace is followed by a couple of long rock gardens and a long pool. At the end of this pool, look for a railroad trestle on the left and the point where the river necks down on the right. This is the signal for some

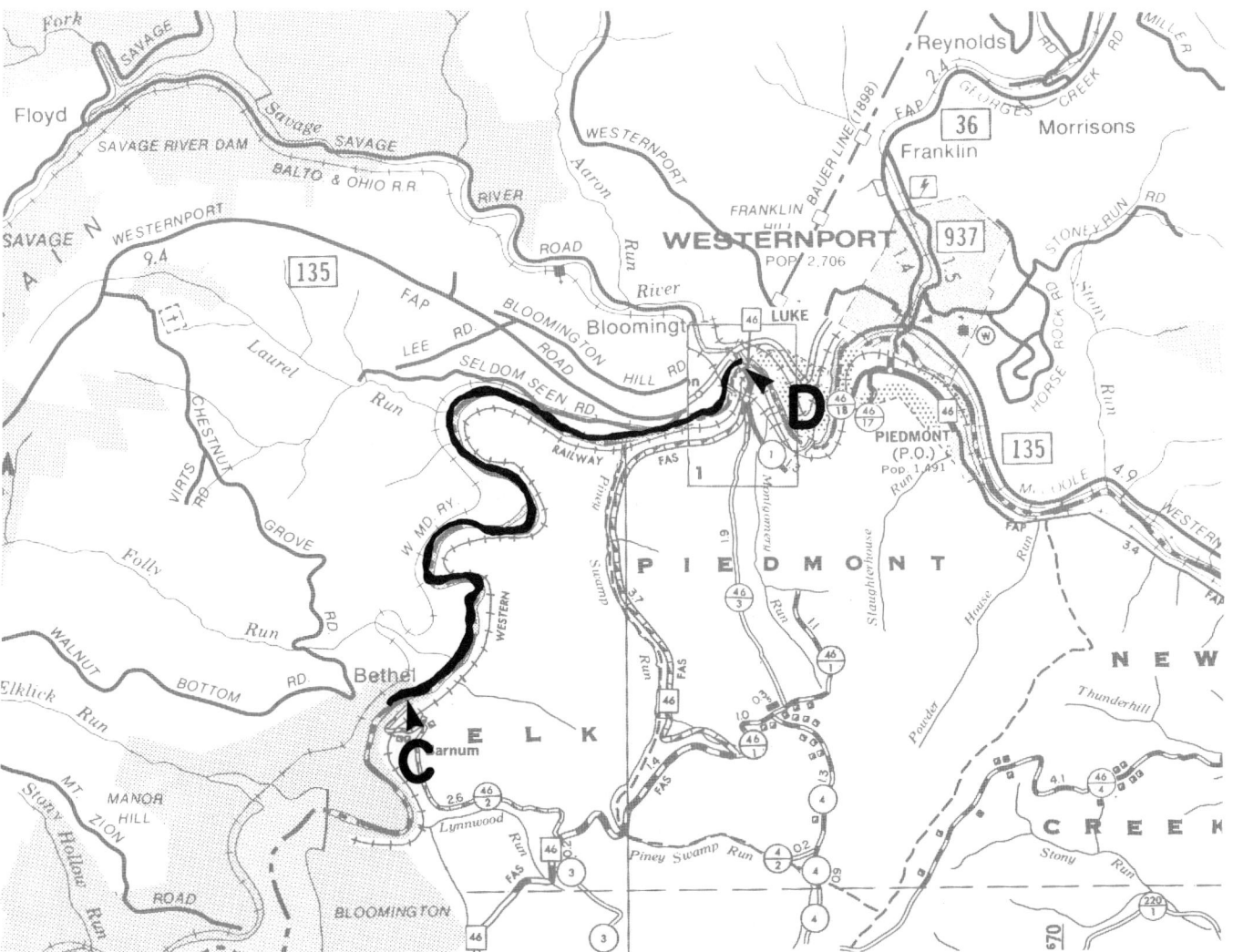

Bob Opachko surfing one of the two holes between the cobble bar and railroad tracks described on the preceding page. Photo by Ed Grove.

good low Class III twisty waves on the right at 1,000 cfs Try them, you'll like them—particularly if your balance is good.

After another pool the river necks down slightly on the left and you're faced with a second helping of standing waves not quite as dynamic as those just upstream. However, there is a vigorous surfing hole and two good surfing waves at the end of this rapid.

Next you will encounter a long pool and another island. Go right. Pools and long Class I–II rapids alternate until you reach a railroad bridge a half mile from the take-out. The bridge is followed by another Class I–II rapids, a long pool, and then the river splits. Go left this time. About five minutes later you will approach a concrete-and-stone-block railroad bridge. The concrete is located on the upstream face of the bridge and the stone block on the downstream face. The take-out is only 50–100 yards below this bridge on the left—just above where the Savage River joins the North Branch.

It's a shame that sufficient water on this delightful section is now solely generated by dam releases. As of this writing, water is released only four days a year in the period from August through early October. Remember, this water comes from the bottom of a big dam and therefore is very cold. Decked boaters in particular should pay attention if the day is brisk and cloudy.

As described above, this section of the North Branch at 1,000 cfs makes for a very pleasant trip. At 600 cfs the river is somewhat gentler and pickier. All rapids except one are no more than straightforward Class II's, and even the double ledge exception softens to an easier Class III. Conversely, at 1,250 cfs the river clearly is pushier, and some of the wave trains develop more of a Class III character.

Sideling Hill Creek

This section of Sideling Hill Creek is a Class I–II pure delight for good novice paddlers. However, the scenery and frequency of mild whitewater action on this 13-mile trip are sufficient to attract more experienced boaters. Most of the trip wanders near the base of 1,600-foot-high Sideling Hill, which has 200- to 400-foot-high cliffs and sharp slopes made of crumbling shale, a soft sedimentary rock. Because of the poor shale soil with nutrients leached away by quickly draining precipitation, only the toughest trees grow here — pines and eastern red cedar. Sharp-eyed paddlers can spot columbine as well as prickly pear cactus along the way. In early May red columbine flowers give a bright touch while yellow prickly pear flowers add their own bit of dazzle in the latter part of June. The rapids are gravel bars and broken ledges which can be rather spicy when they occur on tight turns. Reasonable boat control and a solid brace are important in these situations.

The first half of the trip passes primarily through woods and a gorge that are partially included in the Sideling Hill Wildlife Management Area. In the latter half, the river skirts abandoned farms and traverses the Lillie-Aaron Straus Wilderness Area of the Boy Scouts of America. The main hazard of note is a deteriorating low-water bridge about a mile below Zeigler Road near the take-out by Lock 56 at Pearre. Other hazards include the occasional log in the river and the multitude of anglers during spring trout season.

The put-in for this trip is located at the Old US 40 bridge, just downstream or south of the newer US 40 highway. On the downstream side of the bridge you can find an old Randy Carter canoeing gauge. A more rustic gauge is the U-shaped root growing in the old stone bridge abutment on river right at the put-in. The bottom of the root is about nine inches above canoeing zero and should so equate with the nearby Randy Carter gauge.

Shortly below the put-in the paddler wanders through a pretty gorge of woods and scenic shale cliffs. Roughly a mile into the trip, after a bend to the right and a nice Class I–II rapids, a pretty waterfall appears on the left. The only real sign of civilization in this gorge is a telephone line two miles or so after the put-in. The cliffs and Class I–II rapids on this winding stream continue with a pleasing frequency until one reaches a Class II ledge just as the river turns sharply left. This ledge should be run on the left and is roughly four miles into the trip. Here in the gorge, the gradient is a bit steeper—up to 25 feet a mile at one point. Following the ledge, cliffs and Class I–II rapids continue for another mile or so. After five miles the gorge ends and the paddler soon reaches Norris Road, a rough ford-type take-out not recommended except in emergencies.

Just below Norris Road the creek splits around a couple of islands, and more nicely spaced Class I–II rapids continue for a mile or so. You will see farmland on the right and Sideling Hill above on the left, followed by a pretty

Sideling Hill Creek. Photo by Steve Ferendo.

145

146 Sideling Hill Creek

Section: Old US 40 to Potomac River (Pearre, MD)

Counties: Allegany (MD)

USGS Quads: Bellegrove

Suitable for: Day cruising

Skill Level: Accomplished novices

Months Runnable: Winter and spring after wet spell or hard rain

Interest Highlights: Bluffs and cliffs; Sideling Hill; 1848 C and O canal aqueduct

Scenery: Beautiful for most of the trip

Difficulty: Class I–II

Average Width: 15–30 feet

Velocity: Moderate

Gradient: 16 feet per mile; 1 mile in gorge 25 feet per mile

Runnable Water Levels:
  Minimum: Wier runnable below Ziegler road; 0 feet Randy Carter gauge at put-in; 3.2 feet on Saxton gauge (Raystown Branch of Juniata River) is a very rough correlation—call the U.S. Weather Bureau in Harrisburg (717) 234-6812
  Maximum: Flood stage

Hazards: Deteriorating low-water bridge 1 mile below Ziegler Road; occasional logs in stream

Scouting: Approach the low-water bridge carefully

Portages: Low-water bridge 1 mile below Ziegler Road

Rescue Index: Remote

Source of Additional Information: None

Access Points	River Miles	Shuttle Miles
A–B	13	11.0 miles west 13.5 miles east

Access Point Ratings: Put-in and take-out are very good.

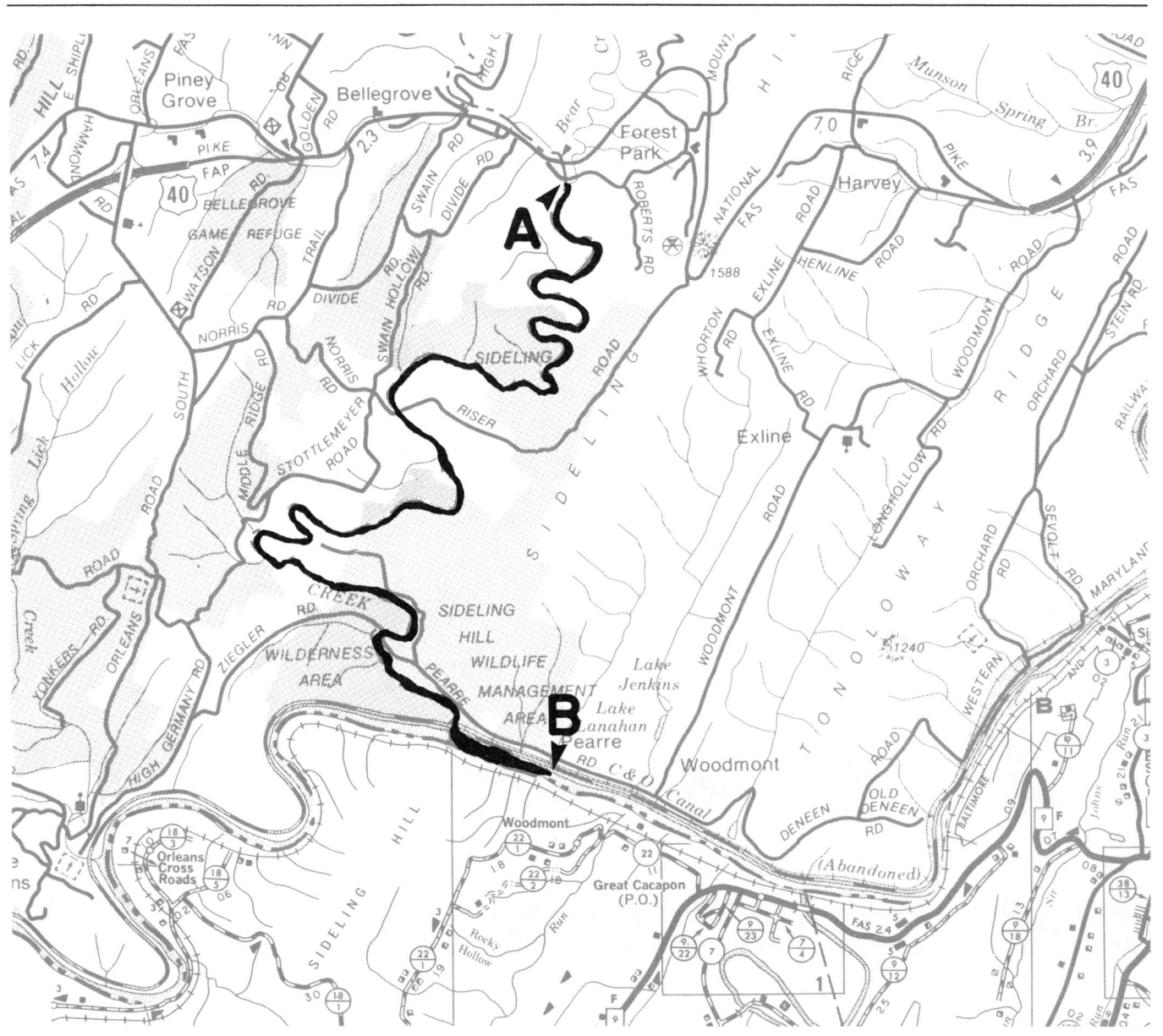

rock wall on the left. Over a mile later, past three bends and Stottlemeyer Road on the right, you'll encounter another Class II rapids. At that point paddle almost due east—straight toward Sideling Hill—for about a mile. After a right turn below a high bluff is another Class II rapids, followed by high cliffs on a second right turn.

Below the cliffs one crosses Zeigler Road. You can take out here if you are pooped and want to avoid a portage downstream. Immediately following Zeigler Road is an easy Class II weir. If you haven't yet seen the Randy Carter gauge upstream, there is enough water for the trip if the weir is runnable. About a mile below Zeigler Road lies the aforementioned disintegrating low-water bridge that must be approached with care and carried on the left. Roughly a quarter mile below the low-water bridge is the 110-foot arch of a picturesque C & O Canal Aqueduct built in 1848. Just past the aqueduct, Sideling Hill Creek enters the Potomac. The take-out is about a half mile downstream opposite Lock 56 of the C & O Canal at Pearre.

Because much of the Sideling Hill Creek area is remote, this is a good opportunity to spot wildlife. Deer are often seen, as well as beaver, muskrats, racoons (early morning), and squirrels. Bird life includes wild turkeys, turkey vultures, hawks, and an occasional bald eagle.

Incidentally, if you prefer a big winding river to a little winding stream, the serpentine 25-mile section of the Potomac from Paw Paw to Pearre (Class A-I) is worth consideration—particularly for low-key paddlers who like weekend canoe campers. There are periodic "hiker-biker" stops provided on the C & O Canal along the way with such colorful names as Sorrel Ridge, Stickpile Hill, Devils Alley, and Indigo Neck. Sorrel Ridge is near the scenic Paw Paw tunnel on the C & O Canal and most preferred by canoeists. These stops provide campsites, outdoor restrooms, and potable water as the Potomac snakes its way between Paw Paw and Pearre. There is also a 14-mile canoeable stretch above this section of Sideling Hill Creek, but it is not nearly as spectacular, and the rapids only reach Class I in difficulty.

Finally, when you run this creek the first time, try to go with someone who has run it before. You will need some intelligent help to guess the water level before arriving at the put-in. Although Sideling Hill Creek is up several times during the year, there are no gauges that reasonably correlate to those on the river. Also, the shuttle roads on the western side of the creek are not marked, and one can easily make a wrong turn. The shuttle roads on the eastern side of the creek are much easier to follow but are longer and require the substantial effort of crossing Sideling Hill.

Antietam Creek

Because of the numerous bridges crossing Antietam Creek from below Funkstown to Antietam, this is a roll-your-own Class I–II novice trip that depends on how many of the 22 miles between these two towns you wish to paddle. The Class I's are numerous riffles formed by gravel bars and small ledges. The Class II's are primarily the remains of old mill dams thoughtfully spaced over much of this section. The only hazards are located in the Devil's Backbone Park area: a six-foot dam followed a mile later by a three-foot dam. Also, you should scout the rapids at each bridge and dam; high water in recent years has carried trees into the entrances of rapids around the bridges, making them hazardous. Paddlers should watch for trees in the river (sweepers) below some rapids when the water is high.

On this 22-mile stretch, farmhouses, bridges, old mills, and stone walls complement rather than detract from the rural setting. There are scenic lunch stops galore. The remains of dams that were used to provide water power for the mills have formed good Class II rapids at Poffenburger Road (the first put-in), Wagaman Road, and Roxbury Road during the first third of the trip. There is also a triple ledge two and a half miles downstream from Wagaman Road.

After this ledge and about eight and a half miles into this 22 mile section, paddlers must portage the six-foot dam at Devil's Backbone Park just upstream of Route 68. A mile below the six-foot dam is a sharp three-foot dam that is now breached on the sides; the right side can be run with care.

The next five and a half miles from Manor Church Road to Keedysville Road are easily paddled and isolated, which gives you the opportunity to watch for ducks, beaver, and your favorite songbird. The minimum level for the 14-mile upper stretch is three feet on the Burnside Bridge gauge farther downstream.

The last seven and a half miles below Keedysville Road (Hicks Bridge) are quite interesting. For starters, a beautiful waterfall appears on the right about one mile below Hicks Bridge, and then you enter that stretch of the river that wanders through Antietam National Battlefield. Roughly two miles below Hicks Bridge you will reach Route 34 and a nice Class II ledge formed by the remains of an old mill dam. For those who don't have a lot of time or for winter paddlers, the remaining five miles or so downstream from Route 34 make for a scenic short trip.

A mile below Route 34 is Burnside Bridge, where paddlers can further admire Antietam Battlefield and its striking markers. Also, there is a surfing wave formed by a two-foot V-shaped dam that is easily run. The Burnside Bridge gauge is located just above the dam and should read at least 2.6 feet for the lower section. Before running the upper or lower sections of this creek, check this gauge because the Frederick gauge gives only a rough correlation.

Only four miles remain to the take-out. The main Class II rapids on this final stretch is the rock garden slalom just above the Harpers Ferry Road take-out on either right or left.

Sharp-eyed folks can spot a surprising amount of domes-

Furnace Rapids on Antietam Creek. Photo by Walter Foster.

tic and other wildlife on this trip. In addition to cows in the pastures along the riverbanks, there are great blue herons, ducks, woodpeckers, kingfishers, quail, deer, rabbits, beaver, and signs of river otters. One other interesting feature about this creek is that it continues to flow after other rivers ice up. So if you crave some winter paddling when ice has your favorite river in its frosty grip, check out Antietam Creek.

Section: Poffenburger Road to Harpers Ferry Road
Counties: Washington (MD)
USGS Quads: Funkstown, Keedysville
Suitable for: Day cruising
Skill Level: Novices
Months Runnable: Winter and spring
Interest Highlights: Picturesque bridges, old mills and farms; Antietam Battlefield
Scenery: Pretty to beautiful in spots
Difficulty: Class I–II
Average Width: 50–100 feet
Velocity: Moderate
Gradient: 7 feet per mile
Runnable Water Levels:
  Minimum: 3.0 feet (upper) and 2.6 feet (lower) on Burnside Bridge gauge; roughly 4.0 feet (upper) and 2.8 feet (lower) on Frederick gauge
  Maximum: 7.0 feet (upper) and 6.5 feet (lower) on the Frederick gauge
Hazards: Six-foot dam at Devils Backbone; three-foot dam one mile downstream
Scouting: Recommended if running three-foot dam and at rapids formed by bridges/dams; look for trees in chutes
Portages: Six-foot dam at Devils Backbone
Rescue Index: Accessible
Source of Additional Information: National Weather Service, Frederick gauge (301) 899-7378

Access Points	River Miles	Shuttle Miles
A–B	6.5	4.0
B–C	2.0	3.0
C–D	2.0	3.0
D–E	3.5	4.5
E–F	2.3	2.0
F–G	1.0	2.0
G–H	4.2	3.5

Access Points: (All points are rated as good.)
 A: Poffenberger Road
 B: Roxbury Road
 C: Route 68
 D: Manor Church Road
 E: Keedysville Road
 F: Route 34
 G: Burnside Bridge Road
 H: Harpers Ferry Road

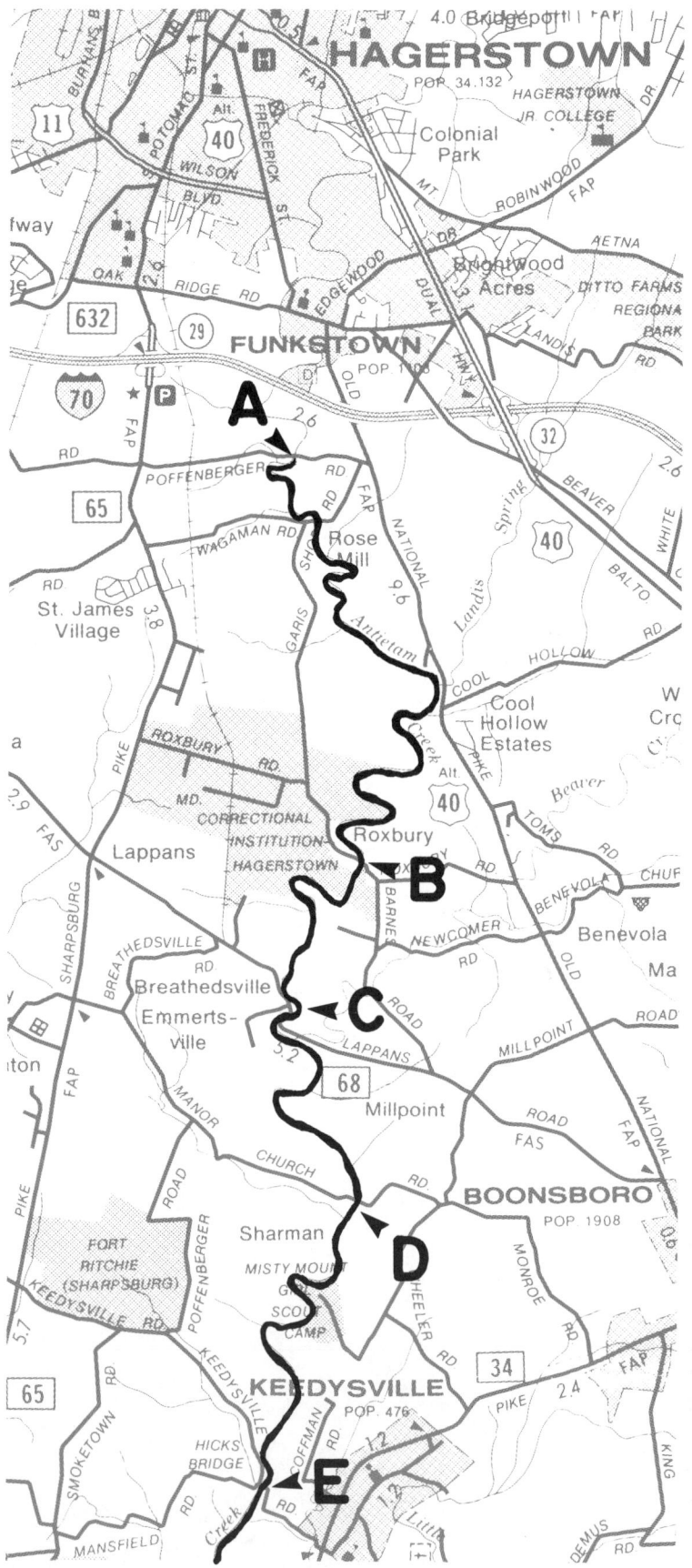

150   Antietam Creek

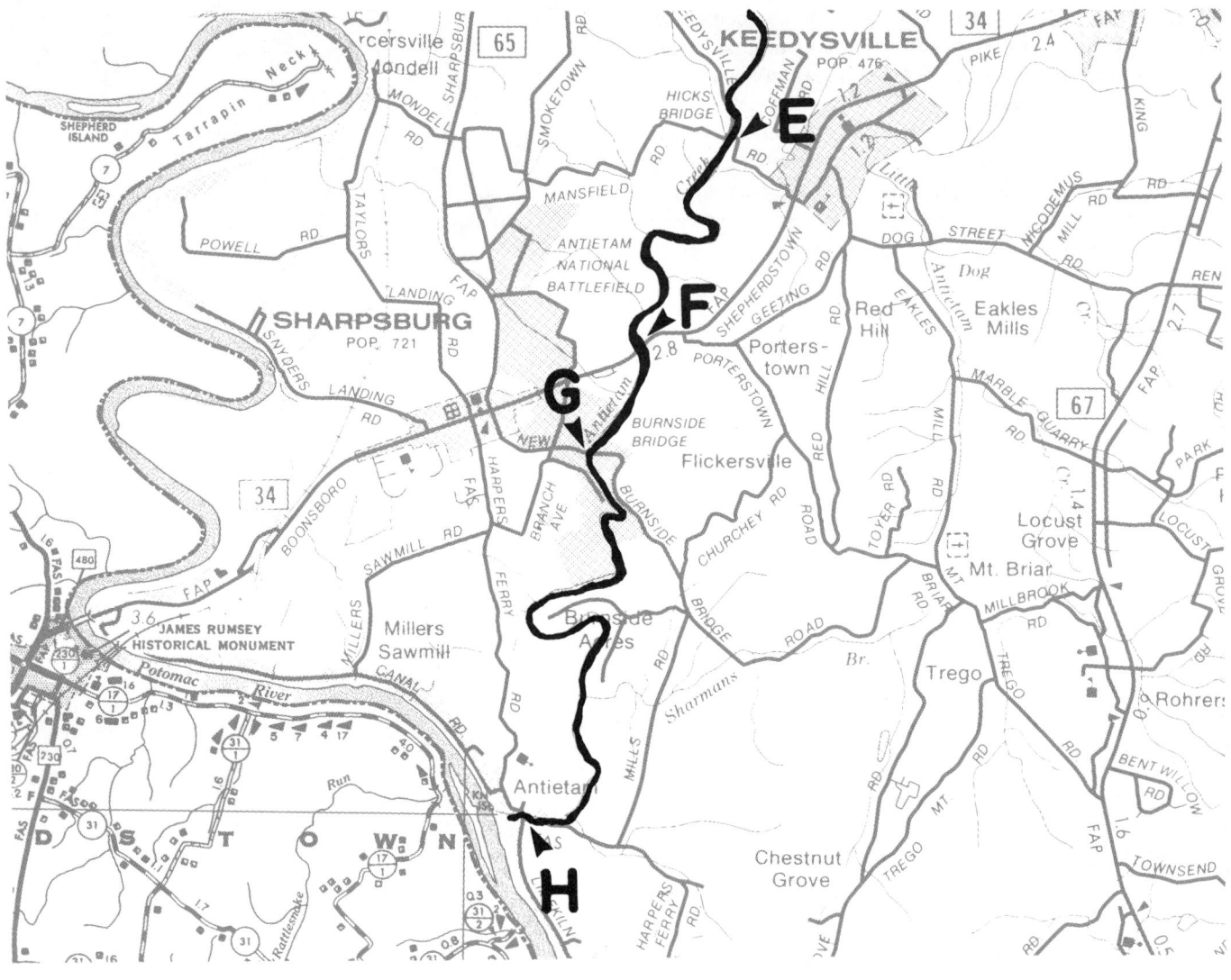

Shenandoah and Potomac Rivers

Bull Falls and the Staircase

One of the true classic Class II–III trips for accomplished intermediates and shepherded novices who want to sharpen their paddling skills is Bull Falls and the Staircase. If you are willing to pay the admission price of two to three miles of flatwater, the remaining three and a half miles of whitewater make the trip worthwhile. But the flatwater also has a positive side: It's a lazy start for rafters, boaters, and experienced tubers as well as a perfect opportunity to sharpen novices on whitewater strokes they will soon need.

Almost halfway through the trip, Bull Falls (Class III) starts off the more serious whitewater with a bang. Below Bull Falls there are fairly continuous Class I and Class II rapids through the Staircase until the first possible take-out at Harpers Ferry is reached. Below this point there still is Whitehorse Rapids (Class II–III) before the final take-out at Sandy Hook.

The trip from Millville to Sandy Hook is a very scenic one. The low hills where the Shenandoah and Potomac rivers merge are very pretty, and there is the charming and historic town of Harpers Ferry to poke around in after the trip. Also, this is a dependable trip because the rivers hold their water for virtually the entire year. The only dangerous time is when the river is too high on occasion in winter and spring and rarely during other times of the year.

For the put-in on Bloomery Road, launch underneath the power lines by the transformer station on the outskirts of Millville, or, to avoid some of the flatwater, put in farther downstream. About the last put-in is River and Trail Outfitters—a good one and a quarter miles below the transformer station. However, you should get permission from the Outfitters and join an organized club trip if possible. Finally, be careful about leaving shuttle cars at isolated spots on Bloomery Road; thieves have broken into unattended cars on numerous occasions. Having a gracious camper or outfitter keep an eye on your shuttle cars would probably be very wise.

Wherever you put in along this stretch, notice that there are many camping spots on river left. Also, silver maples, sycamores, cottonwoods, box elders, and occasional ashes line the riverbanks. The Route 340 shuttle road is lined with royal paulownia trees which are breathtaking in midspring when they are covered with large, light purple flowers. From the put-in to Bull Falls two to three miles downstream, the river is popular for fishing in canoes, johnboats, and other watercraft. Smallmouth bass, bluegills, channel catfish, and the omnipresent carp are the primary fish that swim these waters. Also, be alert for bird life: Great blue herons, turkey vultures, ducks, geese, and swallows dart above the paddler. On one trip a rare and majestic piliated woodpecker was even sighted.

Bull Falls. Photo by Ed Grove.

Just below the power-line put-in the paddler has the choice of running a Class I channel between two islands in the center of the river or continuing down the left to Class I riffles at the end of the second island. About a half mile downstream, you will pass the Millville gauge on the left, which is followed by the put-ins for various outfitters on the left and summer homes on the right. The river is about 100 yards wide here.

Over two miles from the power-line put-in, some small islands appear on the right, and you will be heading straight toward a hill roughly 200 feet high. Approaching this hill several minutes later, you'll see rocks across the right and center of the river with a long Class II rock garden on the left. Notice the nice stone wall supporting the railroad track and the interesting rock formations on the left when passing through this rapids. There are also one or two mild surfing spots near the bottom of this slalom.

Then, in the pool below this rapids, look for an exposed broad, flat ledge blocking most of the river. This is your signal to stop on the 50-foot-long section of the rock ledge between the current flowing through a narrow notch on the right and diagonally from right to left over a more powerful drop to the left.

Congratulations. After three miles of warm-up you have arrived at Bull Falls and novices can now start quivering. At low and medium levels the long, low ledge here is a perfect place to beach boats, rafts, and tubes before scouting, eating lunch, or watching the continuous parade of boats and bodies go over the falls.

The most classic route here is the three- to four-foot Class

152 Bull Falls and the Staircase

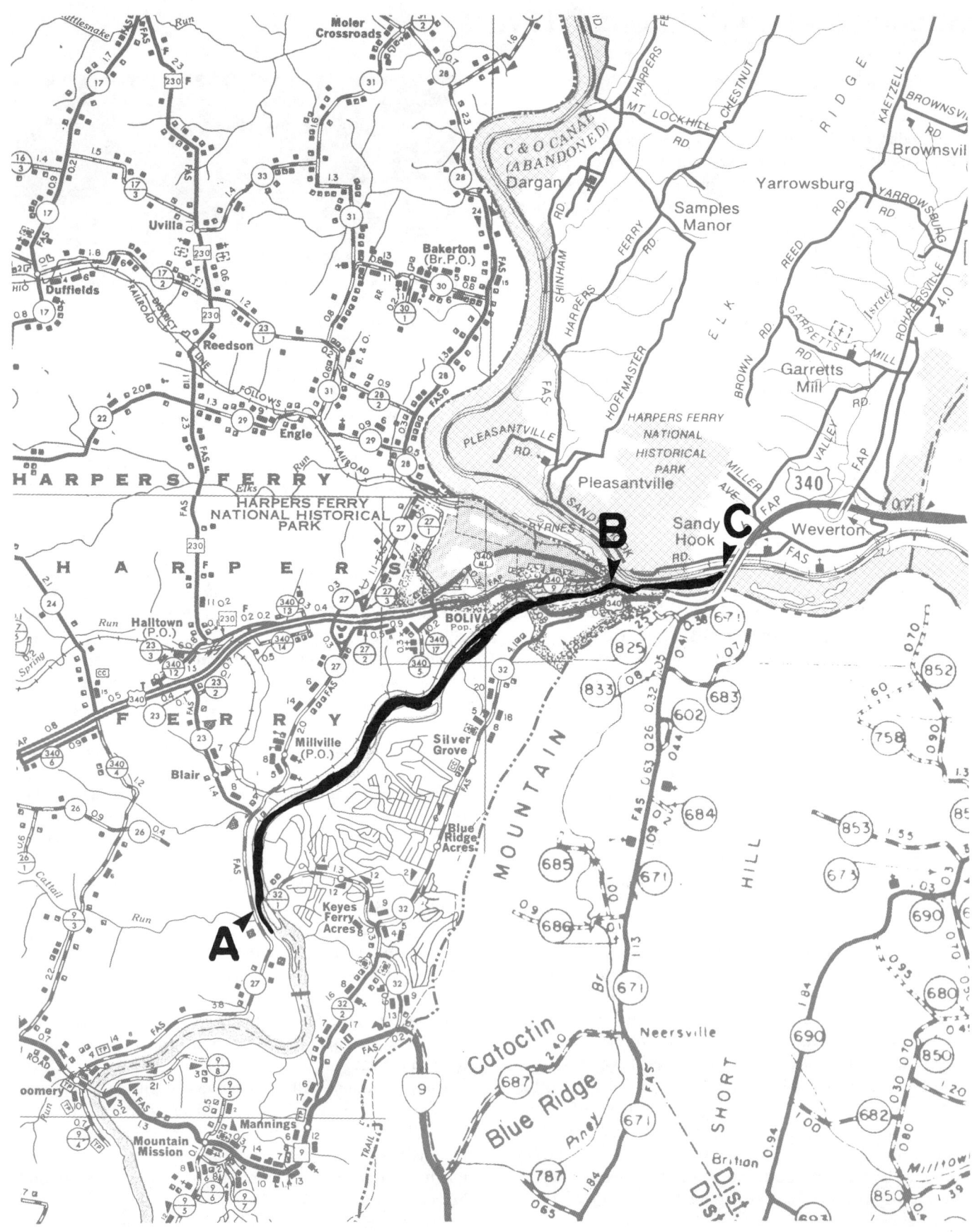

III drop immediately to the left of the large, low scouting ledge. The paddler should start this run reasonably close to the scouting ledge to prevent being carried too far left by the current. Upon reaching the drop notice that there is a just-exposed rock (low water) or a roostertail (higher water) about five feet from the scouting ledge. Turn hard right 90 degrees and run this drop on the tongue just to the left of this rock/roostertail. The reason for running this drop tight right is simple: The farther left one goes the more chance there is of hitting a submerged rock in the channel.

After running this drop, keep your boat parallel with the current because at lower levels a hydraulic about 25 feet below can flip those who drop into it sideways. Incidentally, this hydraulic is a great teacher for those who want to explore the world of sideways hole sitting. It is gentle enough not to be a keeper but tough enough to bounce boaters around a bit; sometimes considerable effort is required to exit. If you plan on sitting in it sideways, have floatation in your boat and wear a helmet—the ledge is shallow. Also, have a rescue boater nearby to pick up the pieces in the pool below. As the Millville gauge reaches three feet, this hole starts to wash out and is not as grabby.

Getting back to Bull Falls, the classic drop described above is actually the third runnable slot from the left bank. To run the other two, either scout them from below after running Bull Falls the classic way or look them over from the railroad tracks on the left after beaching your boat upstream. The drop closest to the railroad tracks is basically two drops (Class II–III) which can be run center. The second drop from the left (low Class III) can also be run, but scout it first to avoid a nasty rock near the bottom.

The fourth slot (on the right of the scouting rock) is a Class II–III rapid with a one-foot ledge on the top into a narrow slot below that drops two to three feet. Novice paddlers and tubers too nervous about the classic drop just to the left of the scouting rock can run this one if they have some boat control. Incidentally, this slot also has a small surfing spot near the end at moderate levels.

The adventurous can explore other drops farther to the right on this riverwide ledge. The first of these is a straight drop which used to have a tree lodged in the normal runout. The next drop is a narrow slot with a nasty rock to dodge immediately below entry. There are perhaps four other possibilities farther to the right that are unrunnable at low water and may be possibilities at high water—particularly a rocky slalom on the extreme right.

The great thing about Bull Falls is that the easy carry over the scouting rock allows paddlers many opportunities to run this rapids. They can either take alternate routes or try again if they don't run it right the first time. However, at really high levels, this riverwide ledge is covered, and parts of Bull Falls take on Class IV characteristics.

After a hopefully invigorating stop at Bull Falls, one reaches a 50-yard pool before hitting 50 yards of Class I–II standing waves. These are followed by another 50-yard pool and a Class II ledgy drop best taken on the far right at lower levels. A nice long pool follows, and then the river splits in several places. Going from right to left, the first three splits are straightforward Class I–II drops over covered cobbles with some riffles below. The last alternative on the extreme left, a small Class I–II slalom, gives one the feeling of running a creek.

From the long pool located below the splits you can clearly see the first Route 340 bridge. You are now about to begin the well-known Staircase—so named because it is a stairstep-like series of ledges which continue for a good mile. At lower levels this mile is generally Class II, but at high levels it starts taking on Class IV characteristics because of its length, strength, complexity, and the big holes that develop.

The Route 340 bridge marks four and a half miles from the transformer station put-in and is about halfway down

---

Section: Millville, WV to Sandy Hook, MD

Counties: Washington (MD) and Jefferson (WV)

USGS Quads: Charles Town, Harpers Ferry

Suitable for: Day-trip cruising

Skill Level: Shepherded novices and intermediates (moderate levels); advanced paddlers (high levels)

Months Runnable: Most of the year except for extended dry periods

Interest Highlights: Scenic confluence of Shenandoah and Potomac Rivers; historic town of Harpers Ferry

Scenery: Pretty to beautiful in spots

Difficulty: Class II–III at moderate levels; Class III–IV at high levels

Average Width: 250–1,000 feet

Velocity: Moderate to fast

Gradient: 10 feet per mile; 3.5 miles at 15–20 feet per mile

Runnable Water Levels:
  Minimum: 1.8 feet Millville gauge
  Maximum: 5.5 feet Millville gauge

Hazards: Occasional trees in river

Scouting: Bull Falls (Class III)

Portages: None

Rescue Index: Accessible

Source of Additional Information: National Weather Service, Millville gauge (301) 899-7378; commercial outfitters near the river

Access Points	River Miles	Shuttle Miles
A–B	5.0	5.5
A–C	6.5	8.0

Access Point Ratings: A, excellent; B, very good; C, fair

the Staircase. At low levels the upper half of the Staircase tests one's water-reading ability because it is very picky. Perhaps the best route at lower levels is to start on the left and then work toward the center. Just above the center abutment of the bridge is a one-and-a-half-foot ledge which can be run to the right or left of the abutment. The ledge also offers surfing opportunities.

After getting a breather by the center bridge abutment, paddlers can continue their Staircase descent. Just below the abutment to the right is another nice one-and-a-half-foot ledge followed by 100–200 yards of little ledges. Then there is a spicy Class II–III double drop in river center over two one-and-a-half-foot ledges called Hesitation Ledge by local paddlers. Another 100 yards of small ledges follow, and you then find yourself in a series of nicer Class II ledges and surfing spots until you reach a ten-foot-high wall with a ten-foot circular hole in it on river left. These are the ruins of an old cotton mill. Just below this wall is the Harpers Ferry beach.

Having come five miles below the transformer put-in you can take out at the massive parking lot on river left in scenic Harpers Ferry. However, if you are not in a hurry, continue downstream and within a half mile you will reach the confluence of the Potomac and the Shenandoah. Greeting you at this confluence are the abutment remains of an old bridge on the Shenandoah, a working railroad bridge over the Potomac, a striking hill 1,200 feet above the river, and a railroad tunnel. Once past the confluence, look back upstream at the pretty village of Harpers Ferry nestled in the trees.

The last mile begins with an easy Class I set of waves, with a good surfing spot on the left. A couple of minutes later you'll encounter a pleasant 50-yard run of Class I–II waves. Shortly below these waves the river flows between two large rocks on the left with some impressive waves below. This is Whitehorse Rapids. At the top left are a couple of surfing possibilities at reasonable levels and below are about 50 yards of vigorous Class II–III waves, which become Class III at higher levels. There are also two routes to the right of Whitehorse that should be looked at before being run.

Just below Whitehorse, pick up any errant boats and boaters and begin looking for a wall on the left. The second Route 340 bridge looms just below. After several minutes, you will notice a sandy beach and a three- to four-foot sandy hill instead of a wall. This is the first possible take-out at Sandy Hook, but if you go a couple of minutes farther downstream and remain about 100 yards or so upstream of the bridge, you will find another beach. This is the preferred take-out because the walk takes you over more gradual terrain. This 125-yard portage first goes over the C & O Canal towpath (which is also the Appalachian Trail here), then continues down across some broken crossties over a muddy stream (the old canal), and finally over the railroad tracks to

Bull Falls. Photo by Mark May.

Sandy Hook Road. Be very careful when crossing the tracks here; freight trains pass frequently at a good clip.

One can also take out on river right just above the Route 340 bridge, but the portage is longer and you have to carry up a nasty little hill at the very end. On the other hand, a nice little cascade from a nearby stream provides welcome wet relief on hot days.

Unlike the first take-out at the Harpers Ferry parking lot, it is hard to find a place to park cars at Sandy Hook. You basically have a few sloping places next to the railroad track or in people's driveways on the other side of Sandy Hook Road, but parking in driveways is not recommended unless you get permission. So leave as few cars as possible and watch your valuables; there have been some thefts here, too. Perhaps the best way of dealing with the shuttle for this trip is by conning a couple of shuttle bunnies to do the chore. While you meander down the river, they can visit scenic Harpers Ferry and pick you up later in the day.

Harpers Ferry is rich in history. The first settler, a trader named Peter Stephens, arrived in 1733 and set up a primitive ferry service at the junction of the Potomac and Shenandoah rivers. Robert Harper, a millwright and the man for whom the town is named, settled here in 1747 and built a mill. The original ferry and mill are long gone. In the 1790s George Washington was instrumental in establishing a national armory here. By 1801, the armory was producing weapons, and arms produced at Harpers Ferry were used by Lewis and Clark on their famous westward expedition of 1804–1806. The arrival of the C & O Canal and the B & O Railroad in the 1830s generated prosperity, and by the 1850s Harpers Ferry had 3,000 residents.

In 1859, however, John Brown's raid on the eve of the Civil War thrust the town into national prominence and set the stage for its eventual decline. When the Civil War began in 1861, the armory and arsenal buildings were burned to prevent them from falling into Confederate hands. Because of the town's geographic location and railway system, both the Union and Confederate forces occupied the town intermittently throughout the war. Discouraged by war damage and fewer jobs, many people soon left. The finishing blow to the town was dealt by a series of devastating floods in the late 1800s.

Harpers Ferry has since been restored by the National Park Service and today is a delightful place to visit. Besides restored streets, shops, houses, and public buildings, there are other points of interest. On the Shenandoah side above the town is Jefferson Rock. Here, in 1783, Thomas Jefferson was so taken with the view he thought it was "worth a voyage across the Atlantic." Not far from this rock is the grave of Robert Harper and a very interesting cemetery. On the left side of the Potomac River across from Harpers Ferry is the Appalachian Trail and the C & O Canal towpath for day hikers and backpackers.

Victim of the old Wier Dam remains, Staircase section of the Shenandoah River. Photo by Steve Ferendo.

Gunpowder Falls

Gunpowder Falls is a pleasant Class II-III trip at moderate levels for good intermediate boaters. A 3.3-mile run from Route 1 to Route 40, it passes through a pretty but shallow wooded gorge and has only one drawback: It's too short. One can put in at Lower Loch Raven Dam upstream, but this would mean an additional seven-mile scenic paddle over flatwater with only occasional riffles.

The falls line of Gunpowder Falls begins just below Route 1. You can warm up by running the Class II rapids at the put-in and doing some elementary surfing at the bottom of this rapids. About a quarter mile below is Pot's Rock, a nice long Class II-III rapids entered by way of a rock garden 50 to 100 yards long. Then, move right with a quick cut back to the left just before dropping over a two-foot ledge. Adding spice to Pot's Rock, a fun surfing spot is located just below the ledge. Decked boaters can get enders here at one and a half to two feet on the Route 1 gauge. Shortly below Pot's Rock is a Class II rock garden.

The next rapids of significance occurs as the paddler reaches the I-95 bridge. Here a 100-yard Class II rock garden (Class III in high water) appears just above the bridge and continues well beyond. The rock garden ends and a pool is reached just as you pass under the nearby Route 7 bridge. You'll also hear an impressive roar at this point, which is your signal to get to river right and scout because you have a long, strong Class III rock garden of over 100 yards to run. There are surfing spots toward the end of the rapids. At higher levels it becomes a Class IV because of its length, strength, and complexity.

One can take out at the Route 7 bridge, which is the most convenient take-out, but this makes the trip only a couple of miles long. Also, the long Class III rock garden and a couple of other nice rapids will be missed.

Below Route 7 there are two good drops. The first is a relatively short Class II rock garden known as Finger Rock. The second is a Class II-III drop with a ledge on the left and (with enough water) a tight S turn on the right. First-timers should scout from river right. The second rapids also has reasonable surfing opportunities here and there.

The Route 40 bridge take-out follows. Take out on river left, and here you encounter the only problem with this otherwise pleasant trip: no legal parking near the bridge. The nearest place is a quarter to a half mile southwest of the bridge, so a shuttle driver to meet you or a willingness to hike is necessary.

There is a gauge on the Route 1 bridge put-in. Read it carefully above the mark of zero. The "perfect slalom" level (one foot) is a nice Class II-III run. However, the "perfect" level (four feet or so) is a real flush, and the trip should be considered in the Class III-IV range. At this level pay particular attention to the long rapids just below Route 7.

The Gunpowder is basically a winter or spring trip following a recent rain when the Loch Raven reservoir is full of water. This will usually produce runnable levels for a week. There is reasonable bird life along the river, such as herons and turkey buzzards, and the scenic gorge is restful. It's too bad this delightful trip isn't longer.

Long rock garden rapids just below Route 7, Gunpowder Falls. Photo by Ed Grove.

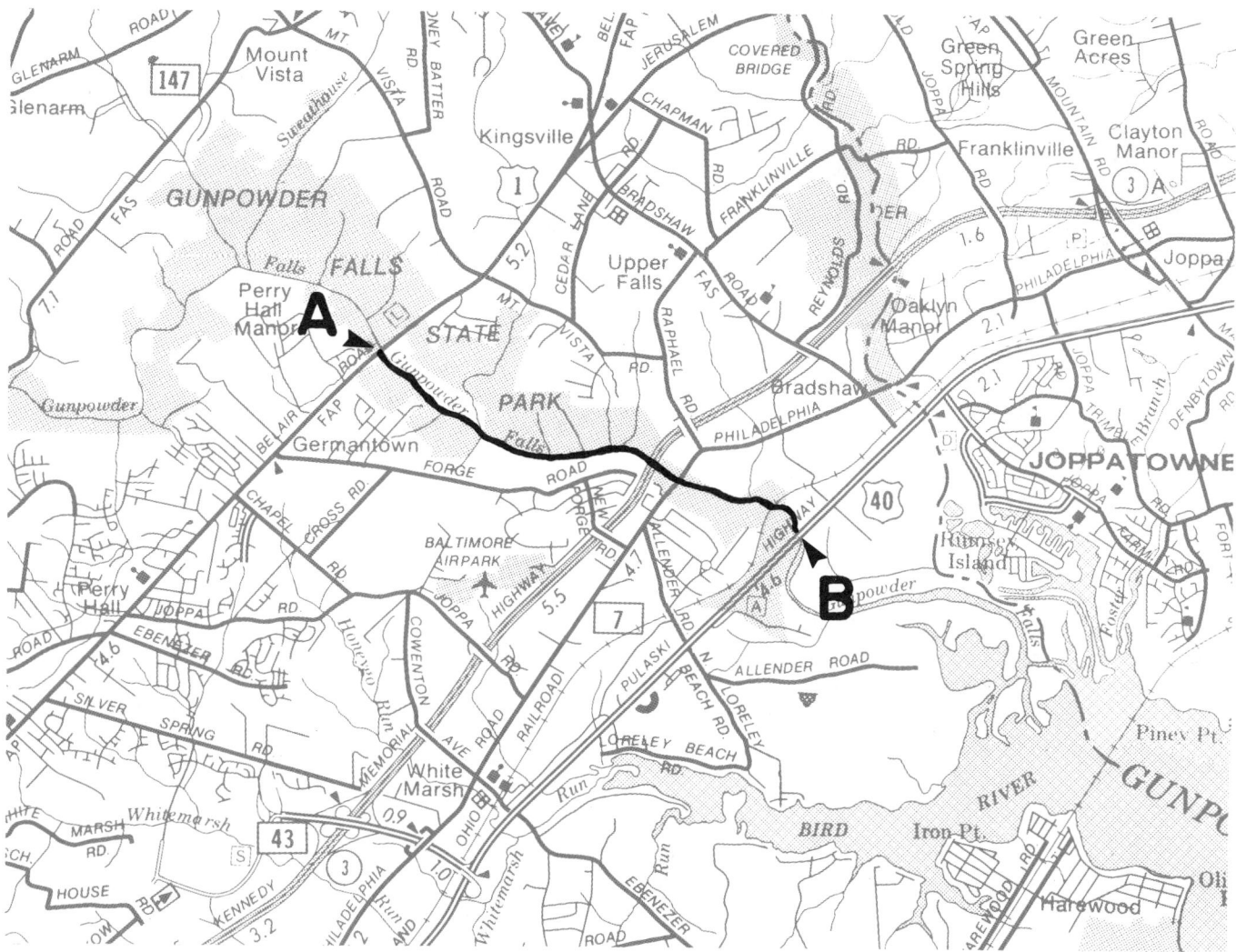

Section: Route 1 to Route 40

Counties: Baltimore (MD)

USGS Quads: White Marsh

Suitable for: Day-trip cruising

Skill Level: Intermediate boaters (moderate levels) and advanced boaters (high levels)

Months Runnable: Winter and spring after a hard rain when the reservoir is full

Interest Highlights: Nice wooded gorge

Scenery: Pretty in most spots

Difficulty: Class II–III at moderate levels; Class III–IV at high levels

Average Width: 50–100 feet

Velocity: Moderate to fast

Gradient: 20 feet per mile; 1/2 mile at 40 feet per mile

Runnable Water Levels:
  Minimum: 0 feet on Rt. 1 gauge
  Maximum: 4 feet on Rt. 1 gauge (very heavy water)

Hazards: Occasional tree in river

Scouting: Long rapids just below Rt. 7 are Class III (moderate level) or Class IV (high level)

Portages: None

Rescue Index: Accessible but difficult

Source of Additional Information: None

Access Points	River Miles	Shuttle Miles
A–B	3.3	5.0

Access Point Ratings: Put-in, very good; take-out, fair (no legal place to park)

Prime Hook Creek

Delaware Route 1 to Refuge Headquarters

For open and closet bird lovers Prime Hook Creek is a delight, but other folks will like it, too. Although there is no whitewater here, this seven-mile trip through a 9,000-acre National Wildlife Refuge is filled with variety and beauty for novice paddlers and their families. A good half day should be allowed for a leisurely paddle through this swamp forest in a vast freshwater marsh to enjoy fully the wildlife and scenery. Time should also be set aside in the first part of the trip to thread one's way through a series of long ponds with contiguous dead-end nesting ponds scattered here and there.

The put-in is located on the southern side of Waples Pond just behind a tavern on Route 1 near its junction with Route 5. Because this is private property, be sure to check with the managers of the tavern before leaving cars at the put-in. Here an eight-foot-wide stream exits the smaller eastern section of the pond, which has been split by Route 1. Look for a white National Wildlife Refuge sign which promises better things to come.

Just a couple of minutes from the put-in you will enter the first of a string of long ponds. As you begin paddling across the first pond, look for a white sign at the far end that says "To Blinds 27 and 28." Follow the sign, which refers to one of the numerous duck blinds in the refuge.

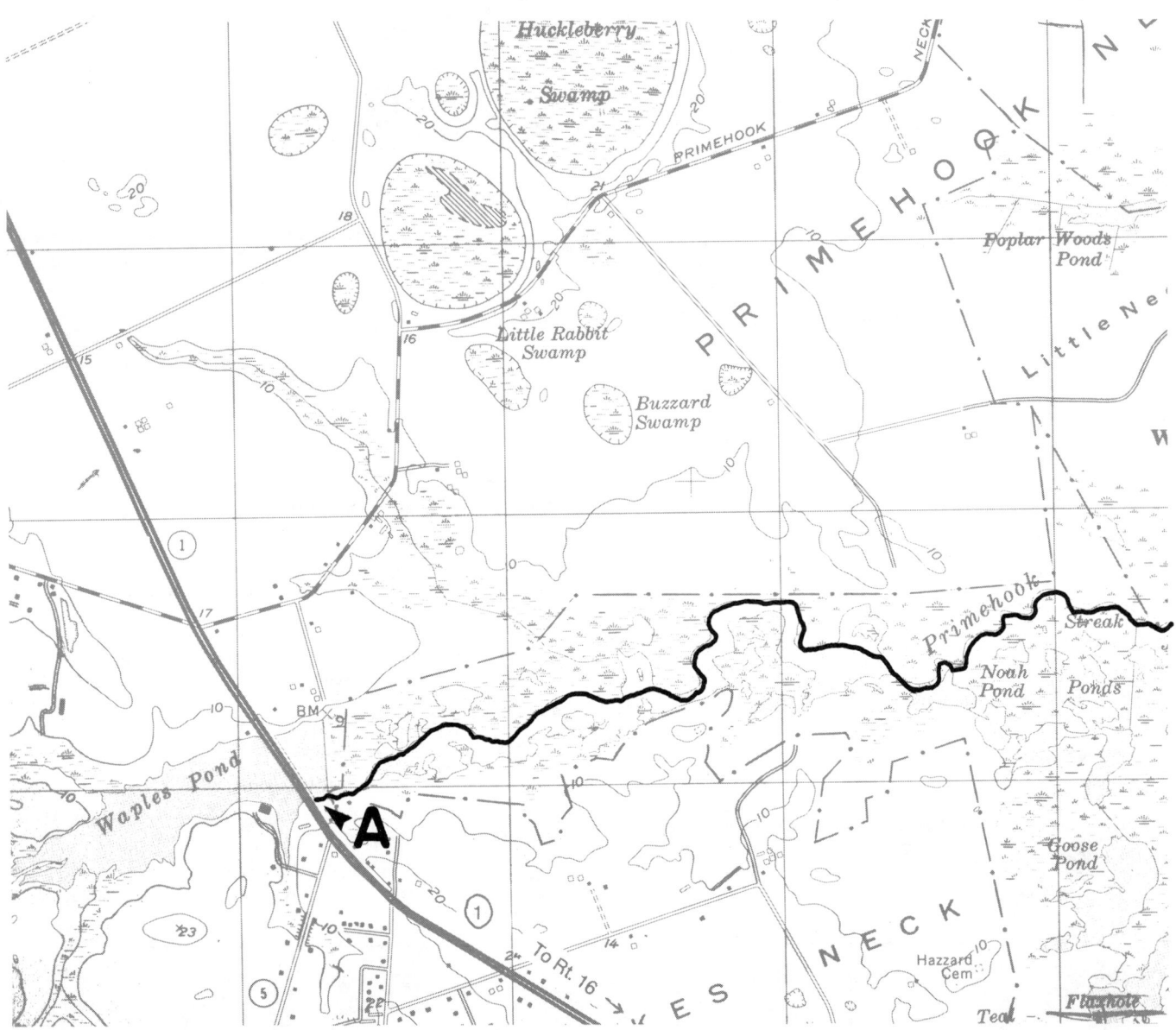

Section: Rt. 1 to Refuge Headquarters

Counties: Sussex (DE)

USGS Quads: Lewes, Milton

Suitable for: Day-trip cruising

Skill Level: Families and beginners

Months Runnable: All year except for extended dry periods

Interest Highlights: National Wildlife Refuge; swamp forest in freshwater marsh; many birds

Scenery: Very pretty to beautiful

Difficulty: Class I

Average Width: 15–200 feet

Velocity: Slow

Gradient: 0 feet per mile

Runnable Water Levels:
  Minimum: Not applicable
  Maximum: Not applicable

Hazards: Duck hunting blinds should be avoided

Scouting: None

Portages: None

Rescue Index: Accessible

Source of Additional Information: Refuge Manager, Prime Hook National Wildlife Refuge (302) 684-8419

Access Points	River Miles	Shuttle Miles
A–B	7.5	5.0

Access Point Ratings: Put-in and take-out are excellent.

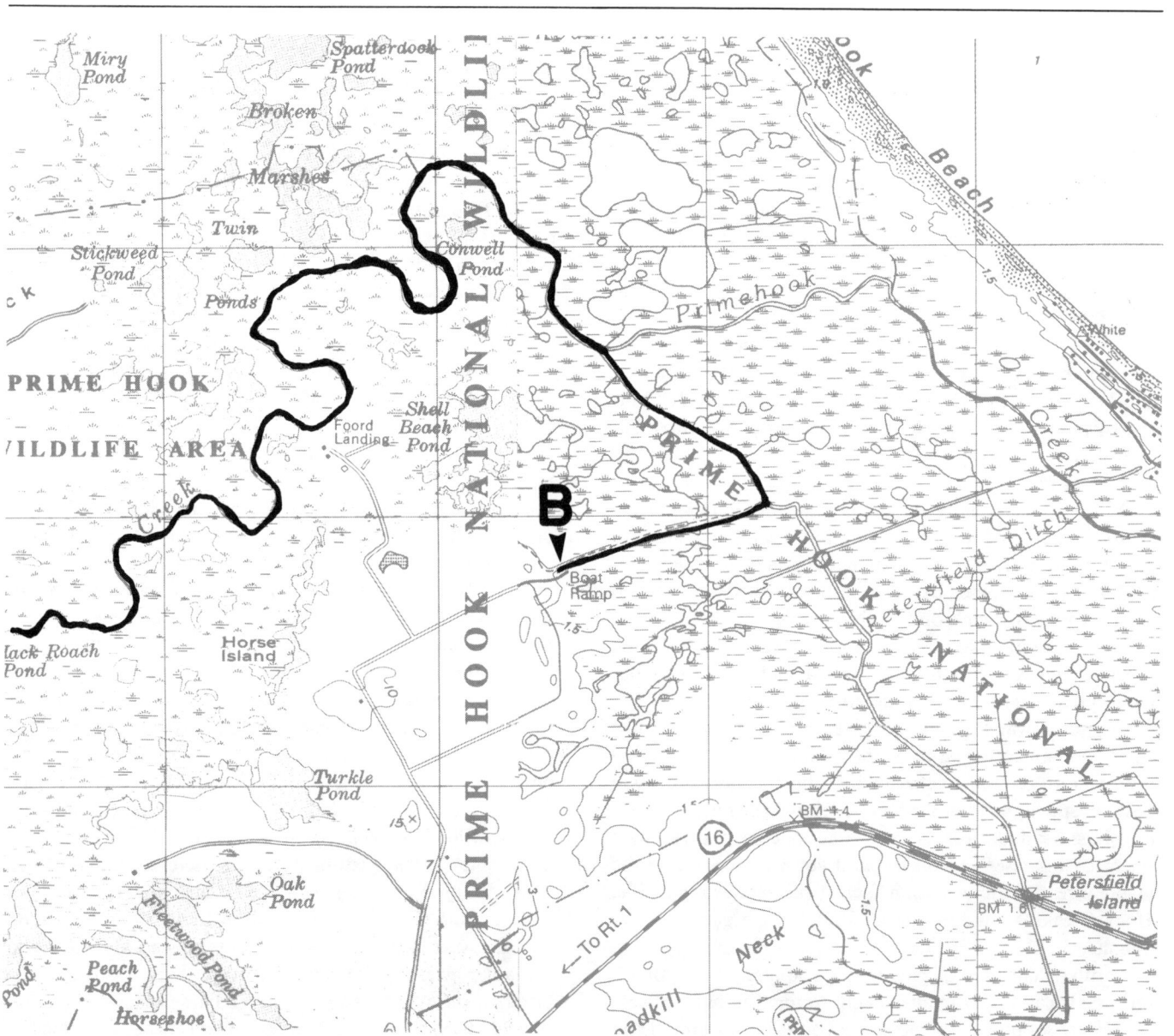

Prime Hook is a prime duck-hunting area and is usually open for hunting a week in early November, and from Thanksgiving through New Year's Day. During this period there may be nearly 20,000 ducks and geese on the refuge. However, if you paddle during hunting season, don't be alarmed; the duck blinds are located a good distance away from Prime Hook Creek and the other main channels you will be canoeing. Also, the blinds are so widely spaced that there is little chance that the hunters will deplete the very large duck and goose population in the refuge.

You will then pass through several other ponds while paddling generally east. As you paddle, take note of the several side ponds that are dotted with bird-nesting houses on poles. Although these birdhouses are primarily built for ducks during nesting season, starlings and even owls may make their nests in them. From March 1 to July 1 paddlers must stay 150 yards away from any active nest. These shallow nesting ponds also contain large carp which make impressive wakes as you paddle by. Don't look for the main channel to continue from these ponds, however; they are dead ends, as one of the authors discovered one day while racing the sunset through this area.

Paddle on the left side as you cross the first few main ponds until you reach an island of trees. Bear right around this island. (If you go left, you will find a narrow channel that dead-ends into a nesting pond.) Shortly after passing this island, you should see another sign in the distance at the end of the next pond that says "To Blinds 27 and 28." Follow it and you will soon pass Blind 28 going off to the right, followed by a sign for Blind 27 also going to the right and another sign on the left saying "Refuge Headquarters." Follow this latter sign and you will be paddling on a small 20- to 30-foot-wide channel. At this point you will have paddled about two miles.

With a dense marshy woods encroaching on this narrow twisting stream of inky-appearing but clear water, be prepared to see more bird life than on the ponds. On one beautiful warm December day one author flushed at least ten small groups of black ducks which were hiding within 50 feet of his passing boat. He also spooked several other duck species, numerous kingfishers, a red-tailed hawk, and a couple of great blue herons on this stretch.

About halfway through this seven-mile trip you will pass a shed and an access point on the right called Foords Landing, which is closed to the public. Shortly thereafter, you pass several signs to other blinds. Keep following the signs to refuge headquarters. About a half mile beyond the shed the left bank rises several feet and you will notice that the woods are becoming a thin facade of trees along Prime Hook Creek. Beyond this facade stretches a large freshwater marsh.

Another half mile of paddling and impressively tall 12-foot reeds called phragmites begin to line the bank. These reeds may soon be gone, however; because they provide no food for the resident wildlife, they are being sprayed so more nourishing vegetation can take their place.

At this point the channel is not as twisting or as narrow as the intimate swampy woods. This open channel, roughly 30 feet wide and with straightaways of 100 yards or so, makes for an interesting change and can be exciting. For example, when one of the authors was once paddling this stretch at the end of a warm winter day, a gigantic flock of starlings, redwings, grackles, and other blackbirds were muttering in the tall reeds and nervously gathering in the few remaining trees along the riverbank. As he continued to paddle, the birds suddenly broke from the reeds and trees in kaleidoscopic groups—forming and dissolving patterns as they wheeled directly in front of him. At the same time he was experiencing a magnificent sunset of bright pink, orange, and red clouds across the open, crystal-blue sky.

Shortly, the channel straightens more and becomes slightly wider. After passing more duck blind signs and having paddled a total of six miles, you will come to a side channel and a sign indicating that the refuge headquarters is to the right. This is Petersfield Ditch. A half mile later another side channel and sign directs you around a second right turn toward refuge headquarters. This is Headquarters Ditch. From this turn it is only a half mile to the take-out at the dock by the refuge headquarters.

When paddling this section, be sure to complete your journey before dark because the roads to this National Wildlife Refuge are closed at sundown. Also, if there is a chance you will be caught on the river at sunset (particularly during duck-hunting season), please advise the resident ranger if possible and bring a flashlight. Duck hunters coming from their blinds in motorboats may not clearly see a slower canoe ahead of them, and you risk either a collision or being hit by a heavy wake.

Prime Hook Creek is indeed a superb trip—particularly on a mild fall or winter day when the leaves are off the trees, enabling you to observe better the wildlife, and when insects or sultry heat will not hassle you. If you go in the summer or late spring, be warned: Mosquitoes are bad beginning in mid-May, and green-headed flies and brownish deerflies are bad in June, July, and August. Insect repellent keeps the mosquitoes away but doesn't stop the deerflies. However, these latter pests are primarily landlubbers and don't bother paddlers as much on the water. Also, be on the lookout for poison ivy, which festoons certain bank areas on the twisty, narrow stretch of the creek that follows the long ponds.

The wildlife is teeming in this refuge. In addition to a large black duck nesting grounds, there are blue-winged teals, pintails, buffleheads, scaups, widgeons (or baldpates because of their white "cap"), mallards, gadwalls, and wood ducks. Other waterfowl periodically present are snow and Canadian geese, great blue and green herons, kingfishers, bitterns, ibises, and snowy egrets. These birds can put on spectacular displays and have given one author fond memo-

Bird-watching on Prime Hook Creek. Photo by Janet Kegg.

ries. For example, late one December afternoon we were watching a large flock of Canadian geese which covered the field next to the refuge headquarters, when suddenly, just at sunset, they took off with a magnificent honking and whirring of wings.

Concerning predatory birds, red-tailed hawks and great horned and screech owls are found in the refuge. In the spring ospreys are common, and one may even get a rare glimpse of a bald eagle. In winter golden eagles are present, which feed on geese still remaining on the refuge.

Migrating waterfowl concentrate in March and November, providing excellent bird-watching. Also, many waterfowl winter on the refuge. May is the best time for viewing shorebirds such as gulls, terns, sandpipers, plovers, and willet. In drier parts of the refuge you can find quail, pheasants, downy and hairy woodpeckers, woodcocks, snipes, and songbirds such as cardinals, goldfinches, mockingbirds, meadowlarks, catbirds, thrashers, wrens, and warblers—including the striking golden-yellow prothonotary warbler.

Mammals in the area include the white-tailed deer, river otter, muskrat, opossum, gray squirrel, eastern cottontail, striped skunk, woodchuck, and both red and gray foxes. Deer are seen most often. You can also fish in Prime Hook Creek and Petersfield Ditch as well as in nearby Turkle and Fleetwood ponds for largemouth bass, chain pickerel, white perch, catfish, and crappie. As of this writing, we understand that Delaware's second largest crappie was caught in Turkle Pond.

The vegetation is also interesting. In addition to red maples in the swamp forest, there are the rare seaside alders, cherry trees, persimmon trees, water lilies, sweet pepper bushes, and blueberries. In wet areas, insect-eating pitcher plants are found as well as cattails, wild millet, and wild rice in the marsh.

A lower stretch of Prime Hook Creek and other watery channels can be paddled in a ten-and-a-half-mile circuit. This is not recommended as a first trip, however, because the scenery is not as striking, and tidal changes may make more work for the paddler. Additional information, maps, and guidance for this enjoyable trip can be obtained from the rangers at the refuge headquarters Monday through Friday from 7:30 A.M. to 4:00 P.M. Also, please check with the refuge headquarters at (302) 684-8419 about hunting and fishing seasons; they are subject to change from year to year.

Pocomoke River

The ten-mile section of the Pocomoke River from Whiton Crossing Road to Snow Hill flows through a cypress swamp and is a delightful paddle for novices and families. There is a comfortable variety to the journey. The trip begins on a short channelized section of the river, and then narrows to a small twisting stream with surprising current (but no rapids) in the midst of the cypress swamp. Finally, the river slowly broadens and straightens so much that one ultimately gets the feeling of paddling on a long narrow lake with cypress trees dotting its scenic shores.

The water on this trip is primarily tea colored because of the cypress swamp. Indeed, the word *Pocomoke* is Indian for "black water." The banks are primarily sand or loam. Paddlers need not worry much about fallen trees; they have mostly been cut away so duck hunters and fishermen can travel up and down the river. On a recent trip by one of the authors there were no carries over fallen logs, and hopefully this situation will continue.

At the easy Whiton (pronounced White'-on) Crossing Road put-in, with a mixed cypress and hardwood forest on both sides, the river is about 50 feet wide and channelized straight as an arrow. After nearly a mile or so the river suddenly narrows to a twisty channel of 20 feet and the current picks up. This is indeed amazing because the overall gradient of this ten-mile section is only two feet per mile. Along here the predominant trees on the bank are not cypress but river birch, maple, holly, oak, and sweet gum. Only slowly do the stately cypress trees with their numerous knobby "knees," which glean oxygen from the air, make their presence felt. You have to paddle another mile and a half beyond the channelization, however, before sighting a profusion of these knobby appendages on the right bank.

Another mile farther the paddler will view an even nicer cypress stand on the left. Here the river straightens and widens to perhaps 60 feet for a short stretch before narrowing again. One not only notices occasional ducks and hears the honking of geese during migration season but also sees numerous duck blinds constructed next to the stream in varying stages of repair and disrepair.

The bridge for Porters Crossing Road is reached about one and a half miles later, which marks the five-mile halfway point. The paddler can take out here if necessary; however, when setting the shuttle, be warned that the road sign marking the Porters Crossing Road turnoff from Route 354 was still missing as of this writing. So while driving on Route 354, look closely for this blacktop road if you put in or take out here. Actually, though, because of the greater number of cypress trees gracing the banks, a take-out at this point would be foolish unless the paddler is really tuckered out. The leisurely slalom through the cypress swamp continues for another mile or so, and then the river widens and the forest recedes. This is a nice change, and one can now admire the numerous stately cypress trees from a more respectful distance.

After another mile, you will pass under a set of power lines—the first sign of civilization other than Porters Crossing and the duck blinds. Here the river is 75 to 100 feet wide. A few minutes beyond the power lines a 25-foot-high bank rises on the right. Once you are past this bank be on guard because the river is quite wide here, and you'll need to carefully watch the distant banks in order to stay in the main channel. As of this writing, there was a striking duck blind in the center of the river a little farther along that had a good-sized pine tree growing sideways from it. Just a few minutes later, the paddler will spot a house on the distant left bank of the river about three and a half miles below

The short, channelized section just after the put-in, Pocomoke River. Photo by Ed Grove.

Porters Crossing. The main channel is to the right here and very wide.

You are now in the home stretch. After another mile and a half of paddling, you'll spot the Snow Hill water tower on river left and then reach the take-out at the white Route 12 drawbridge in Snow Hill. Take out above or below the bridge on river left near the Pocomoke River Canoe Company building, or you can continue a half mile farther and take out on river left at Snow Hill City Park.

The presence of many fishermen and duck hunters attests to the abundance of wildlife on the Pocomoke. During a recent winter trip, numerous ducks were seen and honking geese were heard; there were also several sightings of great blue herons, and a flock of turkey vultures had gathered in a tall cypress near the river. Predatory birds such as hawks are also present. In the winter snow geese cover the fields near Snow Hill while numerous migratory species are seen in spring and fall. Deer and other four-footed critters are nearby, while the Pocomoke itself contains chain pickerel, white and yellow perch, crappie, and bluegill sunfish. In the spring, fishermen come out in droves to catch spawning herring which run all the way up to Porters Crossing.

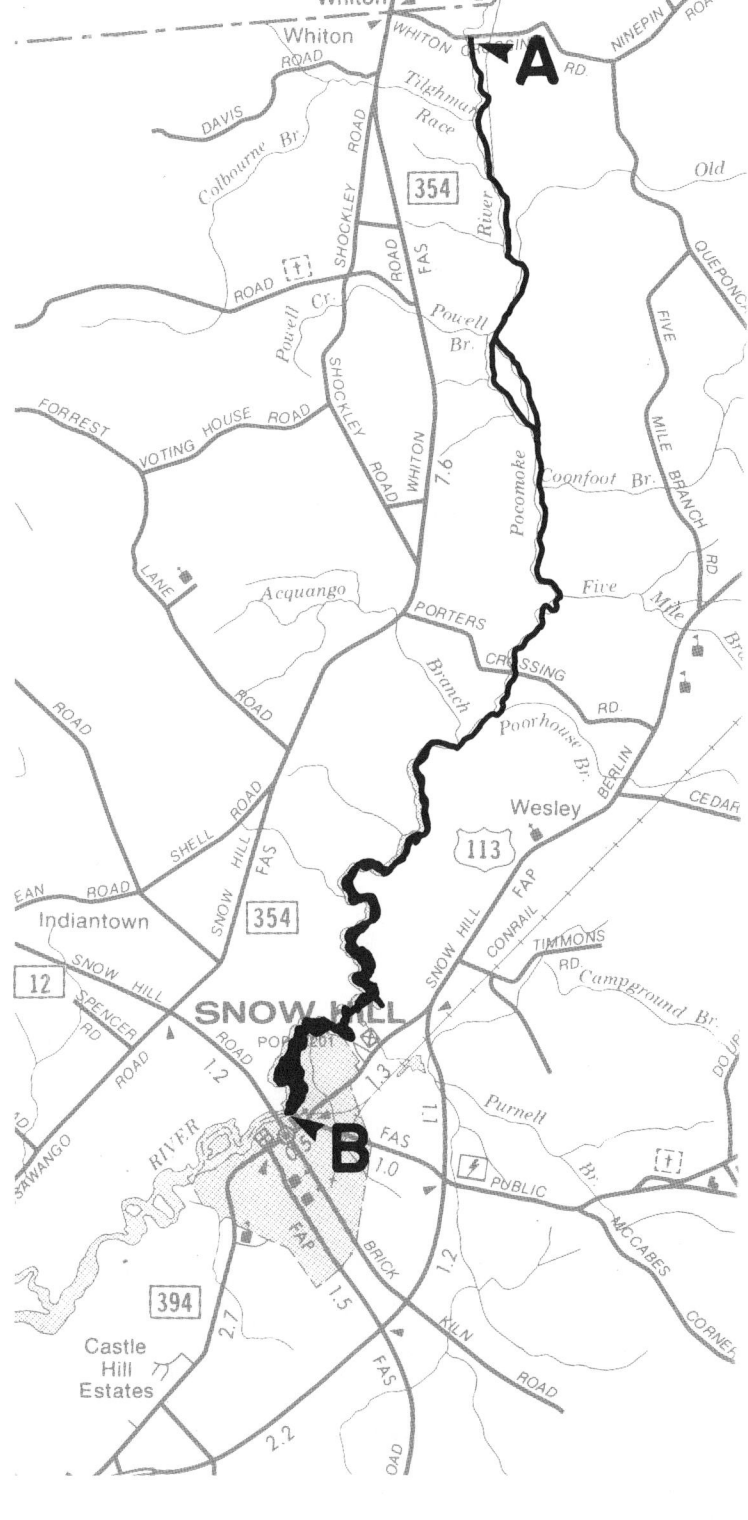

Section: Whiton Crossing Road to Snow Hill, MD

Counties: Worcester (MD)

USGS Quads: Wango, Snow Hill, Ninepin, Public Landing

Suitable for: Day-trip cruising

Skill Level: Families and beginners

Months Runnable: Entire year except for prolonged dry periods

Interest Highlights: Cypress swamp

Scenery: Pretty to beautiful in spots

Difficulty: Class I

Average Width: 20–200 feet

Velocity: Slow

Gradient: 0–2 feet per mile

Runnable Water Levels:
  Minimum: Not applicable
  Maximum: Flood stage

Hazards: Possible downed trees across river; duck hunters in season

Scouting: None required

Portages: None

Rescue Index: Reasonably accessible

Source of Additional Information: Pocomoke River Canoe Company (301) 632-3971

Access Points	River Miles	Shuttle Miles
A–B	10 to 10.5	9 to 10

Access Point Ratings: Put-in excellent; take-out, very good to excellent

Route 12 drawbridge near the take-out for the Pocomoke River, Maryland. Photo by Ed Grove.

Virginia

South Fork of the Shenandoah River

The Shenandoah River is legendary throughout the world. In song, story, and among canoeists it is part of the vocabulary of the English-speaking world. The valley through which it flows is synonymous with agricultural richness, particularly in apples, and the very name conjures images of pastoral serenity and farm living. For the paddler the Shenandoah offers little in the way of whitewater but it does provide a beautiful river experience, running through a combination of scenic farmland and steep mountain forest. This section of the South Fork has probably been paddled by more beginning, as well as veteran, paddlers than any other stream. Boy Scouts have wetted their paddles in the South Fork for generations and outing groups of all varieties continue to do so in droves. For any Virginia paddler a trip down the South Fork of the Shenandoah continues to be an essential part of the Old Dominion experience.

The Shenandoah Valley was beloved by the Indians who lived and traveled here before the coming of the Europeans. The valley seems to have been largely conserved as a hunting ground in the years immediately preceding the arrival of colonists, although prehistoric villages continue to be found along the South Fork. The aboriginal villages were very small and tended to revolve around cave dwellings in the limestone cliffs of the valley. The inhabitants of these villages greatly predated the Susquehannocks and Catawbas of popular legend and were apparently not related culturally or racially to these later Indians.

The identity of the first European to see the Shenandoah Valley is a matter of controversy. There is evidence that French Jesuits visited the area before 1632. John Lederer, the early geographer, certainly was there in 1669. The most entertaining account of the early explorations of the valley, however, is that of Governor (of Virginia) Alexander Spotswood and friends in 1716. History records that Spotswood was not much of a geographer or explorer but he certainly knew how to have a good time in the Virginia mountains, a skill pursued still by paddlers from all over. Accompanying Spotswood was the young John Fontaine, ancestor of Mathew Fontaine Maury. His diary records the particulars of Spotswood's journey. The expedition consisted of many gentlemen of Virginia, along with servants, slaves, women, drovers, etc. and the party carried with them, according to Fontaine, "Virginia red wine and white wine, Irish uisgebaugh [whiskey], brandy shrub, two sorts of rum, canary punch, cider, etc." [Blair Niles, *The James*, Rivers of America Series, Farrar, Strauss & Giroux, 1940] Crossing the Blue Ridge at Swift Run Gap, the present site of US 33, Fontaine says they "all drank the King's health in champagne, and fired a volley . . . the Princess' health in Burgundy, and fired a volley . . . all the rest of the Royal Family in Claret, and fired a volley . . . then the Governor's health, and fired a volley." Thus was established the honorable tradition of guns and booze at all Appalachian mountain parties which continues to this day. The Governor's expedition did little to further the cartographic knowledge of the valley but it did draw attention to the valley as a site of future development. After his expedition German, Dutch, and Scottish immigrants from Pennsylvania began settling in the valley of the Shenandoah. The names of their descendants are still evident on the mailboxes along Route 11 and other roads in the valley.

During the Civil War the Shenandoah Valley was of critical importance to both sides. The farms of the valley provided a large portion of the foodstuffs necessary to keep the armies of the Confederacy operating, and the strategic location of the valley meant that an army unchecked there could

Section: Bixler Bridge to Karo Landing

Counties: Page and Warren (VA)

USGS Quads: Luray, Rileyville, and Bentonville

Suitable for: Cruising

Skill Level: Beginners

Months Runnable: Year round except for an unusually dry summer

Interest Highlights: Scenery, wildlife, history

Scenery: Beautiful

Difficulty: I (II)

Average Width: 80–150 feet

Velocity: Moderate

Gradient: 5 feet per mile

Runnable Water Levels:
 Minimum: 300 cfs
 Maximum: 1,500 cfs

Hazards: None

Scouting: None

Portages: Low-water bridge at Bentonville Landing, three-fourths' way through the trip

Rescue Index: Accessible

Source of Additional Information: USGS gauge recording (202) 899-7378. 1.3 on the Front Royal gauge is minimum for this section. There are a number of canoe outfitters active in the area. Check with phone company information.

Access Points	River Miles	Shuttle Miles
A–B	7.5	9.5
B–C	8.5	6.0
C–D	4.5	3.0
D–E	7.0	5.5
E–F	9.0	5.5

South Fork of the Shenandoah 167

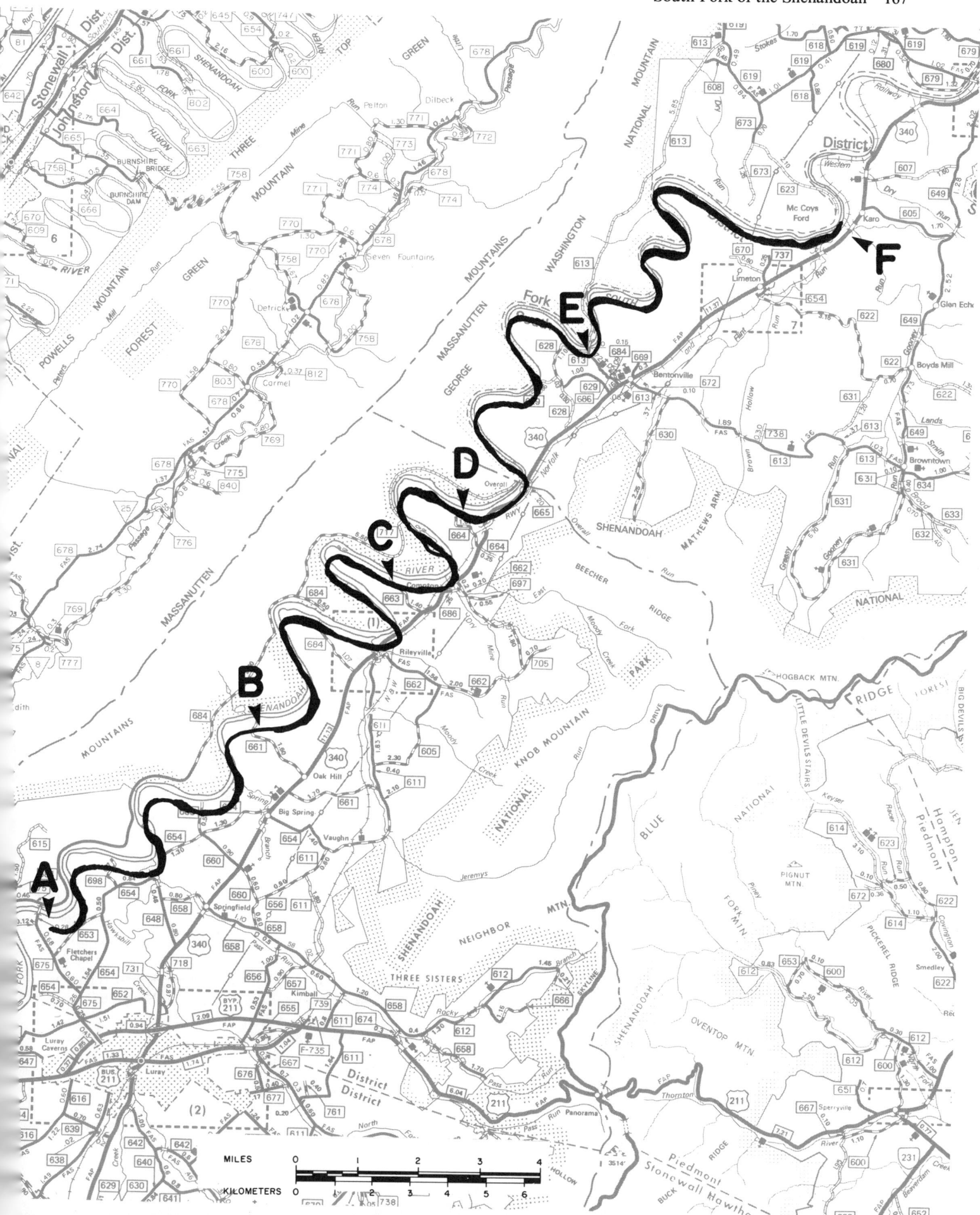

Shenandoah River Valley. Photo by Bill Kirby.

easily threaten Washington, D.C. As a result the valley was the site of constant fighting throughout the war. The most famous of the campaigns fought there was Stonewall Jackson's campaign in the spring of 1862. During this period Jackson tied up Federal armies of several times his own strength, weakening the Northern attempt to take Richmond and keeping the Federal leadership in constant anxiety for the safety of the Northern capital. Later in the war, when Southern fortunes began to sink, Federal General Philip Sheridan was charged with the duty of reducing the valley to such an extent that "a crow flying over the valley would have to carry his own rations." [Mark M. Boatner, *the Civil War Dictionary*, David McKay Co., Inc., 1959] Following a scorched earth policy, Sheridan destroyed every barn, burned every crop, and killed all animals throughout the length and breadth of the valley, causing great hardship among the inhabitants. When, as predicted by Stonewall Jackson, the valley was destroyed, so went the Confederacy.

The present-day paddler on the Shenandoah will see things much as they might have been before the Civil War, with the addition of the occasional concrete bridge, power line, and tractor. The business of the land, farming, takes place in much the same area it did during earlier years. Some of the fields have been plowed within the same fencerows for generations. Battlesites can be visited that are nearly identical to their wartime appearance, not due to protection, but because the land is still being used for the same purpose. The river contains numerous fish dams built by prehistoric Indians. These structures, only visible at low water, are V-shaped arrangements of rocks pointing downstream. The people of the hunter-gatherer culture would place nets at the downstream end of the V and gather the fish funneled in from upstream. Some paddlers grumble about running man-made rapids but who can be offended by a ripple produced by a thousand-year-old pile of cobbles. Interesting to think that the stones placed so laboriously by hand long ago now bear the multi-hued streaks scraped off the aluminum and plastic pleasure craft of today.

This trip on the magnificent Shenandoah is not really a whitewater trip. The only rapids of any significance is Compton's Rapids, encountered 16 miles from the put-in. This drop is a ledge with nice standing waves at the bottom, the height of which increases with higher water levels. Compton's is recognized from upstream by a high rock wall that appears to block the stream ahead and by the unusually loud rumble of the rapids. Compton's is not dangerous at reasonable levels but it has swamped many open canoes and soaked a lot of clothing and bedding. Make sure everything is battened down before running this drop.

The balance of this stretch of the South Fork consists of tiny ledges and ancient fish dams, beautiful vistas of the Blue Ridge and Massanutten mountains, and relaxed paddling. The river is a sterling example of a geomorphologically mature stream and it meanders back and forth between the above-named ridges. As a result, the view and the orientation of the light is constantly changing, and the paddler is presented with a feast of visual entertainment alternating between steep forested slopes, limestone cliffs, cow-tenanted fields, and shady bowers between sandy islands. Camping is possible in many places along the river, although the "No Trespassing" signs proliferate more and more each year. If there is any doubt as to whether camping is permitted in a particular spot it would be wise to locate the nearest farmhouse and inquire. The river is heavily used in this area and littering is a severe problem for some of the landowners; therefore, protect the relationship between paddlers and riparian landowners by utilizing courtesy, discretion, and a large trashbag.

Seven miles below Compton's Rapids a low-water bridge appears that will probably require a short portage. This bridge at Bentonville Landing signals the final quarter of the trip, as Karo Landing is just nine miles below. Karo Landing, on Gooney Run, is not marked by bridge or other unmistakable landmark so be sure to study it while running the shuttle to insure that it will be recognized from the river.

Passage Creek

The northern part of the Shenandoah Valley is bisected by the intimidating massif of the Massanutten Mountain. From Harrisonburg to Strasburg the Massanutten holds apart the respective valleys of the North and South Forks of the Shenandoah until at Strasburg the North Fork abandons its northeasterly course and turns east to join the South Fork near Front Royal. From the floor of either valley the Massanutten appears as an abrupt, even-topped wall separating the lowlands surrounding it. A look at a map, however, reveals that the Massanutten is itself cleaved throughout its northern half by the defile of Passage Creek. As Passage Creek tumbles from its high repose in the Fort Valley to join the North Fork of the Shenandoah it becomes briefly a cascading torrent which will delight the whitewater paddler. Only slightly over an hour from Washington, D.C., Passage Creek rewards the paddler with clear water, easy access, towering cliffs and rock formations, rhododendron thickets, and tight, intricate rapids. There is a price, however, and that price is an ever-changing maze of fallen trees in the lower part of the run. Fortunately the worst part of this labyrinth is in relatively calm water so it is more of an inconvenience than a death trap, as it might be otherwise. State Route 678 follows the creek throughout the length of the trip, although it occasionally wanders some distance from the stream, so rescue or a walk-out will not be a disaster.

Passage Creek meanders along peacefully over a sandy bottom in the miles above the Elizabeth Furnace Recreation Area. Upon reaching the picnic area, however, the mountain closes in on both sides and the creek begins to head downhill. Putting in at the picnic area the paddler is treated to a swift current and occasional Class I–II gravel bars and rock gardens for a mile or so. Soon the good stuff begins, with a Class II–III ledge series where the creek closely approaches the road. The stream continues dropping at a rapid pace through ledges for a few hundred yards and when it turns away from the road to the right and a high rock wall appears on the right bank, Out-of-Sight Rapids is fast approaching. A scout from the bank will be in order here, especially if you are not following a paddler familiar with the route through this rather complicated drop. At higher levels some good surfing waves appear partway through the series. The eddies are small, however, and a flip could put the boat against some angry rocks, as the distance between the individual ledges is very short. Out-of-Sight is followed by another Class II–III ledge series and then the creek turns back against the road. Against a masonry wall supporting the road on the left is a series of entertaining ledges. Soon the fish hatchery dam is reached, a six-foot high weir. The right side of the dam looks like the proper portage route but this is not the case! Years of paddlers walking over this area have severely eroded the soil there and portaging on the right side of the dam is prohibited. Carry on the left side with care. In high water beware of the flow going over the dam.

Passage Creek. Photo by Bill Kirby.

170 Passage Creek

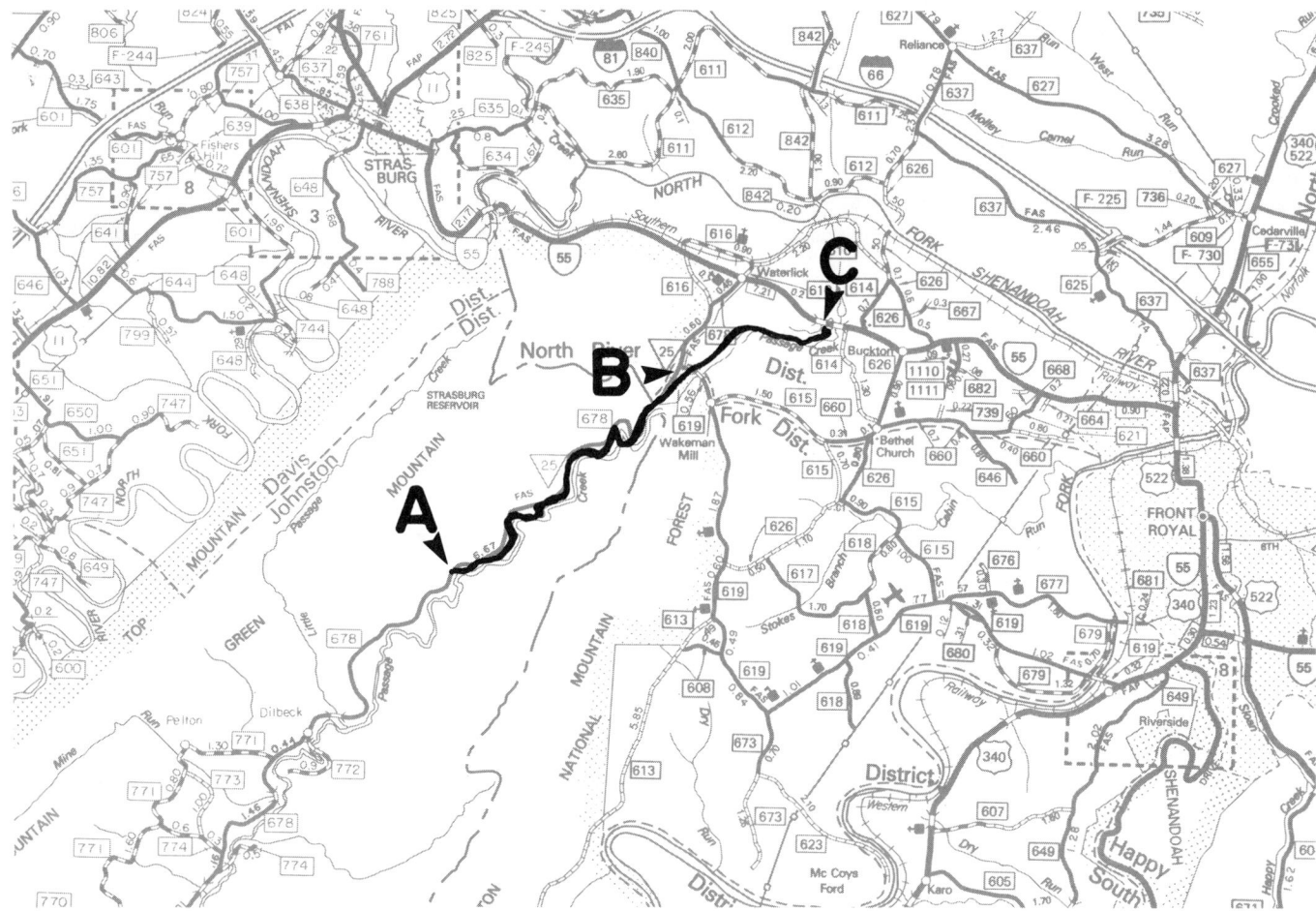

Below the hatchery dam the stream begins to flow with a decreased gradient and the load of rock rubble and timber carried by the creek through the steep section above is deposited. Passage Creek divides around numerous small islands and between these islands there may be tangles of fallen trees, debris, and branches. Use extreme care when choosing which route to run between the islands and always be prepared to get to shore quickly. The route through this maze changes with every high-water season so the paddler is on his own in negotiating the puzzle. Below the jackstraw pile the creek flows swiftly between wooded banks until the Route 55 bridge at Waterlick heaves into view. This road is a heavily used truck route so be cautious in walking along the shoulder with a 15-foot-long boat slung over your shoulder.

Passage Creek is a heavily fished trout stream, stocked, as one would expect, from the hatchery at the exit from the steep section. Along with most of the small streams in the state, we highly recommended that Passage Creek not be paddled on opening day of trout season, which is usually the first Saturday of April. A high-speed collision with a wading fisherman would be a disaster in both the physical and public relations areas, especially since there are certain to be hundreds of canoeist-hating fishermen standing by in the event of a mishap. As an indication of how totally the nimrods take over the area during the height of trout season we offer the following anecdote. During the research for this book one of the authors packed his kayak on top of his car and headed for Passage Creek to take some photographs. Upon arriving in the area he immediately realized that this was not the day to attempt a descent of Passage Creek as evidenced by the vast number of vehicles parked in every possible nook and cranny of the normally empty woods. Wide places along the shoulder of the road that wouldn't appear to allow space for a bicycle managed to accommodate two or three pick-up trucks. The stream, where visible from the road, was so crowded with rubber-trousered anglers that it looked like a cocktail party in a flooded basement. Upon attempting to leave the area the author discovered, via a painfully obvious traffic jam, that the State Police had set up a roadblock on Rt. 678, the only road out of the canyon. The author, upon reaching the head of the line, was politely asked to produce his "license," and still not grasping the true situation, he dutifully handed the trooper his driver's license. Glancing at the proffered documentation, a frown crossed the face of the officer until he examined the peculiar craft on top of the author's car. Evidently deciding that anyone who hauled such a contraption about the countryside probably wouldn't know a trout from a tricycle, the officer silently handed the author his permit and waved him through the blockade. A glance in the rearview mirror as the paddler drove away showed the trooper talking to his partner across the road, pointing to the author's car, shaking his head, and laughing uproariously.

For those with a propensity for hiking, a trip to Signal Knob via the Signal Knob Trail will certainly be worthwhile. The trail begins at a small parking area off the road on the west side of the canyon near the Elizabeth Furnace campground and leads to a prominent peak used as an observation post by both sides during the Civil War. The Massanutten Trail heads south from the Fish Hatchery and follows the crest of Massanutten Mountain all the way to Route 33 east of Harrisonburg. This entire area lies within the George Washington National Forest, which is a public hunting area, so wear bright clothing when hiking during hunting season. And don't have a white handkerchief hanging out of your back pocket. A local hunter was once heard to say that the deer hunting was so poor that the only shot he had gotten off that year was a "noise shot"(!), presumably a rifled shotgun slug sent flying through the brush at whatever it was that made the noise of breaking twigs. So don't walk like a deer, either.

Passage Creek is located between Front Royal and Strasburg on State Route 55. From I-66, go south on Route 340 toward Front Royal and go right (west) on Route 55 for about five miles. The creek is crossed one-half mile before the left turn onto Route 678.

Other streams in the area include Cedar Creek, flowing into the North Fork from the north nearby; South Fork of the Shenandoah to the south; and the Lost River just over the West Virginia line to the west.

Section: Elizabeth Furnace Picnic Area to Route 55

Counties: Shenandoah and Warren (VA)

USGS Quads: Strasburg

Suitable for: Cruising

Skill Level: Advanced intermediate

Months Runnable: January to mid-May or following heavy rains

Scenery: Beautiful

Difficulty: II-III+

Average Width: 20-45 feet

Gradient: 40 feet per mile avg.; 60 in steepest section

Runnable Water Levels:
 Minimum: 150 cfs
 Maximum: 600 cfs

Hazards: Difficult rapids, logjams, strainers, fishermen, dam

Scouting: Scouting from road possible for most difficult rapids

Portages: Dam at fish hatchery; probably some logjams to carry around

Rescue Index: Accessible

Source of Additional Information: USGS gauge recording (202) 899-7378. The Cootes Store gauge should be in the high 3-foot range, though this is not an exact reading for Passage Creek, which is in a different watershed. There is also the Randy Carter gauge on the Rt. 55 bridge.

Access Points	River Miles	Shuttle Miles
A-B	4.0	4.5
B-C	2.0	3.0

Potomac River

The Potomac River forms the northern border of Virginia, separating the Old Dominion from Maryland and the District of Columbia. Throughout the history of the United States the Potomac has functioned as an important highway for communication and commerce as well as a barrier to the many military forces, foreign and domestic, that have campaigned throughout this area. In more recent years the Potomac has found new duties as a premier recreational area for the millions that live in the region. Whitewater paddling is the most recent of these activities, but the old river has proven to be a superlative location for the enjoyment of this relatively new sport.

The Potomac provides whitewater of all degrees of difficulty throughout its length, from the small headwater streams of West Virginia and western Maryland, through the Blue Ridge at Harpers Ferry, and across the Piedmont between the mountains and the coast. The most heavily used section, however, and the section that is discussed below is the stretch between Great Falls and the tidal estuary at Washington, D.C. Access to the river in this area can be had in many spots. The C & O Canal follows the river on the Maryland shore between Washington and Cumberland, Maryland, and provides public access and parking at many locations. The Virginia side of the river is almost entirely in private ownership and public access is rare. Between Great Falls and Washington the most important access points are Great Falls, Maryland, the Old Anglers Inn, both on Mac-Arthur Boulevard, and the old Lockhouses number 10 and 6, on the Maryland George Washington Memorial Parkway and Canal Road respectively. All of these points are accessible via the Capital Beltway (I-495) at the Maryland George Washington Parkway exit. Note: There is a George Washington Memorial Parkway on the Virginia side, too, but that provides no access to the river. The original plan called for the parkways to be joined by a bridge at Great Falls but this plan was fortunately scrapped, due in large part to the efforts of the late Chief Supreme Court Justice William O. Douglas.

Along the northern border of Virginia lies the largest rapid in the state and one of the largest runnable rapids anywhere. This drop was named by the earliest colonists and has retained through the centuries the designation given to it by them: the Great Falls of the Potomac.

The Falls are created where the Potomac, like all other rivers that flow eastward into the Atlantic, drops over the edge of the continental bedrock onto the sedimentary soil of the Coastal Plain. The falls line proper is actually located farther downstream, at Roosevelt Island in the estuary between Rosslyn, Virginia, and the District of Columbia. The entire section of the river between this spot and the Great Falls, a distance of some nine miles, is a result of the headward, i.e., upstream, erosion of the riverbed by the stream. The present location of the falls represents the latest manifestation of this unending process. All of the rapids down-

Whitney Shields running the first drop on the Maryland side of the Great Falls of the Potomac (level was 2.96 feet on the Little Falls gauge). Photo by Ed Grove.

stream, Observation Deck Rapids, S-Turn Rapids, Rocky Island Rapids, Wet Bottom Chute, Difficult Run Rapids, Yellow Falls, Stubblefield Falls, and Little Falls, are the locations of particularly resistant strata of rock where the falls may have once paused in their ever-slow but inexorable upstream migration. The present-day Great Falls of the Potomac display the steepest and most spectacular display of a falls line rapid of any of the eastern rivers.

Before beginning a description of the Great Falls section it must be pointed out most emphatically that this area is extremely hazardous. The danger of the rapids is probably the highest of any rapids currently run. The most advanced paddlers in the country examined these drops for years before the first attempt was made, and although the passage of eight years since has increased the number of paddlers completing the run, it has not decreased the objective hazards presented by these falls, as proven by the hundreds of documented deaths that have occurred here. No one should attempt such a run without the highest degree of skill and confidence, particularly a very fast and sure roll and previous experience in vertical waterfall running. Most importantly the newcomer should only paddle the Falls with someone who has previously completed a successful run; the choice of the wrong route would almost surely be fatal. Finally, the park rangers who administer the land on both shores request that runs be made only before 10 A.M. and preferably on weekdays to avoid a public spectacle and the encouragement of unqualified individuals to emulate the paddlers they see but don't understand. A run that turns into a circus or results in a death or costly rescue operation by the Park Service would almost surely cause the law- and rule-makers to close this incredible resource to those who are best able to appreciate it.

The Potomac flows along lazily all of the way from Harpers Ferry, some 35 miles upstream, across the Piedmont with only the lightest riffles disturbing its placid green surface. Seneca Breaks, five miles upstream from the falls, marks briefly the new sentiment of the river but the Potomac resumes its pastoral quality below Seneca. Only four miles from the Capital Beltway and without further prelude the river drops over the Great Falls Dam, a six-foot stone structure built in the 1850s to provide drinking water for the District of Columbia. The structure still serves in its original capacity, the water thus stored being pumped by gravity through the aqueduct running under the equally aged MacArthur Boulevard into the city. The Potomac pools briefly below the dam and then begins its rush to the estuary in earnest.

The area below the dam for a quarter of a mile, and generally lumped together under the designation of Great Falls, begins with gentle rapids. Immediately the channel, 2,500 feet wide at the dam, is split by the long and narrow Falls Island, which separates the main part of the Falls from the so-called Fish Ladder, adjacent to the Maryland shore.

Just downstream, the Fish Ladder channel is split again by Olmsted Island, which separates the Fish Ladder from an equally steep but unnamed channel between Olmsted and Falls Islands. In years past Olmsted and Falls Islands were linked with the Maryland shore by footbridges, allowing visitors to the Maryland Great Falls Park, known officially as a unit of the C & O Canal National Historic Park, the opportunity to walk across the Fish Ladder channel and the previously mentioned unnamed defile to Falls Island to view the main section of the Falls. In June of 1972 the flood caused by Hurricane Agnes destroyed these extremely sturdy steel and reinforced concrete bridges, located 25 to 40 feet above normal water level, and made the islands and their spectacular views of the Falls the exclusive preserve of the wildlife and whitewater boaters in all but the lowest water levels. Plans to reconstruct the bridges were still uncertain as of this writing. Both the Fish Ladder and the unnamed channel were altered by the Corps of Engineers around the turn of the century in an attempt to allow fish to migrate upstream of the falls. The resulting channels have concrete ramps which have weathered to expose the aggregate rock and look like magnified views of emery cloth, knife-edged boulders in mid-channel and impossibly tight turns. These hazards, combined with the extremely high gradient, make both these channels horrifyingly dangerous and they should not be considered.

The main channel, separated from the Fish Ladder channel immediately below the dam, falls over unnamed drops of increasing severity for a couple of hundred yards. These drops, reaching Class IV in difficulty, would be significant enough to be named and paddled often anywhere else, but here they are mere prelude to and warning of the main event which awaits just below.

The Falls proper begins on a front approximately 600 feet wide. The Maryland Falls, running alongside Falls Island, reach their full development first, running swiftly to the brink of a convex-curved 20-foot vertical drop. The river immediately regathers its strength and within a few boat lengths drops over a straight-lipped ten-foot drop that is not quite vertical. The river again "pools" while moving at a rapid pace and turns sharply right and drops over a concave-edged ten-footer that has a very wicked hydraulic at the bottom amid many broken boulders. This hydraulic has kept boats and boaters for uncomfortably long periods of time. Indeed, while there had been no boater fatalities here at the time of this writing, the hole had kept a couple of pilot-less boats on a permanent basis, tearing them to pieces in lieu of releasing them to their bedraggled owners.

To the right of Maryland Falls the channel known since George Washington's time as the Streamers extends its flat section a few dozen feet farther downstream of the Maryland Falls and then proceeds to drop through a chaos of boulders, narrow twisting chutes, and vertical falls that defies description. At the top of this channel is a very interesting phenomenon: a small chute drops a distance of several feet and apparently runs onto a sharply sloped rock at the base, causing the flow to bubble straight upward in a natural water fountain fully as high as the height from which the water originally fell. This entire section of the river is ridiculously dangerous-looking and, to our knowledge, has never been attempted. The name of this section apparently comes from the last drop in the sequence. A relatively small amount of water, at summer-type levels, falls over a rocky lip which is fairly regularly notched at the top, creating dozens of tiny waterfalls at intervals of one foot or so, falling a vertical distance of about ten feet.

Even farther to the right, against the Virginia shore, is the section known as the Spout, named possibly by George Washington or at least current at the time of the writing of his diaries. The Spout is separated from the Streamers by a 100-yard-long unnamed rock island. This channel extends even farther downstream than the Streamers before becoming unruly, but it makes up for any tardiness with extra effort at being horrendous, awesome, and even downright bodacious. After the initial pool the channel flows over a drop of seven or eight feet from a lip that has the shape of about 120 degrees of a circle; the paddler drops from the outside to the inside of the circle. This concentration of the resulting hydraulic makes it extremely strong and it tends to back-pop-up or back-ender the paddler, thoroughly frustrating the carefully constructed plans the paddler has made for surviving the following drops. Most paddlers of this falls

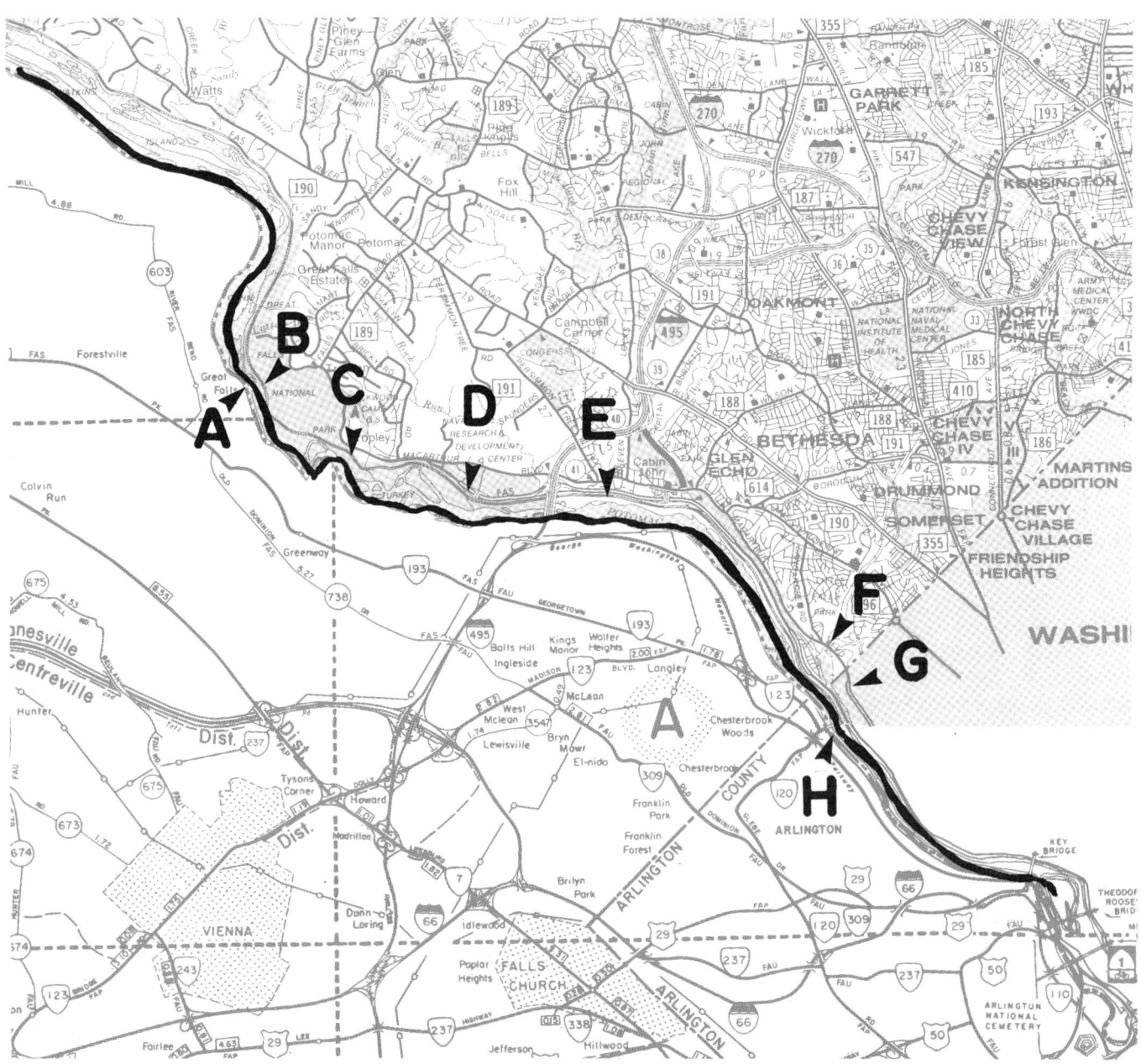

eschew the entire left side of the drop and enter on the far right, even though this necessitates a very sharp right turn at the bottom.

The channel runs straight downhill to the next drop, which splits at the top. The right two-thirds consists of another conclave lip and a very nasty-looking hydraulic at the bottom. The far left side is a rightward-slanting slide and is actually easier than it looks. Immediately the channels converge and crash together violently against a rock wall straight ahead. The paddler must make a 90-degree turn to the left, proceed over a five-foot drop, make an immediate 90-degree turn to the right, and then drop a couple of feet. The whole sequence of this rapids from the slanting drop through the two sharp turns, usually lumped together as the second of three major drops in the Spout, occupies the linear space of only about three boat lengths and drops some 10 to 12 feet. A flip here, even with the quickest and surest of rolls, could be disastrous, particularly in view of what lies downstream.

After twisting through the described second drop the Spout forms a moving pool of 60 feet in length before delivering the coup de grace. The third and final drop consists of a single vertical falls of about 20 to 25 feet. The right two-thirds of the falls drops onto a slanting ledge halfway down and then strikes a flat boulder or ledge at the bottom. The exact configuration of the slanting ledge and flat ledge at the bottom are unknown but the surrounding rock is heavily fissured and potholed, suggesting the presence of many nooks and crannies in which the bow of a boat might become wedged, trapping the paddler under an enormous weight of water pouring over his boat and body. Rescue from such a situation would appear to be quite impossible due to the steepness of the shoreline and the tremendous power of a large amount of water flowing over a lip only about 12 feet wide. Only the farthest left portion of the falls drops into clear water. Reaching this clear slot requires a turn at the top of nearly 90 degrees, virtually in mid-air. In addition, the paddler must simultaneously raise the bow of the boat to avoid a tiny, almost invisible rock at the bottom which is hidden by the curtain of water at all but the lowest levels. This small rock has taken a heavy toll in sterns from those who failed to notice it and achieve some degree of arch to their fall from the lip. Fortunately, within the very narrow range of water levels in which runs of the falls are possible, the hydraulic at the base of the last drop is not a safety problem. The long fall, however, results in a deep penetration of the pool at the base and the water pressure at these depths has popped the seams of some fiberglass boats.

After this orgy of descent the river pools very briefly and runs down to the heavy but more normal rapids of Observation Deck or "O-Deck" as it is known locally. The origin of the name "the Spout" will be obvious to any who view this huge rapids. Survivors of such a run will certainly know that they have done something. We must again emphasize that for anyone but those who just can't sleep nights without having run Great Falls once in their lives the best advice is to forget it. Or to repeat a phrase heard repeatedly on many rivers, "Let's not, and say we did."

For years the myriad of paddlers who played in the rapids below the Falls gazed up from Observation Deck Rapids and wondered about the possibility of a successful run through some section of the very complex drops of the Falls. Many hours were spent discussing the merits of each of the almost infinite number of possible routes through the maelstrom. Most paddlers considered any attempt to verify these hotly contested assertions to be tantamount to suicide, a

---

Section: Great Falls to the estuary below Little Falls

Counties: Fairfax and Arlington, VA, Montgomery, MD, and Washington D.C.

USGS Quads: Falls Church and Washington West

Suitable for: Cruising

Skill Level: Beginners to experts based on section and water level.

Months Runnable: All year.

Interest Highlights: Scenery, wildlife, geology, whitewater, history.

Scenery: Good to beautiful.

Difficulty: Great Falls proper, VI; Below Great Falls to Little Falls, II–IV; Little Falls proper, III–VI.

Average Width: 60–2000 ft.

Velocity: Fast

Gradient: 14 feet per mile average

Runnable Water Levels:
  Minimum: none
  Maximum: 15,000 cfs

Hazards: Large rapids, wide river, difficult to swim out of, vertical walls in some sections, waterfalls.

Scouting: S-Turn, Yellow Falls, Little Falls.

Portages: Great Falls, Little Falls Dam.

Rescue Index: Accessible except for Mather Gorge section.

Source of Additional Information: USGS gauge recording (202) 899-7378. The Little Falls gauge is the indicator. The Potomac is never too low but watch out when the gauge reaches 4.0 feet. At these and higher levels greater skills will be needed. Ten feet is official flood stage and you shouldn't be near the river at anything approaching this level. The Canoe Cruisers Association, P.O. Box 814, Annandale, VA 22003 (301) 656-2586.

Access Points	River Miles	Shuttle Miles
A–B	0.0	14.0
B–C	2.0	3.0
C–D	2.5	2.0
D–E	2.0	2.0
E–F	3.5	3.5
F–G	0.5	0.5
G–H	1.0	1.5

Nolan Whitesell running the last drop of the Virginia side of Great Falls of the Potomac, July 1986. This was the first run of Great Falls in an open canoe. Photo by Steven Michael Lowe. (Level: 2.96 feet on Little Falls gauge)

notion reinforced by the steady incidence of fatalities incurred by ill-advised swimmers and rock scramblers. Each year several of these unfortunates were swept accidentally into the Falls and without exception met death in the foamy green chaos of the two-hundred-yard-long stretch of whitewater. For many years it seemed that the Great Falls of the Potomac would forever remain outside the ken of whitewater paddlers, unexplored and unknown. In 1976 this changed.

Two internationally known local paddlers, who prefer still to remain anonymous to the general public, studied the Falls along with many others and wondered whether a run was possible and, if so, which route would be the most feasible. These two, one a C-1 paddler and the other a kayaker, chose a route down the Spout section and, based upon experience gained in running smaller waterfalls during the development of waterfall running during the early 1970s, decided to attempt it. An additional factor in this decision was their plan to run a steep river in the Himalayas in the near future and their feeling that the Great Falls bore a resemblance to the 300-foot-per-mile gradients they would encounter in the canyons of Asia. Thus, the first run of one of the most feared drops in the region was, in point of fact, a mere training run for more severe rapids in Nepal!

After the initial run it was two years before another attempt was made, in 1978. In late August of that year two more paddlers, both kayakers this time, successfully ran the spout. The following year the Maryland Falls was successfully run for the first time. Since that time the number of paddlers completing the run and the variations of route and water level have multiplied. No one has been killed purposely running the falls so far, but there have been an increasing number of close calls and many destroyed boats. As mentioned above, the first fatal run could be the last legal run of all, so let's be careful out there.

Below the falls the Potomac drops over Observation Deck Rapids, named for the tourist overlooks on both sides of the river. At levels of around three to four feet on the Little Falls gauge this rapids provides large, ender-sized waves for the delight of the paddler. The sure presence of hundreds of amused, awed, and puzzled spectators on sunny weekends provides the hot-dog paddler with an unparalleled forum for the display of his skills. One such kayaker, a few years ago, apparently in search of female companionship, painted in large letters on the stern deck of his boat his name and phone number, preceded by the message "For a date call. . . ." The effectiveness of this technique is unknown to the writers.

Below O-Deck the river turns 90 degrees left and runs toward the reentry of the Fish Ladder on the left. Just before the Fish Ladder drops into the mainstream, the river drops over a three-foot ledge that produces fun surfing waves at lower water levels. Where the Fish Ladder enters bizarre currents are created in the deep water, which can be fun or frightening depending on the skill level of the paddler. Immediately after receiving the Fish Ladder's flow the river enters the S-Turn, a back-to-back set of right and left turns. At higher levels the Potomac splits again just below the Fish Ladder, with the left fork running hard up against the Maryland shore for one-fourth mile before reentering below Rocky Island Rapids. The upper portion of this Maryland channel is called the Catfish Hole and is a popular put-in spot accessible via the C & O Canal towpath from Great Falls, Maryland.

S-Turn Rapids is a strange little place. The rapids are created not so much from a high gradient as from the concentration of the entire Potomac River into a channel only 60 feet wide. At levels between 3.2 and 4.7 feet on the Little Falls gauge a nasty hole forms behind a boulder on river right at the beginning of the S-Turn. At lower levels this boulder, known as Judy's Rock after the late Judy Waddell, a local paddler and Great Falls Park Ranger, becomes exposed. At any level the whole S-Turn sequence is full of moving waves, whirlpools, and cross currents. After straightening out of the S-Turn the river flows more or less quietly for 200 yards to Rocky Island Rapids.

Rocky Island Rapids is probably the most heavily used

rapids on the river. When the gauge reads between 3.8 and 4.7 feet paddlers flock here to surf the wide, smooth five-foot waves created here. Shortly below Rocky Island Rapids the Maryland channel from Catfish Hole reenters and the reunited river runs through Wet Bottom Chute, a four-foot ledge offering surfing waves and a nice bouncy ride. For the next mile the Potomac flows placidly between vertical rock walls 50 to 200 feet high on both sides with spectacular scenery and abundant wildlife. It is difficult to believe in this section that one is only a few miles from the Washington, D.C. city limits and right in the middle of a suburban community. The land on both banks is part of national park areas and is thus preserved for recreational enjoyment.

As the vertical rock walls recede, the paddler approaches the confluence with Difficult Run, a creek entering from the Virginia, or right, side of the river. Just upstream from the mouth of Difficult Run is the rapids named for that creek. Difficult Run Rapids consists of three chutes, separated from one another by rock islands. The left channel, called the Maryland Chute, is a three-foot ledge offering a small hydraulic and two-to three-foot waves. The center channel, appropriately named the Middle Chute, is a longer, gentler rapids with boulders and small ledges scattered over 100 yards. The Virginia Chute, on river right, is a narrow two- to three-foot ledge with a very smooth surfing wave at the top. All three of the chutes are heavily used as a training area by Washington region paddlers.

Below Difficult Run the river flattens and runs placidly between wooded shores. One-half mile below the rapids the Angler's Inn put-in appears on the left shore. A parking area on MacArthur Boulevard across from a restaurant called the Old Angler's Inn provides access to the river. Paddlers park here for trips both upstream and downstream on the river and on the C & O Canal. Hikers, bicyclers, birdwatchers, and other outdoor types park here also, so in anything approaching good weather arrive early to secure a parking slot. Be certain not to block the emergency gates in the lot because the rescue squad and park rangers use these accesses regularly on busy weekends. Also, forget getting a drink or a bite to eat at the Angler's Inn in paddling clothes. The place is strictly for the carriage trade and gnarly-looking river rats will be shown the door immediately.

Below Angler's Inn the river continues flowing calmly for about a mile until the Yellow Falls–Calico Falls area is reached. The river is now being split by high rock islands with vertical walls. When a modern design home is seen on the right, Virginia, shore a choice must be made as to which channel to run. Yellow Falls on the right is the steeper, more entertaining of the two. Calico Falls to the left is a longer, cobble-strewn sequence with no distinct drops. Yellow Falls should be scouted by first-timers because of the nasty hidden boulder located at the bottom that has wrapped up and destroyed many canoes.

Below Yellow and Calico Falls the river channels merge once again and soon the Carderock Picnic Area is passed on the left, another access point. On the Virginia shore opposite Carderock, Scott Run enters, creating a picturesque little waterfall. Bathing in the cascade is often done but cannot be recommended since Scott Run watershed is entirely urban and suburban. Immediately below Carderock, Stubblefield Falls is encountered. This is a gradually steepening cobble rapid with entertaining standing waves and whirlpools.

The Cabin John Bridge carrying the Capital Beltway is now in sight and without this reminder the paddler would think he was still in some remote mountain location. Below the bridge the Potomac flows tranquilly through a maze of low wooded islands for some three miles until Little Falls is approached. On river left below Cabin John Bridge access to the river is gained at Lock 10 on the C & O Canal. The take-out spot is well hidden among small channels along the Maryland shore so the paddler new to the area should seek guidance from a local paddler before attempting to take out here. The river between Lock 10 and Little Falls is interesting and scenic but contains no fast water so most whitewater afficionados seldom paddle it.

The Little Falls section of the river is a blessing to whitewater paddlers in the area but it can be an extremely hazardous place under the wrong conditions. The beginning of this section is marked by the Little Falls dam, a low concrete dam that is deceptively simple looking. The smooth flow over this three-foot barrage creates an absolutely lethal hydraulic at the base that has killed dozens of people over the years. The river is nearly a half mile wide at the dam so rescue from shore or boats in the event of a mishap is virtually impossible. From upstream the dam is not easily seen but can be inferred by the concrete pump building on the left. If one is paddling down the river and this structure becomes visible, start moving left to exit the river well above this dangerous construction.

Immediately below the concrete dam is the old Little Falls dam, a rock-fill structure built to provide water for the canal on the Maryland shore. This dam has no hydraulic but at reasonable levels the rocks are thinly covered in most places and iron bars poke dangerously through the rubble in some areas. Choosing the proper channel is difficult but crucial.

Below the twin dams the river narrows rapidly and drops over several small ledges before reaching Little Falls proper. This rapids is a straightforward ledge at the lowest levels but even the slightest change in water height can alter Little Falls into a thundering, boiling monster. At high levels the normally short Class III drop stretches into a Class VI killer with 15-foot exploding waves stretching for half a mile. No detailed explanation of Little Falls is attempted here since it is essential to only attempt this stretch in the company of paddlers who have experience with this rapids. It is interesting to note that the highest water velocity ever recorded in nature was seen at Little Falls during the massive flood of 1936.

Thornton River

The Thornton River forms at the confluence of its North and South Forks in the tiny historic village of Sperryville. Both tributaries of the Thornton cascade eastward off the Blue Ridge in Shenandoah National Park. The butternut clad legions of the Confederacy traveled over Thornton Gap and along the South Fork of the Thornton. Southern troops camped beside the Thornton at Sperryville on several occasions and must have certainly drunk the clear waters of the stream. The tiny creek that now provides recreation was once, like so many of the streams of Virginia, a source of sustenance, a geographic barrier, a highway, and an important landmark for the men who fought and bled across the state.

After gathering its forks the Thornton slides between Turkey Mountain on the north and Poortown Mountain on the south and then runs hard up against Red Oak Mountain on its eastward course. After passing Fletcher's Mill the stream continues in a southeasterly direction before joining the Hazel River shortly before the Hazel flows into the Rappahannock shortly above Remington. One of the most enjoyable aspects of the Thornton is that the drive to and from the river, from any direction, is through some of the most attractive and prosperous countryside in Virginia. The Skyline Drive is just a few miles west of the put-in and should not be missed by anyone new to the area. The apple orchards and horse farms of the surrounding region are scenic and pleasant. Sperryville is an apple-processing center and good local jams and cider may be gotten there in the fall. A native wine industry is also beginning to grow in the region, for which all enthusiasts of the grape may be grateful. Perhaps what Jefferson referred to as "a champagne country" may soon become so, as literally as it is now figuratively.

Although the entire Thornton is canoeable the whitewater enthusiast will want to select the best portion for his use. The best hassle-free and consistent whitewater section of the Thornton is between Fletcher's Mill and Rock Mills. This is a generally scenic trip where the river plays tag with rolling pastureland and increasingly large rocks or cliffs covered with hemlocks.

Above this section there are problems and below it the Thornton becomes too tame for real whitewater action. Between one and two miles upstream of Fletcher's Mill (along US 211) there is nearly always too little water and simply too many fences, low bridges, and back yards to contend with, even though the gradient is double that of the section below Fletcher's Mill. One mile above Fletcher's Mill, where Route 522 meets Route 211 (next to a big store called The Sperryville Emporium), the fences and bridges are gone, but there often is not enough water. Indeed, the gauge at Fletcher's Mill clearly refers to downstream, and when it says zero, the only way one can paddle upstream is with hiking boots or (for the one mile just above) with incessant scraping and continual trying to squeeze a three-foot-wide canoe through shallow, rocky two-foot chutes. Also Beaver Creek at the put-in usually adds a significant volume of water to the trip.

Boulder Ledge Rapid, Thornton River.
Photo by Lou Matacia.

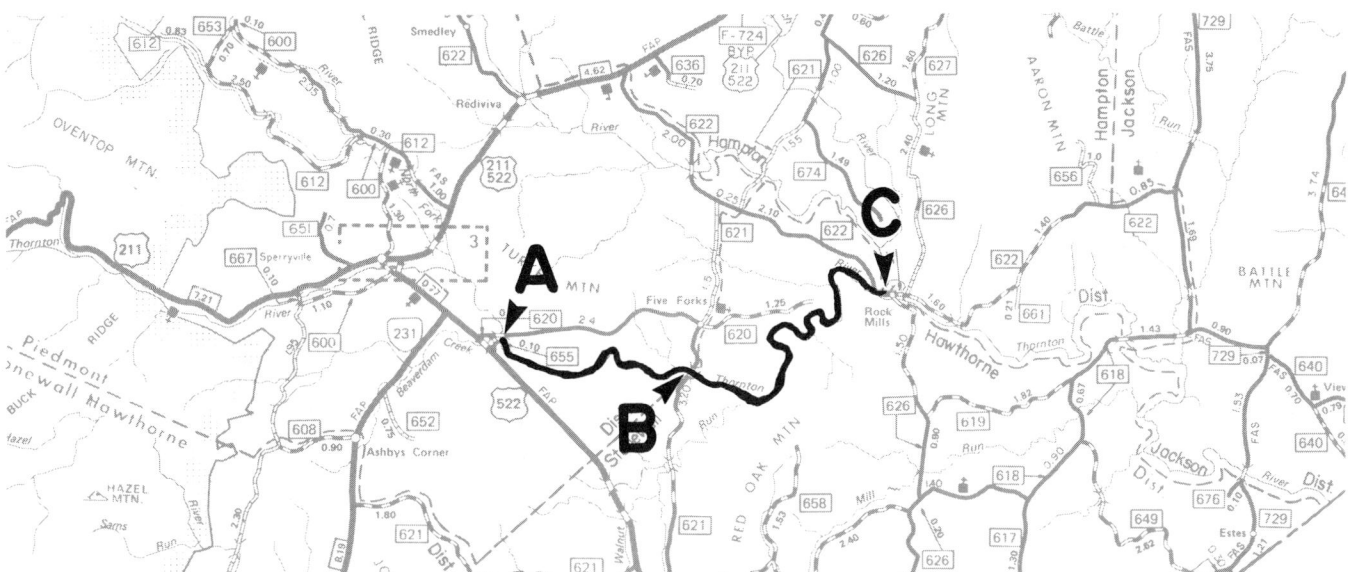

This very pleasant, basically Class II run has lots of moderate action beginning with the rapid below the put-in. Paddlers will be pleased to note that the fences referred to in previous literature have (at least as of this writing) been removed. However, be alert for at least one downed tree across the river.

The rapids for the first few miles are basically ledges (one a two-footer) interspersed with short rock gardens and one hard turn. However, about one and one quarter miles into the trip (after almost 30 minutes of paddling in low water) one comes to the lone Class III of the section (which is a marginal Class III in low water). Boulder Ledge Rapids, a descriptive if slightly redundant name, can be recognized by a long pool and a short rocky cliff forming the right bank as the river makes a hard right turn. Also, about 50 to 100 yards back from the left bank of the river is a much higher rocky bluff. The novice/intermediate paddler should get out and scout this rapids on river left. One should not only observe the main four- to five-foot bumpy drop (usually run right to left) but also look downstream to see if any other obstacles are lurking.

There is a nice little double ledge several minutes later followed by the first of several pretty lunch stops where the riverbank on one side or the other becomes huge rocks with hemlocks growing out of them.

The first bridge (Route 621) is reached after two and a half miles or as one approaches the halfway point of the trip. Just above this bridge there is a picturesque cliff on the left with a small surfing wave below at moderate levels. For the remaining four miles below the bridge the small ledges and pretty cliffs and boulders adorned with hemlocks and evergreens become more frequent. In particular, halfway between the Route 621 bridge and the take-out, below a

Section: Fletcher's Mill to Rock Mills

Counties: Rappahannock (VA)

USGS Quads: Washington

Suitable for: Cruising

Skill Level: Intermediate

Months Runnable: January to mid-April

Interest Highlights: Scenery, whitewater

Scenery: Good

Difficulty: II

Average Width: 20–30 feet

Velocity: Fast

Gradient: 24 feet per mile

Runnable Water Levels:
  Minimum: 100 cfs; 0 on Fletcher's Mill gauge
  Maximum: 500 cfs (estimate); 3 feet on Fletcher's Mill gauge

Hazards: Strainers, cattle fences

Scouting: Boulder Ledge

Portages: None

Rescue Index: Accessible

Source of Additional Information: USGS gauge recording (202) 899-7378. The Culpeper gauge should be over 2.0 ft. for a reasonable run. The Culpeper gauge is not on the Thornton so is only an indicator of runoff in the general area. There is a Randy Carter gauge on the bridge at Fletcher's Mill, which should read at least 0 feet.

Access Points	River Miles	Shuttle Miles
A–B	3.0	3.0
B–C	4.0	4.5

beautiful cliff, the river funnels to the left for an entertaining 50-yard run with a hole at the bottom left at lower levels. Two nice ledges with a surfing hole follow about ten minutes later. The Class II action with cobble bars, ledges, and very good scenery continues to the take-out bridge (Route 626) on this very relaxing trip.

If there is not enough water on the Thornton, check the nearby Hughes River as an alternate; the Hughes usually holds its water longer than the Thornton.

Zach the schnauzer on the Thornton, assisted by Tom Kopczyk. Photo by Bill Kirby.

Aquia Creek

Aquia Creek is one of those poorly known gems that delight the heart of the whitewater paddler. Located only 30 miles south of Washington, Aquia (pronounced uh-KWYE-uh) Creek promises little based on the land surrounding it. The environs of the creek are mostly agricultural land to the south and the Quantico (pronounced KWAN-ti-co) Marine Base to the north. The take-out is on Route 1, the famous north–south road that runs from Maine to Florida, encrusted for the whole route with the most tacky developments imaginable. While enroute to the river and while driving the shuttle the paddler will despair of any enjoyment for the day. But ignore all that. Ignore the trailer courts, the auto graveyards, the places along the road with names like Al & Nick's Tire World. Once on the river the jaded paddler is in for a day of surprise and delight. Aquia Creek is one of the most scenic and enjoyable small streams east of the Alleghenies.

The stream at the put-in does not arouse particular hope. Aquia Creek at Route 610 is a tiny sand-and-mud-banked creek. The flow moves along swiftly over a sandy bottom, but the only drops are where the stream flows over fallen logs. Fallen logs of the nonsubmerged variety are something of a problem for the first couple of miles but at most water levels one should be able to lift over them or pass underneath with little trouble. A couple of miles into the trip a concrete bridge is approached with three large culverts running through it. Barring any accumulation of debris in the pipes, and sufficient clearance depending on water level, any of these passages may be run safely. Be very sure of clearance before entering because, although the current through the bridge is not particularly swift, a broach in the pipe could be very serious indeed. The idea of being wedged with your boat into a debris jam in a culvert is the stuff of paddlers' nightmares. This bridge is property of the Marines and if you break it they'll be very mad at you. It was built to handle heavy military traffic and looks it. After passing under the bridge Aquia Creek begins to gradually steepen. This process continues all of the way to the lake near the take-out. Also, in the vicinity of the bridge several tributaries enter and the stream doubles in width, becoming a much more respectable size.

Soon the paddler begins to notice that the banks are showing some rock mixed in with the sand and clay and eventually the rock begins to predominate. The slopes on the left bank rise high above the stream and rhododendron begins to populate the stream's edge, serving notice that the geomorphological environment has changed significantly. Aquia Creek has entered the falls line area, where all of the eastward-flowing streams drop off the bedrock of the continent onto the sedimentary soils of the Coastal Plain. Some of the small streams in this area pack all of their drop into a small area, like Accotink and Pohick creeks, creating rapids with four- and five-foot drops. Aquia Creek, however, distributes its gradient more evenly, creating a stream more suitable to the intermediate paddler. As the creek passes downstream the slopes rise higher and higher on both sides, spectacular rock formations appear, and hemlocks tower over the stream, jutting dramatically from the rock. Rapids become steeper, but not nasty, and the relaxed paddler will find his or her adrenal glands beginning to stir into activity. The drops consist mostly of ledges up to three feet in height, some with rather complicated routes, many dropping over very tight turns into picturesque little pools at the bases of high rock cliffs. On the inside of bends white sandy beaches invite the paddler to linger and soak up sun.

Approximately two-thirds of the way through the trip the Route 641 bridge is reached. While this bridge would make a convenient take-out, doing so here would deprive the paddler of the very best part of the trip. Between this bridge and the lake Aquia Creek has all of the pluses and none of the minuses. The downed trees of the far upper section are gone, the gradient continues to steepen, and the cliffs, hemlocks, and rhododendrons are at their most spectacular. The wildlife in this area is equally pleasing. On one trip we saw beaver, deer, kingfishers, ospreys, hawks, great blue herons, and various and sundry waterfowl. The scenery is reminiscent of some of the upper Cheat tributaries in West Virginia, such as Red Creek, subtracting the high mountains in the far distance. The action builds to a crescendo for the final mile, which is almost without quiet water, until the Aquia drops into the lake. Now the paddler must pay for his enjoyment upstream with a two-mile paddle across the lake.

The route across the lake is not immediately obvious since the dam is earth fill and has the same look as the rest of the shoreline. Just keep paddling straight ahead and look for a cut in the bank in the distance on the left. This is the concrete spillway on the left edge of the dam. Give the entrance to the spillway a wide berth, as there are no warning signs or buoys. Beach the boat on the earthen dam and walk up the bank to scout the best route to drag the boat over the dam to the outflow channel. The dam itself is about 100 feet high and rather impressive. The lake is relatively small for such a large dam, indicating that the gradient of the creek under the reservoir must be quite large. Doubtless some fine rapids were sacrificed to create the water supply for Stafford County. The upstream end of the reservoir is silting in very heavily, so whitewater paddlers may look forward to the distant day when the lake will be filled by sediment and the creek will reassert its authority over its own destiny.

Below the dam Aquia Creek is rather unattractive. Although it still drops at a good rate the creek passes by some dismal scenery and the odor of sewage as one passes a trailer

182 Aquia Creek

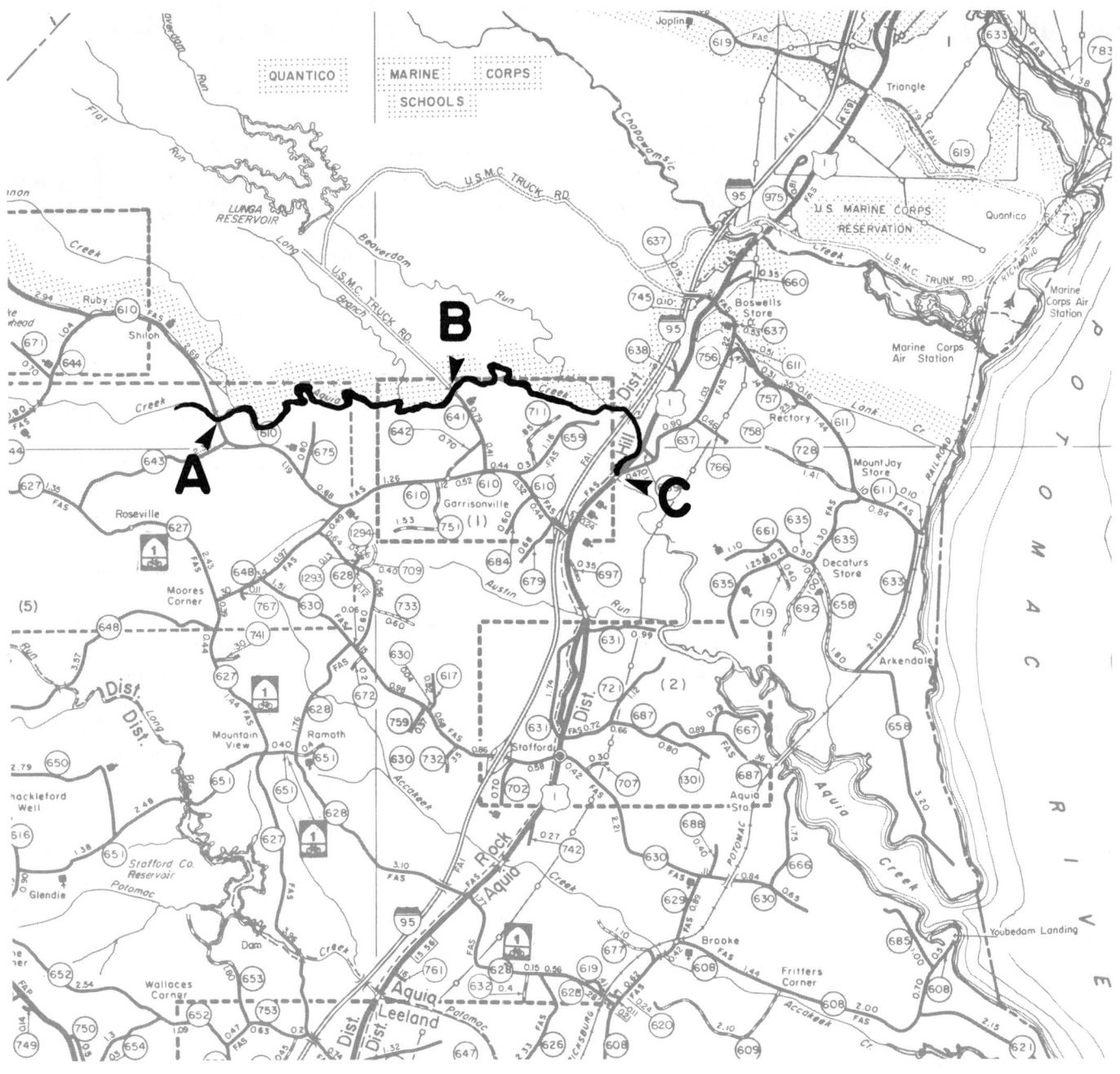

Section: Route 610 to Route 1

Counties: Stafford (VA)

USGS Quads: Stafford

Suitable for: Cruising

Skill Level: Intermediates

Months Runnable: January to April

Interest Highlights: Scenery, wildlife, whitewater

Scenery: Beautiful

Difficulty: II

Average Width: 15–50 feet

Velocity: Fast

Gradient: 15 feet per mile

Runnable Water Levels:
  Minimum: 35 cfs
  Maximum: Unknown

Hazards: Strainers, strainers and more strainers at certain times

Scouting: None

Portages: None except around downed trees where necessary

Rescue Index: Accessible

Source of Additional Information: None really. This is a hard stream to catch up. Roger Corbett states that a reading on the Remington gauge of 5.0 feet (202-899-7378) indicates a runnable level, but this is not reliable. If in the area check out the creek. If it looks runnable at the put-in on Rt. 610, it's runnable all the way.

Access Points	River Miles	Shuttle Miles
A–B	6.0	5.5
B–C	4.5	3.5

court on the left is depressing. At lower levels paddlers will have to carry over a large pipe running across the river just upstream of the take-out. The pipe is leaking badly but the wise paddler will refrain from examining the effluent from the pipe too closely. Some things man was not meant to know (unless he wants to heave his lunch). Fortunately the take-out is only one mile below the dam so this sort of abuse need not be endured for long.

The land on the left bank for most of the trip is part of the Marine base and is posted against trespassing. It would seem best, then, to arrange lunch or suntanning spots on the right bank to avoid any possible federal entanglements. Just as with Aquia's neighbor to the north, Quantico Creek, the Marines will occasionally entertain the paddler with low level jet and helicopter flights over the creek. What you thought was the blood pounding in your ears may turn out to be the sound of huge helicopter blades.

Rappahannock River

The Rappahannock River shares the distinction with the James and the Potomac of being inextricably intertwined with the history of the state and the nation. Some of the earliest settlements on the continent were founded on the banks of the Rappahannock estuary. George Washington warned Congress during his presidency that if measures were not taken to improve the navigation of the James below the falls at Fredericksburg then the day might come when that city would be overshadowed as a seaport by the upstart village of New York. It is the Rappahannock over which Washington in his youth, according to legend, threw a silver dollar. Throughout most of the Civil War the Rappahannock and Rapidan formed the de facto border between the Union and the Confederacy. Today many Virginians who live on both sides of the river feel that the state legislature in Richmond still views the Rappahannock as the border between the "real Virginia" south of the Rappahannock and the Yankee country north of that stream, and appropriates state monies for roads and other services accordingly. Along the banks of the Rappahannock four major battles were fought during the war. The battles of Fredericksburg, Chancellorsville, the Wilderness, and Spotsylvania Court House resulted in the deaths of over 100,000 Americans between December 1862 and May 1864. John Wilkes Booth, having murdered President Lincoln, ran south through Maryland, crossed the Potomac near what is now the Route 301 bridge and entered Virginia. Passing through King George county he crossed the Rappahannock to Port Royal, on the banks of that river, and was shot in a burning barn near the village.

The Rappahannock begins its existence in the coves and gaps of the eastern slope of the Blue Ridge in Fauquier, Rappahannock, and Madison counties. The waters of the Rush, Covington, Thornton, Hazel, and Hughes rivers join the upper Rappahannock near Remington while the Conway and South rivers join the Rapidan near Stanardsville and the latter mingles with the Rappahannock near the battlefield of Chancellorsville. The tributary streams are steep and rocky as they tumble off the Blue Ridge but flow sluggishly across the western Piedmont. The Rapidan and Rappahannock, before their confluence, run between sandy or mud banks with farmland straddling the streams for many miles. Downstream of Remington, however, the Rappahannock begins to tilt downward slightly and the stream accelerates adequately to add some sporty action to the pleasant scenery.

After putting in at the Remington bridge the paddler is teased by the river with a jaunty little ledge under the railroad bridge within sight of the put-in. After this brief chute through the remains of an old canal dam the river remains quiescent for about two miles before rewarding the efforts of whitewater fans. This flat section is scenic, however, and runs along swiftly over a sand or gravel bottom. The wooded banks provide a sense of intimacy and shield the river from the fields surrounding the stream. Only the occasional sound of farm machinery or the mooing of the local beef population will intrude on the paddler's privacy. The ambience of this section invites the paddler to swing his feet over the gunwales, rest his back against the thwart or aft deck, and drift with the gentle current, watching the trees wheel overhead. This relaxation continues for two and a half miles before the sight of exposed rock notifies the voyager of a new mood of the river.

The remaining two miles to Kelly's Ford is an entertain-

Kelly's Ford, Rappahannock River. Photo by Bill Kirby.

ing trip through rock gardens and over complex ledges requiring good boat control. At low water skill will be needed to locate the best routes through the low boulders and ledges without scraping and dragging inordinately. At higher levels the route will be less intricate but waves and hydraulics will require forceful paddling and probably some bailing in open boats. At very high levels the obstructions disappear but the turbulence becomes severe and only very experienced paddlers should venture out. The river is rather wide in some sections and would present a swimmer with a dangerous and long flush through continuous rapids. The addition of cold water would make this trip a hazardous one indeed for the unqualified. The exposed rocks and remote-seeming setting of this section give a wildness to the scene and the abundant wildlife, especially birds, make for a satisfying afternoon of paddling. All too soon the Kelly's Ford bridge comes into view, signaling the end of the trip. For those with the time and inclination the river is canoeable all the way to Fredericksburg, a distance of 29 miles. The next public access, however, is at Motts Run Landing, 24 miles from Kelly's Ford, so be prepared for a long paddle if continuing below Kelly's.

Kelly's Ford is a very historic spot, having been utilized many times during the Civil War as a crossing spot by troops of both sides. Many small battles were fought near the ford, signifying its importance as a strategic river crossing for the large armies. Kelly's Ford is still a scene of action but of a different sort, being a popular local party spot. During one of the author's first trips on the Rappahannock he and a paddling partner had intended to camp there on a Friday night after the drive down from Washington, preparatory to meeting more friends from out of town for a trip from Remington to Motts Run. Pulling into the parking area on the south side of the bridge around dusk, however, they discovered a party beginning to form. Inquiring as to the nature of the occasion they were told that Kelly's Ford was known throughout the surrounding counties as the locale for a traditional informal party every Friday night during warm weather and had been so for generations. Camping plans ruined, author and friend bent to the winds of fate and enjoyed a long evening of leaning on the hoods of various highly powered automobiles, sipping from the shared bottles of Jack Daniels, and listening to and creating lies and stories of increasingly exaggerated proportions as the night wore on. The canoe trip next day was slightly fuzzy but swift water and sunshine soon restored their vigor.

Section: Remington to Kelly's Ford bridge

Counties: Culpeper and Fauquier (VA)

USGS Quads: Remington and Germanna Bridge

Suitable for: Cruising

Skill Level: Intermediate

Months Runnable: January to May

Interest Highlights: Scenery, wildlife, whitewater

Scenery: Good

Difficulty: II

Average Width: 35–150 feet

Velocity: Fast

Gradient: 12 fpm

Runnable Water Levels:
  Minimum: 400 cfs
  Maximum: 1,500 cfs

Hazards: Strainers, hydraulics at higher levels.

Scouting: None

Portages: None

Rescue Index: Accessible

Source of Additional Information: USGS gauge recording (202) 899-7378. The Remington gauge, located at the put-in, should read between 4.0 and 5.0 feet for a reasonable run. Several outfitters in the Fredericksburg area can be of help.

Access Points	River Miles	Shuttle Miles
A–B	5.0	6.0

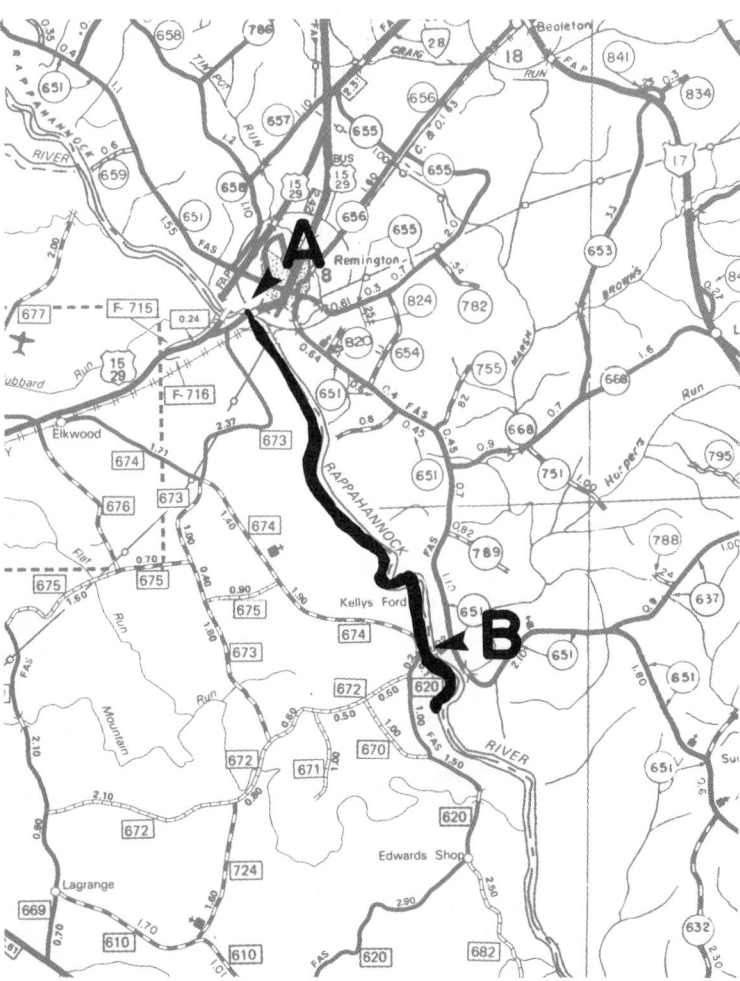

Tye River

The Tye River packs a lot of variety into a comparatively short area. Beginning at Nash, just a mile or so below the mouth of Crabtree Creek, the Tye starts in a mountain pass, cuts through foothills, and then settles into an open valley. A cross-sectional view of its gradient would be very close to a parabolic curve, a classic geomorphological landform.

In the first couple of miles below the confluence of the North and South Forks at Nash the Tye is a steep boat-buster with abrupt drops and tight turns through boulder-strewn chutes. The scenery in this section is spectacular, with high rock formations and steep forested slopes on both sides. The road follows the river closely on the left but is not intrusive, and the paddler may bless its presence in the event of a rescue effort or boat salvage operation. Rapids are almost continuous in this stretch but there are four memorable ledges that may have to be scouted depending upon water levels. The difficulty of these drops will be Class III in low water and Class IV at higher levels.

After passing under the first bridge at the confluence of Campbell Creek the Tye relaxes a bit. Rapids continue to appear at regular intervals but they are not so threatening as those above Campbell Creek. The river valley has widened somewhat and the gradient has lessened as the Tye leaves the mountain pass it has carved through Pinnacle Ridge at Nash and approaches its alluvial fan east of the mountains.

The rapids in this section consist of gravel bars and occasional sizable ledges where the Tye runs up against rock bluffs on either bank. The difficulty of the rapids in this section is a step down from the upper region, in the Class II–III range. The scenery is still good but a few cabins and cleared areas begin to intrude on the view.

As the fourth bridge crossing approaches, the Tye leaves steep terrain behind and begins meandering through a broad valley full of orchards and cattle. The river flows primarily through a channelized trough with bulldozed banks, only occasionally dropping over a Class II ledge, a shallow gravel bar, or through a narrow chute around a small island. The channelization in this section is not overwhelming since the river has been kept in its natural course. Hurricane Camille in 1969 caused great damage in the Tye River valley and the flood caused the stream to relocate its course in this lower section, according to locals. As Massies Mill is approached the river broadens out over a gravel bed and at low-water levels the paddler may find him or herself sliding and/or hiking for short stretches.

The water on the Tye is usually brilliantly clear and clean. The river is a popular trout stream and paddlers should make all possible effort to avoid conflict with these fellow friends of our rivers. As with many small streams in the state, it is probably best to avoid it on the first weekend of April, the opening day of trout season. On one trip paddlers were threatened by locals with having their cars towed away because "this is private property and canoeing isn't allowed." This sort of comment is hard to swallow when the banks are lined with dozens or hundreds of fishermen who don't seem likely to have secured permission from all the riparian landowners, but remember, the quiet word turneth away wrath. Getting into a shouting match on the banks of a stream is

Ed Grove on the upper Tye River. Photo by Bill Kirby.

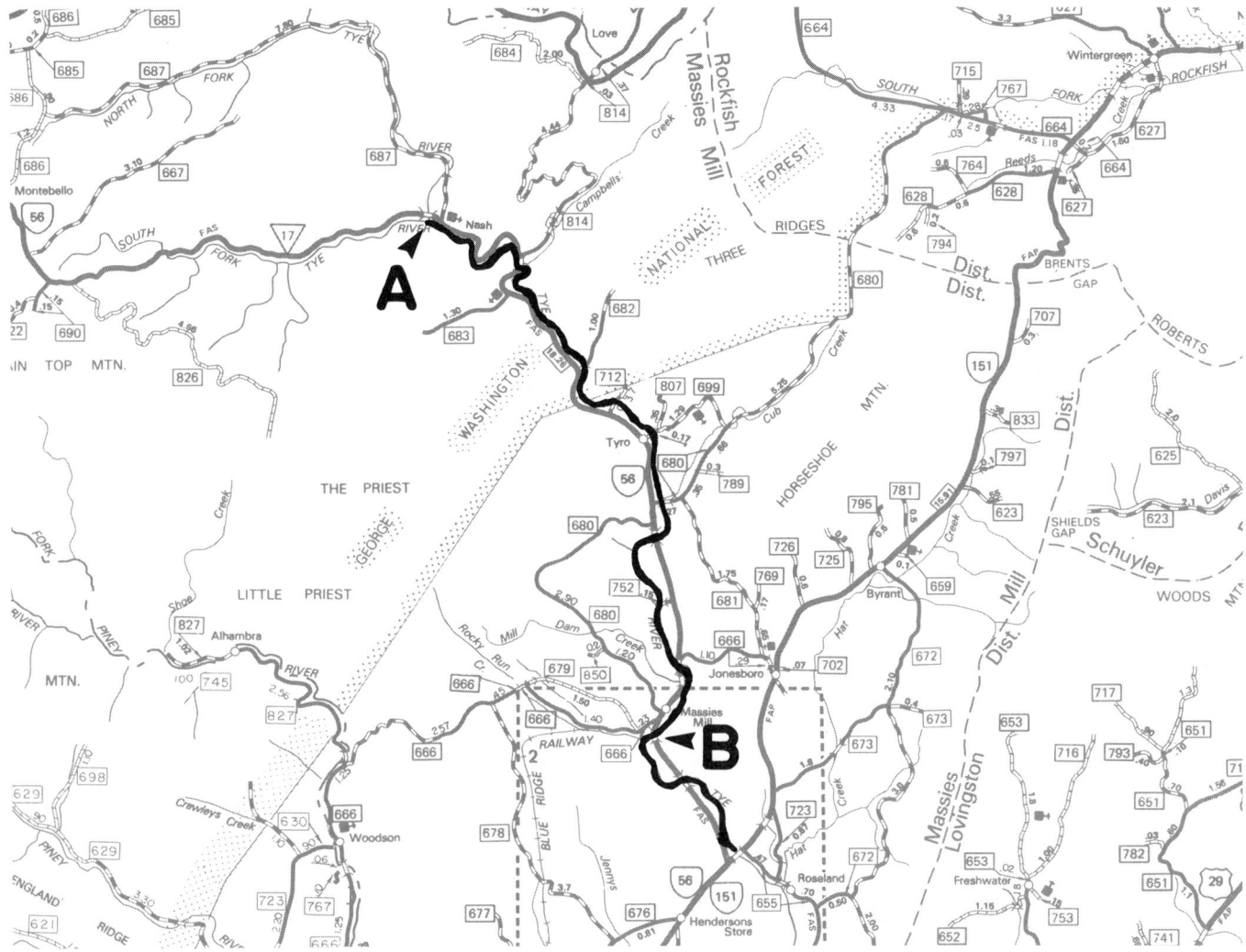

Section: Nash to Massies Mill

Counties: Nelson (VA)

USGS Quads: Massies Mill

Suitable for: Cruising

Skill Level: Advanced

Months Runnable: January to April only following a very heavy rain

Interest Highlights: Scenery, geology, whitewater

Scenery: Beautiful

Difficulty: IV in the upper section, II–III in lower reaches

Average Width: 20–40 feet

Velocity: Fast

Gradient: 56 fpm avg.; 85 fpm in upper 1.5 miles

Runnable Water Levels:
Minimum: 250 cfs
Maximum: 600 cfs

Hazards: Strainers, steep rapids, pinning possibilities on boulders, cold water

Scouting: All major rapids scoutable from road

Portages: None

Rescue Index: Accessible

Source of Additional Information: USGS gauge recording, (202) 899-7378. There is no USGS gauge on the Tye. Roger Corbett states in *Virginia Whitewater* that 4.5 on the Cootes Store gauge indicates a runnable level on the Tye. The correlation between the gauge and the level on the Tye is indirect at best and cannot be relied upon. In general, when everything else is ripping and roaring, go take a look at the Tye.

Access Points	River Miles	Shuttle Miles
A–B	8.5	8.0

worse than useless. In this particular instance the cars were not towed away, nor have any cars ever been towed according to all paddlers consulted concerning this question. There are "No Trespassing" signs at the put-in parking area at Nash. An elderly gentleman who lives in the house across the river states that people cross the property all the time to put boats in but it would probably be best if boaters put in on the upstream side of the bridge where the land is not posted.

The Tye drains a very small watershed which, even though it is virtually completely forested, seems to lose water very rapidly. As a result the Tye can go from too high to too low in a day and the paddler must be alert and determined to catch this stream with a suitable flow. By the time the Cootes Store or other gauges show sufficient water to indicate that there may be flow in this area the Tye has most likely waxed and waned and may be unrunnable. But go take a look anyway; if there is sufficient water it will be worth it, and there are plenty of alternatives in the area if you miss the Tye. Alternatives in the general area include the Piney River, the Pedlar, the Buffalo, and, somewhat farther away, the Maury.

When in the neighborhood of the Tye, a short hike is a must for all lovers of falling water. Above the runnable section of the Tye, along Route 56 toward the Blue Ridge Parkway, lies a small Forest Service parking area. From here a trail leads up Pinnacle Ridge along Crabtree Creek to a spectacular cascade high on the mountainside. Crabtree Falls consists of a steeply sloping curtain of water some 100 feet high where Crabtree Creek ends its meandering along the top of the ridge and falls abruptly into the valley of the upper Tye. The hike to the falls from the parking area is short but very steep, following innumerable switchbacks beside the swift and clear creek. Those who struggle all of the way to Crabtree Falls are amply rewarded by their beauty and by the breathtaking views available from the top of the rock dome over which the creek cascades.

The Tye River. Photo by Bill Kirby.

Maury River

The Maury River is formed just above Goshen Pass where the Calfpasture and Little Calfpasture rivers join. These two streams flow on parallel courses in a southwesterly direction along opposite sides of Great North Mountain until, near Goshen, the Calfpasture turns southeast. Just as the streams merge the now-sizable Maury cuts across the spine of Little North Mountain and drops precipitately into the Valley of Virginia. This happy circumstance of a reasonably large amount of water flowing through a steep mountain pass provides whitewater paddlers with excellent scenery, easy access via interstate roads, splendid rapids, and sparkling water quality in a combination unsurpassed anywhere in the East. Luxuriant rhododendron stands, steep rock cliffs lining the river, and cascading tributary streams create a superb arena for the enjoyment of our sport. The Maury is therefore the quintessential Virginia whitewater stream and, if one were forced to choose the finest among the ten best streams of Virginia, the Maury would be the odds-on favorite for such a title. The only negative aspect of this stream is that it is too short.

One aspect of the Maury that may be considered a mixed blessing is the presence of a paved road closely paralleling the river throughout the length of the Goshen Pass. The road, State Route 39, is usually dozens of feet above the stream, however, and so does not detract from the wild character of the scenery to a great degree. The presence of this artery will be appreciated by many who may require assistance, may be forced to walk away from the river sans boat, or who have friends or family who wish to see what the devil their friend or relative has been doing on weekends for all these years. In addition, the fortunate location of the road provides the Maury with a delightfully short shuttle route, allowing multiple runs of the river in a single day if so desired.

The put-in is shortly below the confluence of the Calfpasture and Little Calfpasture Rivers, where the river runs up against the road and turns left into Goshen Pass. There is a dirt road here which leads the short distance from the paved road to a convenient pool. Parking here is limited, so arranging the shuttle so that most vehicles are at the bottom of the run is recommended. Below the put-in the Maury flows swiftly over some entertaining riverwide low ledges for a few hundred yards, a few short rapids and quick ledges, and another 100-yard rapid to the first of the named rapids, one-half mile below the put-in.

Undercut Rock, one-half mile below the put-in, is a three-foot ledge, broken on the right and more abrupt on the left. Either side may be run but beware of the boulder on the bottom right which gives this rapids its name.

Shortly below Undercut Rock is Roadside, recognizable by a jumble of low boulders on the left forcing the river to the right against the roadside bank. Take a left course through this drop, easier at high levels when room is created for the passage of conservative boaters. This rapid is a long

Goshen Pass, "Devil's Kitchen," Maury River. Photo by Bill Kirby.

wave field (100 yards) with a nice surfing wave three-quarters of the way down. Excellent surfing waves are found at the bottom of this drop.

A long and pleasant Class II–III boulder garden appears below Roadside. This is an example of the good nature of the Maury for this rapids seems to be provided as a morale builder for the nervous paddler in preparation for the serious business that lies below. At the bottom of the boulder garden is a pool known as the Blue Hole. Running out of the Blue Hole the river disappears to the left, the road retreats high up on the right bank, and an unusually basso profundo roar may be heard from the stream ahead. These clues and the sight of various numbers of people in brightly colored helmets and nylon clothing scrambling all over the riverbanks should indicate that something unusual lies ahead. Rest assured that this is indeed the case.

Devil's Kitchen is the object of all of these grave portents and it deserves them. This drop is a 100-yard-long heavy Class IV with almost every conceivable river hazard packed into a short distance. The river drops about 20 feet in this span, with steep drops, limited visibility, strong holes, undercut rocks, tiny eddies, fallen trees, and the possibility of strainers making this by far the most serious rapids on the trip. The complexity of the series makes a detailed descrip-

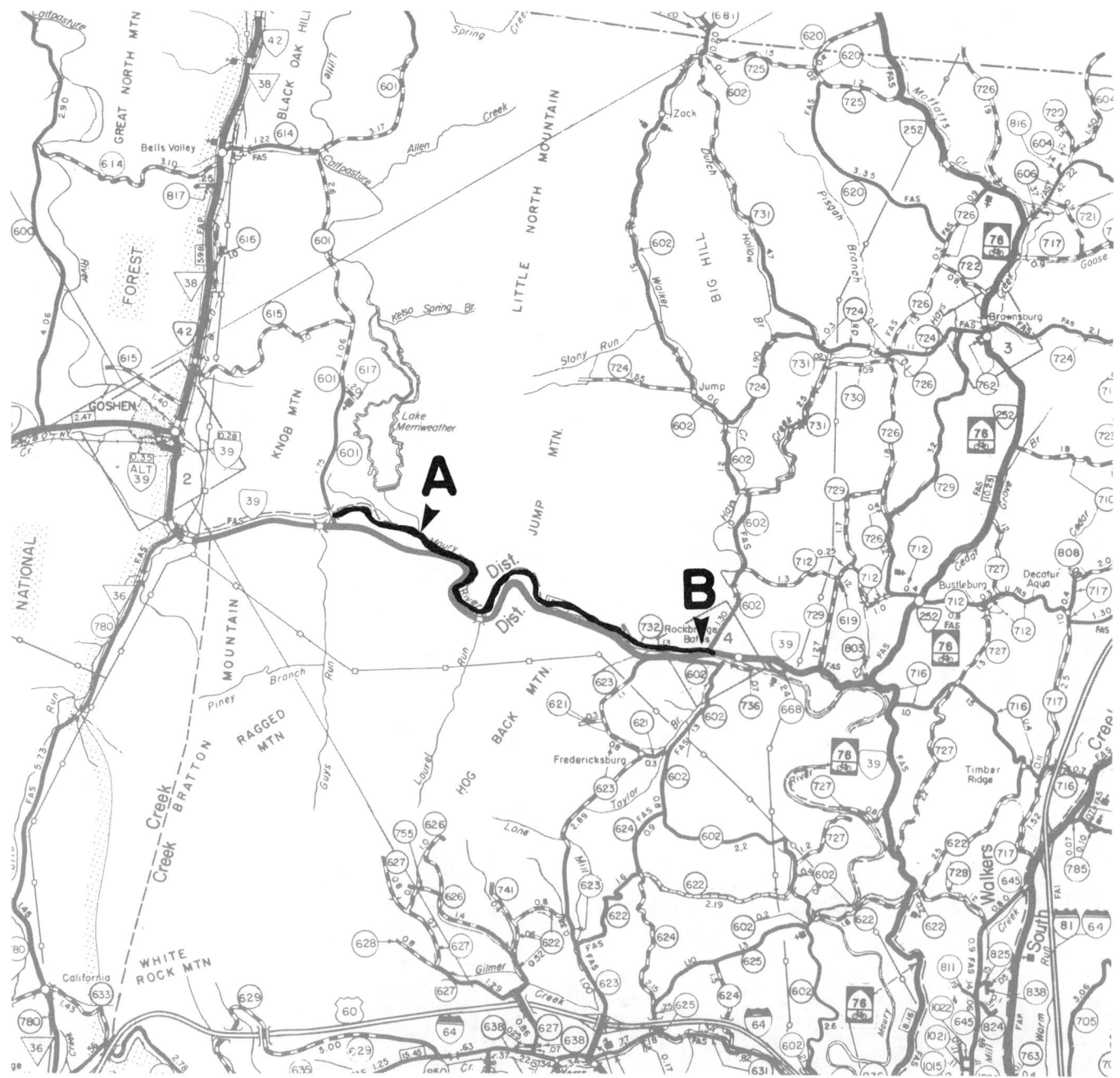

tion of the route impractical, but the general path is to the *left* of a quasi-island made up of bus-sized boulders on the right; you should be working right to end up on river right at the end of the run. Avoid the temptation to sneak the heavy stuff by running through the more lightly watered channel to the right of this island because it is festooned with strainers and studded with undercut rocks. Land above the entrance of Devil's Kitchen on the left and take a long hard look at it on foot.

Below Devil's Kitchen the Maury provides another of the delightful Class II-III boulder gardens that make this trip such a pleasure. When these drops are navigated the paddler will find himself at the picnic area where, after Devil's Kitchen, some may wish to make use of the restrooms near the road. Leaving the picnic area, the highway, perhaps sensing more accurately than paddlers what lies ahead, again retreats away from the river and remains cowering high above the canyon floor for over a mile. More small ledges follow the picnic area and culminate in a four-foot drop that requires an S-shaped course.

Soon Laurel Run falls off the right mountainside and enters the Maury, but it isn't noticeable unless you look for it. There are three small drops below Laurel Run that afford nice play spots. Corner Rapid, located after a sharp bend to the left, is formed from boulders cut from the cliffs on the right. The river is squeezed to the left and through a boulder jumble. Paddlers should run the upper section on the left and then get to the right for the lower section. This section has lots of large holes to punch or avoid depending on the skill or inclination of the paddler. Scrupulously avoid being pushed too far right at the top as you'll be squeezed into one of two violent channels; the lower left is ugly, with pinning spots and scrapy channels.

A couple of hundred yards of Class II follow and soon a smoothly sloping rock wall will be seen on the right. This indicates Sloping or Sliding Rock Rapids, a 100-yard-long ledge series. The route is straight through on the right. The channel is directly next to the sloping rock wall, which runs uninterrupted into the water, and zooming down this bouncy channel with the rock within arms' reach on the right is reminiscent of looking out the window of a speeding subway. The eddies against the wall are very entertaining if they can be caught, and they provide opportunities for dynamic eddy turns, exciting surfing chances, and the possibility of customizing your boat by grinding off the bow on the unyielding stone. There are easier eddies on the left. There are also some nice surfing holes here.

Downstream is a long Class III rapids that has some very nice surfing waves toward the end. About 100 yards later, the paddler will reach a calm spot known as the Indian Pool, recognized by a picnic table, a stone stairway, and the road. Below Indian Pool is another Class II-III rock garden almost one-half mile long that becomes rather bony at lower levels. This long rapid has several play spots and a new four-foot drop about two-thirds of the way down on river left. It is possible to take out at the bottom of this rapid where the road reapproaches the river, but we recommend continuing into Rockbridge Baths for the sake of tradition if nothing else.

Below Indian Pool the canyon opens out into the valley but the river has tenaciously retained enough gradient to keep the paddler entertained a while longer. Class II-III boulder gardens and ledges continue for a mile, with the river occasionally splitting around islands. These islands are deposited material, occuring where the steep gradient of the

---

Section: Goshen to Rockbridge Baths

Counties: Rockbridge (VA)

USGS Quads: Goshen

Suitable for: Cruising

Skill Level: Intermediate except for Devil's Kitchen, which is for advanced paddlers only

Months Runnable: January to May or other times following a moderately heavy rainfall. The Maury retains water longer than many other rivers in the area.

Interest Highlights: Scenery, wildlife, history, geology, and whitewater

Scenery: Exceptionally beautiful

Difficulty: Class III (IV)

Average Width: 40-60 feet

Velocity: Fast

Gradient: 48 feet per mile average; 71 in the Goshen Pass

Runnable Water Levels: USGS gauge recording (202) 899-7378. The Buena Vista gauge should read at least 3.0 for a decent run. Note that the gauge on the Rt. 39 bridge at Rockbridge Baths is 4 or 5 feet off and the needs to be reinstalled; Maury River General Store in Rockbridge Baths, phone (703) 348-5500
  Minimum: 300 cfs; 1 foot at Rockbridge Baths or at James River Basin Canoe Livery (703) 261-7334
  Maximum: 1,500 cfs; added congestion makes swims at levels above 3 feet hazardous; runs up to 5 feet are not too difficult for advanced paddlers, and 6 or 7 feet are possible for crazed experts.

Hazards: Strainers, keeper hydraulics at high levels, difficult rapids. Lots of jagged rocks that have been broken off or rolled up and exposed during the November 1985 flood.

Scouting: Devil's Kitchen, Corner rapids below picnic ground, Brillo rapids just above Rockbridge Baths

Portages: None

Rescue Index: Accessible

Source of Additional Information: James River Basin Canoe Livery, RFD No. 4, Box 125, Lexington, VA 24450 (703) 261-7334

Access Points	River Miles	Shuttle Miles
A-B	5.5	5.5

Route 39 bridge over the Maury River after the November 1985 flood. Photo by Bill Kirby.

Goshen Pass has receded, reducing the capacity of the stream to carry rock, rubble, and sand. This excess material settles out of the flow and forms the islands and braided channels of this section. These characteristic formations are found wherever a steep stream reaches a level of temporarily decreased gradient. The drops in this area tend to be technical and require careful channel hunting at lower levels. At high levels just blast ahead and Devil take the hindmost.

The last two notable drops on the run are easily recognized. They are both within a few hundred yards of the Route 39 highway bridge. The first is called Lava Falls, after the igneous rock intrusion that forms the rapids. Lava is a Class II-III chute, run on the far right. Good surfing waves are found at the bottom. Shortly below is Brillo, an abrupt four-foot ledge. Scouting here is in order since the channel is difficult to see from above. The route of choice at low and medium levels is on the far left but even a perfect run will likely be accompanied by a grinding sound on the hull of the boat, providing an immediate answer to the question of the origin of the rapids' name. (There is a temporary bridge between Lava and Brillo. Presumably it will be dismantled after the Route 39 bridge is repaired.)

The Route 39 bridge is now in sight signaling the end of the run. Do not take out at the bridge, however; this is frowned upon by the landowners. Instead, continue downstream to the General Store on the left bank in Rockbridge Baths, a distance of a few hundred yards. There is a 150-yard long Class II rapid before the store.
Now go back and do it again!

The Maury River is referred to on old maps and in old texts as the North River of the James. In 1742 there occurred the first bloodletting between Indians and the colonists in the upper James Valley, on the North near its confluence with the James, near present-day Glasgow. A band of Indians from the north traveled, as was common at the time, along the Great Warpath to attack their enemies the Catawbas in North Carolina. This Great Warpath was used also by the early colonists and later grew into the Valley Turnpike, now State Route 11. The marauding Indians apparently took some property from white colonists on their way to the south and the local militia gathered to punish the Indians for this transgression. John McDowell, commander of the local militia, intercepted the Indians on North River and was killed along with seven of his men in the ensuing battle.

The North River was renamed in honor of Matthew Fontaine Maury, born in Virginia but raised in Tennessee. Maury obtained a commission in the U.S. Navy as a young man and sailed out of Newport News, Virginia. Over the succeeding years he began a study of ocean winds and currents which was to earn him the title of "Father of Oceanography." The Civil War interrupted his scientific career, however, and he devoted his efforts to strengthening the miniscule Confederate Navy and to the destruction of the ships on which he had formerly served. After the defeat of the South, Maury became a professor at the Virginia Military Institute at Lexington on the North River. There he fell in love with the Goshen Pass and requested that upon his death his remains be carried through the pass. An honor guard of VMI cadets carried out this wish, and a monument to him stands on the road in the pass today.

While in the area of the Maury those with a historical bent will not want to miss a side trip to Lexington, Virginia, one of the most historically rich towns in a state that thrives on its past. The Virginia Military Institute, where Stonewall Jackson was a professor before the Civil War, Washington and Lee University, where Robert E. Lee spent his last years after the close of the same war, as well as a wealth of historic buildings, monuments, and cemeteries will bring the past alive to those who are in tune with such things. The James River and Kanawha Canal reached as far as Lexington until 1895 and provided reliable transportation between the Tidewater and the mountains. Despite the engineered safety of the canal, river travel in those days had the same attendant hazards it has today. The famous tale of Frank Padget, a black slave employed on the canal, is a timeless story that whitewater paddlers of today are most equipped to appreciate. For a detailed account readers are referred to Blair Niles's *The James, From Iron Gate to the Sea*, (New York: Farrar, Straus & Giroux, 1940) but the outline is as follows: A canal boat Clinton was attempting to pass across the mouth of the rain-swollen Maury on its way up the James to Buchanan drifted into the James when its towline broke. It accelerated toward the Balcony Falls section, which is run by whitewater paddlers today, at lower water levels, for sport. The boat was headed for a dam and seven people jumped off the boat and swam for shore. Four reached shore but three were swept over the dam and drowned in the hydraulic. The packet boat then, with some 50 people on board, successfully ran the dam and continued on toward the rapids. Volunteers were called for to save the people who had jumped from the boat onto any nearby rock and those still on the boat itself, which was hung up on a rock in midstream. Five boat hands, including Frank Padget, took a bateau from the canal, dragged it over the towpath, and put on the river. They rowed the boat into the middle of the river, by all accounts using techniques of ferrying and eddy turns in heavy water as modern as this year's slalom boat, and retrieved most of the victims after several trips out and back. On the last trip, however, the bateau broached and wrapped firmly about a rock and all were thrown into the river. Frank Padget and the man he was attempting to rescue drowned in the flooded James. The contemporary account, from the *Lexington Gazette*, is astounding to read and shows evidence of whitewater technique that most present-day rescue squads would do well to emulate. A monument to Frank Padget still stands today along the railroad tracks that replaced the canal towpath near the scene of the accident.

The Maury lies virtually at the intersection of I-64 and I-81 and so is easily reached from any area of the state. Route 39 crosses Route 11 at the ramp for the latter road off of I-64.

Other rivers in the neighborhood include the Cowpasture, Calfpasture, Bullpasture, and Jackson, all due west of Goshen Pass; the Upper James to the south; and the Tye, Piney, and Pedlar over the Blue Ridge to the east.

James River

The James at Richmond qualifies as one of the great whitewater streams of Virginia by virtue of its popularity with paddlers from all over the area, especially those from the southern half of the state. This river defines the concept of proximity to a populated area, as the run described lies entirely within the city limits of Richmond. The river is never too low to run and thus provides the water-craving summer boater with a place to maintain his skills and sanity when most of the smaller streams in the state are dry as a bone. Indeed, the paddler should beware of levels of too much water during the winter and spring. The James can rise extremely rapidly to a dangerous level. The ledges and broken dams that create the whitewater sport on this section of the James can become deadly when large amounts of water pour over them, creating dangerous hydraulics of great width.

As with the rest of our eastward-flowing rivers, the James meanders for many miles through farmland with no appreciable gradient before it reaches the edge of the bedrock underlying North America. Here the river tumbles off the continent onto the Coastal Plain, creating whitewater for our enjoyment. The city of Richmond was located here in colonial times to take advantage of the free power available from the falling water. Many low dams were built across the river to collect water for use in running various mills and industrial operations. Most of these have fallen into disuse and now are broken out, creating chutes and broken ledges. The nature of the rapids on the James is largely determined by these structures, the original nature of the river bottom having been overwhelmed by the man-made alterations. The resulting run is as unique as it is convenient and the paddler must take care to realize the unusual hazards attendant to a primarily artificial whitewater course.

The James River comprises the heart of the state of Virginia. Along its banks were created the earliest settlements in the western hemisphere. The tidewater planters created a society modeled on English laws and traditions, establishing the pattern for the continent-wide society which grew from these initial plantations. Nathanial Bacon, an early settler of the Richmond area, led his neighbors in a revolt against a disinterested and aloof aristocracy in 1676, burning the capital of Jamestown to the ground, and striking the first

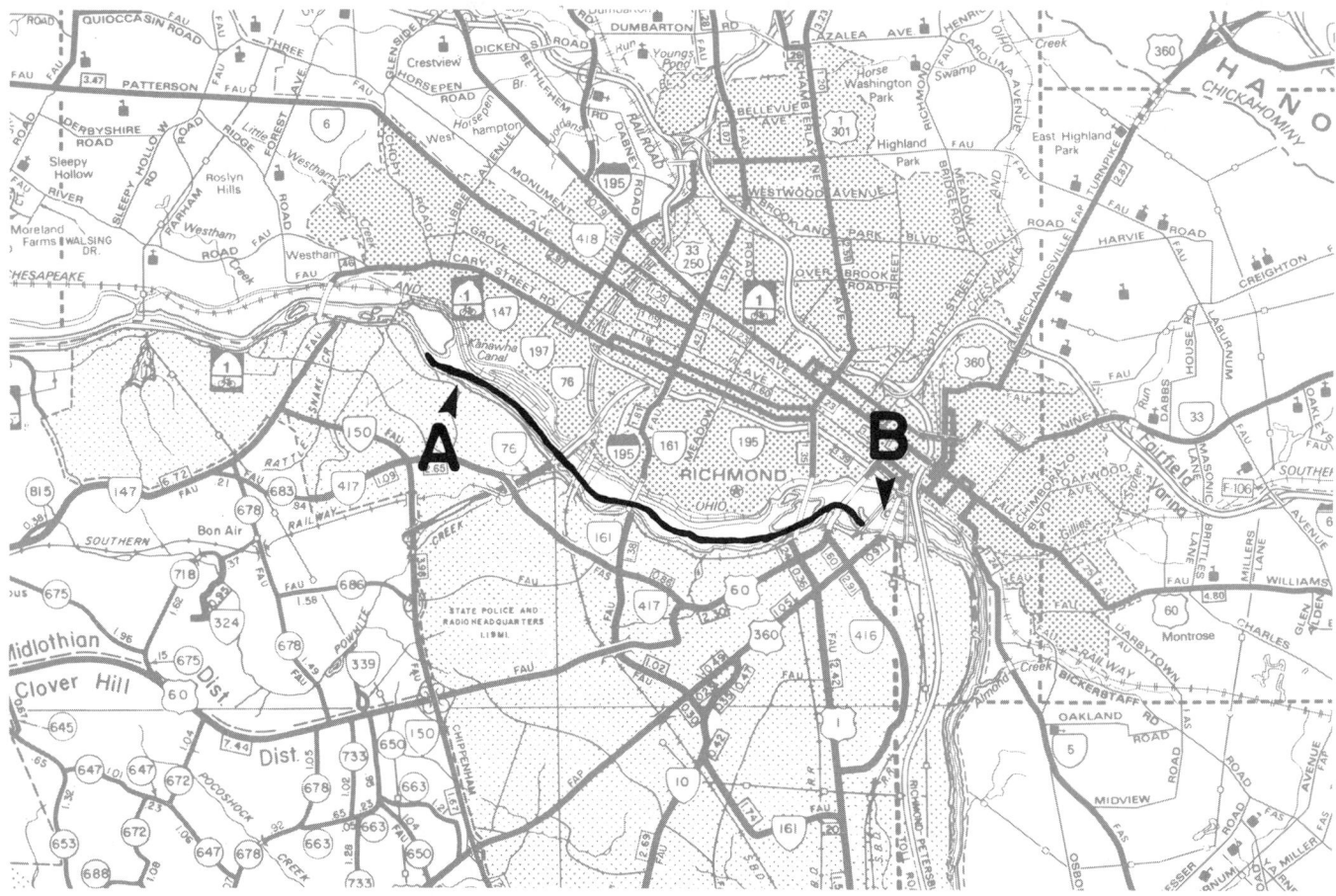

blow in the struggle against colonialism that would culminate one hundred years later in the establishment of the United States. Patriot and English armies marched and countermarched through the James basin in the War for Independence, establishing Virginia as the birthplace of the American nation and presaging it as the cockpit in a later war which nearly destroyed that same nation.

When the Southern states seceded from the Union in late 1860 and early 1861 Richmond was chosen as the capital, both to bring the border states into the war on the Southern side and to emphasize the preeminence of Virginia among her Southern neighbors. As a result of this decision the state became the center of the most destructive event in the history of the country. The banks of the James became the goal of the Northern armies for four years of insane destruction, and Richmond would lie in ruins at the end of this struggle. Factories on the falls line in Richmond churned out weapons, gunpowder, and supplies for the Southern armies, and Yankee prisoners were incarcerated at Libby Prison on the left bank of the James and on Belle Island in midstream. In the end the greater strength of the North prevailed and the nation, begun in Virginia and symbolically rent asunder there, was restored to its previous state of unity. Students of ecology will notice while traveling through the countryside between Richmond and the Potomac that the land of Virginia is still recovering from the depradations suffered during the Civil War. Think of these things while paddling through the modern metropolis of Richmond on the James River.

The put-in is on Riverside Drive on the south bank of the James, at a parking area called Pony Pasture. Below here the river flows quietly for a mile or so to the first of the

Section: Riverside Drive to Mayo Island

Counties: Henrico, Chesterfield (VA), and City of Richmond

USGS Quads: Richmond

Suitable for: Cruising, training

Skill Level: Intermediate–advanced

Months Runnable: Year round (watch out for high water in winter and spring!)

Interest Highlights: History, whitewater

Scenery: Fair

Difficulty: II–V

Average Width: 200–400 feet

Velocity: Fast

Gradient: 15 feet per mile

Runnable Water Levels:
  Minimum: 1,000 cfs
  Maximum: 3,000+ cfs

Hazards: Iron bars, broken dams, hydraulics, strong rapids

Scouting: None essential, but when in doubt, get out

Portages: None

Rescue Index: Accessible

Source of Additional Information: USGS recording (202) 899-7378 should be between 4.0 and 6.0 feet. Coastal Canoeists, c/o Les Fry, 2008 Charleston Ave., Portsmouth, VA 23704. There are several rafting outfitters operating on the James who can provide valuable assistance.

Access Points	River Miles	Shuttle Miles
A–B	5.5	7.0

Diana Kendrick at the James River put-in. Photo by Paul Marshall.

Members of a local rescue squad practice dam rescue on the James River at Richmond. Photo by Bill Kirby.

rapids. For a couple of miles the river flows through rocky islands and over numerous small ledges and rock gardens. This is a warm-up for the first of the major drops, known as First Break. First Break is actually two breaks in the old Belle Island Dam, a masonry structure. The upstream-most of the two breaks is dry in low water. The more highly used lower break is a three- to four-foot drop into nice waves, a good surfing spot. Watch out for submerged rocks immediately below the surfing waves. Catch the eddy on the left to get back into the waves. Below here stay to the right, up close to Belle Island, to enter Hollywood Entrance.

Hollywood Entrance is a pleasant Class II–III set of drops at normal levels. There are several nice surfing spots in holes and waves. Don't come out of your boat, however, because the big'un, Hollywood, lies below.

Hollywood Rapids consists of a five- to six-foot ledge, broken and runnable on the right, followed by a mess of wet boulders in the outflow. The preferred route is to the left at the bottom but you will have to scamper to get there. The boulders can also be avoided on the right with some speed. Go either way, but make your mind up early. There are lots of entertaining waves and holes here.

After passing under the Robert E. Lee Bridge the Vepco Levee Rapids is reached. This is an easy ledge, but with more boulders in the outflow of the best channel. Soon the Manchester bridge is seen overhead and the Second Break Rapids looms. Second Break is a four- to five-foot drop through a break in an old Vepco (Virginia Electric Power Company) dam. A straightforward drop, but dead ahead at the bottom are broken out chunks of concrete with exposed steel-reinforcing bars (re-bar). Just as with Hollywood, go right or left but know before you go and don't mess with the re-bar. Stick toward the left to enter Pipeline Rapids.

Pipeline consists of four distinct drops. The third of the series contains a great ender spot at reasonable levels, accessible from the eddy on the left at the bottom. From the eddy, just poke your bow into the hole and hang on tight. Again, don't come out of your boat because the fourth drop lies just below and would cause an unpleasant swim. The take-out at the bridge over Mayo Island lies shortly downstream.

It should be noted that the above description is a brief treatment of the most commonly paddled route through the falls of the James. There are many variations on this route and some entertaining rapids not covered by this description. Also there are an almost infinite number of potential put-ins and take-outs available due to the urban nature of the landscape. Those interested in the many variations available should contact local paddlers. Indeed, this river is so complex that the first trip down the falls of the James should be in the company of locals if at all possible, for both safety and enjoyment reasons.

Appomattox River

The Appomattox is another of those gems of the eastern seaboard, a river that meanders over a mature landscape through rather boring if pleasant scenery for many miles before dropping off the continental shelf. Where once were located mills and other industry the river now flows through spectacular scenery and drops over entertaining ledges and boulder gardens. America's abandonment of the rivers as foci of industry and development has preserved many streams in a semi-wild state without the protection of law and regulation. The Appomattox and its sisters, the Potomac and Rappahannock, are in this fortuitous category.

The Appomattox is replete with the history of Virginia. Like the Rappahannock, the Appomattox played host to some of the earliest settlements in the hinterlands of North America, in the days when the area west of the falls line was the frontier. Pre-Columbian Indians populated the area heavily, unlike the area north of the Rappahannock, and place names testify to their influence with early colonists. The Petersburg area was the site of the denouement of the Civil War, the city enduring a ten-month-long siege which produced severe civilian casualties in addition to those of the combatants. The Petersburg campaign is considered by many historians as the beginning of the concept of total warfare which reached its full development in the wars of the twentieth century. The siege is interpreted by the National Park Service at the Petersburg National Battlefield south of the city. Following the break of the siege by Union forces, Robert E. Lee and his Confederates retreated west along the Appomattox, attempting to reach Danville and a source of much-needed supplies at the railroad there. The ragged remnants of the forces of the South were caught and surrounded at the town of Appomattox on the river of the same name and the four-year struggle was over for all practical purposes.

Putting in at Chesdin Dam the paddler is allowed a mile of flatwater paddling to warm up on before reaching the first obstacle: a six-foot dam, with a required portage on the left. Reentering the river the paddler is welcomed by two entertaining Class II rapids. Following a swift water section without distinct drops another Class II rapids is encountered. The paddler may elect to run straight ahead or enter an old canal channel on the left and reenter the river proper via a stronger, steeper drop where the canal bank has broken out.

Continuing downstream the paddler is treated to a wider river with many islands and intricate passages through boulder garden rapids and small ledges for a couple of miles. The bird-watcher will find many examples of his interest in this section. The largest rapids in this section lie below, within a few hundred yards of the take-out bridge. An eight-foot dam, broken on the right side, provides the first entertainment for the paddler. A less severe boulder garden immediately follows the Broken-Dam Rapids and then a Class III rapids appears, signaling the end of the action. Just below the last rapids an old millrace reenters the river on the left, creating a steep drop of ten feet. Those with the energy and nerve may wish to portage to the top of this drop and run back into the river.

Stephen Ensign on the Appomattox River. Photo by David Whitley.

198 Appomattox River

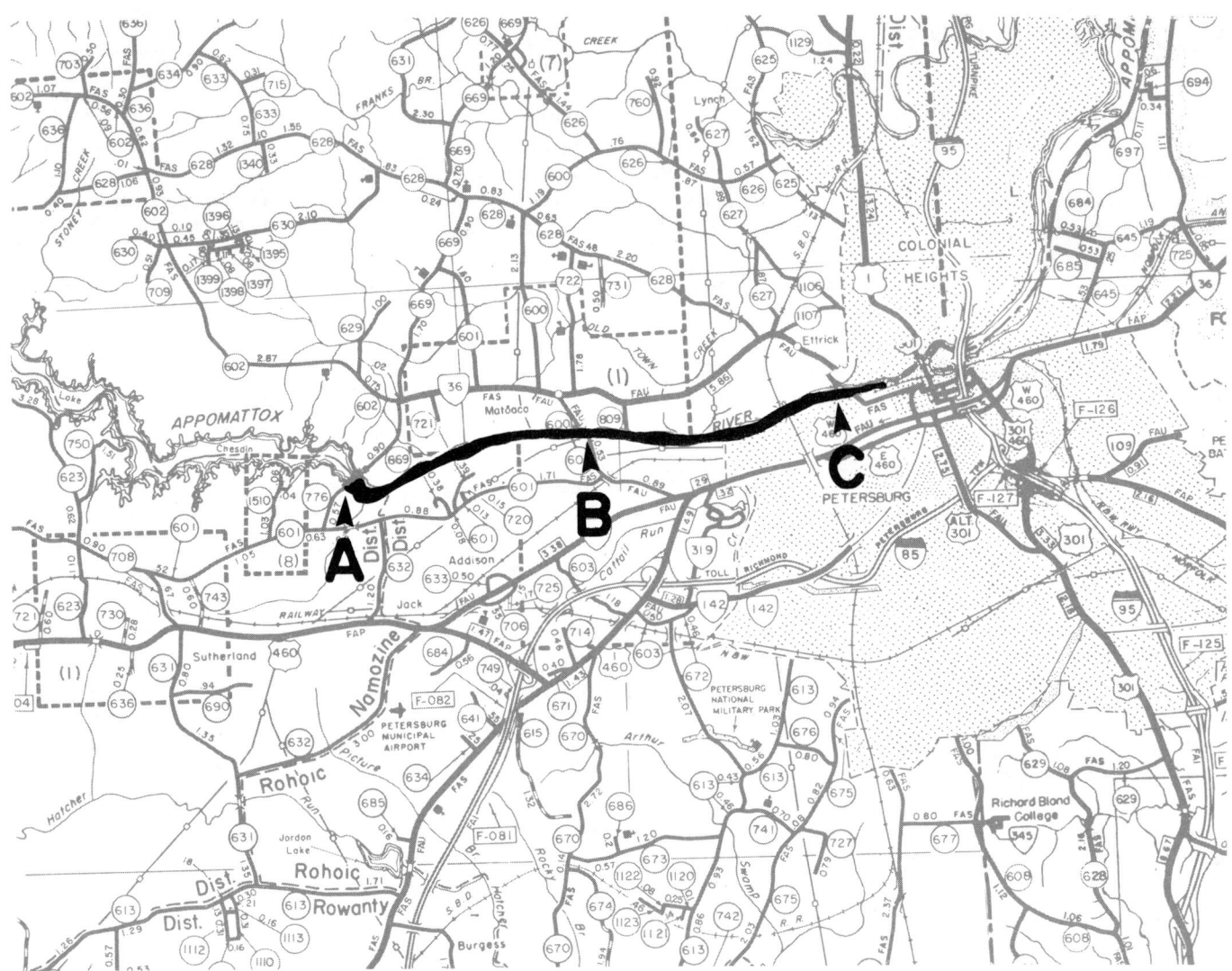

Section: Chesdin Dam to Petersburg

Counties: Chesterfield and Dinwiddie (VA)

USGS Quads: Sutherland and Petersburg

Suitable for: Cruising, racing, training

Skill Level: Intermediate

Months Runnable: January to June

Interest Highlights: Scenery, whitewater, history

Scenery: Good

Difficulty: II–III

Average Width: 40–90 feet

Velocity: Fast

Gradient: 15 feet per mile

Runnable Water Levels:
  Minimum: 500 cfs
  Maximum: 1,800 cfs

Hazards: Dam 1 mile below put-in

Scouting: Broken Dam Rapids just above Route 36 bridge

Portages: Dam below put-in

Rescue Index: Accessible

Source of Additional Information: Appomattox River Company, 610 N. Main St., Farmville, VA 23901 (804) 392-6645. A reading of the Matoaca NWS gauge is available by calling (804) 226-4423. This gauge should be above 2.0 feet for a run.

Access Points	River Miles	Shuttle Miles
A–B	3.0	4.0
B–C	3.5	5.0

Johns Creek

This section of Johns Creek is a superb run for the advanced paddler who is in good physical shape. It should only be undertaken with careful attention to the gauge for the river, and paddlers doing it for the first time should go with someone who knows this tight, tough technical stream well. Paddlers familiar with earlier guidebooks should note that the gauge on the Route 615 bridge in New Castle was revised in 1981 to give a more honest reading. A level of "zero" is equivalent to three inches of water on the old version. Also, please note that a change of a few inches on this gauge can dramatically increase the difficulty of this river.

What can be seen of Johns Creek from the road is misleading. At the put-in, it looks like a drainage ditch, while the section immediately above the take-out looks like the Class II–III Nantahala River in western North Carolina. In between, hidden from view, is a ruggedly beautiful gorge which has an average gradient of 60 feet per mile, with some places exceeding 125 feet per mile. This gradient combines with a heavily obstructed riverbed to create about three miles of very lively water. The rapids in the gorge range from Class III to Class V and are mostly continuous, with only a few short flat stretches offering a breather. Where possible, all these rapids should be boat or land scouted.

After the put-in at the Route 311 bridge, there are about two miles of flatwater leading into the gorge. The arrival of the heavy section is heralded when the paddler reaches an overhanging rock wall on the right. Then, the river takes a sharp left bend and immediately picks up to Class III. After a couple of these "smaller" rapids, the proverbial bottom drops out.

The first major rapid in this hot and heavy section is a steep Class III–IV S-turn from right to left over a succession of rocks, drops and holes for about 75 yards. Locals have christened this "Sirius, the Dog Star," an abstract but somehow very appropriate name.

The paddler is soon confronted with the picky entrance to Class III+ "Royal Flush." The entry requires a slalom around rocks and pourovers, setting the stage for a fast blast from left to right where the main flow piles into a boulder on the left. Some very fast ferrys and dynamic eddy hopping can take place at the bottom of this drop.

Immediately after this is an island which splits the river again, with a shallow channel on the left and a steep, blind chute on the right. (The left channel is not floatable if the Route 615 gauge is below two feet.) After dropping down on the right there is a small eddy in front of a large rock. This rock blocks the view of what is below—a fast moving

---

Section: Rt. 311 bridge to New Castle

Counties: Craig (VA)

USGS Quads: Potts Creek, New Castle

Suitable for: Day cruising

Skill Level: Advanced or expert

Months Runnable: Usually in winter or spring or after heavy rains

Interest Highlights: Beautiful gorge

Scenery: Beautiful in gorge

Difficulty: Class II at beginning; Class IV for 3 miles in the gorge (with one Class IV–V); Class II–III at the end

Average Width: 25–35 feet

Velocity: Fast

Gradient: 50 feet per mile; one mile in the gorge is 150 feet per mile

Runnable Water Levels:
  Minimum: 0 feet on Rt. 615 gauge
  Maximum: 1.5 feet on Rt. 615 gauge

Hazards: Bambi Meets Godzilla (Class IV–V); numerous Class IV rapids; Fool's Falls; trees in river

Scouting: Boat or land scout all major rapids

Portages: Optional

Rescue Index: Remote (and there are hostile landowners)

Source of Additional Information: None

Access Points	River Miles	Shuttle Miles
A–B	5.5	6.0

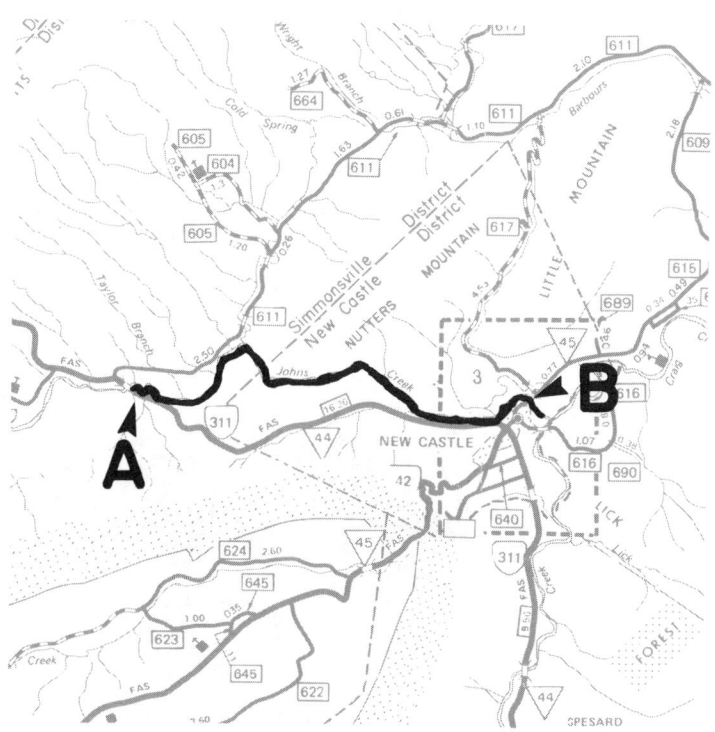

chute which drops over a ledge and divides around a large boulder. This tough Class IV rapids has informally been called "Coke Island" as it is surely "the real thing."

Shortly thereafter is another strong, steep Class III–IV sequence terminating with a large padded rock dividing the current into two chutes. The right chute is more easily run by dropping off at an angle and surfing down a wave/hole into the bottom eddy. The left chute is more difficult and should be looked at carefully before attempting it. Locals have dubbed this rapid "Little Heinzerling" due to its similarity to Heinzerling rapids on the Upper Yough in Maryland.

Just below is the granddaddy of the rapids on Johns Creek. One colorful name (among several) applied to this Class IV–V rapids by local paddlers is "Bambi Meets Godzilla." One may assume that "Bambi" is the innocent paddler. This is a real heart pumper with a total drop of about 15 feet in 30 yards. Here the flow channels to the right and narrows, with a tongue that drops over a five-foot slide into a boiling hole. Then comes another drop next to a boulder and a final drop into another hole before reaching the pool below.

"Blind Man's Bluff" is around the next bend. This Class IV rapids is simply a jumble of boulders. The paddler's predicament is to guess which channel is clear and safe. Watch out for log jams blocking the path. Run on the right.

Next is a Class IV rapid called "The Separator." Here the river funnels to the left and plunges steeply over a jumble of rocks. Halfway down is a three-foot drop. Immediately below is a screaming right-hand turn to avoid a pillowed boulder. The current then continues over another drop into a hole that requires a sharp left turn. The final chute deposits paddlers into a small pool where they can regain their breath and composure.

After this, the river tones down somewhat and begins dropping over low ledges and chutes. However, a smooth horizon line soon announces "Fool's Falls." This is the last and biggest individual drop; it has been described as unrunnable by certain previous guide books. However, with proper care and appropriate water levels, a path can be found over this Class IV five-foot drop into a rock garden. In popping over the drop and overshooting its hydraulic immediately below, proper boat angle is critical to avoid a vertical pin. Run right with your boat pointed to the right. Be really cranking when you go over the drop.

The river changes character immediately after this drop and becomes very much like the Class II–III Nantahala River. The take-out is roughly one mile below "Fool's Falls" at the rescue squad station near New Castle or the Route 615 bridge in town.

The only difficulty with this delightful trip are recent problems with local landowners. Certain landowners, particularly on the right bank and near "Fool's Falls" are very hostile to paddlers; there have been instances of paddlers being threatened by at least one of these landowners brandishing a shotgun. When planning a run down Johns Creek, check with local boaters to ascertain the latest information about this situation.

E. G.

Liz Garland runs Found Paddle Rapid on Johns Creek. Photo by Ron Mullet.

Glossary

Blackwater Stream. A river with waters dyed a reddish color by tannic acid from tree roots and rotting vegetation.

Bottom. The stream bottoms described in this book allude to what the paddler sees as opposed to the geological composition of the river bed. From a geologist's perspective, for example, a river may flow over a limestone bed. The paddler, however, because of the overlying silt and sediment, perceives the bottom as being mud.

Bow. The front of a boat.

Broaching. A boat that is sideways to the current and usually out of control or pinned to an obstacle in the stream.

By-pass. A channel cut across a meander that creates an island or oxbow lake.

cfs. Cubic feet per second; an accurate method of expressing river flow in terms of function of flow and volume.

C-1. One-person, decked canoe equipped with a spray skirt; frequently mistaken for a kayak. The canoeist kneels in the boat and uses a single-bladed paddle.

C-2. A two-person, decked canoe; frequently mistaken for a two-person kayak.

Chute. A clear channel between obstructions that has faster current than the surrounding water.

Curler. A wave that curls or falls back on itself (upstream).

Cut-off. *See* **By-pass**.

Deadfalls. Trees that have fallen into the stream totally or partially obstructing it.

Decked boat. A completely enclosed canoe or kayak fitted with a spray skirt. When the boater is properly in place, this forms a nearly waterproof unit.

Downstream ferry. A technique for moving sideways in the current while facing downstream. Can also be done by "surfing" on a wave.

Downward erosion. The wearing away of the bottom of a stream by the current.

Drainage area. Officially defined as an area measured in a horizontal plane, enclosed by a topographic divide, from which direct surface runoff from precipitation normally drains by gravity into a stream above a specified point. In other words, this is an area that has provided the water on which you are paddling at any given time. Accordingly, the drainage area increases as you go downstream. The drainage basin of a river is expressed in square miles. (Also known as a "watershed.")

Drop. Paddler's term for **gradient**.

Eddy. The water behind an obstruction in the current or behind a river bend. The water may be relatively calm or boiling and will flow upstream.

Eddy line. The boundary at the edge of an eddy between two currents of different velocity and direction.

Eddy out. *See* **Eddy turn**.

Eddy turn. Maneuver used to move into an eddy from the downstream current.

Eskimo roll. The technique used to upright an overturned decked canoe or kayak, by the occupant, while remaining in the craft. This is done by coordinated body motion and usually facilitated by the proper use of the paddle.

Expert boater. A person with extensive experience and good judgment who is familiar with up-to-date boating techniques, practical hydrology, and proper safety practices. An expert boater never paddles alone and always uses the proper equipment.

Fall line. The line between the Piedmont and Coastal Plain where the land slopes sharply.

Falls. A portion of river where the water falls freely over a drop. This designation has nothing to do with hazard rating or difficulty. *See* **Rapids**.

Ferry. Moving sideways to the current facing either up- or downstream.

Floatation. Additional buoyant materials (air bags, styrofoam, inner tubes, etc.) placed in a boat to provide displacement of water and extra buoyancy in case of upset.

Grab loops. Loops (about 6 inches in diameter) of nylon rope or similar material attached to the bow and stern of a boat to facilitate rescue.

Gradient. The geographical drop of the river expressed in feet per mile.

Hair. Turbulent whitewater.

Haystack. A pyramid-shaped standing wave caused by deceleration of current from underwater resistance.

Headward erosion. The wearing away of the rock strata forming the base of ledges or waterfalls by the current.

Heavy water. Fast current and large waves usually associated with holes and boulders.

Hydraulic. General term for souse holes and backrollers, where there is a hydraulic jump (powerful current differential) and strong reversal current.

K-1. One-person, decked kayak equipped with spray skirt. In this book, this category does not include nondecked kayaks. The kayaker sits in the boat with both feet extended forward. A double-bladed paddle is used.

Keeper. A souse hole or hydraulic with sufficient vacuum in its trough to hold an object (paddler, boat, log, etc.) that floats into it for an undetermined time. Extremely dangerous and to be avoided.

Lateral erosion. The wearing away of the sides or banks of a stream by the current.

Ledge. The exposed edge of a rock stratum that acts as a low, natural dam or as a series of such dams.

Left bank. Left bank of river when facing downstream.

Lining. A compromise between portaging and running a rapids. By the use of a rope (line), a boat can be worked downstream from the shore.

Logjam. A jumbled tangle of fallen trees, branches, and sometimes debris that totally or partially obstructs a stream.

Low-water bridge. A bridge across the river that barely clears the surface of the water or may even be awash; very dangerous for the paddler if in a fast current.

Meander. A large loop in a river's path through a wide floodplain.

PFD. Personal floatation device, e.g., life jacket.

Painter. A rope attached to the end of a craft.

Pillow. Bulge on surface created by underwater obstruction, usually a rock. Remember: these pillows are stuffed with rocks.

Pool. A section of water that is usually deep and quiet; frequently found below rapids and falls.

Rapids. Portion of a river where there is appreciable turbulence usually accompanied by obstacles. *See* **Falls**.

Riffles. Slight turbulence with or without a few rocks tossed in; usually Class I on the International Scale of River Difficulty.

Right bank. The right bank of the river as you progress downstream.

Rock garden. Rapids that have many exposed or partially submerged rocks necessitating intricate maneuvering or an occasional carry over shallow places.

Roller. *Also* **curler** or **backroller**; a wave that falls back on itself.

Run. *See* **Section** and **Stretch**.

Scout. To look at rapids from the shore to decide whether or not to run them, or to facilitate selection of a suitable route through the rapids.

Section. A portion of river located between two points. *Also* **Stretch** and **Run**.

Shuttle. Movement of at least two vehicles, one to the take-out and one back to the put-in points. Used to avoid having to paddle back upstream at the end of a run.

Slide rapids. An elongated ledge that descends or slopes gently rather than abruptly, and is covered usually with only shallow water.

Souse hole. A wave at the bottom of a ledge that curls back on itself. Water enters the trough of the wave from the upstream and downstream sides with reversal (upstream) current present downstream of the trough.

Spray skirt. A hemmed piece of waterproof material resembling a short skirt, having an elastic hem fitting around the boater's waist and an elastic hem fitting around the cockpit rim of a decked boat.

Standing wave. A regular wave downstream of submerged rocks that does not move in relation to the riverbed (as opposed to a moving wave such as an ocean wave).

Stern. The back end of a boat.

Stopper. Any very heavy wave or turbulence that quickly impedes the downriver progress of a rapidly paddled boat.

Stretch. A portion of river located between two points. *See* **Section** and **Run**.

Surfing. The technique of sitting on the upstream face of a wave or traveling back and forth across the wave when ferrying.

Surfing wave. A very wide wave that is fairly steep. A good paddler can slide into it and either stay balanced on its upstream face or else travel back and forth across it much in the same manner as a surfer in the ocean.

Sweep. The last boat in a group.

TVA. Tennessee Valley Authority.

Technical whitewater. Whitewater where the route is often less than obvious and where maneuvering in the rapids is frequently required.

Thwart. Transverse braces from gunwale to gunwale.

Trim. The balance of a boat in the water. Paddlers and duffel should be positioned so the waterline is even from bow to stern and the boat does not list to either side.

Undercut rock. A potentially dangerous situation where a large boulder has been eroded or undercut by water flow and could trap a paddler accidentally swept under it.

Upstream ferry. Similar to **downstream ferry** except the paddler faces upstream. *See also* **Surfing**.

Appendixes

A. Commercial Raft Trips and Expeditions

Several commercial raft outfitters operate through Central Appalachia. All operate on whitewater streams of varying difficulty and most are reputable, safety conscious, and professional. There are, however, several companies that will rent rafts or other inflatables for use on rated whitewater to individuals who are totally ignorant and naïve about the dangers involved. These companies normally do not run guided trips but rather send unsuspecting clients down the river on their own to cope with whatever problems or hazards materialize. It is our position that safe enjoyment of whitewater requires education and experience, and that attempting to paddle whitewater in any type of craft, privately owned or rented, without the prerequisite skills or without on-river professional guidance is dangerous in the extreme. That various companies will rent boats or rafts to the unknowing only proves that some people are unscrupulous, not that whitewater paddling is safe for the unaccompanied beginner.

All of the reputable raft companies throughout Central Appalachia operate guided raft excursions only, where professional whitewater guides accompany and assist their clients throughout the run. This type of experience has an unparalleled safety record in the United States and represents an enjoyable and educational way of exposing the newcomer to this whitewater sport. Through professional outfitters, thousands of people every year are turned on to the exhilaration of paddling. Spouses and friends of paddlers, who are normally relegated to enjoying our beautiful rivers vicariously through the stories of their companions, are made welcome and provided the thrill of experiencing the tumbling cascades firsthand.

Choosing a commercial outfitter is made somewhat easier by the Eastern Professional River Outfitters' Association (EPRO), the professional organization for commercial river runners in the eastern United States and Canada. Through its devotion to safety and its strict membership admission requirements, EPRO ensures that its member companies epitomize the highest standards in professional river outfitting. A directory of EPRO outfitters can be obtained by writing to EPRO, 530 South Gay St., Suite 222, Knoxville, TN (615) 524-1045.

B. Where to Buy Maps

As indicated in the introductory material, maps included in this book are intended to supplement rather than replace U.S. Geological Survey topographical quadrangles and county road maps. Maps can be purchased from the following locations:

United States Geological Survey (USGS) Topographic Quadrangles

Eastern U.S.
USGS Map Distribution
Box 25286
Denver Federal Center
Denver, CO 80225

County Road Maps

Delaware
Delaware Dept. of Transportation
Division of Highways
P. O. Box 778
Dover, DE 19901

Maryland
Map Distribution Sales
Maryland State Highway Administration
Brooklandville, MD 21022

204 Appendixes

Pennsylvania
PENNDOT Publication Sales
Forms & Publications Warehouse
Building 33 Harrisburg International Airport
Middletown, PA 17057

Virginia
Virginia Dept. of Highways & Transportation
attn: Information Services
1221 East Broad Street
Richmond, VA 23219

West Virginia
West Virginia Dept. of Highways
Planning Division, Map Sales
1900 Washington Street East
Charleston, WV 25305

Whitewater River Maps

William Nealy Maps
Menasha Ridge Press
P. O. Box 59257
Birmingham, AL 35259-9257

C. Other Menasha Ridge Press Guidebooks

A Hiking Guide to the Trails of Florida, Elizabeth F. Carter

The Squirt Book: The Manual of Squirt Kayaking Technique, James E. Snyder, illustrated by W. Nealy

Chattooga River (Section IV) Flip Map, Ron Rathnow

Nantahala River Flip Map, Ron Rathnow

New River Flip Map, Ron Rathnow

Ocoee River Flip Map, Ron Rathnow

Youghiogheny River Flip Map, Ron Rathnow

Kayak: The Animated Manual of Intermediate and Advanced Whitewater Technique, William Nealy

Kayaks to Hell, William Nealy

Whitewater Home Companion, Southeastern Rivers, Volume I, William Nealy

Whitewater Home Companion, Southeastern Rivers, Volume II, William Nealy

Whitewater Tales of Terror, William Nealy

Carolina Whitewater: A Canoeist's Guide to the Western Carolinas, Bob Benner

A Paddler's Guide to Eastern North Carolina, Bob Benner and Tom McCloud

Wildwater West Virginia, Volume I, the Northern Streams, Paul Davidson, Ward Eister, and Dirk Davidson

Wildwater West Virginia, Volume II, The Southern Streams, Paul Davidson, Ward Eister, and Dirk Davidson

Diver's Guide to Underwater America, Kate Kelley and John Shobe

Shipwrecks: Diving the Graveyard of the Atlantic, Roderick M. Farb

Boatbuilder's Manual, Charles Walbridge, editor

Smoky Mountains Trout Fishing Guide, Don Kirk

Fishing the Great Lakes of the South: An Angler's Guide to the TVA System, Don and Joann Kirk

A Fishing Guide to Kentucky's Major Lakes, Arthur B. Lander, Jr.

A Guide to the Backpacking and Day-Hiking Trails of Kentucky, Arthur B. Lander, Jr.

A Canoeing and Kayaking Guide to the Streams of Florida, Volume I, North Central Peninsula and Panhandle, Elizabeth F. Carter and John L. Pearce

A Canoeing and Kayaking Guide to the Streams of Florida, Volume II, Central and South Peninsula, Lou Glaros and Doug Sphar

Appalachian Whitewater, Volume I, The Southern Mountains, Bob Sehlinger, Don Otey, Bob Benner, William Nealy, and Bob Lantz

Appalachian Whitewater, Volume II, The Central Mountains, Ed Grove, Bill Kirby, Charles Walbridge, Ward Eister, Paul Davidson, and Dirk Davidson

Appalachian Whitewater, Volume III, The Northern Mountains, John Connelly and John Porterfield

Northern Georgia Canoeing, Bob Sehlinger and Don Otey

Southern Georgia Canoeing, Bob Sehlinger and Don Otey

A Canoeing and Kayaking Guide to the Streams of Kentucky, Bob Sehlinger

A Canoeing and Kayaking Guide to the Streams of Ohio, Volume I, Richard Combs and Stephen E. Gillen

A Canoeing and Kayaking Guide to the Streams of Ohio, Volume II, Richard Combs and Stephen E. Gillen

A Canoeing and Kayaking Guide to the Streams of Tennessee, Volume I, Bob Sehlinger and Bob Lantz

A Canoeing and Kayaking Guide to the Streams of Tennessee, Volume II, Bob Sehlinger and Bob Lantz

Emergency Medical Procedures for the Outdoors, Patient Care Publications, Inc.

Guide and Map to the Uwharrie Trail, G. Nicholas Hancock

Harsh Weather Camping, Sam Curtis

Modern Outdoor Survival, Dwight R. Schuh

Stream Index

Antietam Creek, 148–50
Appomattox River, 197–98
Aquia Creek, 181–83

Back Fork of the Elk River: Three Falls Section. *See* Elk River, Back Fork of the
Big Sandy Creek, 109–12
Blackwater River, 107–8
Bull Falls. *See* Shenandoah and Potomac Rivers

Cacapon River, 122–23
Cheat River, 113–19; Laurel Fork of the, 105–6

Dark Shade Creek, 31–33
Delaware River, 55–59

Elk River, Back Fork of the (Three Falls Section), 84–86

Forks of the Greenbrier. *See* Greenbrier River, Forks of the

Gauley River, Lower, 71–74; Upper, 64–70
Greenbrier River, Forks of the, 86–95
Gunpowder Falls, 156–57

James River, 194–96
Johns Creek, 199–200

Laurel Fork of the Cheat River. *See* Cheat River, Laurel Fork of the
Lehigh River, 44–48
Little River, 86–87
Lost River, 120–21
Lower Gauley River. *See* Gauley River, Lower
Lower Youghiogheny River. *See* Youghiogheny River, Lower

Loyalsock Creek, 38–43

Maury River, 189–93
Middle Fork River, 96–97
Muddy Creek, 60–62

Nescopeck Creek, 49–50
New River, 75–77
New River Gorge, 78–83
North Branch of the Potomac. *See* Potomac River, North Branch

Passage Creek, 169–71
Pine Creek, 34–37
Pocomoke River, 162–64
Potomac River, 172–77; North Branch of the, 138–44
Prime Hook Creek, 158–61

Rappahannock River, 184–85

Savage River, 134–37
Shade Creek, 31–33
Shenandoah and Potomac Rivers (Bull Falls and Staircase), 151–55
Shenandoah River, South Fork of the, 166–68
Sideling Hill Creek, 145–47
Slippery Rock Creek, 26–27
South Fork of the Shenandoah River. *See* Shenandoah River, South Fork of the
Staircase. *See* Shenandoah and Potomac Rivers
Stony Creek, 31–33

Thornton River, 178–80
Tohickon Creek, 51–54
Top Youghiogheny River. *See* Youghiogheny River, Top
Tye River, 186–88

Tygart River and Gorge, 98–104

Upper Gauley River. *See* Gauley River, Upper
Upper Youghiogheny River. *See* Youghiogheny River, Upper

Wills Creek, 28–30

Youghiogheny River, Lower, 22–25; Top, 126–28; Upper, 129–33

About the Authors

Ed Grove has enjoyed canoeing for over 30 years. A decade ago, he became a true whitewater enthusiast after taking a course from Louis Matacia, the legendary Virginia paddler. A graduate of Stanford University, with two degrees in International Relations, Grove has worked for the federal government. Before retiring early to spend more time with his family and paddling, he was the Deputy Budget Officer for the Department of State. He is now a consultant and lives with his wife Carol and two sons in Arlington, Virginia. Paddling is only one part of his deep and abiding love for the outdoors.

Bill Kirby began canoeing with the Canoe Cruisers Association of Washington, D.C. in 1969. He took up kayaking in 1972 after watching the Olympic Trials on the Savage. As a park ranger with the U.S. National Park Service, Kirby primarily supervised the River Safety Team at Great Falls Park in Virginia. He has also served as editor of the journal of the American Whitewater Affiliation, *American Whitewater*, and has written articles on outdoor subjects for *Downriver* magazine, the *Washington Post*, and various association newsletters. Currently in the construction wholesale business, he can still be found roaming the central Appalachians with boat on car. He claims to have swallowed more Potomac River water than any other living human.

Charlie Walbridge is an active paddler in both open canoe and C-1. He began canoeing in 1960 and became involved seriously with whitewater in 1971 in central Pennsylvania. He worked as a schoolteacher and raft guide while running rivers and training for the U.S. Whitewater Team. He is currently president of Wildwater Designs, a mail-order retailer of canoe and kayak gear. He is one of the originators of the throw-line rescue bag and co-designer of the HiFloat PFD. In addition to paddling rivers throughout the country, he is the safety chairman of the American Canoe Association and is active in instruction and conservation efforts. He has contributed to *Canoe* and *River Runner* magazine and is author of *The Boatbuilder's Manual* and *The River Safety Report*.

Paul Davidson, Ward Eister, and **Dirk Davidson** are the authors of *Wildwater West Virginia, Volume I, The Northern Streams* and *Volume II, The Southern Streams*.

Quantity Sales

Most Menasha Ridge Press books are available at special quantity discounts when purchased in bulk by corporations, organizations, and special-interest groups. Custom imprinting or excerpting can also be done to fit special needs. For details write: Menasha Ridge Press, P.O. Box 59257, Birmingham, Alabama 35259-9257 or call 800-247-9437, Attn: Special Sales Dept.

Individual Sales

Are there any Menasha books you want but cannot find in local stores? If so, you can order them directly from us. You can get any Menasha book in print. Simply include the book's title, author, and ISBN number, if you have it, along with a check or money order for the full retail price plus $2.00 to cover shipping and handling. Mail to: Menasha Ridge Press, P.O. Box 59257, Birmingham, AL 35259-9257.

Note to Our Readers:

Your comments, corrections, and any information you have about material contained in this book would be greatly appreciated. Please feel free to write us or the authors care of Menasha Ridge Press, Post Office Box 59257, Birmingham, AL 35259-9257.